THE LIFE OF DAVID A PROSSER

A Brummie

David A Prosser

Best Wishes
Dave

Pen Press

First published in Great Britain by
Indepenpress Publishing Ltd
25 Eastern Place
Brighton
BN2 1GJ

ISBN13: 978-1-78003-295-5

Printed and bound in the UK

With kind permission from Carl Chinn
the photographs on pages 294, 307, 337 and 338.
are from the Birmingham Lives
The Carl Chinn Archive

With kind permission of Birmingham Library Services
photograph on page 286, Bulls Head Pub

I wrote this book for my three children,
Anthony, Wendy and Matthew,
who I love deeply.

I dedicate this book to my ex wife Irene who saw this book through with me to fruition.

My grateful thanks to the two artists
for the line drawings they did
throughout this book

Mr Alan Waite

and

Mr Graham Wilson

MY WIFE

Before you read this book I feel I must make it known that my ex wife, Irene, encouraged me to do whatever I said I couldn't do. She sat down with me when I felt low and thought I would never be any good and amount to anything, she taught me more than any of the teachers that had me for ten years. She put up with my illiteracy, stupidity, my ignorance and the poverty we endured because of me. She suffered with me and our children and never complained – she always said, "So long as I am with you, I would live in a shed in the middle of nowhere." She poured faith, happiness and love into my children and me; she is the backbone of my family. Irene, my devoted ex wife who never ever gave up on me, I owe her for what I am and have now. She was my tower of strength, my back bone. "Dave," she told me, "I love you so much I would give up my life for you," which brought tears to my eyes. She still says that to this very day – even though we are divorced.

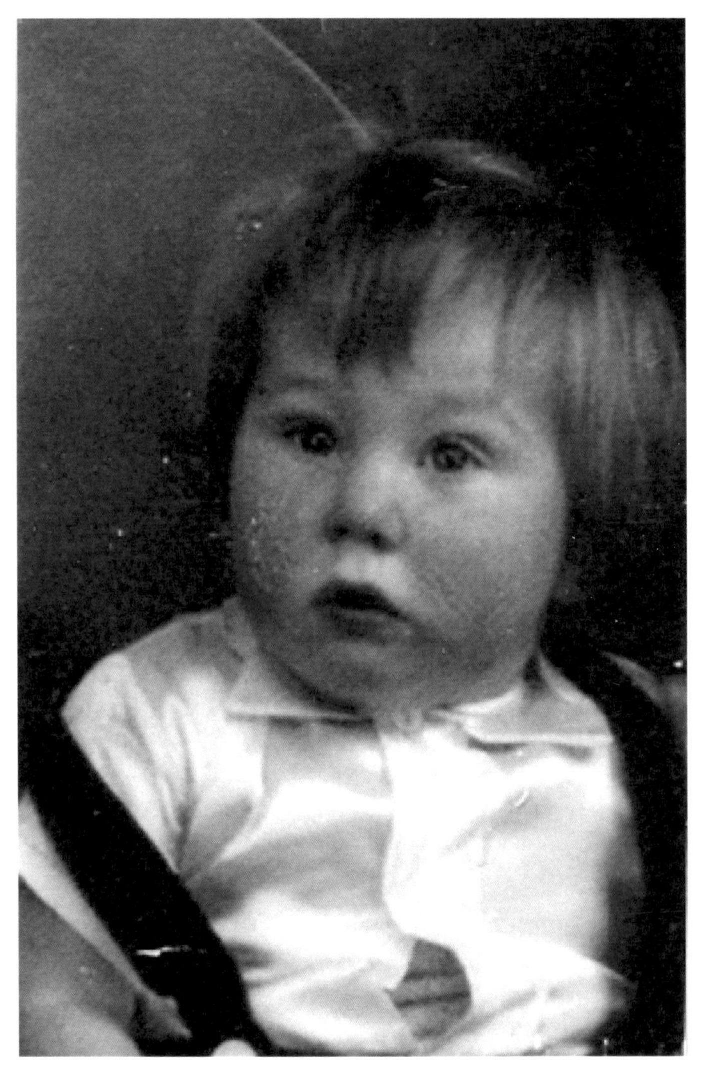

The author at the tender age of eighteen months
(born 30th October 1943)

The author with his sisters.
left to right: Kathleen, Janet, Doreen

My mom on a rare day out

CONTENTS

MY EARLY YEARS

An Autobiography

ABOUT THE AUTHOR

David was a real Brummie born to a very loving mother. His family lived in a council house in the Stechford area of Birmingham, where nearby there were fields, trees to climb, a river to play in and lots of places to explore.

He spent 1948 to 1958 at Audley Road School being very sporty, playing in goal at football and representing the school all through his school days and he excelled at high jumping.

As a young boy, known as Pross to all his friends, he had a poor but very colourful childhood. His life was filled with many adventures that hopefully you will enjoy reading about.

(Comments from a friend)

INTRODUCTION

I WAS BORN IN THE YEAR 1943, October 30th, at 38 Plowden Road, Glebe Farm, Birmingham 33. My Mother being Dora Louisa Prosser (née King), and Dad was William John Prosser, who everyone knew as Jack or Snowy because his hair went pure white at the age of 21.

We were a family of six; at the time of my birth, my two eldest brothers went in the forces so I rarely saw them, but I remember well the times when I did see them when on leave from the forces for the pain I suffered at their hands. Then they got married. So growing up until the age of five there were only four of us, me and my three sisters Kathleen, Doreen and Janet. My younger brother John was born five years after me.

My young life was surrounded by poverty and hardship, but after saying that it bred into me a sense of 'make do and mend and survival', with a mother so loving and caring she always put us first before herself, and a dad who mostly thought of himself (the majority of his money went on drink and women, so he created the hardship we suffered). Our house consisted of three bedrooms upstairs; downstairs a living room, a kitchen, a pantry, bathroom, coal hole, a cubby hole under the stairs and a cupboard next to the bathroom. A Belfast sink in the kitchen where Mother sat me as a child and bathed me more times than I remember. There was a wooden draining board that rested on the wall to the sink, under the draining board was a boiler where Mom boiled up the water for us to have a bath, if on that Saturday or Sunday evening she had three spare pennies for the gas meter, if not we had no bath just a wash-down in the sink in the kitchen. At that time it was the only sink in the house, the water was lukewarm from the boiler behind the coal fire that was in the living room, if we had a fire that is.

Plowden Road
(showing author's house, last one on the right)

Showing the bottom of Plowden Road
where it meets Swancote Road

We weren't allowed to boil the kettle some of the time as Mom could not let us use the gas when money was tight, so a wash-down was in cold water – OK in the summer, not so good in the winter, it was more difficult for the girls of course. Us boys didn't like washing anyway, we tried to avoid washing no matter if the water was hot or cold. We had an outside toilet that wasn't so nice in the winter.

I was a little terror. I often had cuts and broken bones my mom had several names for me, most of which I can't repeat. When I was born until the age of two I was known as 'grizle arse'. I cried so much and moaned so much my mom had to feed me continually (my wife said I haven't changed!). Most children have one bottle at feed time, I always had two my sister Janet who is eighteen months older than me was always hungry. My mom couldn't understand why this was, until one day she saw me taking Janet's bottle from her and drinking it all.

As I was born two years before the end of the war, poverty for our family was there in all its glory, Dad being unemployed before the war made all our lives all the more harder. It was taking my parents a long time to recover in the post-war years so everything was make do and mend, meaning my life and my sisters' did not improve for many years. Mother, bless her, could do wonders with six pence (6d). Buying spuds for 1d (one penny) a pound, veggies 2d, two pence a pound, and 2d worth of bones from the butcher's I had to say, "they were for the dog", which we never had. Mom fed us for days with all those vegetables in the form of what we called a stew, yes it was stewed for days.

I adored playing football, hopscotch, skipping, running, tip cat, table tennis and any games going. At the age of four and a half I was playing in the horse road, drawing with a lump of chalk that was once a statue, with six girls – Jacqueline Farrington, her sister Beryl, Rita Hill, Ann Hill, and my two sisters Doreen and Janet, as there were no boys living by me at that time.

YOUR LIFE

What makes life worthwhile?

As children we think that having lots of toys is the ultimate in life, having lots of cuddles, being told you are nice, sitting with your family, walking together down a country lane, seeing Mother Nature, looking at the trees, seeing the birds and knowing their names, learning to tell one from the other. To sit by a river and hear the sound of rippling water and feel the sun gently warming your back, to laugh and smile with your friends, to be with loved ones, to sit quietly sometimes and think how lucky you are.

The ultimate in life is to be told I love you, and for you to tell people you love them. These things in life cost nothing but fills the whole of your life with all the gifts you will ever need.

MY LIFELONG FRIEND

One afternoon (I was coming up to my fifth birthday) I was sitting in the middle of the road opposite my front garden gate, drawing on the concrete road. I remember drawing a matchstick girl with a skirt on. My two sisters Doreen and Janet were playing with Ann Hill from across the road and the two girls from next door Beryl and Jacqueline Farrington, when I saw a lady walking down the road with a little boy:

"Who is the lady?" I asked my sister Doreen.

"They're moving into that empty house there," she said, pointing over the road. I was so excited at the thought of having a boy as a friend instead of soppy girls, well that's how I was thinking at that moment in time.

The next day I knocked on the door and asked if the little boy could come out and play. That was the very start of a lifelong friendship. We did a lot together from tatting, taking coach journeys, carrying coal, running errands, gardening and many, many more crazy things, we really enjoyed our childhood in spite of the poverty we grew up in. We were only interested in making money because we never got pocket money in those days.

His name is Trevor Kendall. We are friends to this very day. I can remember that day I saw him with his mother so well it's as clear to me like it was yesterday.

Audley Road Secondary Modern School

Showing the entrance from Swancote Road, to the Infants and Juniors School Playgrounds. At the age of five, on my very first day of starting school, I walked up this entrance with my mom, across the Juniors' playground, through the tunnel to the Infants' playground.

This was the Infants' playground.
This tunnel is where my mom stood and watched me on my first day at school in 1948

This was my first classroom on my first day at school.

This wooden hut was two classrooms. On the right was the Infants, on the left the Juniors. I was in both those classrooms which have now been demolished.
There were steps and two doors in the middle of the hut, they have been closed off and put on the other side of the hut

This was the entrance I had to use
when I went into the Senior School
As you can see it's on the other side of the school.
This entrance is off Audley Road.

My Mom (on the left) with her best friend Lizzie (Trevor's mom)

2oz OF SWEETS

My earliest memory is when I was three years old. I used to stand on the windowsill to watch the children coming out of school. As we lived on the corner of our road I had a clear view of the school entrance where the children came out; I climbed on the chair, then the table, to get to the sill. Mom always told me off for climbing but she never took me off there, I did it every day.

The school entrance was half way up Swancote Road; just a bit further up the road were our local shops, I went every day to those shops with my mom because we were quite poor. I rarely got sweets. One day I was playing my face (as my mom put it) for some sweets; Mom bought me 2oz of sweets, "Now don't tell your sisters you've had sweets." Being very greedy I ate them very quickly. As Mom was putting dinner on the table because it was dinnertime, twelve noon, my three sisters came home for their dinner. My sister Doreen walked in and I immediately said, "I haven't had any sweets have I, Mom?" "Yes you have or you wouldn't have said that," said Doreen, then she played her face something awful till Mom gave her a good hiding with a smacked bum. I was told I wouldn't be given any sweets again, nor did I for a very long time. It was a long time after that little episode, three years I bet it was, Mom bought some sweets and shared them between my two sisters and me, Doreen and Janet. I thought, I will wait for them to finish theirs then I will start to eat mine; it was killing me not to eat mine, then when they had finished theirs I put a sweet in my mouth and made a sucking noise and saying, "Mmm, these are nice." Doreen shouted, "Mom, he is playing us up with his sweets because we have eaten ours!" "I know, I heard him," said Mom, so with a smack across the back of my head, my sweets were taken off me and shared between my two sisters; I ended up with nothing, well only the one I had in my mouth that I had been tormenting my sisters with. Well I cried my little heart out, but I never did it again – once bitten as the saying goes.

DROPS

Once a week my mom took me to a welfare clinic, which was situated an area called Kitts Green; I was three years old my mom told me some years later how old I was.

What I do remember, the first time I went to that clinic, was that I had drops down my ears, throat and up my nose and in my eyes. I've no idea what was wrong with me and I never thought to ask my mom as the years passed. I think I just wanted to forget about it. So whenever I was taken to that clinic I screamed and fought like my life depended on it. They said, "If you're good you can have a bottle of this orange juice," smacking her lips to show me how nice it was. I was sold, that bribe worked every time (I always was thick). Unknown to me she always gave mom a bottle of Cod Liver Oil which she hid away from me, and I was held down at home to be given a spoonful of that horrid cod liver oil (they would have to hold me down these days as well!). After, I was always given a spoonful of orange juice straight away. I loved that welfare orange juice, it was thick and sweet.

Mom's friend Winnie called at our house one morning with her son John who also became my friend. Mom said, "Come on, son, we're going for a walk." That excited me, and as we were walking I would keep asking, "Where are we going?" She would say, "Just for a walk, son." As we turned the corner I saw the bridge, I then knew what was on the other side of that bridge, the welfare clinic. Hurt and pain lay the other side of that bridge.

I pulled, shouted, cried very loudly, if I could have got free of Mom's grip I would have run off. I was what these days is known as 'throwing a wobbly'. "Please, Mommy," I was saying, "Don't take me in there." Every time I saw that bridge I threw a wobbly, even to this very day when I see that bridge I get a horrible feeling in the pit of my stomach; those feelings do not seem to want to leave me.I do remember.

Mothers then used to get baby food called National Dried Milk free – well, I *think* it was free – for their children. I don't think in those days there was an air raid shelter, shed, coalhouse or pantry that hadn't got a National Dried Milk tin in there – I've seen them with nails, screws, tools, drills, car bits, motor bike bits, you name it those tins housed it. We had a couple of those tins in our house, I was informed by my better half. National Dried Milk full cream was a silver tin then later white with blue writing. Half cream was silver and again later white with red writing. I have even seen those tins made into toys. I've seen a lorry and a train, I bet there are hundreds still out there in the shape of every toy you can think of (I want one!).

A tin of dried milk

The back of a dried milk tin

The tin above was acquired on the 3rd October 2012 from an antique shop in the town known as Atherstone – north Warwickshire.

Most mothers obtained these tins of dried milk from their Welfare Clinic. I remember my Mom getting them when she got the dreaded cod liver oil, and of course the Welfare orange juice.

The dreaded bridge to the Welfare Clinic

The Welfare Clinic as it was at that time.

SHORT BACK AND SIDES

The first time I went to the barbers I didn't go to school then as I was only four and a half years old. Mom took me for a hair cut known as short back and sides, the name of the barbers was Tranters, he was our local barber. As Mom walked in with me Mr Tranter said, "Leave him here while you do your shopping." I said, "I don't want my hair cut, Mom." "You'll be OK, son," she said, so off she went shopping. I was terrified.

Well he fought with me to get me into that chair; just when he thought he had won he was puffing and blowing, I jumped out of that chair and ran into the street outside to find my mom. He came running after me and caught hold of my arm, so I kicked him as hard as I could – I cannot print what he said to me! He dragged me back inside, threw me into the chair and I mean threw, I must have bounced about two foot into the air. With a very loud voice he yelled down my ear, "Now sit still," so I did because he scared me. Comb and scissors no problem – I remember thinking, this is all right, then he turned the electric clippers on and started to shave by my ear. I flew out of that chair, ducked under his arms and ran outside with the sheet still wrapped around me. He got hold of me, so I kicked him again, he shook me and dragged me back into the shop. He was much rougher with me that time than the time before, and again I was thrown back into that chair. I think I bounced four foot that second time. He said to me, "OK, son, I won't use the electric clippers, I will only use the comb and scissors." I was still terrified but I calmed down when the scissors were being used.

So finally I got my haircut. When he had finished cutting, he put me on a chair where all the men were sitting waiting for their hair to be cut. The room was full of cigarette smoke, it was like sitting in a fog, my eyes were smarting and it made me cough. They were talking about football. I remember there were three men cutting hair, those same men were there for years. It was a dark mysterious sort of room, well to a youngster anyway, dark oak panels everywhere, the ladies was on the left as you walked in, a narrow passage lead to the men's at the back. Mom walked in, looked at me and said, "That's a nice hair cut, you do look smart, has he been OK, Mr Tranter?" "Yes, Mrs Prosser he was fine." She paid him, I think it was 6d (six pence). "Bye David," he said as he patted me on the back of my head very hard, "Come again," he said as we walked out. The other barbers started laughing, they knew he didn't really want to see me again. My mom never knew till years later what that poor barber went through!

SATURDAY MATINEE

The first Saturday matinee I ever went to was at the Atlas Cinema in Stechford, Birmingham, it was just down the road from my house. I went with my sister Doreen, my mom gave her strict instructions not to take me to the back of the cinema where the tip was and not to go through the park after the films had finished.

It was like a stampede to get out, I had never seen so many screaming kids. Doreen took me over the tip, the one Mom said not to (as I got much older I spent many hours on that tip); my sister said, "Don't tell Mom we came the park way home. Will you promise?"

"I won't honest."

As we walked over the tip we came across a big hole at the edge of the tip with a corrugated sheet of metal across one corner of it, someone had been making a den. "I'm going inside," Doreen said, "you stand there and don't stand on this tin it's not safe." As she went in I looked at the tin sheet – it's OK, I won't fall if I stand on it, I thought, so I stood on it; it swivelled because it was resting on two opposite corners. I fell into the hole catching the inside of my left knee on the corner of the tin sheet, it sliced though my leg like butter, the blood was cascading down my leg, the cut was an inch wide and four inches long.

Thinking a lump of flesh had come out, me and Doreen were searching for the lump of flesh, we thought if we put the flesh back in the hole it would heal up and be OK. "It's gone, Dave," she said, "come on I'll take you to the park keeper." She wrapped her handkerchief round my leg, the blood still cascading down my leg. When the parkie (that's what everyone called him) saw my leg he went white. He wrapped it up with loads of bandages, but the blood came through as soon as he put it on, "You must take him straight to the hospital, that's a very bad cut," he said. In those days the park keepers only had push bikes as we called them (bicycles) so he couldn't take me to the hospital.

Doreen was crying and by this time I was very pale, losing my strength to walk and feeling very poorly. Doreen had to carry me and she got covered in blood. Poor Mother had a shock, "Oh my god, my baby, what have you done now?" I can remember Mom saying that, why I can I have no idea. I can't remember any more, whether it's because I passed out from loss of blood I'm not sure. I had eleven stitches and the scar is still very visible to this day. I've never known to this day if Doreen got a good hiding or not. I have discussed it with Doreen since, I asked her if she can remember getting a belting off Mom but she can't remember. I'm sure if Mom had belted her she would have remembered.

ACCIDENT PRONE

Every summer holiday when I was off school for six weeks my mom, bless her, would pray and ask the Lord, "Please don't let David hurt himself this holiday." I was accident prone, it started when I was four years old just before I started school. In our back garden we had a lean-to shed with a flat roof; it was constructed by my older brother Donald, with a chicken pen incorporated in it. As children we climbed on the shed and jumped off it for what we thought was fun and enjoyment. There was me, my two sisters Doreen and Janet, and their friend Rita Hill, and my then new-found friend Trevor. This was 1947, it had been raining and the ground was very muddy. I was too scared to jump so my sister Janet told me many years later she had pushed me. When I hit the ground I did the splits; I heard a crack, the pain was bad. I lay in the mud screaming. My mom was up the road shopping, my sister Kathleen carried me in to the house. A neighbour came in to the house to see if she could help, "Where does it hurt?" she asked me. I'm lying on the settee in agony and she asked where does it hurt. By this time the house was full of people, the lady kept touching my leg asking, "Does it hurt there?" I said, yes, yes every time she touched me. I heard her say to a woman next to her, "He is stupid, he is saying it hurts no matter where I touch him," (it did). My mom came rushing in, "Oh my baby, what have you done, son?" she was hurting more than I was, "I must take him to the hospital." Mom had no money for the bus fare; she tried to borrow the money for the bus, but no one had any money. The people where we lived, well all the ones I ever knew, were not much better off than my family. When my cousin Arthur who lived with us at that time (because his mom, Margaret, who was my mom's sister, was killed in the bombing in the Second World War – she lived at number 53 Ash Road Saltley in Birmingham) came home from work he said, "I'll take him on the bus to the hospital, and give my name and address," (that was the done thing then when people had no money). "OK, you do that, take him to the accident hospital, and I'll meet you there as soon as I can," said Mom.

After Mom found someone to look after my sisters, with my leg bent in a permanent position – it was less painful I found when kept bent – my cousin took me on the number 14 bus to town. We got off the bus in the old square, he waited a while, then Arthur got back on the bus. Why he did that I have no idea and neither did he. He got back off the bus at Alum Rock and sat on the wall outside a factory called Southhalls. Why he did what he did I have never known (he could have taken me to any hospital). As he sat on the wall my mom passed on the bus and she spotted Arthur sitting on the wall. Full of panic and anger, she got off at the next stop and ran down the road to where she had seen Arthur. My cousin never saw Mom; as the bus passed, he crossed over the road, got back on the next bus and took me back home. When Mom got to Southhalls only to find he had gone she asked a lady if she had seen a man carrying a little boy; "Yes," she said pointing, "he has just got on that bus that is disappearing round the bend." She too headed back home crying, and as she walked into the living room she flopped in to the chair saying, to Arthur, "Why did you bring him back home?" My cousin replied, "I didn't know what to do," (he wasn't very bright, I was told all this by my mom about the bus saga). Mom was worn out saying as she took a deep breath, "I can't do any more today, I will take him myself tomorrow."

So I was in agony all night. Mom said I couldn't have any asprins as I was too young. Still with my leg bent, next day at the hospital the doctor asked, "When did he break his leg, Mother?" "This morning, Doctor," she replied. "I don't think so, Mother, it's started to set, I think he did this last night. Wait outside, Mother," he told her. "I will look after him," he said. With a smile he put his right hand at the back of my left foot, his left hand on the front of my knee, pushed down with his left hand and up with his right – did I scream! Mom came running in, "My baby, my baby, what are you doing to him?" "It's all right, Mother, I've only straightened his leg," he said as though it was nothing, "Now we can X-ray it; he is a big strong boy, Mother." That didn't help the pain, it turned out I had dislocated my ankle and my knee cap and broken the long bone up the front of my leg from the foot to the knee cap. I have no recollection of getting an injection, I would remember if I had as I hate injections. My leg was plastered and I was given a pair of crutches. The nurse said, "Come with me, David, I will show you how to use the crutches," so in the corridor she showed me the best way to use them. Feeling very weak and tired out I found it very difficult to lift my plastered leg. The nurse started to lose her patience with me, "Lift your leg, you are leaving chalk marks all along the corridor," she said in a, well how can I put it, in an excitable sort of voice. When I looked around it looked like those white lines you see in the middle of the road, broken white lines that is. When Mom came to collect me the nurse's voice went very calm, "Bye, David," she said, "you are a brave little boy. He will be all right, Mother," she said as she put her hand on Mom's shoulder. That two-faced nurse, my mom would have been very angry if she had heard that nurse speaking to me in the manner in which she did. We went back into the waiting room and waited what seemed like for ever when a man called out, "Ambulance for Mrs Prosser." We got into the ambulance, and you know I can remember that ambulance like it was only last week. I loved that ambulance ride! All the children that came to see me had a play with my crutches, they had as much fun with them as they did when playing games in the street. I wish I could say my mom was happy but she wasn't relieved, maybe I really wish I hadn't given my mom so many problems.

At the age of four if you don't do as you are told by your mother, this is what can happen to you. I never did as I was told – look what happened to me!

HANDFUL OF PENNIES

I loved going to the fair, it was always and still is in the same place; we always called it the Bulls Head Fair, Stechford. The Bulls Head was a pub, I say was because it has now been demolished like so many other pubs in the area.

I'd only had my broken leg out of plaster for a week and I was going to the fair with Trevor and Tony (Trevor's brother). We got off the bus the stop after the Atlas Cinema. It was evening time and the road was very busy, I suppose they were coming out of work. Tony and Trevor ran across the road. I looked across and Tony shouted, "Stay there," but I thought the road was clear and I ran across the road gripping my 9d (nine pennies) in my hand. A car hit me, I went up in the air doing a somersault and landed on my back, the car had hit my left leg (the one I'd had in plaster), how it never broke again I will never know. The man was shaking, "Get in the car," he said to me, he didn't know what he was saying, then he said, "Get out of the car," so out I got. I was very shaken, fortunately not hurt, even though I was crying my little heart out.

A lady came up to me and said, "Here you are, son, I've picked your pennies up for you, here is your seven pence (7d)." "There were nine pennies (9d)," I said. "That's all I found," she answered. I'm not making up excuses because I had been in a road accident, my manners were bad. I never said thank you to that kind lady for picking up my pennies, all I started to think about was getting to the fair. There were crowds watching me, I was famous for ten minutes. I limped off to the fair to spend my 7d and the man drove off, I bet it took him a long time to get over that accident, poor man. After a few minutes at the fairground I soon forgot all about it. I'm lucky to be alive. I never, even as the years passed, told my mom about that accident, I thought she had been through enough with me as a child.

MY ROCKING HORSE

On my fourth birthday I was given a rocking horse, I remember being so excited, I also remember my sisters were playing on it and they wouldn't get off and let me on it. I stood there crying my little heart out, Mom came into the living room from the kitchen and told them to get off it so on I got and was very happy. My sister Janet was on the back, Doreen on the front, we were having a great time. I will never know how that rocking horse stood up to the treatment we gave it, we treated it very rough. It was a toy and I enjoyed it for many years. I was Hopalong Cassidy one day, Roy Rogers the next, Tex Ritter another, my imagination ran wild. There was one draw back to that rocking horse – if I tried rocking too fast the back legs came up, locked, and threw me over its head.

My mom kept that horse in the coal house; the coal house had a brick-built shelf with concrete slabs on the top which was covering the water pipes, my rocking horse went on there. It just fitted, trouble was it got black from the coal dust, when we had coal that is. If I came off that horse because I rocked too fast Mom would say, "I told you didn't I, if you came off it I would put it back in the coal house, you little bugga," she always called me that, "you will break your neck one of these days," she would say. Every few days I would ask if I could have my horse out to play with, a lot of times she said, "no," because it needed cleaning and she was busy getting the dinners ready for my sisters to have when they came out of school at dinner time. When I did get to play on it Mom would once again say, "if you come off it, back in the coal house." I came off it and back it went. I usually got a nice big lump on my forehead from hitting the floor or the wall. OK, I would think, after mom had put it back in the coalhole, I will ride my pretend horse, and much to the annoyance of my mother I would hold out my left arm as though I was holding the horse's reins and slapping my backside with my right hand, I would gallop all round the house – I was the sheriff, a cowboy, an Indian, an outlaw, all rolled into one. I think Mom sometimes wished she had let me play in the living room with my rocking horse.

My dad made the horse, he got all the wood from his works. He worked at the Metropolitan Camel Carriage Works, Saltley, Birmingham, where he was a Radial Driller. How Dad got the wood out I have no idea, it was all cut to shape when he brought it out; it was well-seasoned timber and was the same timber they used when building the railway carriages, that's what Dad's firm made – everything to do with railways. My mom's brother Bob, my uncle of course, was a manager at the same works; whether he helped my dad get the timber out I don't know. The metal rockers or stays as my dad called them were made from 5/16 of an inch round steel which were also bent to shape. Dad did tell me he had a few goes at making the rocking horse before he got it right. Dad made four other horses for our neighbours, this was ideal for him as my birthday was in October, and the neighbours had seen my horse and asked him to make one for each of their children, and he had time to make all the horses for Christmas. He got everything he needed from work to complete all the horses, even the paint, but he made the mistake of getting paint that needed a coat of special varnish to make it dry, but he didn't know this at the time. After Christmas one of the fathers complained saying their daughter on Christmas morning got paint all over her and ruined her new clothes; my horse was OK, he must have used different paint for mine. Janet my sister had my rocking horse for twenty years, my brother John took a pattern off it and made some horses, he gave me one so I took it to Janet's and swapped it for my horse – it sits in the corner of my bedroom now, and every time I look at it the memories of my childhood are fondly remembered. You can see from the pictures how the legs locked and threw me over its head.

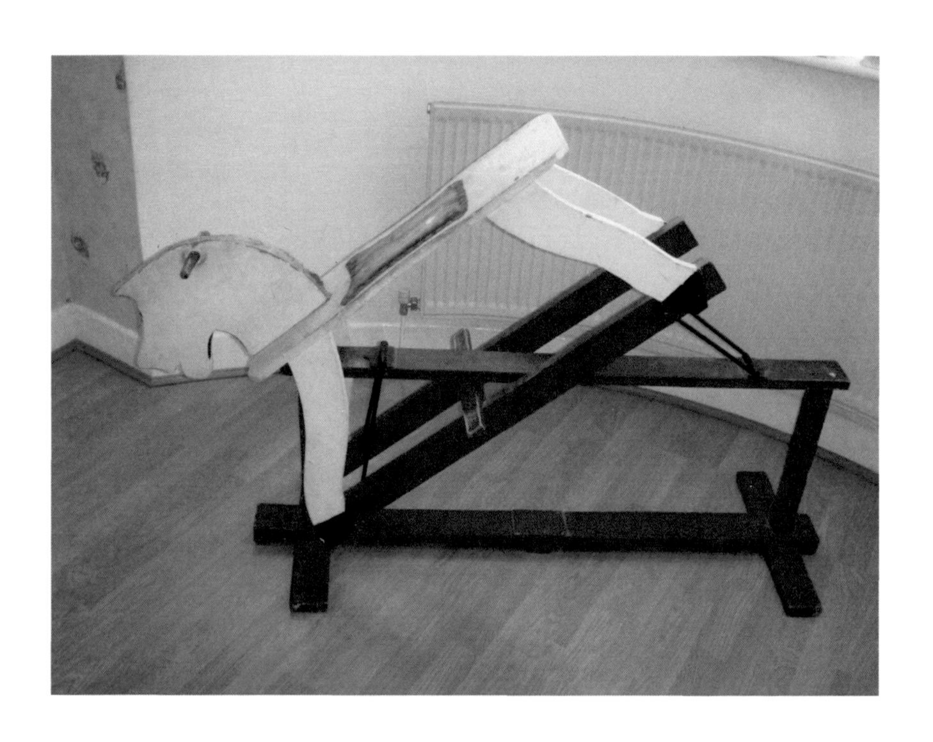

My rocking horse – showing the locked back legs.

Every time I played on my rocking horse I would go too fast and was thrown over its head. I always got told off by my mom, and the horse was put back in the coal house.

LEFTOVERS

I have heard people say when they were children all the food their parents had always seemed better than what they had. I was just the same when my dad came home from work, which was usually late because he always dropped in to the Tote, which was a club by his works. Dropped in means he was drinking. When he sat down to dinner I used to stand and watch him eating, this used to annoy him, "What do you want?" he would say in a stern voice. "Can I have some meat please?" he handed me his fork with the meat on it and said, "Gad Blimey," that was his favourite saying and the other two words that went with that I just cannot repeat, or do not wish to, it was his way of saying, I am annoyed. He would cut a piece of meat and hand it to me, attached to it was his fork, it always tasted much better to me than mine just because it was Dad's. I would stand there chewing and he would order me to go and play, so I always went into the kitchen waited a couple of minutes and strolled back into the living room and sat on the settee, this was facing forward to where the dining table was. I just kept a low profile, thinking he wouldn't notice. When he had finished eating he would always push his plate away from him and wipe his fingers on the tablecloth. Quick as a flash I would jump up and look on Dad's plate to see if anything was left; if there was, I would say, "Please can I have that, Dad?" I had to be quick for fear someone else in the room would get there before me, "Go on," he would say as he rose from the dining room chair to the easy chair by the fire. No matter what was left I ate it – greedy no, hungry yes I was.

As soon as Dad sat in his easy chair by the fire he lit up his Woodbine cigarette, and as it got dark the flickering flames from the fire danced all over the ceiling, that holds such special memories. Cosy and feeling very secure. I would play 'I Spy' with my sisters, we only had a wireless, we didn't have a television for several years. Playing 'I Spy' was a laugh because I couldn't read. My sister would say, "I spy with my little eye something beginning with H." I would say, door, window, rug – they were very patient with me.

I also remember a lot of times when the fire was aglow and kept glowing by putting one lump of coal on at a time, it was those times when I went out and pulled the palings off the neighbours' fences for firewood. When we did have five hundredweight of coal delivered, Mom would on a Sunday, "have a nice fire going." When evening came, curtains drawn, once again those flickering dancing images on the ceiling, even on the walls, on a cold winter's night would warm me right through. Many times we would all sit in the dark with the fire aglow – Kathleen, Doreen, Janet, John in his pram, Mom and Dad and me. Dad smoking his Woodbine; my mom would be knitting most evenings, and when all is quiet the clicking of the knitting needles sounded very loud; the rest of us just staring into the fire, not a word being said. It's a warm feeling remembering those family evenings. When I'm sitting in my lounge with the light off and the glow from my open fire is dancing on the ceiling it takes me back to those wonderful days sitting with my mom, dad, brothers and sisters. It's a warm feeling I'm getting typing up this page. Go on, close your eyes and think back to your childhood and remember the happy times in your life with your mom, dad, brothers and sisters – then the sad ones don't seem half so bad. The best time I find is when one is alone and quiet.

JACK FROST

Every year when winter came round, our house was very cold and damp. Every morning, as we were returning to the land of the living, we knew it was very cold outside because our breath as we breathed would look like steam coming out of the boiling kettle. So the bedclothes were wrapped even tighter around us to keep in the warmth, and our mother had one hell of a job getting us out of bed. One thing I do remember well, were the beautiful patterns in the ice on the inside of our windows, the colours were sparkling when the sun shone on them, the ice was so thick when I tried to scratch it with my nail nothing happened. I couldn't make a hole in the ice to see what the weather was like outside and I always hoped it had snowed. We had lino on the floor and when I got out of bed half asleep and put my foot on the floor I soon woke up, it was like standing on ice. I only possessed one shirt, I hadn't any pyjamas so I slept in my shirt. I slept with my younger brother, he wet the bed every night, so every morning I was soaking wet. My mom lit the oven so we could stand in front of it, steam rising off us. I had to go to school every day with that same shirt on. I tucked my collar inside my shirt so I could wash my neck. One shirt, a pair of pumps with holes in, socks that had more holes in them than there was material and a coat I could not fasten because it was too small, that was my entire wardrobe. We only possessed one towel in our house at that time, and for a long time after that, so being the two youngest when we came to use the towel it was soaking wet. On a very cold snowy or frosty morning, feeling very cold and drying oneself on a wet towel was, to say the least, not nice. Mom would say, "You will be all right, dry yourself." I went through that longer than I care to remember. It must have been heartbreaking for my mom. We had a blue long family comb, which sat on the windowsill next to the back door; again we only had one and it was used by the whole family. We had that comb for years, it was made of nylon.

I got two slices of toast most mornings; on rare occasions we got porridge. I always, all through my school years, took two pieces of toast for my lunch wrapped in some of the bread paper; I put them in my coat pocket and by break time they were all screwed up like someone had twisted them round. Funny really thinking about it, I always really enjoyed that toast – I can smell it and taste it as I'm typing up this page. I bet as you are reading this chapter you wished you had lived like I did, ha, ha.

Years earlier I slept in a bed with my two sisters, they were at the top of the bed, I was at the bottom; yes we had arguments about feet every night, most times I did it on purpose. In the winter Mom put a house brick in the oven, wrapped it up and put it in the bed, even a pop bottle filled with warm water was used when we had one. On occasions the water would leak out of the bottle and wet the bed because we hadn't screwed the stopper up tight enough. Of course bottles weren't used that often, in fact it was rare we had pop but when we did they were taken back because there was a deposit on pop bottles then. I've taken them back to get the deposit for my mom, then bought two pounds of spuds with the 2d I got off the bottle at first in those early days, then it went up to 3d (three pence). When my eldest brother came home on leave from the army his overcoat was put on our bed, it felt very heavy and very warm. I was told many times by my mom, "There are people out there worse off than you, are," all I can say to that is they must have been naked and lived under a tree.

Our toilet, being outside, froze up every winter. My mom took a bucket to bed; we all would go into her bedroom to use it, we shivered all the way there and back. My mom worked so hard for her children as most mothers do, she was always first up and suffered those cold 'jack frost bitten' mornings to warm the kitchen up for all her family and do the breakfast for us and Dad's lunch for work. As we all left school and joined the ranks of workers Mom still did the same every morning but now she had lunches to do as well. How those mothers cope, I have no idea, but they do, my hat goes off to those brave ladies, all of them.

IN ALL ITS GLORY

Barry's parents who lived next door to our house sometimes took me with them when they had a picnic, and the males including Barry, would be fishing. This trip was a short time after I fell in the river at Colsehill when I went with Barry, and his dad took us home in his Scammel Scarab that being his three-wheeled Railway Iron Horse.

We got on the 14 bus at Glebe Farm, where we went I've no idea, wherever it was we were there all day while they were fishing. I wandered off, I don't like fishing, still don't. I got bored, still do, well young children do don't they. And adults like me, ha, ha. There was a barbed wire fence; what's in there, I thought, so under I go, caught my trousers on the barbed wire and heard the sound of ripping material. Well it had torn my trousers, how can I say, like an upside down U, it made a flap. I had no underpants on, (the reason being that I didn't possess any), so I tucked in the hanging piece of material the best I could and made sure no one could see. I headed back to where they were fishing and sat on the grass by the men fishing. When all was packed up off we went, me walking at the side of them holding my trousers where they were ripped. On the bus, liking the bus ride and enjoying all that, boy my mind was full of all sorts which made me forget about my ripped trousers. I got off the bus and not a thought about my trousers. I was walking in front of Barrie's parents with Barry, they were all laughing, I looked round to see why they were laughing. Barry's mom, holding her stomach while in fits of laughter, said in muffled voice through the laughter, "What have you done to your trousers?" By this time they were all in fits of laughter, Barry's two sisters, his older brother and mom and dad. Of course I was showing both cheeks of my bare bum, it must have looked a sight, and my face felt red.

On arriving home my mom was not too pleased as she had to find something to patch those trousers for me to wear when I went back to school. The only material she had was red so the patch was red on my grey trousers, she had tried very hard to find some material that was suitable, she even asked her friend Lizzie but she didn't have anything and the trousers had to be patched as they were the only ones I possessed, so she had no choice but to patch them as I needed them for school. Even though we lived in poverty I had a wonderful childhood and my mother always did the best she could. It's easy to criticise when one is brought up with better living standards, I always remember my mom saying if you only have a penny you cannot spend two.

SUFFERING

I remember one very cold winter's evening in 1949 or 1950; the fire in the grate was only just glowing. The five of us we were very cold, Mom was rubbing our hands and giving us a cuddle to warm us up. Dad was nowhere to be seen. I remember seeing my mom cry because her little children were cold and hungry. It was very hard for a child to see how his mother was suffering, I wanted to help and I remember thinking I wish I could help my mom so I sat and thought of ways I could help, then it came to me.

That evening started me on the road to pulling off the palings in my garden and down my road. It was snowing and without gloves my hands soon got cold, no overcoat, no wellingtons, and only worn-out pumps. The fence then was low, it was feather-edge fencing about two and a half feet high. All the front gardens at that time had the same fencing, it was put there by the council. I was able to pull off the palings which were about four inches wide; some came away with no trouble, others I used one of the palings to put behind them and prise them off. With an armful I took them home thinking Mom would be pleased, but I got a severe telling off and told, "Never take what isn't yours." I cried like a baby, she kissed and hugged me. After that I used to break them up and put them in the coalhouse; we had no coal so I knew Mom wouldn't go in there. I became quite good at getting those palings off. At the end of that winter the palings in my road had a lot of gaps. Mom asked me to go to the tip to find some old shoes so she could burn them on the fire – with slack and potato peelings they made a good fire. I found many shoes on that tip, I even went there with my friend Trevor. I made a trolley and a bike off that tip, but that's another story.

I can say though, I loved my childhood; the freedom to roam, to explore and I am very grateful for that.

LAUGHTER

When my mom used to tell me my eldest brother Donald was coming home on leave from the army, I used to shake with fear. I think he loved to hear screams with pain attached to them. But only if they were painful screams of other people, I think if it had been him in pain he would not have done it to others. Mom would say, "Oh that's good," as she read his letter, "he's coming home for the weekend." "Oh no," I used to say to myself. I used to try and hide and stay out of his way.

When I was out playing I completely forgot about Donald coming home from the army. In I went to have my tea through the back kitchen and into the living room. Then absolute and total fear stormed through my little body. Sitting on the chair by the living room door was Donald. "Got you!" he would say as he grabbed my arm. "You forgot about me didn't you," he would say. "Have you been playing up?" he would ask. "No," I would reply. He would turn me over his knee and bite my bum. I'm not going to cry, I used to think to myself, but the pain was unbearable. I held back the tears and Donald would say, "Oh tough are we now!" Over his knee again, and boy did he bite. "YES!" I screamed very loud and cried for a long time. I had big teeth marks and very bad bruising, it was tender and very sore for a long time. He laughed very loud and thought it was funny. I didn't think it was funny. It turned out he had been told not to hit the kids. He would say, "Well I haven't hit him, I only bit his bum." One afternoon my two eldest brothers were throwing my sister Janet up to the ceiling and catching her as she was coming down; she was laughing and having a good time, enjoying every moment of it, I was saying, "My turn, do it to me, do it to me," so they threw me up in the air and as I hit the ceiling they turned and walked away. I hit the floor, and started to cry as I was crying from the pain that I got from hitting the floor. They seemed to think this was very funny as the two of them were laughing. Mom said, "Why don't you leave him alone and Donald replied, "We're only playing, he's alright." It seemed they thought what they did to me didn't matter.

MAGGOTY BROOK

At the age of five my sister Doreen (aged eight) took me and my sister Janet (aged six) over the park to what was called the white bridge, which was so called because it was painted white. This was in the Bucklands End area. At that time in 1948 all the new houses were being built; we explored the unfinished houses without doors so it wasn't a problem getting in, it was fun to me. I had never seen houses being built, I was really fascinated. Just by the end house we had been looking at was the River Cole, the white bridge spanned it of course, and about eight yards from the bridge was what I was told was a spring with its fresh water flowing, known as Maggoty Brook. Everyone, well all the children, called it that, but I've no idea why or who gave it that name. We all drank from that flowing clear water spring, myself on many occasions as I was growing up. That spring was only a few yards away from the road and ran into the River Cole. The name of the road is Cole Hall Lane.

All those houses I saw being built at the age of five have, in the last couple of years, been demolished and now new houses stand where they were; such a short time for houses to stand 1948–2008. I wonder if Maggoty Brook is still there? I must go and look and relive my memory of a five-year-old. I may see you there. By the way, the white bridge is no longer there. One year we had very bad storms, the swollen river broke its banks, lifted that old white bridge and floated it down the river. A temporary bridge was erected, single line traffic only, traffic lights each end of it. I was told it was temporary, but it is still there years later. I wonder how much longer it will be there across the river, will it outlive the new houses? At least it slows the traffic down which is a good thing, especially at night as it is very dark in that area. After writing this chapter that bridge has been taken down and a beautiful bridge now stands there, a credit to whoever constructed it.

My sister had a den under all the overhanging trees, brambles and shrubs on the river's edge, it was great, I really loved it. I went there a few times with a friend of mine; to think then I was six years old, being allowed to go all over the place and play in the river, and to think it was full of pollution. They used to allow the sewage into that river instead of into the sewage farm. All Mom used to say and she said it all the time was, "Mind the horse road," and behave yourself and those sayings never changed. I bet those sayings are still said today by some of the older generation to young children. Mom would say things like, "Where have you been?" the answer was always, "Nowhere." Mom would usually ask, "What you been doing?" our reply was always, "Nothing." "I don't know, you have been out all day, been nowhere and done nothing," she always replied. Been down the park to me was going nowhere, playing was doing nothing, not like running errands or going up to town.

So many things we do as children that as adults gives us such wonderful memories to look back on, especially in an evening sitting alone in a darkened room with just the reflection of the fire flickering and dancing round the room, just like the evenings when we sat with our mother. What wonderful feelings run through my mind when remembering those halcyon days. What freedom, boy was I a lucky little lad. Of course as a child I didn't realise how lucky I was to have such freedom.

FAMILY PUDDINGS

Mom was a wonderful cook, self-taught on most recipes, but my nan of course showed her how to do many dishes. Her bread pudding was so tasty, I used to help her to mix it up, I loved the feel of that mixture on my hands. Fruitcake we sometimes had, I was never allowed to touch that. My brothers and sisters used to stand around the kitchen table and we would fight to see who could get the bowl and scrape out the mixture that was left. If I was lucky enough to be there on my own, Mom used to let me scrape out the bowl to myself.

The food I didn't like eating was tripe, chitterlings, brains and kidneys. Even if I was hungry I couldn't eat those items of food. Apple pies were my favourite. It was fascinating to watch Mom doing the pastry. She used to use a sterilised milk bottle as a rolling pin, sprinkling flour everywhere; it used to be all over the floor and all over Mom's piny, I can see her doing that now. I would help to peel the apples; I used to eat all the apple peel, the core, pips as well. All the pastry that was left after doing the apple pie, Mom used to allow one of us that was there at the time to make jam cakes with it. She always put a pattern around the pies and a pattern in the middle, also a slit in the middle to let the steam come out. I used to feel very clever when I made the jam cakes with the leftover pastry and say to my sister, "I've made this." My mom used to always make me share it. When she made mince pies, after rolling out the pastry, she would get a set of metal cutters that she bought from Woolworths for 6d (sixpence). These were used mostly at Christmas for mince pies. She always allowed her children to use the cutters to cut the shapes out of the pastry, and it was very exciting to me to see the shapes they made.

Another pudding I used to love was suet pudding, known as Spotted Dick. After mixing the mixture Mom would always place it into a pillow case or a tea towel and put it into a pan of water to boil. One pudding I hated was Yorkshire Pudding with jam on it. I

Used to eat it but never liked it. I was never keen on rice pudding but I loved semolina and still do.

One food item that I did like that Mom made was brawn. Mom used to buy pigs' heads from the butcher's, scrub them clean, put her fingers in the eyeball sockets and pull out the eyes. The head was then boiled in a pan and that was one smell I hated. The brawn, when it was done and set, was even better than when it was brought from the butcher's. Cooking is one thing that I have never taken to, I used to watch my mom do all the baking. All the ingredients were never measured, she just guessed them, she was so good she got the weight close enough to the nearest ounce.

If we knew Mom was going to bake the next day my sister Janet and Trevor's sister, Nanette, Trevor and myself would go scrumping apples when it was dark.

The one time I remember as we crept out of one of the gardens, my sister Janet had filled her knickers with apples, me and Trevor put them down our shirts and Nanette, to our amazement, was dragging behind her a branch full of apples. When we asked her why she had broken off a branch she replied, "I couldn't be bothered picking the apples and filling my knickers with them so I broke off this branch." We were all surprised at the amount of apples that were on the branch, we ate some of the apples and we took the rest to our moms. Our moms always told us off but seeing that we couldn't take them back Mom made a beautiful apple pie. Of course it always depended on whether Mom had enough flour, lard, eggs and whatever else one needs to make pies with, usually we got our pie.

It must be the end of the season

"OK, Trev, that's enough. I hope they are sweet. I'll take some home to my mom – she might make an apple pie."
"Yeah, me too, Dave. I'll take some to my mom as well."

A PERFECT RIGHT HAND

In 1949 I had been in school for about seven months; I started in the January of that year, a tender five-year-old. I was asked with all the other boys and girls to take home a letter telling parents about a day out at Whipsnade Zoo, and would they sign the consent form to allow their sons or daughters to go on the coach and would they pay 3d (three pence) a week or more as the cost of the trip was 10/- (ten shillings). I don't recall paying the 3d every week, I do however remember saying to my teacher on one occasion that I hadn't any money to give to her and she shouted at me in a very loud voice and shamed me in front of the whole class, by saying that all the other boys and girls had paid, so why couldn't I? What did they expect a five-year-old to do at that time when children relied on their parents? It was all my mom could do to feed us.

Anyway I did go on the trip, my teacher and the headmistress came with us. I can still see that screwed-up face of that headmistress – I hated her, talk about ruling a child with a rod of iron, that headmistress had two iron rods and a whip, her voice was the whip, her hands were the rods of iron, her right-hand slap could make you have nightmares for a fortnight. I remember nothing of the day at Whipsnade Zoo, only that one incident that is burned in my memory. Can't remember that head teacher's name nor do I want to.

There was a fairground ride which had a barrier all round it so no one could walk into the ride and get hurt; being five years old and very small I put my hands on top of the rail and ducked my head under it. I was about six feet away from the ride going up and down and round and round. I remember the horses on the ride because I was wishing I could sit on one and have a ride, when I was suddenly violently dragged away by my hair, screamed at and slapped around the face from left to right until I felt sick and giddy.

That's what I remember about that day at Whipsnade Zoo. I've tried but I remember nothing, only that part of the day. I had only been there ten minutes when that happened. I do remember wanting to go home to someone that loved me, my mom.

DINNERS – ONE DAY ONLY

My first week at school I heard the children saying how much they enjoyed the dinners and puddings they had had that day, the thought of puddings made me want school dinners. The boy who became my friend stayed for school dinners and told me all about them. His name was Michael Luckman, we were never apart, he never once made any comment on my appearance, sadly he died of Leukaemia at the tender age of 14. I think of him even to this day. We were in the junior football team, we won the league in 1955; he is standing next to me on my left, right as you look at the photograph (see on page 214–6 back row far right).

My mom had to plead and beg the headmistress to let me stay for school dinners (Mom told me that) because Mom didn't work so I wasn't really allowed. Only certain children got free meals; my mom paid for that week. I heard girls taking the mick out of the children who had free dinners, saying, "Our moms have to pay so why should you get them free, your parents are scroungers."

So for my first school dinner, I was a little excited, we had to line up in the corridor to go into the hall where all the table and chairs were placed out in two rows. As I stood in the queue the girls were saying to me, "You can't stand by me, don't touch me, stand away," so I moved, then I was told by another girl, "I don't want you by me," so I ended up at the back of the queue. In we went in single file; every time I went to sit down I was told, "You can't sit by me." I was feeling very low and very much alone by this time. The teacher must have seen what was going on, she told me to sit there, pointing to a vacant chair, and I sat opposite the cruellest girl I have ever known who said, "Why did she put you opposite me? I told you in the queue I don't want you by me, and don't look at me while I am eating my dinner." She made me feel terrible, "You sit somewhere else tomorrow, I don't want you looking at me." We had fish for dinner; on the table was a bottle of parsley sauce, I never knew what it was then, I saw a boy pick the same type of bottle up on the next table so I thought it must be OK to put it on my dinner. So I picked up the bottle that was by me and shook it hard, just like the brown sauce we had at home, I always had to shake it hard to get the sauce out, I thought this sauce must be the same, well it smothered my dinner, I was horrified! The girl started at me again, "I bet you never have sauce in your house, bet your parents can't afford it, you only put that much sauce on because you are a pig! Miss, miss," she shouted to the teacher, "he has put lots of sauce on his dinner now he is not eating it." The teacher I remember was very kind, she said never mind to me and walked away. That horrible girl kept saying, "pig, pig, anyway you shouldn't be here your mom doesn't work, I bet you haven't paid for it like my mom paid for me, pig." I never said a word to that girl all through dinner. I tried to eat it but found I didn't like it, the sauce that is, so I didn't have any dinner. We had apple pie and custard for desert and the girl opposite said, "I see you have eaten all that and you ate it quick, you pig, I bet you never get puddings at home."

The reason I shook the parsley sauce bottle the way I did, I explained to the teacher, was because at home we always had to shake the brown sauce like that. With a calming hand on my shoulder she said, "It's all right, David." The last words I remember that horrid girl saying to me were, "Anyway you shouldn't be here, your parents don't look after you." She was so cruel I had tears in my eyes. When you stayed for school dinners you weren't allowed to leave the school premises so I sat in the corner of the playground to stay away from that girl, even then I saw her pointing to me as she was talking to some other girls.

When I went home that evening from school I told my mom I wasn't staying for school dinners anymore. My mom went mad at me, saying, "After all the pleading and begging I did to your headmistress and now you don't want to stay for dinners any more and I paid for the whole week." "I don't like the school dinners," I said. I never told her the real truth. The truth was I was too afraid to sit opposite that cruel girl and be tormented. That was my first and last school dinner. That girl was right about the pudding; we rarely got them at home. Well not in the week days, sometimes we did on a Sunday. I wonder what she is like now? I bet she doesn't remember what a horrible cruel girl she was. I would like to think she does remember and regrets what a horrible little girl she was.

AN APPLE A DAY

When I started school, the second teacher I had was called Miss Pitt, I loved that teacher. I was in her class till I went into the juniors. One day while she was telling us something she suddenly said, “David, come here.” I remember this moment so well. When I got to her desk she opened the drawer of her desk, well it was more a lid than a drawer. She took out an apple, held it out to me and said, “Here is an apple for you,” placed it in my hand and started to say, “but,” but the apple went straight to my mouth that fast I think she was going to say, “don’t eat it until playtime. Oh all right, David, go and sit down and eat it as quick as you can.” I wonder if any of the other children were wondering why they never got an apple, if it had been me seeing another child being given an apple I would have thought why can’t I have one.

What a wonderful lady. With me, devouring the apple, she said, again, “Quietly as you can, David.” I think I must have been slurping and making sucking noises as the juice was running from the apple. I was so thin and so poorly dressed, I think maybe I was malnourished and she could see that, maybe I just looked malnourished, I don’t know for sure. Every day that very thoughtful wonderful lady brought me an apple. After that first day she gave me an apple she would say, “I’m going to give you an apple at playtime,” which she did. I do so love that lady; thank you, Miss Pitt, and God bless you wherever you are.

My teacher, Miss Pitt, giving me an apple

MY FIRST TRAM RIDE

It's funny the things that trigger your memory. My first tram ride was to the Lickey Hills, this I remember very well after my wife jogged my memory. I was five years old, before my younger brother John was born. Mom took me and my three sisters Janet, Doreen and Kathleen to the Lickey Hills on a tram. We travelled on a number 14 bus from Audley Road, Glebe Farm, Stechford Birmingham 33, into Birmingham city centre. I can remember getting off the bus in the Old Square, from here we walked through the Minories which fascinated me because the road had been laid with rubber blocks. We walked under Lewis's bridge across Bull Street along Temple Row until we reached St. Phillips church (this was the church I attended for my school leavers' service at the age of fifteen), we crossed over the church yard leading us to Colmore Row, walked along this busy road to the end. Across the road on the left-hand side stood the Post Office with what to me seemed a very large revolving door; on the left of this building was Hill Street, which was quite a steep hill going down, crossing over the railway bridge the walls of which were much too high to see over but at least I could smell and hear the trains. At the bottom of this hill we turned into Navigation Street and to my amazement a wonderful sight to see all the trams lined up with queues of people waiting to get on, what seemed to me at that time hundreds of people.

Once I was on the tram, I was so excited; even at the tender age of five I loved trains, the clickety-clack sound they made on the rails. I had never been on a train at that time. Me and my new friend Trevor went to Stechford railway station to watch the trains go by, we were allowed to roam all over the place and at such a young age, so going on a tram seemed to me like going on a train. The swaying and the clickety-clack was just a dream to me, I can still see those polished wooden benches with the reversible back rests. I was sitting by the window looking at the world going by, I was so happy, what I thought I was doing was whistling. My sister Kathleen who was sitting on the other side of the tram opposite me shouted to me, "David, for God's sake shut up." Mom said to her, "Oh leave him alone, he's just happy," so I stopped whistling, I bet to the delight of the passengers!

When we arrived at the terminus this was situated at the bottom of the Lickey Hills, well almost. I remember what seemed to me like a thousand steps to go up, and I ran up those steps in my excitement to see what was at the top, it was all trees all around. Mom being a large lady struggled to climb those steps (I bet they are still there). Mom took sandwiches and a bottle of pop. I thought I would roll down the hill and I went much faster than I thought I would – it made me very giddy, and as I stood up I fell over, my sense of balance was all over the place. As I finally regained my senses I went exploring; I remember thinking, I'm going to be an explorer, as boys do. I strayed further away from my mom than I should have, when I suddenly realised I was lost. I was quietly starting to panic – how long I was away from my family I'm not sure. I wandered around aimlessly looking for them, then to my delight I saw them through the bushes sitting on a bench eating sandwiches and drinking pop. I waited a couple of minutes to calm myself down then I slowly walked up to them and said, "I've been exploring – can I have a sandwich please, I'm hungry." "I'll give you sandwich, my lad, I've been worried to death," Mom said sternly. "Why?" I asked calmly, trying to act like I didn't know. "Right, you stay where I can see you." "OK, Mom," I replied, no way was I going to explore anymore, I was afraid of getting lost again, so I played with my sisters until Mom shouted, "Come on, you lot, we are going back now." Yeah, I thought, back on that tram.

I was overjoyed. To me that was the best part of the day out, riding on that tram, it's a shame that young people can't experience riding round the cities on a tram the same as the ones I rode on.

IRON HORSE

My next-door neighbours' son was named Barry, he was five years older than me. He loved the small hours of the morning, and boy could he talk, he could talk the leg off an iron pot as the saying goes. No matter how tired I became he just would not go home. I made friends with Barry as soon as I made friends with Trevor he never played in the street till then Barry he was two years older than me, we sort of hit it off from day one, we played together and kept in touch until the day he died, which was in the year 2009 – a sad loss of a very dear friend.

Looking back to his and my childhood, when I was only six years old he took me to a place called Coleshill. He loved fishing, and the thing I remember about that day and the reason I remember it was that there were stepping stones going across the river, one was very green with moss. The river was quite shallow where the stepping stones were, I remember like it was yesterday, his very words to me, "Mind how you step on this stone it's very slippy." Not taking a lot of notice and thinking I knew best I jumped on to that stone, yes jumped! Of course, I slipped and fell in, Barry looked at me and laughed, he said, "I told you it was slippy." To a skinny six-year-old the water seemed to be deep, it came past my waist, Barry waded in, picked me up and carried me to the bank. (That wasn't the last time I went into the river while I was growing up, it happened a few times; that first soaking I got was at the bottom of a hill in Coleshill called Maxstoke Lane, the river is the Blythe. I spent many a happy hour over the following years in that same field, the difference was that I had swimming trunks.)

As we started to walk across the field to head home Barry saw an LMS railway three-wheeler lorry, he ran very quickly to the gate and waved like mad with his coat – talk about luck or coincidence, it turned out it was Barry's dad (he had worked on the railways from a boy, his depot was in Nechells in Rupert Street, Birmingham). Barry shouted, "Come on, Dave, it's my dad." Barry's dad looked at me and smiled, he never laughed, he could see I was distressed because I was soaking wet, "And what happened to you, young man?" he asked as if he didn't know. "I fell into the river," I replied. "Come on, young fella," he said, "I will take you home in my Iron Horse." "Iron Horse?" I said. "Yes, David, that's what they call these lorries, Iron Horses, look," he said, "you sit on the cowling, you'll get dry on there."

I got lovely and warm sitting on that cowling, it was a cover that fitted over the engine, I loved that lorry, I thought to myself I'm going to drive one of these when I grow up. When I did grow up I passed my test on those Iron Horses, I really loved driving them and would you believe it I worked alongside Barry's Dad! When I called him by his surname, which I had done from birth, he said, "David, you're an adult now, call me Bunny." Calling him by his first name was very strange to me because I was brought up to say Mr and Mrs and if I didn't my mom would clout me round the ear, so it was always by their surname which I still do to this day. Incidentally the correct name for the three-wheel Iron Horse is scammell scarab.

TWO BIRTHDAY CARDS

I've sat and thought very hard about this. Did I ever get a present for my birthday? I cannot bring to mind any. I did get a windjammer as they were called at that time, just before my ninth birthday, I felt really smart and very warm, well I could fasten it up. I suppose that could be classed as a present, well it was a wonderful gift, I loved it, being brown in colour and zipped right up to the neck. I was allowed to go outside wearing my new coat to show it to Trevor, I was told I must go back into my house and take it off but I really wanted to keep it on.

Trevor was so jealous, on that same morning I was showing it to him I didn't see him pick up a handful of dirt, and as we werc talking he threw the dirt over my new coat and ran off like the wind into his house. I ran after him, knocked on his back door, his mom came and said, "Trevor told me to tell you he doesn't feel well, he is not playing out today." We laughed about it the next day, we never fell out so I did it to him the first chance I had, which was a long time. After that incident my brother got married in the December. I wore that coat for his wedding, maybe that's why I got the new coat for my birthday. I wasn't allowed to play out in it till after the wedding. Mom bought that windjammer from Evans the club man; he called every Saturday for the money – you know, the glad and sorry, glad to have it sorry you have to pay for it.

One year I remember well, I was ten years old, Trevor's Mom, my mom's best friend Lizzie, gave me a birthday card some years; this year was different, I got a postcard birthday card, that's the type we used to get in those days. That year I was ten she put 2/- (two shillings) in with the card, the first and last time that happened. Some years I got two cards, one off my mom and one off Trevor's mom. I never, as far as I know, got more than two cards, it just never happened. Most years I only got one card. Well, better I ate food than had a toy car or a game.

MY FIRST CAR RIDE

My first car accident was in the year 1950, when cars owned by the working classes were few and far between. How it came about was my two eldest brothers were converting a fish and chip van into a caravanette; the chip van was equipped with all its fryers still in situ and all the fat still in it, it was smelling of old grease and chip fat everywhere, horrible. I don't think buying your fish and chips from this van would have been a good idea. Any road up, I was given a scraper to get as much fat as I could off the walls – "Don't get dirty" was my eldest brother's command. I ask you, fat and grease everywhere. I obeyed his every wish, well I tried to, yes I got grease and fat on me. "Leave that now," he said, "it's OK," so very quickly I dropped the scraper. I stood and watched him sawing slots in a piece of 2x2 inch timber – I want to do that, I thought, and picked up a saw and started to saw one of the slots he had been sawing. I will soon get through this, I thought, he will be pleased with me (secretly I thought he would give me some money for helping him – WRONG). Suddenly a deafening shout of, "Don't cut through that, put the saw down," my nerves took on an Olympic high jump. What he explained when he came back down to earth was when a piece has many slots cut in it you can bend it, pointing to the round front of an old caravan, "that's what these two pieces of wood will do, form a round front over the driver's cab." All this took place on an old farm, not long before it was demolished. The changing face of old England, you would never know there had been a farm there. It looked far better than it does now, it was only a couple of miles from where I lived.

My dad came to see how they were doing with this old van, he was very impressed with them. A few minutes after Dad arrived my eldest brother Donald's friend George turned up (he lived across the road from our house, they grew up together, even evacuated together somewhere, I think it was Nottingham). This friend arrived in a brand new car, he had only had it a week, a bright shiny black car, the smell of the leather interior is something I shall never forget. Sometime later my brother decided to pack up and go home, George said, "Come on, I'll give you a lift in my new car."

I was very excited; a ride in a car, I had never been in a car before! Out of the farm gate, turned right, it felt like we were doing a thousand miles an hour, well it was fast. I remember these words my dad said to me, "Hang on to your hat, son, this is the fastest you will ever go down this road." I'm not wearing a hat, I was thinking, I wonder why he thinks I'm wearing a hat? We were flying, we came to the railway bridge (this bridge has since been widened), and we started to climb to reach the brow of the bridge; there wasn't any way of seeing if there were any other vehicles coming over the bridge on the other side. Just as we reached the brow George was too far over to the right. We slammed straight into an oncoming vehicle and it folded up like cardboard. The poor man sat with a glazed look on his face, his car was absolutely smashed up. George had pushed the car right up against the bridge wall so the man could not get out of any of the doors. My dad told me to go home and tell Mom he would be late home for dinner. I ran like the wind non-stop until I reached home, puffing and panting for breath. I blurted out, "We have been in a car smash, Mom, and it's all smashed up!" Poor Mother went white, staggered to her chair, sat down with tears streaming down her face. "Oh my god!" Mom thought the way I told her was that they had all been smashed up and were all in hospital. "Where are they, where are they?" she kept saying. I was confused, I couldn't understand why she was so upset, she stood up and started running round the room like a headless chicken. "Oh," I said calmly, "I forgot to tell you Dad said he would be a little late home for dinner." Once again she staggered to the chair, nerves all shot. With a stare she says to me, "You silly little bugga, I thought your dad and brother had been seriously injured." I replied in a calm voice, "No, the car's been smashed up not the men, there's nothing wrong with them they're OK." I learned in later years from my brother Donald that even though it was George's fault the insurance company would not pay out. Both men blamed each other for the accident. It turned out that the poor man had repaired his engine, he had no tax or insurance and was out testing the engine he had just repaired. What a shame, I thought, that nice shiny car is all scratched. I remember I was not frightened or shaken at all, I was very calm. That was my first car accident.

The bridge of my first car accident in Church Road, Stechford

Scene of my first car accident,
showing the bridge from the other side of Church Lane.

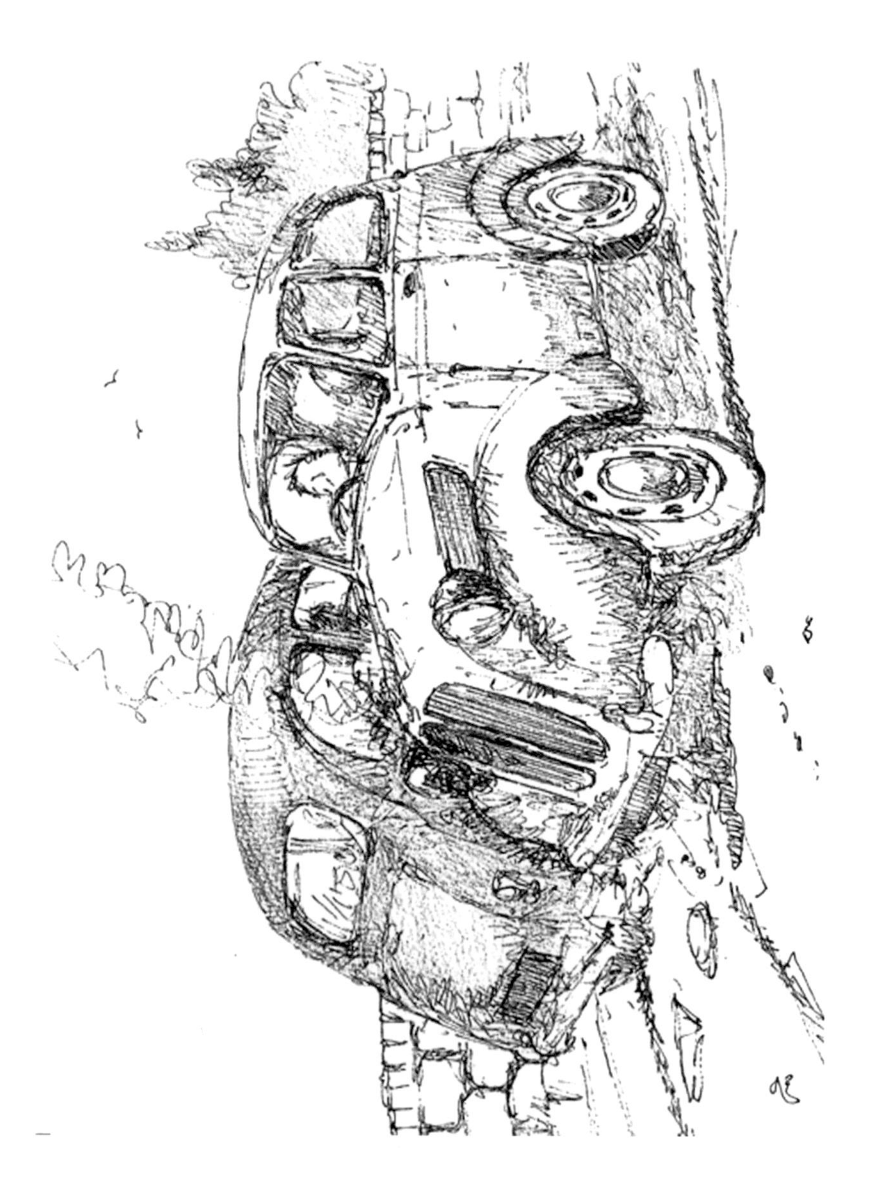

Scraping by

STREAMERS

Stanley James was a hardware shop that was at the end of a row of shops across the road opposite the pub known as the Glebe; in later years it was changed to the Cock and Bull. In the past my mom bought linoleum from Stanley James, we always called it lino, it was the cheapest form of floor covering you could get at that time; it looked beautiful when first laid down, bright vibrant colours, but after a very short time if it carried a lot of traffic the pattern soon wore off. My mom always fitted the lino, never my dad.

Mom even did all the painting and decorating, she was brilliant at wallpaper hanging. Back in the 1940s the edge was left on the rolls of wallpaper, but for a small fee the paper was put on a machine and it cut nearly through the edging. When the roll was tapped on the table the cut edge would fall off. When Mom couldn't afford to pay the extra money to have the rolls trimmed she would sit for what seemed like hours and cut off the edge with a pair of scissors. I have seen Mom leave the edge on, but when put on the wall and overlapped, a bulge from top to bottom of the edge could be seen on every strip. It didn't look too bad, I went in many houses and saw paper hung like that; in fact I helped my mom to hang paper like that. When I was about seven or eight, after she had cut off the edge I always asked to have the edges to play with; she always said no but with a lot of nagging she would give in. I was told, "Don't throw them in the horse road, put it in the dustbin when you have finished playing with them," but after me and my friends had thrown them at each other and had lots of fun I got fed up rolling them up so I left them, streamers scattered all over the road. Yes again I was told to get the cane from the coal house, it was too late to say sorry, three whacks across the bum so I ended up picking it all up after all and binning it. When Mom folded her arms and said to do it, you did it or get the cane from the coal house. Children never learn do they? Well I never did, that's a fact.

GROWING ANOTHER HEAD

Before I started school I had a bubble grow out of the side of my head, you could see the blood pumping round it. I was taken to the Children's Hospital in Birmingham city centre. When the doctor looked at it he was puzzled. He didn't know what it was or why it had happened. I heard him say to my mother, "I won't bandage it, let the air get to it, it looks like an artery that has grown out of his head." He took Mother to one side, he must have thought I was deaf, but in a low voice I heard him say, "Whatever happens, Mother, he must not make it bleed, or he could bleed to death." Well I was frightened to death! Those words frightened the life out of me, as a young child they would wouldn't they and did. After that day I did make it bleed many times and every time I would run to my mom saying, "Mom it's bleeding, am I going to die, am I going to die?" at the same time crying my eyes out. I used to turn over in bed and make it bleed and the pillow used to be covered in blood. The worst time it bled (and boy did it bleed) I was friendly fighting with my cousin who lived with us at the time. He was the one that took me on the bus when I broke my leg. He suddenly said to me, "You're bleeding." I went to my mom, screaming and again saying, "Am I going to die, am I am going to die?" She ran the tap, and with my head under the tap she just kept bathing it with a wet rag. The rag got soaked in blood, it was everywhere. My mom was crying while she was doing it. It seemed a long time being done but it did stop eventually. That was the most worrying time of my young life. But it did go away, it just started to go down. I do believe the doctor was putting some sort of ointment on it to slowly freeze it and it disappeared.

When playing with my friends once they were surprised to see blood pumping from it when I headed a ball. Many years later my mom said that she was worried to death and thought she was going to lose me every time it bled. My mother should never have been put through an ordeal such as that because her life was hard enough.

ICED GEMS

My mom was known by all the local shopkeepers because she used those shops all through the war. People got preferential treatment if they used the same shops. I remember my mom going into Wrenson's (they are no longer trading) asking for a quarter of a pound of iced gems, those little biscuits with a dab of icing sugar in the middle of the biscuit. "Sorry, you are not one of my regular customers," said Mr O, the manager. I believe these were still on rationing because of the sugar that was on them. My mom wasn't very happy to hear him say that to her so she told him a few home truths. I remember I got a little worried because of the way out he raised his voice to my mom. Her friend Winnie (my friend Johnny's mom) used Wrenson's all the time, so she went in and bought iced gems for my mom. Mr O the manager asked Winnie, "Are you buying these for her?" and she replied, "I'm buying them for myself and it's none of your business what I buy or who for!"

My mom was very hard up and she used to make me go to Holidays the local butcher. She used this butcher all through the war and I used to have to go and ask for two or three pence worth of bones for the dog (he knew we didn't have a dog). He always went to the back of his shop and gave me lots of bones wrapped in newspaper and he always said, "Tell Dora, I mean your mom, they haven't been on the floor and there is quite a lot of meat still on the bone." Mom made a stew with them and made it last for three or four days, that's living, eh?

PEG RUGS

Trevor and I were collecting rags from all the houses around our area to make money, and when my mom saw the rags she went through them all to see if there were any coats she could cut up. There were two coats, and after she had washed and dried them I helped my mom to cut them up into long strips, about half an inch wide by six inches long, so she could make peg rugs. The lengths of material were looped through a piece of canvas, and the different colours of the material were sometimes made into a pattern.

It took my mom and me some time to make a peg rug, but I really enjoyed making them with my mom. My sisters loved sitting on it in front of the fire. Mom lined the back with oddments of materials, and when placed in front of the fire it was a joy for me to sit on it, it felt soft and very cosy.

It would have been nice to have one at the side of my bed, it would have made such a difference in the winter months to stand on the rug instead of the icy cold lino. I was sitting on the one by the fire place one day when I saw loads of silver things. I asked Mom what they were, she called them silver fish; I used to watch them running around; if I moved they would vanish very quickly.

I was told sometimes to put the peg rug on the line and beat it with the yard broom; the dust that used to come out of it was from the ashes from the coal fire, and I ended up all grey from the ash dust.

These rugs looked good when down and lasted a very long time. I wonder what people would think these days if they went into a friend's house and saw peg rugs? Would they be talked about I wonder? It wouldn't happen these days, we are all spoiled are we not.

BIRMINGHAM POST AND MAIL

It was my first year of the juniors. As I walked into the classroom I noticed the teacher staring at me and she called me out to go to her. I was thinking, what have I done wrong? I went to the desk where she was sitting writing a letter which she folded and handed to me, saying, "Take this letter and give it to your mother." "OK, Miss," I said. I went to sit down. "No," she said. "Take it home to your mom now." "What, leave school now Miss?" "Yes go straight home now."

I think it was about 2.30–3.00 p.m. Well, get out of school! My feet went so fast through the playground I nearly fell over, I had to run in case she changed her mind. My mom's face when I walked in, "What are you doing out of school?" "My teacher said I could leave school and give you this letter." Well Mom was so delighted when she read the letter she rushed in to the hall for her coat and said, "Come on quick, we can get there in time." We ran up the road and caught the bus. "Where are we going?" I asked. "Shh," she said. I just didn't know what was happening, we got off the bus in the Old Square Birmingham town centre. We were really rushing; I hadn't a clue what was going on.

We ended up in a building with loads of boots and shoes everywhere and that smell you get when in a shoe shop, but this smell was a different from a shoe shop smell you get today of course, it was leather then. I never forgot that smell. My mom handed the letter to the man. (WHY DID GROWN-UPS LOOK SO STERN IN THOSE DAYS?) My mom sat me down, took off my holy pumps (MY FOOTWEAR IN THOSE DAYS WAS VERY RELIGIOUS!) and socks. It was winter, I remember because my feet were wet and I had put on me a brand new pair of socks after mom dried my feet with her handkerchief. They felt so thick and warm with a pattern round the top, they were grey and so was the pattern and to my surprise the man was trying boots on me; "no these are no good," I heard him saying to himself, and he went away. I was horrified, "Mom, I can make them fit," I said to her." "It's all right, son, he is getting a bigger pair for you." Boy was I relived, he tried two different sizes on me before saying, "Yes, these are alright." I asked, "Can I keep them on?" "Of course you can, son," the man said as he patted me on the head, "Yes," said Mom at the same time, she thanked the man and out we went.

Wow can you imagine not having to tuck your sock under your foot to put some space between your foot and the pavement because of the holes in your pumps and not having a soaking wet foot. I used to put cardboard in when the sock was so worn out and there wasn't enough material left to tuck under my foot, but when wet it made my feet wetter plus it went all soggy and fell apart. When the weather was good the pavement rubbed it away to nothing in minutes. I walked out of that building with warm feet and legs but best of all I was walking with dry feet in the rain. I was so happy. I remember that day very well, it felt good. I now know the letter my teacher gave to me was for a free pair of boots and socks from that wonderful establishment known as the Birmingham Post and Mail. I believe they are also referred to as Daily Mail Boots. It turned out that a lot of children at school knew you had your free boots and socks by the socks; if you didn't wear the socks they couldn't tell. I believe the girls' shoes had eyelets in the sides of the shoe, which let other children know where the shoes had come from, and that they were free shoes.

Off to school the next day feeling very warm and proud of my new boots, when two boys came up to me and very loudly said, "Free boots because your parents can't buy you any?" I answered with, "I had these yesterday, my mom bought them for me." "No she didn't, you only get those socks when your parents have no money and you get them from the Birmingham Post and Mail, you are a scruffy scrounger, your parents don't look after you," they teased. I suffered many more comments from a lot of boys but more horrible comments from the girls. Well at least my feet were warm and dry. The teasing ridicule and the torment stopped after a couple of days. I heard one morning another boy getting the same treatment from the boys and girls that I had got from them the week before; children are so cruel especially the ones that were brought up in better living conditions than the boy or girl they were tormenting.

WHITE MICE

The old market hall in the Birmingham city centre, with large steps leading up into what to me looked a massive space with lots of traders selling so many different types of goods, it was just like Aladdin's cave with all the traders shouting at the same time trying to attract the attention of the public as they passed their stall. This shell of a building with arches in the walls every few feet that were once windows made me walk round in awe of the place, and I seem to remember two big pillars either side of the steps at the entrance. I went on a Saturday with my friend Trevor to that old market place, we bought little white mice from there, 6d each (sixpence). Not being able to tell the difference between male and female I ended up with 23 white mice! I gave many of my friends that wanted to keep mice as many as they wanted, free of charge.

When I first started to collect mice, I said to the man selling them, "Mister, can I have that one? Not that one, that one," I said as he picked up the wrong mouse. He picked one up and with a deep breath and a puff and a few choice words he said, "Look, son, do you want this mouse or don't you, I ain't got all day – they are all the same, do you want it?" "Yes, Mister," I said with a trembling voice. He placed it in a box, and feeling very pleased with my new mouse I hurried to the bus stop. I got on the 14 bus to go home to where I lived, and when on the bus upstairs I thought I would take a peep at my new little friend. I didn't know mice were so fast, and as soon as it saw the chink of light, it shot out of the box, ran up my arm, across my shoulders. I just managed to grab its tail, I think it didn't like that because it bit my finger and drew blood, so I threw him back in the box as quick as he came out. I won't do that again, I thought.

Back home I had a beautiful mouse box with a sliding glass lid, inside a well-made nesting box – I felt so proud, I had a factory-made mouse box, with a nesting box, little bowls for food and a bottle clipped to the side for water. In went the mouse, I felt so good I kept looking at it all night. (My mom said I couldn't keep it in the house, so in the back yard it stayed.) Barry who lived next door gave me all the equipment and the mouse box, it was like Christmas come early, I covered it over with a waterproof canvas to keep him warm.

After a few weeks all was well, but one afternoon Barry's cat had slid the glass and got the mouse out before I could get to it, it was so badly cut I was in tears. I called Robert the neighbour who lived the other side of me, I asked, "Rob can you help?" "It's suffering, Dave," he said, "I can't kill it, Rob," I said. "I'll do it for you," he said, and threw it onto the concrete floor, "it's dead now," he said. I buried it in the garden and made a little cross for it. More errands to run, a couple of weeks later I bought another white mouse. I didn't open the box until I reached home, I had learned my lesson, this time I put half of a house brick on top of the box so the cat couldn't slide the glass.

Some time later I got another one just to give my first one a friend, and as I was cleaning them out a week later to my surprise there were 15 (talk about rabbits!). After cleaning them out I forgot to put the house brick back on the glass, the cat killed them one by one, he took them one at a time to his garden next door and they were scattered all round the lawn – he killed all 16. I just sat looking at all those baby mice lying on the grass next door, that was the end of me keeping pets. I shouted to Robert over the back fence, "Rob, do you want my cage?" "Yes please, Dave," he said, so I gave him every item I owned regarding the mice. "Why are you getting rid of them, Dave?" "It's the second time that cat has killed my mice, he won't kill any more of my mice because I won't have any for him to kill!" That surely did kill the pet-saving side of my life.

SHARE NUMBER

The Co-op (Co-operative Society) was the shop that really fascinated me to the point where my imagination ran riot. My mom sent me to the Co-op many times over the years and I went with her many times to buy items from this store. My mom would repeat, "Don't forget to give my share number," that number is burned into my brain 77467 – it rolls off the tongue like poetry. When I got married I could never remember our Co-op number, much to the annoyance of my wife, I gave my mom's number.

I remember those wires that went from the counter to the cash office upstairs, where there were two ladies that could be seen through big glass windows. The ladies serving on the shop floor weren't allowed to handle the cash in those days (it's hard to imagine that now isn't it?). They wrote down the cost of the groceries that had been purchased on a slip with the customer's name on it and what money was given, the slip was then placed in what to me looked like a bomb with the money, they screwed the cylinder, to the lid of the cylinder which was on a wire. (I think that's how it went; my memory is fading a little!) The next operation really got my attention, after the lady had fixed it to the wire she pulled on a wire with a wooden handle attached to it, the bomb would travel upwards along the ceiling and straight in to the cash office, they would sort out the change then send it back to the ladies serving on the shop floor, with the slip and the change. They would call out the name of the person to give them their change, always the surname never by their Christian name. If by this time they were half way through serving another customer, one had to wait for the change till they had finished serving that customer. I don't think that system would work these days do you, everyone seems to be in so much of a rush don't they. It's a shame they didn't leave it in the shop, people would go in just to look at it and of course spend while they were in there.

My mom saved up the dividend until Christmas if she could, which wasn't very often, as that time of her life things were very hard. That dividend book was a life saver at times, I went with my mom a few times to get the money out of that book. We went to the main store in the Birmingham city centre that I believe was the only place Mom could go to for the divi. I remember a couple of times she only got one shilling and sixpence (1/6d) and very glad to have it I might add, times were very hard for Mom in those days. The dividend book was black with hard covers and quiet large I seem to remember; all entries in the book were done by hand when Mom did a withdrawal. She told me if you want quality, shop at the Co-op; they were dearer than most so Mom rarely bought household goods from the Co-op, she had to settle for cheaper goods from other stores, as the old saying goes if you have only a 1/- (one shilling) you can't spend two. My mom said that to me quite a few times through my life. Another saying she very often said was "don't worry, you die if you worry you will die even if you don't, so no point in worrying." She said that to my wife one day when she was worrying about paying the rent because she was short of money and would you believe it, it changed how she thought about things from that day on.

SATURDAY PAY OUT

An occurrence happened every Saturday morning that wasn't anything to do with me directly, indirectly maybe. Mother could not go out on a Saturday morning, that's the time when what we called 'clubmen' came and 'club women'; in the main it was men. Families where I lived, lived on the 'Glad and Sorry' so called because whatever you bought off those club men you paid every week a small amount of money until you had paid back all the cost of the items plus interest, that's why it's called the 'Glad and Sorry', Glad to have it, Sorry to have to pay for it.

Mother could only survive this way in life as most people did in those days – we had shoes, coats, bed linen, and kitchen utensils, even paraffin heaters. Yes, if you were willing to pay weekly those club people were only too willing to sell it to you, so you owed them that much money they kept you in debt for years so they could keep making profit off you. As the amount came down to almost nil this worried them so they would try very hard to tempt you to buy more items off them, they would even make believe they would reduce any item for you because you were a good customer but of course it was all over-priced to start with. Well, on the other hand if those firms had not been around most people would never have been able to buy anything, it was no way to live but it was then the only way for my family.

Every Saturday we had Evans, S and U, Sloanes, the coalman, milkman, plus the insurance man, all calling for some money. To lessen the debt Mom would say to one of them, "I can't pay you this week," boy did they moan, she would say to another one, "I can only pay you 3d (three pence)." "Is that all, Mrs Prosser, it's not enough you know," they would say. I used to like the look on their faces when Mom would say to them, "OK, if you don't want it I will give it to Evans then." "No, I'll take it," they always answered holding out their hand for the money in case Mom changed her mind. Mom did this balancing act with the few pennies she had for years; if she paid 2d or 3d to one, whichever one she missed she would give them double the week after if she could afford it and not pay the ones she gave a few pennies to the week before, and some weeks they were all given nothing at all. I've seen my mom in tears over clubmen pushing for money out of her. Mom always robbed Peter to pay Paul as the saying goes (the good old days, eh!), well they were the good old days for me but not for people like my mother who were trying to survive in this wonderful country we call England. Those clubmen were crooks, they way over-charged for the goods they were pushing to the poor.

FARES PLEASE

My sisters and me, we used to put the dining room chairs together in a row and pretend it was a bus, we would take it in turns to be the driver and the conductor. We did this many times in our young lives. My younger brother John was in his very early years at this time, my sister Doreen would sit him on her lap and make the engine noise to him and rock about to give the feel of the moving bus. My sister Janet would also do this for him. Of course as the years went by he sat on the chairs and made his own noises like an engine, as I did.

Sometimes, but not very often, actually it was quite rare my mom would go with my mate's mom Lizzie to have a quiet drink for an hour. As the saying goes, "while the cat's away the mice will play," that is so true. Our favourite game when no parents were around was to get a pillow and a blanket from the bed, put the blanket over the top stair, sit on the pillow and be pulled down the stairs. (No carpet in those days only lino.) Well, it was great fun for us screaming and shouting, we drove our neighbours to the edge of despair; it must have been a nightmare to live next door to us. The next-door neighbour used to come round and be pulling his hair out. One particular evening we were playing tig and tag – you know, keep your feet off the ground, if touched by the one that's on when your feet were on the ground it was your turn to be on. The only difference this time we were doing it in the house running up and down the stairs, out the front door, round the back, through the back door shouting and I suppose making quite a lot of noise. My mom came in, shouted and told us to play more quietly, children play quiet? Not us lot, that's for sure, but because Mom was home we had to calm it down a little.

My mom, bless her, liked to see her children playing, she always said when she could see her children playing she knew we were happy. The next-door neighbour came round and banged on the door, my cheeky sister Doreen opened the door, the poor neighbour was so fed up he said, "I'm really fed up with you lot,"

My sister was smirking at him as he spoke, "you will smirk on the other side of your face in a minute," then he said, "I suppose your mother is in the bloody pub again." My mom popped her head round the door and replied, "No she bloody well isn't!" A few words were exchanged! My mom's favourite saying then was, "got to play don't they, can't stop kids playing." Well, no way would I like to have lived next door to a family as noisy as we were. Many years later when talking about it to my mom (the years fade the memories for some people) I think she said, "You weren't that bad." Boy, if we weren't I would hate to live by children that were only half as bad as we were, we were very noisy, Mother! But I must agree with you, Mother, when children are playing they are happy, we your children most certainly were.

PLAYING GAMES WITH BROTHER JOHN

As children do, my youngest brother John and I were playing tig around all three bedrooms – running, screaming, shouting, jumping all over the beds having a jolly good time. We hadn't any carpets in our house, only lino (that's short for linoleum) and every time we jumped off the bed on to the floor, well it sounded like thunder.

The next-door neighbours, we really did drive them mad; as we lived in a semi-detached house the floors were joined through the walls, so every time we jumped on the floorboards it sounded like we were in their house. They had four children, well two grown-up lads and two young children, a boy and a girl; we never heard a peep out of them. As we were running from one room to the next, John still trying to tig me, I ran from Mom's room, to the little bedroom across the landing, with brother John close behind me, I pushed the door to the closed position, John's big toe went under the door, his scream was deafening! It made a terrible mess of his big toe, he was taken to hospital.

I got a good hiding, well deserved I suppose, but we were only playing. He suffered a long time with that toe; in fact I took him some time ago to have that toenail off at the foot clinic (the clinic was in an area known to most Birmingham people as the Swan Yardley), maybe that nail gave him trouble because of that accident all those years ago when we were young boys just playing and enjoying life.

"LONESOME"

I came home from school one afternoon when I heard what I thought were the sounds of chicks; I looked in the cupboard at the side of the fireplace, and to my surprise there they were all cuddled together, little balls of yellow fluff, a dozen chicks. I was so excited, Mom told me my eldest brother Donald had brought them home, where from I have no idea – he may have got them from the rag and bone man. Those men had a horse and cart with a box full of chicks, dozens of them, in those days you could get chicks that way by giving the rag and bone man old rags. Mind you, for a dozen chicks he would have wanted a good sack full of old clothes and he would go through them to make sure the clothes or rags were clean. As a child does I kept picking them up – the chicks that is, not the rags – unfortunately one by one they died; after only a very short time only one remained, Mom named it "Lonesome". It grew big, and as it was growing up I noticed that every time I went by it, it pecked me, it pecked me even when I walked into the room and it was the same with my sisters. I played with it a lot while it was growing up, well one could say I tormented it, I suppose it must have been getting its own back.

Our mother was the only one that could do anything with it, it never did peck Mom. I could never go into the backyard without that chicken flying at me, I always ended up the line post screaming, "Mom, Mom, the chicken is pecking me." She would open the back door and shout, "Get in that pen now," (my eldest brother built the pen) the chicken stopped dead in its tracks, its head would go down and look at Mom, "I won't tell you again, get in that pen." It jumped down the two steps and very slowly it walked in to the pen. "I hate that bird," I would say. Mom always said, "It's all right, you must be tormenting it." Every day I would shout through the letterbox, "Mom, is the chicken out?" Sometimes she didn't answer me, another time she said, "It's locked up," when it wasn't, and I would walk in to the back yard that silly bird would either chase me up the line post or into the outside loo. If it was the loo it walked up and down outside the door; there was a gap under the toilet door, and it would pop its head in the gap every now and again making a terrible noise to see if I was still there. I would be shouting at the top of my voice for ages calling, "Mom," when she finally came and locked the chicken up she would smile and say, "I forgot I had let it out." Every time I wanted to go in the backyard I would rattle the gate and shout, "I'm coming in," nothing, all quiet. Good, it's locked up, I thought, in I go. Just as I'm about to open the back door out would fly the chicken from the side of the pen making a terrible noise, pecking me all the way up the line post. It fooled me so many times to thinking it was locked up, it was a cunning bird, it did it to all my brothers and sisters that dared enter our backyard. Even our friends, in the end none of them would go into our back garden not even when told the chicken was locked up. If any chid ventured into the back garden they always ended up the line post. A very good friend of ours, especially of my mom, was a girl that lived across the road from us – her name is Rita Hill. I was talking to her before I published this book and we were having a good old laugh about Lonesome, she remembered being terrorised by our chicken. She said she was up the line post shouting "Pross, Pross, the chicken is biting me," she hated that chicken as much as I did, so did my sisters. I shook the gate one afternoon after school, waiting to get attacked by Lonesome when I noticed Lonesome was hanging over the drain, blood dripping from it. I thought at that time this is the happiest day of my life. As I walked in to the living room my Mom was crying her eyes out, "What's wrong Mom?" I asked. "My chicken is dead," she said. I'm not sorry, I thought, I hated it. My sister Kathleen told me on the 21st September 2009, when we were talking about that chicken and having a laugh, the reason Mom had its neck screwed was because it was egg-bound and suffering. When it was on my plate I sank my teeth into it, I felt like I was getting my own back. The girls, however, wouldn't eat it.

If you walked into our backyard as a child, this is where you would most likely end up shouting "Mrs Prosser, the chicken is pecking me."

NAILED

Whenever Trevor and me went to our park, we sometimes took a short cut down passages between the houses, much to the annoyance of the residents as those passages were for their use only, it was access for the dust men. At the end of the passage was a 6 foot fence; some children had broken a couple of the palings to gain access to the park, as the park entrance was at least a couple of hundred yards away we used those passages whenever we went to the tip or to play in the park. It saved us a good walk.

This particular day we went to the tip; I suppose we were there about three hours looking for pram wheels and bicycle parts. On our way back to go up the passage someone had nailed a big board where the palings were missing. "Gosh," I said, "we now have to walk all that way to the rotten entrance." (Rotten was a word I used all the time.) I kicked the board in temper, and as I did it swung, "Ay, Trev," I said, "look at this." I was pushing it with my right foot and for some unknown reason enjoying it, what I didn't notice was the nail coming out. When it did finally come out the nail went straight through my kneecap and stuck out the back of my leg. The weight of the board knocked me to the ground, for a few seconds I was panicking as I sat wondering what to do. Trevor was more panicky than me. As the fear slowly left me I gathered my thoughts, I looked around for help but not a soul was anywhere to be seen. I took hold of the board and as quick as I was able I pushed the board up and out came the nail, boy that was some pain, I can tell you. I rubbed my knee and limped home.

You know I never washed that wound or put anything on it, it was very sore the next morning. It healed up all on its own, never went septic, I never told my mom, I didn't think she could have taken much more of my antics. That knee is giving me a lot of trouble in the year 2012, now it gives way every now and again, well collapses, I'm not sure if it is because of that nail or just old age.

TRAIN JOURNEY

One year I went with the school to Weston-super-Mare, it was a day trip; we saved 3d a week all year until we had paid (£1). Most times I ran errands to pay my 3d for that trip as my mother could never afford it, well now and again she would give me 2d, but in the main I ran errands and paid for myself. Sometimes, well most times, I would spend my money on going swimming or going to the pictures (cinema that is). On this occasion I was paid up, my mom gave me a one-shilling piece, that's all I had. My clothes were washed and ironed; washing and ironing worn-out clothes didn't help them look good or much better, well a little maybe, but at least they were clean and smelt nice. No children commented on my clothes, they were used to seeing me like that, they were all too excited to even bother I'm glad to say.

So we all gathered at the school, I only lived a few yards from the school, most of the parents were there to wave their little son or daughter off. I used to think how sissy it was to have your mom wave you off, dads were at work. In those days, looking back I would have loved my mom to wave me off. We walked in file from Audley Road School, Glebe Farm, Birmingham 33 to Stechford Station; I loved that station it was all wood, the wooden steps down to the platform were so wonderful to me.

I've loved station buildings and trains all my life. A lot of moms were at the station to wave off their little ones. I looked to see if my mom was there. I knew she wouldn't be because as I left home she was doing the housework. Oh well, I was so excited anyway, a train journey was better than the seaside to me and my mind was on the fish and chips we were going to have at dinner time. We were all talking very loudly, full of energy; I remember they were all telling each other how much money they had to spend. Not one of them had less than a pound, one had £5. I was thinking, how can their moms afford that? I suppose I was thinking they were all as poor as we were in my family but what a lot of money for a child in those days. Yes I was jealous, of course I was. I've thought about this a lot. Green with envy is perhaps a better way to describe how I felt.

When we got to Weston it was a wonderful sunny day, and the station at Weston I loved it and (still do). We walked again in file to the beach, one exciting moment for me was to see and smell the sea that looked to me the giant of a seafront never ending.

What I've thought about all these past years, all day long I was walking around Weston-super-Mare, on my own. I had no one to talk to, was it because I only had one shilling (1/-), or was it that I didn't have enough money to go on the fair with them, or was it that they were so excited they just took off and couldn't wait to spend their money? As far as I know they were in twos or groups. I've never known why I was alone, could be other reasons. I went looking for a present for my mom with my shilling. As I was walking round I hung on to my shilling. As I walked I kept looking in all the shops for a present for my mom, no way was I able to find anything. I kept an eye on the time as we were told to meet by the pier at 12 noon.

We all met up where we were told to on the sea front and the teachers walked us to our dinnertime restaurant upstairs to what I thought was a palace, the waitress came out with a beautiful plate of fish and chips. I was starving; it was a wonderful dinner then a nice cup of tea. Out we all went again and were told where we should all meet up at four o'clock, so in the afternoon I walked around again on my own. Looking for a present for my mom with a shilling, I was hoping wasn't I? I looked in a shop where they were selling ice creams, and bought one for 6d. I thought with the 6d left I could buy my mom a present, whatever could I get for 6d for a present? There wasn't anything for a shilling, how or why I thought I could get her a present for 6d I've no idea. I started to feel quite guilty and ashamed, I had bought an ice cream but a 1/- or 6d would not have got a present for my mom. Almost time to go and meet on the seafront, I had looked really hard for a present and no way could I get one, so I bought another ice cream with my 6d. I felt really sad I couldn't buy Mom anything. All day all that was on my mind was buying my mom a present, then the guilt really kicked in when my shilling had gone, so we all met up at 4pm and started the march back to the station. When we arrived at the station, I was looking at all the iron work the shiny bricks and the woodwork on the station platform, it looked beautiful to me. I was in heaven; I do still love that side of life. On the train going back it wasn't quite as noisy as when we first got to the train in the morning, but still noisy; the noise ceased quite a lot I think after about half an hour. Then it went sort of quiet and they started to say what they had bought for their moms and dads. Some had bought statues, postcards, sticks of rock even novelties. I went nearer the window looking out of it, hoping no one would talk to me, they did of course. I don't know, all day on my own not a soul to talk to, now they wanted to talk to me and I didn't want them to. A girl with red hair, I've forgotten her name, said, "What did you buy for your mom and dad?" I pressed my face up against the window pretending I was looking at something and making believe I couldn't hear her. The boy sitting next to me was pushing me saying "she is talking to you" pointing at the girl opposite me. I'm sure I had a red face, I had to turn and talk to her, again she asked "what did you buy for your parents?" "Nothing," I said, "I didn't have any money. I only had a shilling." "He hasn't bought his mom and dad a present, you are horrible, and mean, did you hear that, he spent all his money on himself and hasn't bought his mom and dad anything. You are selfish." Girls are so cruel at times, I felt terrible. I could have done without her comments I was feeling bad about not getting mom a present as it was, "Well I've bought my mom and dad a present," she then pulled her tongue out at me and turned her back on me. To hide my embarrassment I pushed my face up against the window. By this time I felt really ashamed of myself, so for ages I just watched the telephone wires going up and down, by this time no one was talking to me.

Suddenly we noticed we were approaching Stechford Station, there was pushing and shoving to look out of the window to see if they could see their moms. When the train stopped they all went for the door at the same time. I stood out of the way and let them all get off the train for I knew my mom would not be there. There were moms and dads by the dozens it seemed. I stood out of the way. When I got on the platform, it was very crowded. I heard such wonderful things said to the children by their parents, “Hello darling, hi sweetheart, I’ve missed you, oh it’s good to see you, did you enjoy yourself?” Hugs and kisses, they even brought coats for their little ones. I waited to see if my mom was there, I knew she wouldn’t be. All was quiet, I was standing on the platform on my own, I must confess a little tearful and I felt very lonely at that moment. I waited till they had all gone and looked around to see if mom was there, yes I was standing on that platform and not a soul to be seen. I walked up those wooden stairs and it was now so quiet I could hear myself breathing; as I reached the top of the stairs I was still hoping my mom would be there. Still not a soul to be seen. Oh well, I thought, so I walked home.

I got to my house, not a soul was in sight. Boy I felt so unwanted (I was wanted of course, my mom loved me) but for a child to go through a day with all those people everywhere and not a soul to talk to is, to say the least, soul destroying for a child. So I went round the corner to the British Legion which was just at the back of my house, I walked in (the doorman knew me), my family were there and just to end the day, worse than I thought possible, my mom held out her hand for a present, she must have thought I was trying to hand her something. I think that moment was the lowest point of my young life.

That was the first time I went with the school to Weston-super-Mare. I went to Weston a couple of years after that, but once again I had only 2/- to spend and that was given to me by the headmaster Mr Taylor. At least I had a day at the seaside, which I was very grateful for, as I’m sure many children didn’t have the opportunity to go.

OUR DUCK LONESOME

Again we had 10 or 12 chicks that we had in a cupboard next to the cast iron fire grate. Where they were purchased from I have no idea, my eldest brother Donald always got them. Any road up, one by one they died off, that used to sadden me, a few weeks later there was only one left. The difference being this one turned out to be a duck, it wanted to be the boss. A pen was built in the back yard the same place where that chicken Lonesome had its pen. Lonesome was that fierce hen that I wrote about in a previous chapter. This duck wasn't fierce, it did just what it wanted to do and again the only person that could control the duck just like that hen was my mother. Whatever she told it to do, it did. A little reluctantly sometimes but she always made sure it obeyed her. Just the same as we had to obey her, my mom took no nonsense from anyone; when she said do it we did it, when she folded her arms and gave that, well I can only describe it as a stern look, we knew she meant it and so did her duck.

Now who would have thought you could train a duck. Just proves that animals have brains and like us must be thinking. One day, so my mother told me and this happened a few times, she was walking up the road to the shops when she noticed people were laughing at her. Not being very well off and her clothes looking a little worse for wear, she was thinking that something must be wrong with her coat or (as she put it) her dress was tucked in her drawers. People would smile and say, "Hello, Mrs Prosser," for everyone in those days knew my mom. When my mom turned round to check her clothes were in order, there walking behind her was her duck following her up the road.

She told this story many times over the years, that's how I remember it so well. She would point her finger down the road saying, "Go home." The duck would turn its head and look at Mom who would say, "I won't tell you again, now get home." (That rings a lot of bells in my memory of my mom saying those very words to me over the years.) As the duck looked back at Mom it looked like it was saying, "Please let me come with you," just like me and my sisters used to say to her we got the same response that the duck got from her. Off the duck went straight back home; it never wandered, it went straight into its pen. It's a wonder it was never attacked by any dogs because in those days dogs used to roam around free.

When I got home from school one evening just like that hen, Lonesome the duck was hanging over the drain with blood dripping from it. As I walked into the living room, Mom was sitting at the table crying her eyes out. Mom was very soft like that even with us when we hurt ourselves, she was very strict when it came to good manners and we needed it, Mom. When I asked her what was wrong she replied, "My lovely duck has gone." She cried the same when the hen had been killed. It is wrong to give any animal a name when you are going to eat it. That duck was really one of the family. We never had any more animals after the demise of that duck.

CIGARETTE CARDS

Jimmy, a boy me and my friends usually never played games with, was very good at making a paper aeroplane. He made one, one evening, he threw it and it went round and round and round in circles, it was fantastic. I tried many times to fly paper planes, but every time I tried to fly my plane it just nose-dived straight down.

Anyway, Jimmy had a biscuit tin full of cigarette cards that his granddad had given him, it may have been his dad. He would sell us some cards, about twelve cards for 3d (three pence) but he always insisted we played him skimmers so he had the chance to win them back, he always won them back. What we did would be to stand one card up the gutter and from the middle of the road we had to skim a cigarette card at the card standing up in the gutter and try to knock it down. The one who knocked it down won all the cards that had missed. We could be standing in the middle of that road for hours and never see a vehicle, these days you might get away with three minutes. Thinking back, we were very lucky children, we could play in the horse road all day long playing all sorts of games with no traffic to interrupt us at all. The children these days will never experience the happiness of playing in the street day after day like we did, I loved those days.

I never ever won Jimmy at the game of skimmers and to my knowledge no one else ever did. Every time he knocked the card down he would shout, “JEN” – this was his favourite saying. We must have ruined some rare cards but of course they were worth next to nothing in those days.

BEING A ROUNDSBOY

At the top of my road a man named Arthur, a little wiry man with curly black hair, always wore a brown overall known as a "cow gown", this was because he delivered bread door to door. He worked for a bakery company called Harding's Steam Bakers. Their factory was based in the area known as the Swan Yardley in Birmingham. At that time they had horses as well as petrol vans; I used to love seeing the horses being groomed and cleaned out. I even went to the boss who wore a white coat (that's what most of the bosses wore then) and asked if I could help with the horses. "You are too young, son," was his reply, "you aren't allowed by the horses at your age." I couldn't believe it. Sometimes when the men brought out the horses from the stables they would ask me to hold on to the reins for a short time which made me feel all grown-up.

Arthur drove a petrol van; one day when I was walking home from the shops as I was about to pass his van, he was getting out of it, I approached him and asked him, "Can I help you deliver your bread?" "OK," he said, "I leave the depot at 7.30 a.m." "OK, I'll be there," I answered. Great, I was thinking I can earn some money, but no wages were mentioned. I was there by 6.30 a.m. The face of the bus conductor when I asked for a 3d child's fare! It was just gone 6.00 a.m. when I got on the bus and for a nine-year-old they thought I was just too young to be out at that time in the morning. I think it would be too early for a 65-year-old now. Well for this 65 year old, me. I walked into the bakery and was stopped by a man wearing a white coat, "What can we do for you, young man?" "I'm working with Arthur," I said. "Oh you mean Mo," the boss said. Funny, I thought, why does he keep calling him Mo when his name is Arthur? It was a few days later I asked one of the roundsmen tending the horses, "Why do you call Arthur Mo?" With a laugh he replied, "If at any time we call across the yard to him he always shouts back 'half a mo'," (mo is short for moment). "Oh," I said, not really understanding.

It's strange to think now, that then they allowed children around places like that at such a tender age. Being fascinated by the horses, time sort of flew by, when a stern voice said, "I've been waiting for you, if you don't buck your ideas up I won't let you help me again." It was Mo; I ran to the van, he lectured me all the way to the start of his round saying I had made him late and I would have to run when delivering the bread to make up the time. Northfield, the Lickey hills and surrounding areas, is where we delivered the bread to, and we always stopped at the pub or should I say public house, or boozers as my dad would refer to them. Every dinner time, it seemed like an eternity waiting in the van, he was always over an hour in there, he never gave me a second thought or worried if I had any food. He was a different person when he left the pub, I couldn't talk to him as I could before he went in there. When he had finished and completed the round he would pick a man up who worked on a building site, this man was also a neighbour; he only lived a few doors away from my house. I had to sit in the back of the van squeezed up against the bread trays (which were made of wire) and the back doors – that was the most uncomfortable ride I ever experienced, I was bounced about like a tennis ball. I only suffered it for three weeks, I didn't go again. He only paid me 1/- (a one shilling piece), it had cost me 1/3d (one shilling and three pence) in bus fares to travel there, so I used to walk home and the walk must have been five to eight miles. I'd had nothing to eat or drink, well to be honest I used to pinch the corners off the uncut loaves and hide a packet of morning coffee biscuits and eat them when he went into the pub and dispose of the wrapper down a drain in the road. I asked customers if I could use their toilet just so I could have a drink of water from their tap. Why did I stick it out for three weeks? the promise of more money next time, but that never happened.

Milk rounds, I thought, so I asked the milkman if I could help him as he delivered all round the streets where I lived. It was in the six weeks school holidays so I could work all the week. "OK," he replied and he paid me 1/- (one shilling) for the week. Trouble was I'm a true Brummie (really I suppose you could refer to me as common) I talked using a lot of slang words, he was always telling me off for saying "bo-ul" instead of bottle, "nunk" for nothing, "gew" for going, "belly" for tummy. I got so afraid to speak I would just nod my head when he said anything to me, even that made him have a go at me – "lost your tongue now have we?" I just couldn't win with him, when I told him I couldn't read the notes in the empty milk bottles I got another lecture, he told me his little boy was only five and could read and I should be ashamed of myself, "don't your parents help you?" He went on and on at me all day every day. "I will have you speaking the Queen's English in a few weeks," he told me. Yo wunt, I thought to myself, when you pay me I wunt help yo agen. "Ask your mom to wash your clothes and you have a bath when you get home," he said to me. I was a bag of nerves; I only stuck it for a week, I did that just to get my shilling wages from him. On the Monday I was sitting on my front gate when I heard him shout to me, "come on, I'm not waiting all day for you." I jumped off the gate shouting as I ran down my path, "I ain't helping yo agen," so that was that, as I sat on the gate again after he had gone. As I sat there I spotted the Corona pop man so I ran over to him, "can I help you Mister?" "OK, son, but mind I won't stand any messing about." "OK, Mister, I wunt," I replied. Their bottles in those days had a white porcelain stopper with a red rubber seal and this stopper was held down by a heavy-duty wire that when pulled downwards tight to the neck of the bottle it would seal the gas in which stopped the pop from spilling out. I enjoyed working for him, the first Saturday he gave me a bottle of pop and 2/- (two shillings) but after that first Saturday he gave me 1/- (a one shilling piece) plus the bottle of pop. I could only work with him on a Saturday because he delivered in other areas in the week. He insisted that when I helped him on the next Saturday I must return the bottle; there was a two pence deposit on the bottle. He was very kind to me and he said he liked me because I wasn't cheeky and I worked hard. One time I asked if my friend Trevor could help him as well as me, "OK," he said, "but I will only pay you 9d (nine pence) each and you can share a bottle of pop." Great, I thought, me and Trevor we always worked well together. I know I got a little less money but Trevor was still my closest friend, we shared what we had anyway, in the week we ran errands, we always worked together and worked well. We helped the Corona pop man for a very long time then one Saturday he told us we weren't allowed on the lorry anymore, one of the other roundsmen had a boy working with him, the boy fell off the back of the lorry and badly hurt himself so all the roundsmen were told they could no longer have young children working for them.

One day a lorry was going slow down Trevor's road, a young lad was running backwards and forwards to this lorry and he was leaving paper bags for old clothes to be put in. I just happened to be talking to a boy named Barry who went to my school, and he said, "Let's ask the man in that lorry if we can help." So we asked, "Do you want any help?" "OK, lads, I will pay you half a crown (2/6), and I'll be back in two days' time to pick all the bags up." We worked hard all day delivering those bags to every house in the area. He did come back two days later, we met him at the top of Trevor's road, picked up all the bags filled with clothes and threw them into the back of the lorry, at the end of the day he only paid us 1/- each (a shilling) instead of half a crown. It seemed that children were always taken advantage of by adults; we had always worked very hard for our money.

Corona Bottles

PAST DREAMS

I've been told thousands of times I shouldn't live in the past; I can't help it, poor as I was, knowing hunger, cold, living in well-worn clothes, hard work and running around in the snow until I could no longer stand, frozen fingers, soaking wet feet. I loved my childhood, being with my friends was a joy to me no matter what the weather was doing, the sunny days, playing, earning money. Cycling I really enjoyed, all the seasons with my friends. I sit in the garden on a sunny day, feet up, close my eyes and remember my childhood days with my friends; on cold winter nights I do exactly the same only indoors. Lights out, glow from the fire (now of course it's a gas fire), feet up, all is quiet, nice and warm, my mind's eye goes all through my childhood days that's how and why I remember so much. Things like my friend Trevor and his sisters they used to go swimming with me and my sister Janet. We all ran errands to earn money for swimming. We even went scrumping apples together, not for devilment, that was food to us. We did have our childish moments, like climbing over the railings into our school playground, climbing up the drainpipe and onto the roof; all the roofs were flat, and every time we were on the school roof the caretaker with his two sons and their Alsatian dog would catch us and throw us out. Mind you, thinking about it, he was very good, he never once told the headmaster, we would have got the cane for sure.

Swancote Road, where Trevor lived, was a long road, eighty or ninety houses maybe more. One night, being a bit bored, four of us went to the top of the road, ran, jumped, dived or rolled all the way to the bottom of the road over the gardens. We never trod or broke any plants down – mind you, most people didn't have flowers in their gardens just lawns. Yes every front garden, including Trevor's garden. Tying cotton to doorknockers, pulling the cotton to knock the door and running away, most children did this I would think. Rolling little mud balls and throwing them at the windows or grit if we had no mud. Yes

I was a normal child in that respect. I didn't annoy the neighbours very often. My friends and me would play and enjoy life.

One memory that is very vivid in my mind, I lived in a corner house so from my back garden I could see a lot of back gardens in the next road, four back gardens from mine was a very big apple tree, it grew the biggest cooking apples I have ever seen. One night Trevor and me climbed over the hedges of the back gardens to this apple tree, we got two apples, must have been six inches across, sour but not that bad. Well, I could only eat half of that apple and Trevor only managed about the same, we never wasted any of the apples we saved the half we couldn't eat till the next morning. Next day we were walking down the road and the man whose apple tree it was called us over and shaking his finger at us said, "Don't you ever steal apples from my garden again," (I've no idea how he knew it was us) "if you want an apple you knock at my door and ask for one." Not sure how many days went by, three or four, I knocked on his door and said, "You said if we wanted an apple to knock on your door and ask for one." Well he looked at me and Trevor and in total amazement he replied, "You cheeky little buggers," (lots of adults used that word then) "wait there." He came back with a big apple and said, "Half each and don't ask again," shaking his head as he closed the door, saying again to himself, "cheeky little buggers."

There are so many memories that come back when you sit quiet, close your eyes and start to think of your childhood. The good parts and the bad parts, the freedom I had as a child gave me much happiness.

THE RUBBISH TIP

As a young lad of 6 years I spent many hours on a rubbish tip behind the Atlas Cinema, in the area of Stechford, looking for shoes for my mom to burn on the fire. Also I was looking for old bicycles because I was trying to make up a bicycle, so I could take a tyre off one, if I was lucky that is. A few weeks later I would find a wheel, pedals, chain, frame; it took months. I finally found a saddle with no covering on it, I was so pleased, I wrapped rag all round it so it could be sat on with some comfort. As a small boy I couldn't sit on the saddle and reach the pedals, no brakes on this bike and, oh yes, it was a girl's bike frame so I could stand on the pedals and with my arms up straight I could hold the handlebars. Down the hill I would go, I realise now my sense of balance was so good, very dangerous of course but as a youngster I knew no fear. (I used to jump off when I got to the bottom of the hill.) I ruined the clothes I had on (mind you they were worn out anyway) made worse with me enjoying my life as a youngster. Poor Mother, she used to darn and repair my clothes on an almost daily basis.

Anyway, there were not many cars about in those days, mostly horse-drawn carts, so down the hill with no brakes was quite safe car-wise that is. I had the surprise of my life one day finding an old bike on the tip, all rotten and bent up but brakes on it back and front; well I carried it back to a friend's house whose dad very kindly got the brakes off and saved one of the cables, he put the front brake on for me, I was so pleased, (what wonderful people in those days, always ready to help). It was a very long time before the back brake was fitted; I had that bike many years. Tyres, I always found them on the tip, worn but still OK, no frame just the wheel with a tyre on it. I even found a wheel one day a back wheel, complete with tyre and cog in the river with air still in the inner tube, you know the sort that were usually punctured. I did change the girl's frame to a man's frame, a girl from school gave it to me, it had been left at the back of her shed, it was rusty, front forks

Trying to become a road user

were rotted but there were a lot of good spares on it and would you believe the front tyre was in good condition and still it had air in it, alas the saddle was rotten. I put a lot of parts from that bike onto my bike, I even got a back brake so now I could go downhill feeling a little safer, well it was better than putting both feet on the floor hoping I could stop and my mom wondered why my footware never lasted, if she knew I'm sure I would have been banned from riding that bike.

WE CALL THESE THE GOOD OLD DAYS. I was poor, shabby clothes, but believe me I was a very happy child when away from school hours and those teachers. Good old days (Mmm what do you think?). Of course at that time I wanted better, like a nice bike and good clothes, nearly new would have been nice. I was ridiculed by the teachers had the mick taken out of me, tormented because of my apparel. Looking back at those days now (and I do very often) was it so bad? Would I have liked good clothes, good footwear, been well fed like most kids, had the right apparel when it snowed and was very cold. WOULD I HAVE LIKED ALL THOSE THINGS AND A GOOD BIKE? YOU BET YOUR LIFE I WOULD. On the other hand if I did have all those nice things in my youth, would I have had the freedom that I enjoyed so much? Maybe not.

TEA UNDER THE APPLE TREE

Pype Hayes Park is a park near Erdington. My mom took me there, my little brother was in arms, only a baby. My mom's friend Winnie and her son John, my friend, we were there all day; our moms took sandwiches, bottles of water and a bottle of pop, no sweets or cake just sandwiches. We had a great day, me and my friend John. All there was in the park was a river, well a river to me was the nicest playground any child could ever want. I never went there again, only the once but the memories I have of that day will live with me forever.

The other place my mom took me to was a place called Sutton Park, we went there twice, none of my mates were with me, it was just my mom, my two sisters and my younger brother, and me of course. What a big park, I remember walking for what seemed miles, there was a fair there; the twice I went with Mother there was a train running all round the outside of the fair. I had a ride on the train the first time I went. The second time my mom said, "Don't ask me for anything because I have no money." There is a stream there; I played in the stream all day. Whenever I went anywhere there was always a river to play in. I wonder do children do that sort of thing now?

One place my mom did take me was a place called Chelmsley Wood; there wasn't a river, there were lots of trees to climb, bushes to hide in, millions of bluebells to pick, lots of rhododendrons, it was a magic place to visit. One memory that will never fade about Chelmsley Wood is the first and only time I went with my mom, it was only Mom and me, where the rest of the family were I have no idea. We got on the bus at Glebe Farm, went through Kitts Green, then Lea Village and got off the bus at Tile Cross, walked towards Marston Green Village past a pub called The Bell, up a road to the edge of Chelmsley Wood.

My mom brought me to Chelmsley Wood when it was all a wood. In the grounds of the farmhouse shown in the picture there was an apple tree, we sat under the apple tree and the farmer's wife came out with a jug of tea, not a pot a jug and two cups and no saucers.
Wonderful memories.
The apple tree has been cut down, it was where those two conifers are now. No wall was there at the time I am writing about.

We walked along the edge of a field on the right was what was known then as the mental hospital, next to Marston Green Maternity Hospital. We walked along the path and at the end of it looking straight in front was a farmhouse, in its grounds was an apple tree. My mom told me to sit under the apple tree while she went to the house. She came back and sat down beside me, the sun was shining, a wonderful warm day, no one about, then what I suppose was the farmer's wife came out with two cups and a jug of tea. That's all I remember of that day, sitting under the apple tree with my mom and a jug of tea. I was very happy, that's why I remember that event so well.

Many a year later I tried to buy that farmhouse; I lived, would you believe, in the same road as that house and that apple tree was still there then. I told my family every time we passed the house that I sat under that apple tree with my mom and had a jug of tea. The council bought the house and cut the apple tree down and built a wall all around that old farmhouse. I felt they had taken a little bit of me away.

TIDDLY WINKS

Coronation Day 1953, a magical time. I was very exited, tables all down the road, more food than I ever remember seeing, so much sweet stuff, everyone laughing, smiling, a very happy place to be. I lived in Plowden Road number 38, Glebe Farm, Stechford as I have mentioned before. They had tables for Plowden Road at the top of the hill. I was sitting at a table in Swancote Road, all my friends came from Swancote Road. I really should have been in my road but I wasn't and I have never known why. I would love to see a photograph of Plowden Road and Swancote Road with all the tables in the road, someone must have a photo of them.

Trevor's mom Lizzie, who was my mom's best friend and lived in Swancote Road, squeezed me in to sit with my friends. My friends all had a dickey bow tie that day that lit up, I had nothing, yes I was jealous. I felt left out. I was wondering why everyone had something and I and my sisters and younger brother had nothing, present-wise that is. I made a pig of myself with the food and yet when the people from Plowden Road went to my school for the games, all my family were there, no one from Swancote Road was with us. We were all dressed up for the fancy dress, my eldest sisters Kathleen and Doreen made our costumes out of crepe paper. My younger sister was the Queen of Hearts, I was a clown (I was always told I was a clown by my mom, that's the reason I was dressed up as a clown), my youngest brother was dressed up as Little Red Riding Hood, as you can see us in the photograph.

We didn't win the fancy dress. When it came to the games I entered for the running because I was fast, I thought if I win please don't give me Tiddly Winks, I hate that game (I still do). I was hoping for a gun or a car, but no, what did I win? You've guessed it, a box of Tiddly Winks. I gave it to my sister and she played with it with my little brother and my younger sister but not me.

Coronation Day, 2nd June 1953, author's family from left to right:
Back row Kathleen, Dad, Doreen, Mom,
Janet as the Queen of Hearts, John as Little Red Riding Hood,
author David as a clown.
The costumes were made by my two sisters, Kathleen and Doreen
for the fancy dress parade, out of crepe paper.

Author is third one behind the Queen of Hearts
only face is showing with his crepe paper hat bent down

Coronation Street Party
Neighbours from Plowden Road, Glebe Farm,
in the seniors' playground outside Audley Road School.

We had a big bonfire in the middle of the road some days later, this also was to do with the Coronation; I remember going round all the houses in my road to get any item they were throwing away for the bonfire, 78 RPM WAX records, sideboards, chairs, trees, old timber, I collected all sorts of things even toys. I went to one house where the man said, “Hang on a minute, I’ll look in my shed.” What a shock when he came out with a rocking horse. He saw the look on my face, he then said, “No, I will put it on the bonfire, if I give it you, you will take it home and give it to your little brother.” That’s exactly what I was thinking and he knew it. My little brother would have loved it. I was very disappointed, mind you I still had my rocking horse that my dad made for me, and John played on it from time to time. The bonfire was to celebrate the Coronation; the fire was in the middle of the road, which was shaped like a circle which led to a grove, so lots of room. On the night when they lit the fire there was so much furniture; I wonder how many would-be antiques were burned that day all over England. Fireworks, it was a wonderful time, even potatoes were roasted in the hot embers. While I’m standing there, I noticed the rocking horse burning, what a shame, my brother could have had so much fun on that horse. When we were playing games at my school we all grouped together for a photograph. I still have photos of that day; with me dressed in crepe paper as a clown. I’m glad I have, and I was able to share them with you in this book.

Wonderful time wonderful memories

THE CORN SHOP

In our house we as children were disciplined by our mom, she ruled with a rod of iron, never our dad. Mom was the driving force. Off our kitchen was the coalhouse, that's where Mom kept the cane; knowing it was there made me think twice before doing anything wrong. I still got out of line sometimes, and then Mom would say, "coal house." "Sorry, Mom," I would say. "If I have to tell you again you will get double three whacks across the backside," kept me in check, I needed that discipline, I was a little rogue. I always knew when my mom was angry, she always folded her arms in an austere way, I knew that was it. After I was caned I always had to put the cane back in the coalhouse. When I walked back in she would kiss me on the forehead and say, "Now be a good boy."

I had the bright idea that if I broke up the cane she would not be able to use it, so one day while she was out at the shops I attempted to break the cane up. What I didn't know was that canes do not snap and break like I thought they would and as I tried to pull it apart I got my fingers caught and they bled. I found it to be very springy and I wrestled with that cane for over half an hour. I started to panic, for I knew my mom would be home any minute so I placed it in the dustbin all split rather than broken. I had to place it in a sort of circle, and as I was placing the lid on the dustbin my mom was walking down the path. "I'm going out to play. Mom," I shouted as I passed her. I felt good at that moment in time thinking, that's the end of caning for me. The next day while playing in the road with Trevor, my mom called me into the house and asked me to go to the corn shop, "Here is 3d (three pence), go and buy me a nice thin cane, one with a nice thin end."

The corn shop was called Turners, they sold corn, fertilisers, pigeon food, sacks of oats, I used to buy those oats many times for our family to eat for breakfast. There used to be mice droppings in those oats! A scoop was used to measure the oats into a brown paper bag. This scoop was used for all the animal food, but the person serving did not know they were being eaten by my family and probably other families in the same position as ourselves. So I looked for the finest cane I could find, being very particular about the one I chose, I shook the cane to make sure it had a really good whooshing sound, and gave the money to the man wearing his brown cow gown that I had always seen him wear as far back as I can remember. Walking back down the road I thought, my mom will love this, talk about being thick! Into the house I go, "Here you are, Mom, I picked the best one," I said, and with that Mother bent me over and really gave me six of the best. Hurting, crying and very bewildered I asked her what she had hit me for and told her I had been a good boy. She said, "You broke the cane up and put it in the dustbin and thought I wouldn't see it didn't you, now you can put this cane in the coalhouse," always referred to as the "coal ole". So out to play I went with a backside ringing and stinging. If only I had covered the cane up when I put it in the dustbin, maybe I could have saved all that pain? I would love to be able to say I never got the cane again but that wasn't the case, I got it more times than you can shake a cane at me. I never learn. I think if they could cane me now it would be almost on a daily basis. Ha, ha.

MAKING SLIDES

One very cold winter's day I was playing in the horse road, it was covered in deep snow. All my friends were out playing, it was very cold, in fact it was well below freezing, so we got buckets of water and poured it in the middle of the road the night before. My road was quite a steep hill, we started the slide just outside my house, the slide ran across Swancote Road that ran across the bottom of my road over the pavement and to the garden hedge of our friend Rita Hill. The slide must have been sixty yards long. We all started to slide down the hill across the road; at the bottom the snow was so deep we catapulted over the hedge into the garden at the end of the slide.

The snow in the garden must have been 5ft deep, maybe even more. I remember the hedge next door to Rita Hill's garden, it was very high, the snow in that garden was even deeper than the snow in Rita's garden, and me being the smallest, skinniest kid of them all, I was constantly thrown over the hedge. As the snow had never been walked on I landed in the snow and was buried. I disappeared and found that to be very frightening; at first all the lads had a very good laugh at my expense. This was made worse when the girls came out to play as lads do. I think lads are born to show off in front of girls. I went over the hedge quite a few times. I was by this time very wet and frozen and feeling very uncomfortable. The girls were very well wrapped up, wellingtons, hats, scarves and gloves. The boys never wore scarves like the girls did. Me, I was in short trousers, shirt and a coat, socks with more holes than material (I used to tuck them under my foot, which meant they couldn't be pulled up) and of course pumps with holes in and no gloves. I was enjoying life playing with my friends. Trevor was dressed the same as I was, as he was as poor as me. The lads, of course still showing off around the girls, pulled off my pumps and my worn-out socks held them up in the air and shouted, "Hey, girls, do you want a pair of socks like these!" That was vey embarrassing to see the girls laughing at me.

With all the sliding the ice became like glass, and when the baker came down the hill with his horse and cart, the horse started to slide down the hill. I was so worried for that horse I cried, thinking it was going to hurt itself. The cart went sideways and pulled the horse away from the icy slide. The deep snow in the road brought the cart to a halt. I was so relieved, my nerves were on edge. From that day to this it made me respect horses. In the house I go to try and get dry and warm. My mom asked me to run up the road to the shops. She always said run. I was cold and wet standing by the fire, I just didn't want to move so I said, "Mom, I'm cold," I didn't want to go to the shops. My mom was a large lady so she put her coat and said, "Oh I'll go myself, and it'll be quicker." As she walked across the road she stepped onto our slide fell over and hurt herself quite badly. I felt very guilty, and with tears in my eyes I said, "I will go to the shop." She was laid up for about two weeks after that fall. When I say laid up I mean she was in pain and it took Mom a long time to be able to do the house work and the shopping. Whenever she asked me to run up the road after that, I did.

That same winter Trevor and me made good money shovelling snow from paths. I never liked shovelling snow and still don't. There were six of us lads all together, but it was only ever me and Trevor that tried to earn money as they all got pocket money but Trevor and me didn't until we were much older, this was because my dad was a very heavy drinker and didn't like parting with his money. All the pubs that my dad drank in have now been demolished. (I often wonder if it's because my dad stopped drinking there!) That's why they went broke, ha ha.

WHITE WINTER

IT WAS WINTER AND I WAS SMALL,
NO UNDERWEAR HAD I, NO NONE AT ALL,
THE CLOTHES I HAD WERE IN POOR SHAPE,
I PLAYED IN THE SNOW AND THOUGHT THIS IS GREAT,
NOT FOR LONG FOR I GOT COLD,
I WAS ONLY A CHILD AND NOT VERY OLD,
ALL MY SCHOOL DAYS WERE LIKE THIS,
CHILDREN LOVED TO TAKE THE MICK,
NO WELLIES ALL MY YOUNG LIFE,
HOLES IN MY PUMPS, WELL THAT'S LIFE,
PUMPS IN THE SNOW WELL WE WERE POOR,
THAT WAS MY LIFE, THAT'S FOR SURE.

LAND OF THE SPITFIRE

Castle Bromwich Aerodrome used to have open days, how often I'm not sure. Out front on a stand used to be a Spitfire. I loved going there; to a young lad those type of places were captivating. I always went there with Trevor's brother Tony, I never remember Trevor going. Seeing all the airmen in their uniform made me think I'm going to be in the air force when I grow up.

The one thing that has stuck in my mind was a long glass case with an aeroplane attached to a length of wire that stretched from one end of the showcase to the other with hedges, building and a bell on the bottom in the middle of the scenery. The object of the exercise was to release the bomb from underneath the plane, with finger 'at the ready' on the button the plane came along. When the button was pressed the bomb would fall and you had to hit the bell. After a few goes, I hit the bell every time. The RAF man said, "You are too good now," and stopped me using it.

It was great fun. I watched the paratroopers jumping out of a barrage balloon. I loved to see those big parachutes open, they are bigger than they look when they are on the ground. I didn't know at the time that my wife's uncle was a paratrooper and I watched him jump out of a balloon. Next open day I couldn't wait to have a go on the display model. I went in and said to all the boys there, "I can hit the bell every time." When my turn came I said, "Watch this, I never miss." Well, I couldn't get near the bell, not once did I hit it. Serves me right for being so bigheaded. That day taught me a good lesson.

SNOW HILL STATION

Trains are one of the loves of my life. There were two stations I really loved, both were in the Birmingham area. The one I've so many fond memories of is Snow Hill Station and the other is Stechford Station; both stations are still in use but alas both were knocked down and rebuilt, nowhere near as good as they were before. The old timber and stone work to me were majestic.

One wonderful memory I have of Snow Hill Station is a stamping machine, green in colour with a big brass arrow in the centre of it and the alphabet all round the outside in a circle. When I turned the arrow to each letter in turn and pulled a big lever on the side of the machine it stamped out the letter that had been selected. Me and my friend Trevor printed our name out on that machine every time we went to that wonderful station, it only cost a penny a go and it came out stamped on a strip of aluminium. We always bought a penny platform ticket and were thrown out of that station more times than I care to remember by one of the porters, for no other reason than we were kids. Never playing up, we always said the same thing, "We have a platform ticket, mister." They always said the same thing to us, "I don't care, out you go," that was the normal reply we got on that concourse.

I was in heaven, the smell of the locos, I can smell it now can't you? If only they could bottle it, all train enthusiasts like myself would buy a gallon. I adored seeing the trains coming and going, it was a thrill for me to see the motion of the wheels and the valve gear all moving together, to be honest I still get a kick out of it. The day they started to knock Snow Hill Station down I had a tear in my eye, I can tell you; that was a massive loss to the people of Birmingham, we lost a beautiful masterpiece and I just cannot bring myself to go and look at that modern rebuild. I will live on my memories the original station will live in my mind's eye forever.

IN AWE

Every day Trevor and I went into town we headed for Snow Hill Station. Every time I think of that beautiful station I can never understand why they would wish to destroy what was an icon in the railway world. That station was worth more than money, and I miss that stamping machine.

Trevor and I always liked to walk around the market; one of my favourite places was Nelson's column by St. Martin's church, watching the escape artists trying to escape from the chains they were bound in. The blind lady always fascinated me shouting "handy carriers", she was there for years and I was privileged to buy a carrier from that lady for my mom a time or two – God bless her.

If we had any money we always made a beeline for the man selling baked potatoes, 6d a spud, he always used those white cone-shaped paper bags, same as the ones they used in sweet shops when you bought 2oz of sweets. He always put salt in the bottom of the bag and the spud on the top; we loved buying those spuds in the wintertime, it was great to stand next to the oven and feel the heat from it on a cold Saturday morning. One Saturday we went to see him he said, "Hello, boys, nice to see you again, do you want a potato?" "We only have 3d each," I said. I was expecting him to shout, I'd had my share of being shouted at I can tell you, no Trevor and me were never cheeky. "OK, boys, a small one for 3d." They weren't that small, they seemed as large as they normally were. I think that potato seller was being kind which Trevor and me didn't experience that often.

FAITHFUL FRIENDS

Our dog Rex was a what my mom would call Heinz varieties, he was a cross between I think a Jack Russell and anyone's guess, white all over except for a brown patch on the middle of his back. We went everywhere together, we were pups together. Rex was a very loyal dog.

One day me and my friends were walking to Saltley when they decided we should catch the bus. I forgot my dog Rex was with us. Tony said, "You forgot your dog." I felt really bad that I had forgotten him, boy did he run fast. I was calling him, "Come on Rex, come on boy," he jumped on the platform of the bus and I was so relieved. I took him upstairs, all my friends made a fuss of him, he loved it, and he licked their faces until they looked clean. Where we were going, I'm not sure where we went that day I have no recollection of it at all. I remember that part of the day I've just written about because I felt so bad about Rex, leaving him when I caught the bus.

A long time after that I was round at the shops where I grew up; in the evening we usually walked around the shops or sat on the wall of the Glebe pub, (this was at Glebe Farm, Stechford), when a boy came up to us, me and Trevor that is. I knew the boy by sight because he went to our school; he lived a few yards away from the pub. He asked us, "What are you doing round here?" "Nothing," we replied. "Clear off," he said, "this is my area, not yours." "I will go where I like, you can't stop me," I replied, then he went to punch me. Rex, from a standstill, flew at the boy and grabbed his arm, well I was so surprised, I never knew my dog would protect me like that. I was so proud of him. The boy backing away from us was whimpering with fear. "Come here Rex, good dog," I said, making a fuss of him.

The boy was running away shouting, "I will fetch my big brother to you." I proudly shouted back, "Yeah, I will set my dog on him." I was so shocked, my dog had saved me from a beating up. About five minutes later I saw the boy with his big brother, he looked really angry, I was scared stiff of this big brother I can tell you. "Is that them with that dog?" I heard him say. "Yes," the younger boy said. The older boy went to punch me and again my dog Rex flew at him, well I could not believe how scared of my dog he was. As the dog went for him he half turned in fear. Well I saw something you only see in cartoons because Rex missed his arm and caught the back of his trousers, well the boy was spinning round in circles with the dog outstretched going round and round. This big boy was whimpering louder than his little brother had, who was now running down the road so fast he nearly fell over. The dog gave up his grip and came running to me. The big boy was so scared, as he was running away he was shouting, "I will get the police, they will have your dog put down." Brave boys soon became cowards when faced with a growling dog. I never heard any more about the incident, it never happened again; it made me love that dog for all time.

Funny really, I have a terrible fear of dogs. That dog lived with us for many years; the only food he ate was what we left on our plates. We fed him biscuits, cake, (not often as those two items we only had on rare occasions) bits of chocolate at Easter, in fact no matter what it was Rex would eat it, no fancy tinned dog food in our house, ha, ha, if there had been I think for sure we would have eaten it. On rare occasions Mom bought dog biscuits and I ate some of those. One evening when school was finished for the day, I walked into the kitchen of my house when I heard a loud sobbing noise. Into the living room I go in a hurry, my mom was sitting at the table sobbing her heart out. "What's the matter?" I asked. My dog was dead, I was told, oh no my Rex. We had one car a week or fortnight down our road and it seems Rex saw a cat run across the road, ran after it and went straight under the car, this is what the man told my mom. He very kindly carried Rex and put him in our back garden, I dug a hole in the front garden and buried him there. It's a shame I haven't one photograph of Rex, our faithful dog, but he gave me many happy memories.

Those bullies were not as tough as they thought they were when confronted with my dog Rex.

BUTTERFLIES

At the back of my house a few gardens away on a piece of wasteland was a big hole, I could see it from my bedroom window, I used to catch newts there. I was told by one of the boys that used to use the hole as a scrambling circuit that the hole was made by a bomb, (I think it was a natural hole made by Mother Nature herself) he would ride his motorbike in and around that hole. I was always worried he would hurt the newts. Mind you, it had all sorts of rubbish in it, would you believe bedsteads, old prams, no wheels of course, garden rubbish, how those newts survived in there is a mystery to me. Years later the hole was filled in and they built a British Legion on the ground, since then that building has been demolished; now lots of houses stand there.

Before all those changes took place when it was a big hole with newts breeding in it, I also caught butterflies there. I was chasing a beautiful coloured butterfly with a net made from one of my mom's old stockings tied to the end of a twig, the stocking kept coming off so I held the stocking at the end of the stick so it wouldn't come off anymore. I caught two butterflies, and then I spotted a Bob Howler as we called them. I ran to try to net it, tripped and badly cut my left wrist right down to the bone, off to the hospital, four stitches.

I did make my mom's life hard. SORRY MOM!

FLYING HIGH

Model aircraft was not a great love of mine, I liked them, OK never at that time wished to own one, trains were the love of my life. After running errands one week I did really well, so I went up town to a model shop in Temple Row, opposite St. Phillips church in Birmingham city centre. I loved that model shop, there were aeroplanes hanging from the ceiling and other made-up kits, it truly was an Aladdin's cave. I used to go in to that shop just to look around. I purchased a Tiger Moth aircraft kit, it was all in Balsa wood, I can't remember the cost of it. I hurried home with visions of flying it in four days' time. Allow me to explain the reason I bought a balsa wood aeroplane.

What prompted me into buying an aeroplane kit was as I was walking up the road to our shops with Trevor one morning a boy we knew but never played with came out of his house, well his entry from his back garden, with a model of a Hurricane that was beautifully painted. Trevor said, "Corr, Bobby, can we have a look at your aeroplane?" We walked over to him and asked him what the plane was called. "Hurricane," he told us, he had only finished it that morning, "You can look at it but no touching." He had put an engine in it and with a flick of the propeller with his finger it started. What a row it made for a tiny engine! We walked down the park with him, he started the engine off, cor I thought, I want one of those. Then Bobby said, "If you are really interested I will show you how to put them together and dope them," that was a word used at Trevor and me. I only knew the word dope because that was what I was called all the time, I had no idea it was a term used for making aircraft outer skin hard. So we went back to his house and waited for him in his back garden. Out he came with all manner of items, he got some tissue and pasted the dope on it, that's what you do, then you place it over the frame of the aircraft. He said, "It goes taught when it dries like this," and showed us an unpainted one. It's really amazing how taught it goes.

Did I say flying in four days? Well it looked easy when Bobby was showing me. I was trying to study the plans but not being very bright I just could not work it out. A couple of days later I must try, I thought to myself, so I laid out the plans and tried to glue all the struts together for the wings. I glued them to the plans, I broke some struts, some got twisted, that was the end of that plane. I only got as far as putting the wings badly together. I was wishing Dad would guide me, but no such luck.

A couple of years later I did buy another one but I made the same mistakes again, that kit never got past one wing, it too ended up in the dustbin.

What I needed was an adult's guiding hand but it never happened; trouble as well was I didn't have any craft tools, I only had my mom's carving knife. Talk about doing everything with nothing, but I couldn't have done it even if I had everything.

The flying game, never to be.
Attempting to make a Balsa wood bi-plane.

BACK GARDEN ADVENTURE

Billy, the boy who lived in Swancote Road (he's the one that fell off the scaffold of Kenilworth castle) he lived with his granddad, mom, dad and sister. He was better off than all the rest of us put together; he had a tandem bike, a touring bike, trolley, tent, games, good clothes, binoculars, and new clothes. He was a wiry little fellow. One day he said to Trevor, and me, "I've got my tent up in the back garden, come down tonight you can sleep in it." It was the old green thick canvass type. Off we went at eleven o'clock on the night. I told my mom, "I'm sleeping in Billy's room tonight." She didn't mind, she just said, "You behave yourselves."

We waited for Billy to enter. How he got out of his house without his mom or dad knowing, he climbed out of his bedroom window, slid down the drainpipe and let us in the backyard. Being in the summer it wasn't total darkness. Billy had a torch with him to guide us right across the yard where there was a shed dividing the yard from the garden where Billy had his tent. As he led us through the entrance there was a shed either side. Out in the back garden we slept in that tent all night, it was quite an adventure.

The next morning after his mom and dad went to work Billy came to see how we had liked our stay. "Great," we said. "Good," said Billy, "any time you want to drift in again just let us know." We never did stay there again; when we told the other lads they all said they had done that a few times. I myself only did it once. Great memories of doing those sorts of things As we walked through the sort of archway or covered way, Billy opened the shed to get his bike out and there in all its glory was the oldest motorbike I had ever seen at that time. It was in beautiful condition. I asked, "What's in the other shed?" When he opened the door it was like Aladdin's cave, tools hanging up, what a wonderful workshop. No wonder then whoever it was made Billy's trolley made a fantastic job. He also had stilts. I always wished at that time I could have all those things. But when I got anything I adored it and loved it whatever it was. Billy loved all of his possessions. I wouldn't think he had quite the feelings I got when I acquired anything, when things are got easy. I don't think it's possible to have the same feelings as earning and working hard for them, I may be wrong. What do you think?

That motorbike I saw in Billy's shed ended up in the motorbike museum at Bickenhilll, across the road from Birmingham International Airport.

SCHOOL HOLIDAYS

On one of the days in the 6 weeks school holidays I went to the tip, I could not believe my eyes as I got to the edge of that tip because there in all its glory was the bottom half of a pushchair, all four wheels were still on it and in good condition; being a pushchair and not a pram the wheels were the small type and not the big ones. I was so excited to see those wheels, they were like gold, they were never thrown away not in the 1940s, people always made use of wheels in those days and never ever threw them on a rubbish tip, they were always used to make carts for fetching coal and taking rubbish to the tip. Any road up, I picked up the frame with the wheels still attached and ran all the way home, the reason I didn't try taking the wheels off at the tip I wanted the axles the wheels were attached to, plus I was afraid some bully boy would take them off me. Oh yes, there were those types around even in those days, I had my share of being bullied by older boys, I was a tough little fellow and strong but I was a placid boy, I hated arguing and fighting so I did neither, I like the peaceful life.

When I reached home I set to and started to clean the wheels, I love things to be clean – after saying that, can you imagine the state I was in! Oh yes, in a state all right, but at that moment in time I didn't care, I was the king of our street or so I thought; I had four wheels plus the axles. Right, I thought, now all I need is a plank and two pieces of wood to fit on top of the axles, so I kept going to the tip. It was about six weeks before I found a plank; the one I found was four feet long, one and a quarter inch thick, ten inches wide if my memory serves me right. After finding the plank I needed lots of nails, so back to the tip several more times to find the nails I required. I found half a house brick which I used to get the nails out of the wood, mind you wood was scarce in those days as people used wood daily to light their coal fires, so on a daily basis I looked for nails till I had enough for my trolley, I found that with my hands pushing the nails back and forwards

I eventually got the nails out; it took me days to get the amount of nails I needed, but I did get extra just in case I needed them. With a pocket full of rusty nails I walked home; the nails were in my trouser pocket which was the only place I could carry them, every time I went to the tip, every step I took I was injected in the leg a dozen times. I suffered that because the nails were so important to me as I hadn't a coat at that time so it had to be the trouser pocket, (did you know a boy with half a house brick and a piece of wood can demolish a house HA HA!).

I straightened all the nails in my backyard with my half a house brick; well I hadn't got a hammer. I nailed the two pieces of wood to the axles, I then nailed the axle to the back of the plank and the front. Boy was I proud, I was now the owner of a trolley, I was so pleased with myself. Ah string, I thought, yeah my mom's washing line, lots of spare wrapped round the line post because it was too long, so I went and found Mom's scissors and I helped myself to a long length of it. (I got a good hiding for cutting the washing line.) With mom's poker that she used to poke the coal in the fire grate to make it burn better by way of letting the air circulate around it, I lit the gas stove, put the poker in the flames until it got red hot then burned a hole at both ends of the piece of wood attached to the front axles. I tied the rope through the holes I had made, just the job I thought, and pulled my trolley up to the shops. (I only used the poker to burn the holes in the wood when my mom was out shopping) I saw my dad burning holes in wood with the poker, that's what gave me the idea.

The first shop was called Stockton's, it was our local newsagent; outside of this shop was a good slope so I pulled my trolley right to the front door of the shop, sat on my trolley and away I went. This is great I thought, down the slope I've got to turn the front wheels, they won't turn! What do I do now? So I pulled hard on the rope with my left hand to turn left, and pushed the right-hand side of the front wheels with my right foot and as I did the front axle came off. I went flying, grazed my knee, and as I sat on the pavement rubbing my leg, a man walked past and asked me what had happened, "My front wheels have come off," I explained. "What you need, son, is a nut and bolt, if you make a hole through the plank and the axle, put in the bolt then you will be able to turn the front wheels." "Thank you, mister," I said. What a nice man, I thought, he didn't laugh at me or ridicule me like everyone else does, what a fool I am, I said to myself, of course I need a nut and bolt.

I carried my trolley home, got my mom's poker from the fireplace, lit the gas stove, put the poker into the flames till it glowed red hot like I did before (again I could only do it when mom was out) there were no tools in our house in those days, I then burned a hole in the plank. This took three goes before I got a hole through the plank and a further three times to get a hole through the wood on the axle. I knew my mom was short of money so I put three pennies in the gas meter, it was money I had earned from running errands, she never knew I did it, she couldn't understand how she got so much gas for her one penny. When my dad came home from work I asked him if he could get me a nut and bolt from work, Dad worked for the Metropolitan Camel Train Company so it was easy for him to get nuts and bolts. When I showed him what I wanted it for he was so proud of me, "Did you do this all on your own?" "Yes," I replied. With a pat on the head he said, "Well done, son." I felt very proud, he had never praised me up before, "I will get your nut and bolt tomorrow," he said.

The next evening I kept pestering my mom asking, "is it time for Dad to get home yet?" I must have asked a dozen or more times till in the end she just ignored me. Well, I was excited and very impatient, I just wanted to get my trolley on the road. When he finally walked in I said, "Have you got it, Dad? Have you got it?" "Gad blimey," his favourite saying when he was annoyed, "let me get my coat off." He handed me the nut and bolt with washers and explained how I should fit it. I fitted the nut and bolt that my dad gave me, and up to the shops I go, outside the newsagent's shop doorway, sat on the trolley, down I rolled, pulled on the rope to turn left, round I went. It felt great I was really excited. My friend Trevor saw me, "Cor, Dave," he said, "whose is the trolley?" "Mine, Trev," I answered, "I made it all from the tip when you weren't with me, thought I would surprise you." "Let me have a go, Dave," Trevor asked. "OK, Trev, don't crash it." He loved it, I got quite a big head, well I had never done anything myself before. The next afternoon all my friends had a go on it and my other friend Billy said, “My dad has made me one,” (it might have been his granddad I’m not sure now which one he said made it), “I’ll go and get it.” “We can have a race,” I said to him. Billy laughed at me and said, “What you race me on that old wreck?” “Yeah, come on, Billy,” they all shouted, “OK, OK, I’ll go and get it.”

Well when I saw his trolley my heart sank I can tell you, it was painted green and red with a padded seat and white lining all round it, I thought it was beautiful. All my mates were laughing at me by this time, “Well you threw out the challenge,” said Eddie.” “It’s OK,” I said, “you never know I might beat him.” Well that gave them another good laugh, I was dying inside with shame as we both sat on our trolleys, Billy sat high on his trolley he had big pram wheels on the back, small ones on the front, I only had small wheels all round, his small wheels where bigger than mine. As we sat on our trolleys a young girl walked past, Billy said. “Ay love, he has challenged me to a race, who do you think will win?” I felt my face go red, “Oh yours will easily,” she said. “See, Dave,” he said, “I told you.” I said, “OK, Bill, a rolling start, no pushing.” Off we went and to my surprise and delight I was much faster than Billy downhill, he only passed me when we hit the flat level road. “That was a fluke,” Billy said to me, so we did three more times and I beat him downhill every time. I shouted, “I’m the king of the hill!” Boy did I feel proud, he had a beautifully made trolley that his dad or granddad had made for him, whereas mine was made up from scrap off the tip and it cost me nothing. That taught me a good lesson that day, never to judge a book by its cover as the saying goes. I had years of fun on that trolley. Do you know for the life of me I cannot remember what happened to that trolley. I have sat for hours over the past years trying to remember what I did with it but alas I really can’t remember.

Beating Billy down hill on my trolly that I had made up from the tip made me feel really good.

THE RIVER BLYTHE

Coleshill, a little village in North Warwickshire, the first time I ever went there was with my next-door neighbour Barry, that day I fell in the river. My mom took me there once, I went on the bus with her, then a couple of years later I went to the same spot with my mates on the bike I had made up from the rubbish tip. It seemed like there were hundreds of people walking up and down Maxstoke Lane to the same spot; all it was, was a field with a river running through it. This field was at the bottom of a steep hill, people were having picnics there, children paddling, me and my mates went there to swim. There was a little white cottage known as Cuttle Cottage, the field was Cuttle meadow and the little bridge over the river was Cuttle bridge. Opposite the cottage was a wooden shed that had been turned into a tea hut, that's all there was, a lot of the time the tea hut wasn't open. One hot day we were getting a cup of tea from the hut when Billy went to the dustbin at the side of the hut, he picked up a stone and started to kill the bees that were buzzing round the bin, when he suddenly jumped up screaming as a bee had stung him on the lip. Boy, within seconds his face had swollen up like a balloon. His lip went three times the size it normally was. He was a laugh to be around, he got into more scrapes than I did. Billy always appeared fearless, he was a good friend. I never took a towel to dry myself with; I used to run around till I got dry. One very hot afternoon a man came up to me (I say man, he was a youth in his very early twenties I think), and asked if I would sell him my swimming trunks, "No," I told him. "I will give you half a crown (2/6d)," he said. I was tempted. "All right, five bob (5/-)," he said. I answered with, "They won't fit you." "Yes they will," he replied, "they tie at the sides, OK 7/6 (seven shillings and six pence)," that was a fortune to me. "OK," I said, so with Johnnie's towel wrapped round me I took off my trunks. He gave me the 7/6d and without a care he undressed without covering himself, to say they fitted where they touched is an understatement, he was happy and so was I. I was given those trunks. I think it was Barry my next-door neighbour. Now it meant when I went to Woodcock Street swimming baths I had to hire a pair of trunks from them, I think it cost two pence 2d which was refunded when you returned them. Of course one of the times I kept them I thought it would save me hiring them every time I went there. It worked quite a lot of times till one day the lady attendant caught hold of my arm and asked for them back; the reason she knew I had them that day I was unfortunate enough to be the only boy wearing hired swimming trunks. I did get another pair, I bought Robert's trunks for sixpence 6d as he never used them after he stopped going to Coleshill with me.

I was telling Robert who lived next door (his house was joined on to my house) about the field in Coleshill. "I want to go," he said. "Your dad won't let you," I said. "I won't tell him, Dave, I will take my tent if you let me go with you." "OK," I said. So without his dad seeing, he passed his tent over the fence to me and I tied it onto the back of my bike. It was thick green canvas with wooden poles, and to a young lad it felt very heavy.

Next morning I met Robert round the corner, he sat on the crossbar, off we went. It was a struggle, we kept changing over so we had a break from the pedalling, we got there OK. We erected the tent and Robert was loving it, it was a nice warm day, when to my surprise my mom turned up with Johnny's mom. It started to rain so my mom and Johnny's mom went into Robert's tent, poor Robert stood outside getting wet, he wasn't very happy. Mind you we were dripping wet from swimming in the river anyway.

The rain stopped, the sun came out, it was hotter than before it rained. We had a great time. I took Robert a couple of times after that but without the tent. One of the times as I was swimming against the current Billy, who always played up, picked up a dried cow pat and threw it quite hard; it hit just below the shoulder blades and took all the wind out of me, plus it felt like a thousand injections. I was fighting to stop going under, I swallowed a fair amount of water. I nearly gave up when I felt the bottom of the riverbed, the water only came up to

A day at Coleshill. We used to swim in this river (the River Blythe). The cottage is Cuttle Cottage in the meadow known a Cuttle Meadow. The bridge over the river is also called Cuttle.

my backside as I stood up, I thought it was much deeper as I stood up emptying my lungs of water, shouting to Billy, “You are mad, Billy, I thought I was going to drown.” Billy was on the bank laughing his head off. We never fell out. Billy always did silly things like that, we all were great friends we looked after each other, we had a fantastic childhood.

My mom always said, “These young days are the best days of your life, young man. Enjoy them, son, as much as you can,” so I did. Thank you, Mother. How right she was.

Swimming in the River Blythe
"Come in lads it's great!" I shouted to them

GAS WORKS

Trevor came to me one day, he said, "Dave, Mrs D. wants a quarter hundredweight of coal." We went to Whites coal yard in Church Lane, Stechford, in all weathers, we would carry coal – wind, snow, rain, frost, nothing stopped me and Trevor from earning money; we got 3d sometimes 6d (sixpence), in snow we always got 6d. Mrs D gave us a shilling (1/-), that was a lot of money to us. We never had a wheelbarrow; I used to carry it while Trevor held it at the back. I asked him recently if he did ever hold it to help take the weight off my back, he said, "No I didn't." No wonder my muscles got bigger! I am 68 now, Trevor is 70; we always reminisce about our young days and the things we did to make a penny. When I was carrying the coal I carried it till it got too heavy for me, I used to drop it, have a rest for ten minutes then ask any man that was passing to put it on my back. I got comments like: "it will kill you," or "it will break your back," or "you will get filthy." After it was lifted on to my back I would again carry it until I dropped it. We would do this until we carried it to where it had to be. I remember one day it was snowing and very slippy underfoot, Mrs R asked us if we would fetch a quarter hundredweight of coal which we did many times for her and usually were paid 6d (sixpence); as we were carrying the coal back to her house there were not many men about so it took much longer than normal to get it to the house. The deal was we would get a 1/- (one shilling) that day for fetching the coal because of the bad weather. I feel at this point I must mention that neither Trevor or me had any wellies, gloves, overcoat or underwear on whenever we did any errands, we even had pumps on that were worn out. The reason we always had worn out footwear i.e. pumps was because it was the only footwear we had, and when worn daily they wore out in a couple of weeks or so. Our clothes came from jumble sales and were always too small. Any road up, when we did finally get back to the house, cold, wet and worn out the lady said, "Where on earth have you been?

I've been waiting for this coal to light the fire for when my husband gets home from work, you have been messing about haven't you." No explanation would do, she just wouldn't believe a word I said. "It's the snow, Mrs R, it's slippy and there weren't any men around to lift it on to my back and there was a long queue." "You're lying to me, well I'm only giving you 2d each," she replied. Two pence, we were always polite, "Thank you, lady," I said whenever she asked me or Trevor to run errands for her, but after that we said, "no," but we said it very politely. We were used by a lot of adults who didn't care about our welfare, we worked hard for them but they never appreciated what we did for them. One or two would say, "You are good lads for fetching these groceries for me, I can't pay you anything today, I will see you all right next time," but they never did, and we were too polite to remind them. Mrs R asked me and Trevor if we would go to the Gas Works to get a quarter of a hundredweight of coke, of course we said, "yes," even though we had said we would never run any more errands for her, so she gave us a 1/- (one shilling) that was for the bus fares (3d each way) and said she would give us 6d sixpence for getting the coke. I can't remember how much the coke was, I said, "Trevor, if we walk there and ride back we can save the bus fares." Halfway there it started to rain so we had to get on the bus after all because it was taking far too long to walk. On arrival at the Gas Works there was a very long queue, so like everyone else we had to stand in line; the rain was very heavy and by this time we were soaked through to the skin. We paid at the office, got to where the coke came down a shoot, the man operating the shoot asked if I had another sack, "No, mister, I've only got this one, it's OK." "Shame," he said, "I would have filled another one for you half price." "I wouldn't be able to carry it," I explained. His tone changed then, "Go on get out, there are other people waiting. Bloody kids," he said to the next customer, "you wouldn't think parents would let kids out on days like this." As we struggled to get the sack on my back I heard him say to a man, "Have you got another sack?" so he asked everyone, he made his wages up that way I suppose. I carried the sack of coke across the road to the bus stop; by this time the rain had soaked the coke through the sack, which made black slurry run down my back. As we waited at the bus stop the rain now was heavy, coke or coal wasn't allowed on buses, and when the bus arrived the conductor was upstairs so we got the coke onto the luggage rack, fortunately there were no pushchairs on there. Normally there would be three or four pushchairs on the luggage rack, I suppose because it was raining the ladies stayed at home with their little ones, any road up away we went to the front of the bus and sat down. After a few minutes I looked round to make sure the bag of coke was still there, to my horror there was black slurry running from the sack off the luggage rack along the platform and off the bus. The conductor was going mad, "Who owns this bag of coal?" he was shouting as he ran up and down the stairs, "I will find out whose it is." The conductor hadn't noticed how wet and dirty we were, "Don't look round, don't say anything, Trev." "OK, Dave." "When we get near our stop, Trev, if the conductor goes upstairs I'm jumping off." "But we will have to carry it a lot further then, Dave, if we do that." "I don't care, Trev, I'm jumping off, you stay on if you want to." "No, I'm with you, Dave." The stop before ours a lady got off the bus, fortunately for us the conductor ran up the stairs still shouting, "Whose is this bag of coal?" This gave us the opportunity to jump off the bus without him seeing us, but as we stood up I noticed how wet and dirty the seat was, it was black from the coke that had run down my back. I was very worried thinking someone else would sit on that seat and ruin their clothes. As the bus started to move, I said, "Now, Trev," and with every ounce of strength left in me I grabbed the sack, threw it off the bus and jumped after it. The conductor was fuming, "I will remember you, look at the mess you have made on my bus." It was still raining hard; I got on my knees, got hold of the sack and with Trevor's help I stood up. The black slurry from the coke was running down my back and my legs and into my pumps, I was as black as the coke inside the sack, we were soaking, dripping wet.

When we got to the back door of the house, Mrs R opened the door, she was very angry, "You've been far too long, you've walked to save the bus fares haven't you?" "No Mrs," I said. "Look at the state of you, your mom won't half give it to you when you get home, you are black and soaking wet." "It's the rain, Mrs." "Don't be cheeky to me, young man." I never meant it the way she took it. "Well, I'm not paying you, here is a biscuit each." It was a Rich Tea biscuit, stale and soft; she always gave us a biscuit and they were always stale. Upon that she closed the door. "Look, Trev, we are soaking wet, black, five hours' work for a rotten Rich Tea soft stale biscuit." "Why does this keep happening to us, Dave?" "Dunno, Trev, it's not fair all that work and no money." We did eat the biscuits we never wasted food.

To cap it all a good hiding off my mom, bless her, she had to wash and repair my clothes. Well it wasn't the last time we worked and never got paid.

Going to the Gas Works to get a bag of coke, getting very dirty and soaking wet, then to be told you are not getting paid makes it a day neither Trevor nor myself will ever forget.

TRYING TO MAKE BOTH ENDS MEET

One of the things about Christmas that I loved, as well as getting presents on Christmas Day, was going into town with my mom and seeing all those lights, every shop decorated up, the long queues all round Lewis's out into the street. I only queued once with my mom to see Father Christmas at Lewis's, it took too long and all those people on those concrete stairs, to be honest it used to scare me. I always worried about stairs like that, nothing underneath them just sitting on the floor either end of the stairs. Going through the grotto was magical for children. I much preferred the Co-op Christmas grotto, it always seemed bigger and better to me, all those wonderful toys and me. Like all children, I wanted them all.

I didn't go to see Father Christmas every year, in fact I only remember going to see Father Christmas once, I went up town with Mom every year but most times she had no money to spare. We always went round the Rag Market and the Meat Market; Mom was always looking for cheap presents for her children and cheap meat. I can still see and hear in my mind's eye, dealers holding toys up with outstretched arms shouting, "Only one left 6d, take this toy with this one then you can have the two for 9d – they are here to be sold." I used to think, I wish I had some money I would buy those. The man I loved to watch was Mr Lees, I assume it was Mr Lees, he was the man selling the china with an overturned tea chest and a piece of carpet on top of it; he would bang the plates on it throw them up in the air and say, "These plates will last you a lifetime and they are strong," all the time banging them edgeways on, by hitting them on the tea chests this way they wouldn't break and on the next stall they were shouting about the linen they had for sale. Christmas is a magical time.

One year I was in town with Mom at Christmas, she was really poor that year; she desperately tried to buy toys cheap. I can see her eyes now looking so anxious and watery asking, "Can you do those for

3d or 4d?" but no good, the dealers wouldn't drop the price. She was so worried, the pain she must have been going through just trying to get little presents for her children so we could wake up Christmas morning with something in our pillowcase, yes always a pillowcase. That year I remember seeing tears run down my mom's face and I asked, "Are you alright, Mom?" She said, "I've got something in my eye." I knew she was hurting; it's hurting me writing it down. I had 8d in my pocket and offered it to my mom, "It's alright, son, buy yourself some sweets," she said. I went to a stall and saw a very pretty glass decorated with holly and bells; it was 6d so I bought it for my mom. "Here you are, Mom, I've bought you a present." She broke down and sobbed her heart out, with her arm round me she hugged me very tightly; she never said a word at that moment in time, her actions said it all. How can a child not remember such an occasion? As we walked out of the market she did say, "I love the glass you bought for me, but I can't buy you anything." "I don't want anything, Mom," I replied. I hurt her more than I could ever have imagined by trying to make her happy with a present; I shouldn't have done it should I, but as a child who loved his mom so much I thought a present would make her feel good.

When we got to the bus stop there was a very long queue, it seemed never ending; we waited for over an hour to get on the bus, the bus filled to capacity with people standing from the front of the bus right down to the platform. I hated being squashed and pushed around on those over-crowded buses. As the bus approached the next bus stop there was a very long queue because the bus had filled up from the terminus, it didn't stop the people standing there shouting and waving their fists. I was so relieved to get off that bus. Every year was the same, too many people, and not enough buses in those days at Christmas time, a day in town meant a day that is one Christmas that is burned into my memory.

RATION COUPONS

Stocktons our local newsagent was on the corner of Trevor's Road, Swancote Road, and Mr Stockton ran that shop all through the war and well into the post-war years. One Sunday I was sent to that shop to buy a pound of sugar, it was against the law to sell groceries on a Sunday in those days, and when I asked for a pound of sugar a silence came over the shop. The lady looked around to see if any policemen were about, she very quietly walked to the back end of the shop and still looking around she picked up a pound bag of sugar. It was a blue bag I think, all sugar in those days were put in those blue bags. Covering the bag with both her hands and placing it under my coat she said, "There, keep it under your coat and don't let anyone see you with it," she said all that in quite a worried voice. I was terrified; I put it under my jumper, the same jumper I had from the bag of rags I mentioned in another chapter, and ran like the wind down the road non stop till I got inside my house. I felt like a criminal. I was scared stiff (doesn't one's body goes stiff when scared?). It was a relief to walk into my house, my heart was going like a train, "Here you are, Mom, sugar, I'm not going on a Sunday again," I said. "OK, son," she said very calmly. I'm standing there still shaking. To think these days I could walk all around Birmingham with a wheelbarrow full of sugar and not a soul would even take a second glance, how our England has changed. The nicest memory I have of that shop was the day rationing finished; I was sitting in the house and was told I could go and buy some sweets without ration coupons. My mom gave me 3d (three pence), I ran to Stocktons and very nervously asked for 2oz of sherbet lemons. I have no idea why I remember what sweets I bought, maybe because it was the first time I had ever bought sweets on my own because from birth everything with sugar in it was on ration coupons. With shaking hands I handed over my 3d, she handed me the sweets and said, "There you are, bab." I got out of that shop very quickly; I will go and tell Trevor,

I thought, I would excite him. "Trev, Trev," I blurted out, "you can buy sweets without coupons." "I know, I've been already with my mom, she bought me some," Trevor said. I was so disappointed I thought I was the only one that knew, it appeared all my friends knew before I did, well at least I had my two 2oz of sherbet lemons.

One morning when rationing was still in force I was going through the sideboard drawers looking for some string. My sister Doreen had shown me how to make a gate when the string was tied into a circle, put on each hand and with the fingers put in certain positions through the string then with the hands pulled apart the string took on the shape of a gate. So as I pulled out what I thought was the drawer, I pulled the middle piece between the two drawers by mistake to find it was a secret drawer. I never knew it was there, Mom kept it a secret, I found Mom's ration book in there so I cut two sweet coupons out. I couldn't read or write at that time in my young life but I knew what the sweet coupons looked like, they were the last two sweet coupons so I cut them out of the book. I ran up the road to find my mom, "Mom, Mom," I said, "I've found these," and handed the coupons over. "Sh," she said, "don't let anyone hear." She took me in the sweet shop and bought me 2oz of sweets, Dolly Mixtures I remember. I thought I had been very clever, I thought she will never know; children know nothing do they, I had taken the last two coupons. Funny thing was I was not a dishonest child, I had never stolen a thing nor wanted to.

The next day I was playing with Trevor in the horse road, "David," Mom shouted, "I want you a minute." "Oh, Mom, I'm playing," I said. "Just for a minute," Mom said, so as I walked through the front gate she grabbed my arm and said, "You little bugga, you took those coupons out of my book that you gave me yesterday." "I found them, Mom," I said. "Oh you still want to lie to me, get the cane from the coal house," she angrily replied. She canned me three times for stealing the coupons and another three for lying to her. I never lied to her again. No tea that evening, it was five o'clock in the afternoon, and I was in bed with a very sore bottom. I very much needed that sort of discipline; if my mom had been soft with me I dread to think how I would have turned out. Spare the rod and spoil the child, how true is that saying.

RUN RABBIT RUN

Christmas, carol singing night after night, my aim every year was to earn a pound, I never got to that magic £1 mark, close to 18/11 (eighteen shillings and eleven pence), but never the one pound. Couple of my mates did, it's a magical time for children, Christmas carols, coloured lights, Christmas trees, trimmings, how I loved those magical Christmases. Not coming from a family with lots of money it was make-do-and-mend season, a magical time for me but not so for my mother, the suffering she went through I can only imagine. My mate Johnny came down the road one Christmas Eve, he told me, "Your mom is up the shops crying her eyes out." He heard her say to a lady who wondered if she was alright, "I've got no money to buy my children any presents for Christmas," her heart and soul must have been torn in two. Just writing about it makes me feel tearful, that memory never fades. I actually remember what I got that Christmas, a colouring book with about eight pages in it and six crayons, no nuts or chocolate bar, we usually had these every Christmas but not that Christmas. I kept that book for a very long time. I've no idea why, maybe because I felt there was so much hurt in my mom I kept it to say thank you. I loved it and it was very special to me, I don't really know the reason why I kept it. The pictures in it were of Hopalong Cassidy (William Boyd).The happy times of making paper chains, I remember the horrible taste after licking the gum to stick them together, crepe paper cut into strips and twisted, then they were pinned to the ceiling. Sometimes my sisters would sew cotton right through the middle of the crepe paper strips, then they would gather it up to make it look fancy instead of flat twisted paper. There is one year I remember so well but not what year it was, I was very young. It's strange how certain things in your life stay as vivid memories like it was only yesterday. It was Christmas morning, well dinnertime; I was lying on the floor in the living room, as it was the warmest place in our house. Well actually it was the only sitting room downstairs, the only other room was the kitchen. I had a shooting game that Christmas and I loved it, still do, for my present; a little wire gun which when I squeezed the handle it released a spring that fired a round piece of wood at four animals on a frame. When hitting one of the animals, if you did, you scored points which were shown on the front of the game underneath each of the animals. My mother was putting the dinner out and shaking potatoes from the saucepan onto the plates on the table in the living room, lots of steam, and Mother saying, "You will have to move now, son, and play with that after dinner," just then Flanagan and Allen were singing on the wireless (no TV in our house in those days) "Run Rabbit Run." I loved that song and still do for it burned into my memory that very special Christmas morning and my wonderful mother that memory will be mine to eternity. I love it. Thank you, Mr Flanagan and Allen. One Christmas in 1948 when I was five years old, first year at school, I had a cowboy suit, it meant the world to me. On the first Friday back at school after Christmas that Friday we were told we could bring a toy to school, "I will come in my cowboy outfit," I said to one of the boys, another boy said he would come in his. I heard him telling another boy about his outfit, boy did it sound good. My mom saved 3d a week in a club to get my outfit. Any road up, I didn't go in it to school (to be honest after hearing about the cowboy outfit the other boy had I knew they would laugh at me and take the mick because my outfit was a cheap one, mostly plastic or a material like plastic). I was glad I didn't as his outfit was all sheepskin, leggings, waistcoat, even a cowboy shirt, stones that looked like diamonds all round the hat, guns with pearl handles, gun holsters with diamonds on them, diamond-studded cowboy boots with silver spurs attached, best outfit I've ever seen even to this day. Mine was very basic, but it was mine and I loved it. I did make-believe I had forgotten it, you can imagine the comments I received. "I bet you haven't got one, bet you daint get any presents for Christmas," children are so cruel, he was a spoiled child what's that you say, sour grapes you bet it was! That same Christmas morning my sister Doreen had a doll, she went to walk down the stairs and dropped it, the doll smashed into a thousand pieces, and did she sob. We only got one present, main present, some years we got a game as well. Every Christmas Trevor and me went carol singing, and with the money I got I bought my mom a tin tray and a piny (every year the same present that looked big when I wrapped it) from a shop called Lathams. My Mom was a large lady, I never thought it wouldn't fit, the lady never asked me what size did I want. When Mom put it on I would say, "Oh, Mom, it's too small." She always said, "It's perfect, I love it." Bless her, buying for my mom always made me feel good and very happy.

As a seven year old I lay on the floor in the living room to play with my shooting game as it was the warmest place in our house. I remember that Christmas Day so well, because on the wireless Flanigan and Allan were singing 'Run Rabbit Run'.

I loved it, and still do, it made that Christmas morning stand out in my memory.

Note the piece of wire sticking out at the top of the handle – well it did me no harm.

JUGS OF BEER

The Glebe Pub had an outdoor, alas even that pub has now been demolished. This pub was my dad's second home, (more like his first). My mom, bless her, would have raised the Union Jack if she had seen the Glebe Pub being demolished, as this pub made a big contribution to me and all my family for the poverty we suffered. My dad drank there, any spare money and minute he had he spent there.

As I said, it had an outdoor, lots of children including me would earn money for fetching beer from this outdoor. I've taken beer bottles, jugs, and pop bottles, once even a basin, usually for a pint of mild. They weren't supposed to serve beer to children but they always did. I was given 3d (three pence) by one lady and 4d (four pence) by another; never the men, only ever the ladies used to ask me to fetch beer.

Sometimes the men serving would be very grumpy and in a raised voice say, "Don't keep coming here for beer, I've enough to do," I used to think, why say don't come here for beer because that's what they sold. In the main barmaids were nice; only a couple of times I remember them saying, "I'm busy, you will have to wait," and wait we did for what seemed to be forever. Most times they would say, "I'm not supposed to sell you beer," but they always did.

The Glebe Public House
Sadly now demolished. The outdoor is underneath the Ansells sign

The Glebe Pub as I remember it. It had ornamental gates that were locked every night. There were iron railings all around it as well so one wasn't able to go near its doors till opening time. The gates and railings were taken down and melted for the war, the Second World War

PIG SWILL

A friend of mine whose name was Douglas, he lived at the bottom of the adjoining road to my road the same road as Trevor's Swancote Road, his dad kept pigs in their back garden, they did this all through the war because of food shortage. I loved to watch the pigs being fed, when the food was being poured into the trough the pigs went wild, like they had never been fed, they pushed each other violently. It fascinated me so much I offered to go round the houses with Douglas and collect the pigswill, it was a smelly job but I just loved doing it.

Dougie lived across the road from Billy, two doors away from John, Eddy lived across the road from John, Trevor lived six doors away from Eddy and I lived over the road from Trevor. Six of us, we spent many a year together; we went everywhere together, at one stage we all rummaged on the tip. As we entered our teens we sort of split in half, not completely for we sometimes all got together and went cycling, swimming, football. Me and Trevor were like brothers, we spent every day together, well almost, Johnny sort of mixed with all of us, out with them one day and us another.

About once a fortnight I would help Douglas collect the pig swill, so did Trevor; the pig swill was in dustbins usually at the side of the houses, we could only go to certain houses because there was another family that kept pigs a few doors away from Trevor's house, it was agreed they never touched Dougie's pig bins and he never touched their pig bins. As we were colleting one day Dougie looked really worried, "What's the matter, Dougie?" I asked. "There isn't enough swill for the pigs," his bin round was done in two halves, one set of houses one fortnight and the other half the following fortnight. In those days people didn't waste much food, well it wasn't long after the Second World War and rationing was still on, and times were still very hard for the working classes so pig keeping was even more difficult. "Well, Dougie, let's take one or two and half empty them from the other pig keepers' bins," I said to him. "We can't, Dave, we have an agreement, we don't touch the theirs and they don't touch ours." "Well, if we don't empty the bins, only take a bit out of each bin, Doug." "That should be all right, Dave," so that's what we did. When we got back to his house he said, "I haven't any firewood to boil the swill up," so I climbed over the fence (well it was spiked railings) to the field at the back of his garden to find some wood. Dougie said, "I've looked all over that field, Dave, there isn't any."

I looked and found a small handful in the field, wood was very hard to find in those days, everyone used wood to light their coal fires, so with the few sticks I found and with what Dougie had, he lit the fire under the pig swill. As the wood started to burn Dougie began to throw the bread on to keep the fire going, I never knew bread would burn like it did. "I hate burning the bread, Dave, but it's the only way I can get the swill to boil." All sorts went into that swill and to think how they go on today about hygiene, health and safety, it has to make you smile, I never caught anything, but I never liked the smell of those bins.

As I was walking back to my house the other family who kept pigs, their two sons were walking towards me, they shouted, "You've been taking our pig swill." "I have not," I said. "Yes you have, you were seen and they told us it was you." "Well it wasn't me," I kept insisting. "We will have the same amount back out of your bins next week, we have to feed our pigs as well you know," they shouted. My mom kept the swill for that family but it was more than my life was worth to take my mom's pig swill. I was more afraid of my mom more than any boy. Every Christmas the people who saved the swill all year were given a nice piece of pork to say thank you. The man who kept the pigs went to see Dougie's dad about us taking his swill. Dougie got a good hiding and I was banned from going round to see the pigs; it seemed that it was set in stone never to touch the other family's pig swill.

Enjoying watching the pigs while waiting for the pig swill to come to the boil. It was very interesting to see the pigs fight to get the best position when I poured the swill into the trough. After watching the pigs feed I now know why my mom used to say to me at meal times you are like a pig in a trough.

MY TALKING BOOTS

It was a Saturday morning, I ran some errands for two neighbours I had earned 9d (nine pence). Trevor was going with his mom to the Birmingham Rag Market; his dad worked in the fruit market. The Atlas Cinema had its normal Saturday matinee at 12 noon, we always referred to it as the flicks, so off I went to the flicks. I walked down Audley Road, I completely forgot about my right boot, I think those boots were the same ones I had from the Birmingham Post and Mail, the toe cap was flapping just like it was talking or singing, it was singing 'there will always be an England', more like *Land of Hope and Glory*, it was hanging on by a thin piece of leather; on the left-hand side there was a long piece of leather hanging where the toe cap had been ripped off. I was able to tuck that piece of leather inside my boot under the inner sole, which made the boot look normal and the toe cap OK. Every time I did it I used to think, that's better, so off to the flicks I go. Trouble was I only took a few steps and it was flapping again. I patiently tucked in the leather strip to hold the toe cap constantly thoughout the day, well every day. How long I suffered that boot I've no idea, I know I had to go to school like it but I don't recall any other children taking the mick about my boots when at school. They were showing Hopalong Cassidy that day I loved that cowboy with his black clothes and his silver accessories. At the end of the film we were like a herd of cattle all rushing to get to the bus stop first. I would normally walk home, but I must have been feeling lazy that afternoon. I had 2d (two pence) left, it was only two stops so I waited for the bus, and while I was standing there a boy standing next to me gave me a nudge with his elbow. I turned to see what he wanted, with a snigger and a sneer he said, "Your toe cap is flapping." I felt embarrassed and ashamed, I had completely forgotten about my boot. "Why don't you get a pair of boots like mine," he was sniggering all the time he was saying it, "mine are polished, why don't you polish yours?" "My mom can't afford any at the moment, I'm getting some new ones next week," I told him, I wasn't but I didn't know what else to say to him. By this time there were lots of boys and girls waiting for the bus and they were all looking and laughing. I was praying for the bus to turn up, I even thought of running from the bus stop to get away from the humiliation I was suffering. Just as I was about to run, the bus turned up, I was so relieved I went upstairs on the bus (I always went upstairs) and hid my feet under my seat so my boots were not seen. When I got off the bus I must admit I was close to tears but I held them back. Where I came from boys were tough and never cried, at least not if anyone could see you, I grew up to believe that. As I walked into our kitchen my mom could see I was upset, "What on earth's the matter, David?" she asked, "Nothing, Mom," I replied. "Yes there is, now what's up?" a mother knows her children well. I told her how the boy had laughed at me because the toecap on my boot was flapping and all the boys and girls at the bus stop were laughing at me. She hugged me and said, "You are better than all them, you would never take the rise out of anyone would you, son, that was in the same boat as you." "Never, Mom," I said (taking the rise meant taking the mick, in the same boat meant as poor as I was). I was taught to help people never to belittle anyone; if I did, which I never did, Mom would have belted me till I couldn't sit down; she was a stickler for good manners and respect. "I will ask your father when he comes home from work if he has any money to help me get you a pair of pumps." I felt very happy at that moment; all I wanted was to look normal just like all the other children. I got my new pumps the next day, I felt really good walking around with footwear that looked OK. My thoughts were at that time, now no one can take the rise out of me now. It's not good for children to feel this way, is it? But ay, that's life because when those pumps got holes in the soles, which was not long, because I had to wear then daily so they wore out very quick, I was back to putting cardboard in them and tucking my socks under my feet. Life can be so cruel and hard even for children, for mothers even harder. I have the up most respect for mothers, they really do run the world.

Wish I had some new boots so people wouldn't laugh at me.

FAGGOTS AND PEAS

Carmichaels was what everyone where I lived called “the faggots and pea shop”. Really it was a cooked meats shop; ham, cooked pork, cheese, cereals, biscuits all those sorts of items, but the Carmichaels we knew were famous for their faggots and peas. People would queue for nearly an hour before they opened to buy their famous faggots. There’s been as many as fifty people waiting, if you were at the front of the queue you got plenty of gravy, at the back of the queue and you would definitely get no gravy; in fact many a time you got no faggots because they were sold out, so many a time I was sent to get in the queue early.

I would listen to people talking, not that I wanted to you understand. The times I heard about their daughters having babies and what a bad time they had, and even talking about someone dying, and how they went about laying them out. I never liked to hear about people dying but while in that queue on occasions I endured that type of conversation, even women’s troubles, I heard just about every disease known to man, ha, ha in this case women. We stood outside winter and summer it was a sight to see some of the people, men and women dressed to kill, some in slippers and aprons and Nora Batty’s wrinkled stockings, well you can imagine it can’t you. If you close your eyes and get a picture going in your mind’s eye I’m sure it will make you smile, and scruffy little me usually needing a wash; and to see the different utensils they were holding that always fascinated me, jugs, kettles, yes kettles people really did live on the edge of life in those days, saucepans, big mugs.

Some people went to the hardware shop known as Suches, which was a couple of doors away to buy a basin or bowl (only if they were the better-off type of people) which was always dusty and on occasions the shopkeeper would be asked to wash out the bowl which they kindly did with a smile. That shop did quite a trade because of the faggot and pea shop. I tell you what, I'm proud to have been a part of it, it's my history, those faggots and peas are the best I have ever tasted, yes I've tried the Black Country ones a few times, not to my liking. Carmichaels have never been equalled in my humble opinion.

The one time I went to get some faggots for my mom I was at the back of the queue; I was supposed to get four faggots but because I messed about and was late, I only got three, the last three I might add, and no gravy. It was raining so I got water in with them; well it looked like gravy, only see-through. Well, I got a clip round the ear and no faggots for not doing as I was told. Those faggots were their own recipe, many people my mom told me asked for that recipe but they always said no. They had a daughter the same age as me; I wonder did she have that famous recipe?

ALL GROWN UP

The first time I ever had long grey trousers it was in February; there was snow on the ground and it was very cold. When I went to school everyone noticed this scruffy boy had a new pair of trousers, which to me seemed wide and baggy with turn-ups, they took the mick for the first morning and then it all faded. Well they were really warm after wearing short trousers.

After school had finished and after I had my tea I went with my two friends to Manor Park playing fields where there was quite a slope at the end of the football pitches. We had an old tin tray that we used for sledging down the slope, and lots of children were there sledging, what we called the posh kids as they had real sledges, not a tin one like we did. We had every bit of fun as they did. And all we had was a piece of tin for a sledge. We were jealous of them if I'm honest; I always wanted a proper sledge but never got one. Mind you there were a lot of things I wanted and never got but that never ever stopped me enjoying life to the full as a youngster. I never found a sledge on the rubbish tip. I bet those posh kids never had the freedom of childhood that I had. I called every one that was better clothed than me posh. Jealous, me? How dare you, oh all right I was.

On the way home I looked down and saw a tear in my nice new trousers. One day and I had ruined a new pair of trousers well, there was another good hiding coming my way. Not only ripped but dirty as well. It's no wonder I was called "Scruff", and a few other things I can't print. Boy, I can tell you, when away from school and out with my friends I was in heaven. I'm a very lucky man to have had such a wonderful childhood.

SIXPENCE FOR SWEETS

To go to the cinema in the 1940s and the 1950s was a real treat. Trevor and I used to stand outside the Atlas cinema which was situated in the Stechford area of Birmingham, sometimes until it was it was too late to go in because the second picture had started. Children were never allowed to go in alone if the picture had an "A" certificate. There were three types of certificate films: for children to watch without an adult it was a "U" certificate and when it was an "A" a child always had to be accompanied by an adult. If it was an "X" certificate children were not allowed in at all. So it was "A", "U", "X". I think it has all changed now.

Sometimes I would stand there alone but most of the time Trevor was with me and we would ask anyone to take us in, courting couples, old dears, people with children. Thinking about it, it was rare to see mom, dad and children going in to the cinema at night. To any of the people I would say "take us in, Mister," or "take us in, Lady," hold out my hand with the sixpence in it. If we had to have an adult to take us in because the film was an "A" we used to get a lot of comments, most I can't repeat; those comments or insults only came from men, never the ladies. The most common one was of course was "No", usually quite loud, when some kind couple said "Yes" I gave them my sixpence. Most times I was told to stand at the back of them so we could not touch their clothes and was told on occasions to walk past the kiosk so as not to be seen with them. I must have looked a sight. Only once do I remember a couple allowing me to sit by them. I was told to keep quiet, don't fidget, sit still. I sat there frightened to death to move, well as you know children always fidget.

One evening I was standing there on my own. I can't remember why Trevor wasn't with me, asking, "take me in, Mister, take me in, Lady," when a pretty young lady with very dark shoulder-length hair with a three-quarter length coat on (I remember the coat was sandy-coloured and she was very pretty, she had a scarf round her neck) and to my delight she said, "Of course I will, Bab." I handed her my sixpence and to my surprise she said, "It's alright, Bab, I will pay for you, you go and buy some sweets for yourself." I said to her, "I will sit on my own lady?" "No, Bab, you sit by me," she replied. That had never happened to me before and it never happened again. God bless that kind lady.

You see if you were sitting by yourself and there wasn't an adult either side of you and the picture was an "A" certificate the usherette knew someone had taken you in, she would shine her torch on you and throw you out. They were cruel to children, even when they were quiet and just enjoying the film they would throw them out. I found out years later my eldest brother's sister-in-law was the usherette at the cinema. I was talking to her one day and asked if she ever regretted throwing kids out, she said no they shouldn't have been in the cinema, hard woman. When couples did take you in you were told, "We will take you in but you ain't sitting by us." Even now that thought makes me feel very uncomfortable but of course I was very scruffy so I suppose I can't blame them. I remember some of the courting couples, the lady's hair was always nice and always looked like they were going to a wedding and she always had bright red lipstick on; and the man had a smart suit and Brylcreemed hair, polished shoes and a smart tie, her on his arm and always looked very happy and very much in love. Would you want a scruffy little kid sitting by you when you were in love? Neither would I. (Well I'm not sure, I was that scruffy kid.)

Oh yes, the next day I told Trevor, "A lady took me in and paid for me and I bought sweets with the sixpence." He was so jealous every time we stood outside the Atlas Cinema, and was asking to be taken in, he would say, "Is this the lady that paid for you to be taken in?" He was hoping if we saw her she would pay for us again, secretly so was I also, alas I never saw her again.

It's wonderful remembering the past, even though it was hard but the small things we achieved made us very happy, as they do now.

PLAYING WITH FIRE

As children did in the 1940s and the 1950s, in those days we all played together in the horse road, as my mom always called it. The girls played alongside of the boys, and I very much liked to watch the girls skipping they were so fast and nimble. I tried a few times to join them but my feet were not fast enough, and it wasn't long before they told me to clear off because I was spoiling their game. I was quite good at hopscotch, though never good enough to beat the girls.

I had such wonderful times, those were wonderful years for all us children, we were poor, not well-clothed but when playing in the horse road with all my friends nothing else mattered; we were all good neighbours to one another and that combination can never be beaten. I don't care how rich or poor anyone is, with good friends and neighbours like I had you were opulent.

One day when we were playing in the road I had a box of matches; I'm not sure why I had matches, I think I got them from my mom's kitchen because one of our the girls had one of those fire cans we used to swing round. Anyway, I remember lighting the paper in the can, I think it was on the same day I had those matches, I had matches in my pocket quiet often in those days (I think it was Nanette, Trevor's sister that was playing with the fire can that day), she swung it round till it got red hot and glowed. Some of the girls were as tough as the boys; one girl whose name was Ann Hill said to me, "You shouldn't play with fire, nor should you have matches." I remember I lit a match, I thought I would play her up and singe her hair, boy did I get scared, I never knew hair burned the way it did, her hair went up in flames. Ann's sister Rita rushed over to her and put out the flames. I can't remember what Ann said to me but we all carried on playing after I apologized to her. I remember that day well. I never did anything I shouldn't after that day with matches for fear of it going wrong, yes I learnt a good lesson that day.

I still see Ann and her sister Rita from time to time, Rita like me loves talking about the past. Ann was playing one day with my sister Janet when June a girl who came out to play (she lived two doors away from Ann) she had a blue ribbon in her hair. Ann said, "That's my ribbon she has in her hair, I lost it the other day." So Ann said to June (who now lives in America), "That's my ribbon you've got in your hair, June." She said, "No it is not, my mom bought it for me last week." (I don't think Ann for one minute thought maybe she could be wrong.) "Yes it is," Ann replied, "I've got the other ribbon in the house that matches that one, I will go and get it," and she ran down to the back of her house but when she was halfway down the entry she tripped (I can still hear her screams to this day). She ripped open her top lip and damaged her two front teeth; her top lip is scarred but she is still a nice looking lady.

All my friends that I grew up with are down-to-earth lovely people, it's wonderful to keep in touch with old friends and reminisce, it makes one appreciate old times and one's childhood and one's life.

DAD'S WORKS

Most of the factories when I was a boy had Christmas parties for the children of their workforce. It was great fun, as young children we loved it, it was very special to us to get jelly and blancmange, fruit, even cake. The icing on the cake, as the saying goes, was a present to take home after the party had ended.

My dad worked at the Metropolitan Camel and Carriage Works, they made trains. The factory was at the Gate, Saltley, Birmingham; I went there three times, my dad worked there all through the war. The present was sometimes a gun or a game, one year I got a gun, another year I got a Snakes and Ladders game, the third year I got a book and a compendium of games.

My dad used to put on a show for all the children with my eldest brother, they always did the same play about schoolboys, and they were very good. My dad left that firm for a short while and started to work for a firm called S U Carbareter. At the train works he was a radial driller, at his new company he was a labourer; why he left the train company I have no idea, yet he spent many years with the train company.

Anyway I went twice to the Christmas parties at his new firm, I was given a colouring book both times as a present. He left that firm after about eighteen months and returned to his old firm the Metropolitan Camel Carriage and Wagon Works; his boss was my mom's brother, my uncle Bob. At one Christmas party my sister Doreen got her present, dolls' furniture, but she wasn't happy with it, she thought she was too old for it, so she got in the queue again. The man said, "You've been round before haven't you?" "No," she replied, so he gave her another present, did she moan, another set of dolls' house furniture! Some girls had dolls, some had games, my sister wanted a game. That was the last Christmas party I ever went to at that firm, that year I got a red gun.

My dad was a member of the British Legion; I went there a couple of times to their Christmas parties. The first time was after Christmas, they always had their Christmas parties after Christmas, we were taken to the Aston Hippodrome to see Puss in Boots, it was a wonderful show. The British Legion was at the back of my house, and I got the coach outside the Legion. We were given a bag with sweets, an apple and an orange in it, we got out of the coach and rushed in like a herd of cattle to get to what we thought would be the best seats in the Hippodrome, boy we were noisy that afternoon! The apple was sour; I ate mine because I didn't get fruit very often. The boy sitting next to me threw his apple, it hit a man on the back of his head, it really hurt him, he was very angry, he was looking around hoping to see who had thrown it. I was thinking, I wish he had given me that apple. When the curtains went back it went very quiet, I was in heaven, that was the first and last time I went to see a pantomime, the colours of the costumes were so bright and sparkly it was a treat I will never forget, I shall remember the song they sang till the day I die, THIS IS THE HOUR FOR US TO SAY GOOD NIGHT. I was very moved by it, the colours, the atmosphere, it truly was electric, and while writing this I find I want to go again.

FIRE CANS

Fire cans, I have touched on them in a previous chapter, but this chapter was some time after the other one and tells a different story. I loved playing with those fire cans! I realise now of course just how dangerous they were for young children to play with. If when on the tip we found a treacle tin, we would find a nail and with a stone we would punch holes in it, we then looked for a piece of wire and tied it to the sides of the tin, put paper and wood in it. The paper was lit, then the can would be swung around till the wood was well and truly lit, and we would keep putting wood in until the can glowed red hot. If at home we sorted over the slack in the coalhouse, coal made the can glow red really quickly plus it lasted a very long time; wood on the other hand burned away quiet quick.

My sister Doreen was swinging a can in our front garden one afternoon, "Dave," she shouted, "come here and pick this piece of wood up for me." "Can I have a go then?" I asked. "If you go into the coal house and sort through the slack for some lumps of coal," she answered. "If I do, then can I have a go?" I pleaded. "Yes OK, but only if you find a lot," she replied. So into the coal house I went and came out looking blacker than the coal, with the whitewash off the walls all down my back. Doreen was very pleased with the amount that I had found, after putting it in the can and getting it very hot after she swung it round a few times I said, "Can I have a go now?" Doreen again asked me to pick the piece of wood up that she had asked me to do previously, and as I bent down to pick up that piece of wood while she was swinging the glowing red hot fire can around, it hit me over my left eye and split my eyebrow wide open. Off to the hospital with Mother to have it stitched. On returning home Doreen thinks she was given a good hiding but can't remember for sure, fire cans were banned, never to be seen again, not anywhere near our house anyway. (I loved to hear the swishing sound, as the cans were being swung round!)

Making our fire cans glow in the dark.

HEADING HOUSE BRICKS

There is an alleyway at the rear of the shops in Glebe Farm, the alleyway is the delivery access to the shops; backing on to the alleyway were air raid shelters now demolished, with Audley Road School playground backing onto them. The shelters were for the infants and juniors to use during an air raid in World War Two. I went to this school at the age of five to the tender age of fifteen, when I left in 1958 I thought I was all grown up then.

One morning walking to the shops with Trevor, we noticed a builder's lorry parked in the alley, a builder was working on the walls surrounding the backyards of a shop. We could hear all the banging, rubble being thrown onto the back of the lorry, quick as a flash as the saying goes I said, "Come on, Trev, we might be able to earn some money." Climbing over the rubble without any thought of danger I said to the builder, "Excuse me, Mister, do you want any help?" "Yes, lads, would you start to throw all the bricks onto the back of the lorry?" "Yes, easy," I said. "Good, you start there," he said, pointing to the entrance of the yard. "Nice and steady," I said to Trevor, "if we make it last we might be able to come tomorrow and earn more money." We worked really well together and before long we had cleared the whole entrance. The builder soon made another pile that needed moving so we again started to throw the bricks onto the lorry.

All was going well when our friend Johnny shouted, "Hey, what's going on? How did you get this job?" "We asked if he needed any help and he said yes," I answered. "How much is he paying you?" asked John, "He never said," I replied. "I'm going to ask him," John said, "if I can help as well."

The builder said he could work with us, "You three get in a line and I will throw the bricks to you, then you," he said, pointing at Trevor, "can throw them onto the lorry."

All was going well, we must have moved three or four ton of bricks, the ends of our fingers were very sore by this time. I threw a brick to Trevor but because his fingers were sore he dropped it. I quickly turned to say to Johnny don't throw any more bricks. The chain had broken down, by this time because Trevor had dropped the brick but it was too late; as I turned, a brick that Johnny had thrown flew and hit me on the head, just above my right eyebrow, the blood cascaded down my face. Johnny, thinking he was clever, never raised his head, he just threw the house bricks one after the other. The builder came rushing over to me and I put my finger over the cut, "I'm alright," I shouted, "don't touch me, don't touch me," as I couldn't stand people messing with me when I had been hurt (I'm still the same now).

"I think I can manage on my own now, lads," the builder said, "thanks for your help." Me and Trevor said, "Thanks, John, you spoiled our job, now we ain't been paid because of you." No not a penny did we receive, we had worked for nothing. When I stopped bleeding, we all started playing football in the street. I never cleaned that cut, I had a beautiful big lump the next morning, my eye was closed with the swelling and it was very sore for a week afterwards.

THE QUEEN

One Bonfire Night, well a week before really, me and Trevor were around Castle Bromwich looking for firewood for our bonfire. Well, we found these two big branches, which were quite heavy; we were so pleased to find two braches on the ground, that saved us a lot of work as we were dragging the braches past Bradford Hall, which we all thought was haunted. Facing the Hall are two rows of what I think are Chestnut trees, I think the owner of the hall had those trees planted so when he looked out of his window he looked down the avenue of trees, we all called it the conker woods.

Any road up, me and Trevor were pulling those branches along this avenue of trees, we came to the main Chester Road, you can imagine how dirty and scruffy we were, nearly by the Chester Road, I couldn't believe my eyes there were lots of people waving the English flag and the Union Jacks. To my surprise the Queen was passing! Well I shouted as I ran towards the road dragging my branch, and she laughed as I waved and shouted, "Hi, Queen." We were very close to her. Wonder what she thought when she saw two dirty scruffy kids from Birmingham pulling two big tree branches behind them. I will never forget seeing the Queen laugh at Trevor and me as she waved to us, as there was a large gap in the crowd we were the only ones she could wave to there. Those were my three seconds of fame.

I bet if the authorities had known we were there looking like that we would have been hidden away or cleaned up, and at least it gave the Queen a laugh. That was the day she opened All Saints Church at Shard End. That's the church I was married at because my girlfriend lived at Shard End and you had to get married in the parish where your intended came from and that was Shard End.

Author and Trevor waving to the Queen. As she passed, her head went back as she laughed when she saw two dirty little urchins dragging branches for their bonfire. She was on her way to open All Saints Church in Shard End, Birmingham, in the 1950s.

Bradford Hall is the building in the background. Trevor and I were dragging branches one bonfire night, and as we approached the Chester Road we saw the Queen.

This picture is showing the Chester Road where we saw the Queen.

A PENNY FOR HIM

Two days before bonfire night I called for my friend Trevor and said, "Hey, Trev, I have had a great idea." "Oh yeah? What have I got to do now?" "Well, Trev, I thought if I dress you as Guy Fawkes and sit you in a pushchair I can push you to the bus stop up the road, by the shops you can hold a cup in your hand and I will stand at the side of you and ask for a penny for the guy. Can you get a pair of your dad's old trousers?" "I can get my dad's old coat and his flat cap." "If we go round to the back of corn shop" (this shop was called Turners) "there is usually a lot of straw on the floor by their back gate where they have their deliveries. We could go and pick it up and use it to put in your trouser legs, and in the sleeves of your coat, and out of the cap; then we need to find some string to tie round the bottom of the trousers to hold the straw in and round the sleeves and we can put the straw under your hat but we don't need to tie that." If my memory serves me right I think I blacked his face with coal dust not mud. "OK," said Trevor, "Let's do it." So I dressed him up and stood outside the bus stop with him holding his cup for the pennies. We didn't do very well, only 7d. So I had a bright idea of going around the houses after we had had our tea. So after we had had our tea I told Trevor, "I ain't pushing you in the pushchair, you can walk with me. I will ask for a penny for the guy, you just stand there." This we did, I knocked on lots of doors and asked for a penny for the guy. We got lots of different comments! Some would have a good laugh and give us 2d. Some would tell us to clear off and the main comment was, "Sod off, you bloody little scroungers," or words to that effect. One house I remember going to, the man that lived there was the man that ran our post office; he looked at us, laughed, and said, "which one of you is the guy?" I looked at him puzzled and said, "he is" pointing at Trevor. Still laughing he said, "I was only making sure." Then he gave me two shillings 2/-. As we walked up his path I said to Trevor, "I wonder why he never knew which was the guy, talk about being thick." Nothing deterred us, we were used to adults insulting us. We always used the money we got to go swimming or to go to the pictures (the cinema or the flicks) and of course we would buy sweets my favourites sweets at that time were sherbet lemons, they had sherbet in the middle of them. Funny thing is I can't stand them now.

We also used the money that we collected to go roller-skating. Trevor's brother Tony always came with us. We had great fun; there were lots of rough boys that went to that roller rink. I think they had about three bouncers, it could have been more; I saw many a lad thrown out of there and I mean thrown, those bouncers were some tough guys I can tell you. I mostly stayed in the middle of the rink that's where all us wimps went. Yes I was a wimp! I was knocked flying more than once especially when there were six or more of them holding hands. The one on the end would be flipped round at such a speed it was very dangerous. I was sent flying a couple of times by the one on the end of the line as he couldn't stop. I even saw them hit the barrier and get knocked out because of the speed they were travelling and some got really bad cuts. They only did this when they thought the bouncer wasn't around because it wasn't allowed. It was soon stopped as soon as the bouncers saw it start. Everyone that was in the line would get thrown out. They always knew that they would get thrown out as soon as they started. I think when they were ready to go because they had had enough of roller skating that's when they did the line up, there is a name for it but I'm afraid I can't bring it to mind.

One afternoon, when Tony Trevor and I had earned enough money from Guy Fawking, we went to the skating rink. When they gave me my pair of skates the lace was half missing in the one skate. I took it back to complain but even the ladies behind the counter were as rough as the bouncers and I was told to clear off and make do. At the end of that session which I think was an hour, the next hour was ours, some lads from the previous session would not hand their skates back in and they left them lying around because they had sneaked out of the side doors. So I decided to take a lace from one of boots and put it in my boot, when a bouncer came up to me, grabbed hold of me by the scruff of the

Trevor and I loved doing the things none of our friends would do, and me dressing Trevor up as Guy Fawkes was I think one of them. We had fun, Trevor and I.

neck and accused me of trying to steel the skates. He was shaking me violently and threatening to get the police. Bearing in mind I was only a young whippersnapper at the tender age of about nine, I was almost in tears as I tried to explain that I was only replacing the lace because the one that I had been given was not long enough. I told him I had asked the lady at the counter and she refused to change the boots, so he frog-marched me to the counter to confirm what I was saying was the truth. After the lady had confirmed what I was saying was the truth the bouncer said, "Sorry, son, but we do lose a lot of skates from people stealing them." I said, "I love coming here, Mister, I love to skate." Then in a very stern voice he said, "Do not ever do it again, I shall remember you and if I find you in here and you are taking laces out of the skates, even if you have paid I will still throw you out and you will not get a refund, do you understand!" "Yes, Sir," I said as I was cowering and looking at the floor, I wonder how those type of places would get on these days with the infant generation.

That roller rink was off the Golden Hillock Road, Small Heath; it was actually in Warf Road. We went to that roller rink many, many times and we always walked from our houses in Glebe Farm to that rink which was a very long walk, about ten miles I reckon, all to save the bus fares. It was eventually turned into a bingo hall when I worked for Coca Cola. I had to deliver to that building and the first time I made a delivery there I had a look around at the interior; the memories that came back to me, wonderful memories, then I remembered that bouncer and that half a lace, it was an exciting time for me all those years ago. I believe it's now been demolished, maybe because it was an all timber building, I suppose because the safety regulations had changed. I don't know, if it was good enough for my generation it should be good enough for this generation.

BLOOD, SWEAT AND TEARS

Trevor and I sat on my garden wall, in the front garden, we would put our brains together (which were very few as neither of us could read or write very well) to find a way of making money. We had some, what I now know as hair brained ideas; digging out a drive was most definitely one of them. Where our shops were was a community centre and Trevor suggested we went to that community centre to ask if they needed any jobs doing. In the building was a man who worked for the government; he looked after children who had been naughty and got into trouble. (We had no idea at that time about those sorts of children.) He was called a Probation Officer, I had no idea at that time what that was or who he was at that time. I was off school getting over a cold; I can't remember why Trevor was off school. We knocked on the door, a man opened the door of the community centre, "Do you want any jobs doing, Mister?" I asked. The first thing he said was, "Why are you not at school?" "We are getting over a cold," I explained to him. "Oh I see," he said. As I turned to walk away after he had told us he didn't require any jobs doing, I spotted through a half opened door at the end of the corridor a snooker table so I asked if we could play on it, "Yes you can," he said, to my great surprise, "so long as you are very quiet." "Thank you, Mister," we both said together.

About just over an hour had passed when the man came into the room where we were. "I say, you boys, are you interested in gardening?" Without a second's thought I said, "Yes we like gardening we do it all the time." I replied without thinking, we knew absolutely nothing about gardening; my mind was in overdrive wondering how much money we could make. "I live in Castle Bromwich, do you know where that is?" he asked. Well of course we didn't know. I replied, "We will find it, Mister, if you give us directions." "Tell you what, boys, I will leave early tonight and take you in my car and show you the way, is that all right, boys?" "Yes, Mister," Trevor said very quickly. "OK, boys, you carry on playing snooker." (We were there from about ten or ten thirty in the morning till late afternoon, nothing to eat, we just drank water from a tap in the toilet.)

"Wow, Trev, a ride in a car!" we were excited I can tell you. We got into his car, it smelt of leather; I can still smell that to this very day, it was an Austin. "Boys, you will have to walk back, it's not that far only I have to go out as soon as I've shown you the job." "That's OK, Mister, we like walking don't we, Trev?" "Yeah," we would say anything to earn money plus to get a ride in a car, we didn't know anyone with a car. I was ten, Trevor was eleven, we thought he was a millionaire because he had a car. As we were going along the road I was hoping to see one of our friends so we could wave to them, they would have been ever so jealous but we never passed one of them.

We arrived at his house and he parked the car on the road. "Here you are, boys, this is what I want you to do: I want this Hawthorn hedge taking down and this sandstone wall. I have a wheelbarrow you can use to take the stones round to the back garden. I want it put right at the bottom of the garden; the Hawthorn hedge you can drag round the back. When you have done that I want the soil digging out to a slope so it's level with the pavement and again barrowing round the back to the bottom of the garden, but keep all the items separate so it will be easy for me to move at a later date. The reason for doing this, boys, I want to put my car on my garden to keep it off the road, think you can manage that boys?" he asked. Trevor and me stood by the wall with the hedge on top of it, it must have been twelve foot or more high and for a ten and an eleven year old this was a mammoth task. "Can you start tomorrow, boys? I want it done as quick as possible." "Yes, Mister," I replied.

Next morning we walked from our houses, which were in Glebe Farm, to Castle Bromwich. It was a nice warm day nice for a walk; it took us thirty-five minutes to walk there, or thereabout. As we walked up the path the lady of the house came out to us, "There you are, boys, I've put out the tools ready for you, mind you clean them when you have finished with them, there is a spade, a saw and a pair of secateurs."

(What are those, I thought to myself, I've never heard of them.) "And here is a lump hammer," she explained, "it's for knocking the wall down, and the barrow is round the back when you need it." I asked for a drink of water before we started hoping she would give us pop; we got what I asked for, water.

We started to cut down the Hawthorn hedge; we didn't know it had thorns! We got injected, scratched, both of us had ripped our arms to bits and it took us all day to dig up and cut up that hedge. I was by this time very tired, so was Trevor. We stopped work at 4.30 p.m., I remember that because the lady came out with a glass of home-made Ginger Beer and a fairy cake each, best Ginger Beer I've ever tasted, that might be because I was tired, hot and very dry and very hungry. We only had two glasses of Ginger Beer and two fairy cakes all day. The lady next door asked the time, that's how I remember it was 4.30 p.m. We had left most of the hedge lying on the front garden ready to put round the back next morning.

We arrived home worn out. "Trev, it's harder than I thought it would be." "It is, Dave, ain't it. Shall we not go tomorrow?" "Let's see how we feel in the morning," I said. Next morning feeling good after a good night's sleep I called for Trevor, and like me feeling refreshed after a night's sleep and our normal two pieces of toast he said, "Right, Dave, let's go, we won't let it beat us will we?" "No way, Trev." We worked in the only set of clothes we possessed, our seven-days-a-week suit HA, HA! We were not very clean, our clothes that is.

On arriving we took what was left of the hedge round to the back garden, it must have been 60 yards long, it could have been less but to a youngster it seemed very long, then we started to take down the sandstone wall. This took us two days, I was pushing the wheelbarrow, I grew tired very quick pushing the barrow with two big stones in it, I ended up putting one stone at a time in. Trevor and I found this work to be too much for us both at times. After the hedge and wall were down we started to dig out the soil, which we found to be the hardest job to date – many, many barrow loads – we took just over a week to complete the digging out job, it was a relief taking the last barrow load of soil round to the back garden, without a doubt it was far too big a job for two little urchins like us. But we did it, our clothes were more ruined than they were before we started.

We cleaned up, put all the tools away, "Cor, Trev, I wonder how much he will pay us?" Out came the lady with two glasses of Ginger Beer and two fairy cakes. "Well done, boys, my husband will be pleased, you have worked very hard. He'll be home soon, I've phoned him to tell him you have finished the drive."

We had great expectations, saying to each other bet he will give us 10/- (ten shillings) each, well at least 8/- (eight shillings). We were sitting on the wall the other side of the garden when Trevor said, "Here he is, Dave." We knew it was his car because not one car passed us all day, only the milkman and the baker who both had horse-drawn carts. He drove his car on to his drive for the first time, got out of the car, hands on hips looking up and down his new drive saying, "Wonderful, wonderful, boys, thank you very much you have worked really hard, you should be very proud of yourselves," he said, "thank you very much." He then shook our hands and said, "Any time you want to play snooker you come and see me," he turned, walked into the house and closed the door. I looked at Trevor, we were both in shock. "He will come out in a minute and pay us, Dave." "Yeah of course he will." Wrong, he never showed his face; we waited a good fifteen minutes, all that work for glasses of Ginger Beer and fairy cakes. "In future, Trev, I'm going to ask how much they will pay before we start work." "Yeah we will too, Dave."

Every time I pass that house in my car, whoever is with me I say, "Me and Trevor dug that drive out." "We know, you have told us before," they always replied. My wife said, "Dave, why don't you write it down and put it in book form then you won't need to tell me again that you and Trevor dug out that drive," so I have, that's how come you are reading about it. Trouble is now I've nothing to talk about, ha ha.

This is the drive that Trevor and I dug out
in the Castle Bromwich area of Birmingham.

BIRMINGHAM HIPPODROME

Trevor's brother Tony and I went to the Atlas Cinema; again I have no idea why Trevor wasn't with us as the three of us went out together on occasions. Whenever we went swimming it was the three of us which was quite often. I don't ever remember Tony being with us when Trevor and I went with my sister and Trevor's sister in those days. As time went by we went a lot of times with my sister Janet and Trevor's sister Nannette to Woodcock Street baths near the Birmingham city centre. Any road up, while I was watching the film Tony suddenly said, "Dave, look what I've just found, a wage packet." When he opened it there to his amazement was £2.10/- (two pounds ten shillings) inside of it. Tony gave me the ten shilling note (10/-). Boy, did I feel rich!

We left the cinema and got the bus to Birmingham city centre, and walked around the town for a while. Tony said, "Ay Dave, have you ever been to the Hippodrome?" "Cor no," I replied. "OK, come on then you are in for a treat." So in we go, it was the last performance of the day I think. David Hughes a singer appeared. I was waving to him and Tony looked at me, laughed and said, "Why are you waving to a man?" I felt such a fool! After the singer, Morecambe and Wise came on, I liked them, and when the show had finished I got David Hughes' autograph. That was the first time I had heard of him; it was also the first time I had heard of Morecambe and Wise. When I got married I gave my autograph book to my wife's two little brothers but they ripped it up; thing was, it contained all my school friends' wishes to me and their signatures on the day I left school. I really miss that book, that's one of the reasons I'm putting down all my memories in book form. I can then at least read through it to give my memory a nudge as the years pass and my memory fades, but the main reason I've written it is for my children to know how their dad was brought up and lived and the things I have done throughout my life. It may even be of interest to my grandchildren as they themselves grow old.

THE COAL MERCHANTS

One warm summer's day, around nine o'clock in the morning, I walked to the tip as I usually did looking for old shoes for my mom to burn on the fire to keep us warm. I know it was summer but the summer evenings were sometimes chilly; any road up, the old shoes were saved for these chilly nights. The reason we had no coal was because my mom would pay weekly for the coal but she fell behind with the payments so the coal merchants would not let her have any more coal until the bill was paid in full. It was a treat when finally I watched with much interest the coalman carrying a hundredweight of coal through the kitchen to what my mom called the "coal ole" (a cupboard under the stairs).

One thing has always stuck in my mind and it always used to puzzle me as a young lad of early years, my mom (never my dad) used to whitewash the coal ole walls. I was always sent to the hardware shop, which was called Suches. I used to ask for a ball of white and a washing blue. The ball of white would be broken up in a bucket then filled up with cold water, then the blue would be added. The boiler stick that my mom used for getting clothes out of the boiler after being washed would be used for stirring, what I now know was chalk, until all was dissolved. (This stick was also used a few times on my backside when I played up.) Then with a large brush the walls were whitewashed. It would be brushed onto the three walls, very wet and messy I seem to remember.

As I said, what puzzled me when the coalman went to tip the coal from the bag that was on his back, my mom would say, "I've whitewashed the walls, don't dirty them." The poor coalman would try so hard to keep the coal from hitting the walls, as if his job wasn't hard enough, but he did what he was told and said, "I haven't dirtied your walls, Mrs Prosser." He knew my mom; he only lived a few doors away from our house. A thought just came to me, every time I went to get some coal from the coal ole the white would come off the walls and make a real mess of my clothes, so sometimes when the coal was low it was a real struggle to get the coal without getting the whitewash on my clothes. It was usually down my back and down my right arm.

The house the coalman lived in was number 38 (the same number as our house); his house was in Swancote Road, just round the corner from our house. I remember Mom talking one day to my dad and saying that we should have had that house the coalman lived in; there was a mix-up at the council office because both houses had the same number. There had been a mix-up with the keys and she asked the coalman at the time to swap houses but he wouldn't swap, he said he was happy with his house. My mom always said she preferred the coalman's house, was this because she thought the grass was greener on the other side as the saying goes? I think our house, which was a semi-detached on a corner, was far better than the coalman's house which was a terraced house with an entry for access to the back garden; at least we had our own back gate giving us access without having to go through the front door. Mind you, the coalman's house had a back gate but they had to share the entry.

TWO SHILLINGS 2/- TO SPEND

I found as I was growing up girls were the most cruel creatures on God's green earth. I suppose when one is poorly dressed, even scruffy looking, it would make girls not want to be near you or touch you. (Thinking about it I didn't want to touch me either.) It started in the infants when we had dancing lessons – all the girls would say, "I'm not dancing with you." I usually was left out on my own, you would have thought the teacher would have noticed this and made a girl dance with me; on the odd occasions I did dance with a girl, they would say, "Don't touch me, just pretend to be." One time the teacher did make me put my arms round a girl, she made me feel like I was something she had trod in, as soon as the teacher turned away she jumped backwards and literally shuddered and said, "I hate you touching me, you are scruffy." I think that has hurt me more in life than anything else I can think of (apart from a time when I went to Weston-super-Mare and couldn't buy my mom a present). I remember that tune we danced to, even now I can hear it while I am typing up this book it went, step close, step close, step close, step lar la la… I'm sure you know the rest. I just wanted it to end. I always felt very uncomfortable in that lesson, well all lessons really.

All through school I had that treatment off girls, they just did not like sitting by me, they even asked the teacher to move me away from them. When I was in the juniors we were told our class was going to the seaside and we had to save 3d (three pence) a week till we had paid a pound (£1), this took all year. The place we were going to was Weston-super-Mare, but because my mom could not give me 3d every week, it turned out I was the only one not going to the seaside out of my class. A week before they were going I was told to report to the headmaster Mr Taylor; I was worried to death, I was trying to think what I had done wrong. I even thought of running home I was that scared but I was more scared of getting into trouble for running out of school. I knocked on the headmaster's door, I was praying he wouldn't be in. I was shaking I can tell you and when he shouted, "Come on in" my heart pounded. "Ah, David," he said, "a boy from your class is very poorly and cannot go to Weston next Saturday," (as I got back to my class I looked at all the boys but not one of them was off school) "so his mother told me to give his seat to you and she gave me 2/- (two shillings) for you to spend, so you are going to the seaside with the rest of your class." (I believe now it was Mr Taylor that paid for me to go.) "I have given your teacher the 2/- and she will give it to you on the morning you go on your trip." What kindness those teachers showed and gave to me in the infants and the juniors, (apart from the headmistress in the infants, horrible she was, I can feel the slaps she gave me around my face).

The seniors – that was a whole new ball game, those teachers had a licence to bully children, we thought we were grown-up but we were still children. I can still remember the afternoon we were taken across from the juniors to the seniors to meet the headmaster as we were going into the seniors after the summer holidays. We were sat in rows in the main hall, on the floor, in walked Mr Bradbury the head of the seniors, and for some unknown reason I can see that afternoon like it was yesterday. His first words were, "Good afternoon, boys and girls, you are the big boys and girls of the juniors, after the holidays you will be the little boys and girls of the seniors." That thought sent a shiver down my back; I've no idea why.

Where have the years gone? My mom told me many times enjoy your childhood it's the best years of your life, how right you were, Mother, so that is exactly what I did.

My Mother

I love my mother as children do

She loved me all her whole life through

She was poor not much money had she

But that never stopped her loving me

Seven children she gave life to

She loved us all as mothers do

She shed tears and cried with pain

For she could not feed us all the same

The bigger we were the more we ate

This gave her even more heart ache

Our clothes worn each day the same

For we had no other clothes to change

Shoes were worn till they fell apart

All her heart ache again would start

How to clothe and feed us all was very difficult

For we were poor

On her meager budget she got through

For she loved us all as mothers do

BAGS OF RAGS

It's great to be young and to have had the freedom me and Trevor had and the friends I grew up with. Trevor and me did the most things together. Our other friends got pocket money every week, not much I don't think, Trevor and me didn't at that time.

We had an idea, well it was Trevor's idea really, to go all round our neighbours and ask if they had any old rags. Most people were kind to us, we also asked if they had any woollens they didn't want. Talk about cheek, we knew no boundaries, we had no nerves at all, we would do anything to earn money. We were very surprised at the amount we were given because most people in those days wore their clothes till they were threadbare, just like we did. After we filled two sacks up and sorted the woollens from the rags we were surprised to find better clothes in there than the ones we were wearing, to be honest we swapped our clothes for ones we had been given as rags. We both now had a new set of clothes and we felt good, even though we never got them washed, well that never bothered Trevor and me, we were used to living in a world of make-do-and-mend. Funny thing was mom never noticed my clothes were different, if she did she never mentioned it.

A boy came up to me one day and took the rise out of me, "That was my jumper, we threw it away because it got a stain under the arm," as he pulled back my coat that had also been someone else's, "see, I told you it was mine, you two are scroungers and scruffy." It was at that moment I realised I wished I were a bully just like he was; Trevor and me were nice gentle boys. I took off that jumper and threw it back in the ragbag, found another jumper from the rag bag and wore that (me and Trevor could have won a fancy dress competition without even getting changed!).

We carried our sacks of rags from Glebe Farm all the way to Cuckoo Bridge Aston to the firm we called Raggy Allans. It took us one and a half hours to walk it; we walked along the 14 bus route through to the Fox and Goose through Washwood Heath then to Aston, the man with the scales would weigh the rags first then the woollens and he would say, "Look, boys, that's what they weigh." I would look but hadn't a clue what I was looking at. "Yes," I would say. He wrote the weight down on a ticket, we then walked past a mountain of rags on either side of us to an office that looked like it belonged in the Dickensian times. A glass window was slid open, a hand appeared with a voice at the end of it saying "ticket" we handed a faceless person our ticket, out came a hand again saying "thank you" with our money in it. As we walked out of that rag yard Trevor turned to me and said, "Did you know then, Dave, what weight those scales were showing?" "No I daint, Trev, I thought if he thinks I knew what I was looking at he wouldn't rob us." "Bet he robbed us anyway, Dave, grown-ups like robbing kids don't they." "Well they always seem to take advantage of us, Trev, don't they." "I wish I was brainy, Dave, don't yo, then we could stick up for ourselves."

We did that walk many times to sell our rags, the ones in the sacks I might add, not the ones we were wearing. Sometimes when we took a much heavier sack of rags we seemed to get less money we would say, "Mister, this sack is heavier than the one we bought last week, why are we getting less money?" I remember with a smirk he replied, "The price of rags has gone down, now if you had come this morning you would have got more money for your rags." Yes, robbed again, we would say to each other. We used the money for swimming and bus fares and a cup of Cow & Gate after swimming; we always went Woodcock Street baths. We earned our own money; I think we should feel a little proud of ourselves.

PLAYING GAMES

Games were played every spare minute we children had when we were not running errands, me and my friends played as often as we could, there were six of us and we played every evening in the summer time. I loved the warm summer evenings, the energy we had was endless, we were very fit little fellows, it's only when one gets older you realise just how fit you were; if I had half that energy now I would be happy, mind you I was very fit then so I should be grateful. It's now my turn to be old. These are the games I liked most of all:

Polly on the Mop Stick

Two teams of equal amounts, if there were eight of us we all lined up, we would pick two captains then find an object like a piece of wood or a stone and make one side heads and the other side tails (as none of us had any money, the winning captain would have first pick of the people lined up), we did this for many types of games. To be a mop stick team the leader bends over holding onto the fence with the rest of the team bending forward holding on to the waist of the person in front. The Pollys would run and jump on to the backs of the mop sticks to try and collapse them; the leader of the mop stick had to shout "Polly on the mop stick 1, 2, 3," and win the game. If the mop stick hadn't collapsed when this was shouted they were the winners and the Pollys had to become the mop sticks. Thinking back now this was a very dangerous game to play, it's a wonder one of us never had a broken back.

Kick the Can

This was the same as hide and seek, the only difference was whichever one was on first he or she had to find the ones hiding. We always played this game in the dark. When the person on was looking for the ones hiding, when the ones hiding thought he or she couldn't be seen kicking the can after they had kicked the can they would then run and hide again without being spotted; if the person on saw whoever

Polly on the Mopstick

This is how we played British Bulldog.

kicked the can they would shout that person's name and then they would be on if they got the name wrong then the person seeking would have to keep looking till they got the right name of the person kicking the can.

British Bulldog

If any game was dangerous this one was. Again an object would be used for heads and tails to see who would be the Bulldog. Standing on the side of the pavement would be the rest of us, the Bulldog would stand in the middle of the road, the road was laid in concrete, this was in squares so the lines where the concrete finished were the boundaries. Now the Bulldog would shout the name of the person he wished to tackle, and that person had to try to get past the Bulldog and get to the other side of the road, but you weren't allowed to run until the Bulldog shouted "British Bulldog". When the Bulldog tackled you if he got you down on the ground and shouted "British Bulldog" it would be your turn to be the Bulldog. We got a few scratches and bruises trying to get to the other side of the road. One evening a boy named Derek, who never ever played with us asked if he could play; he lived top end of my road, he was very well dressed, "What about your clothes?" I said. "I don't care," he said, "I want to play." "OK you can play," Billy said. Billy was the Bulldog after two of us had got past Billy, he called out Derek's name, made him wait a while so Derek's adrenalin would be pumping, Billy shouted "British Bulldog," and Derek almost got past him. Billy dived at Derek, got his hands round Derek's legs and he went down, hitting his head on the gutter and split his head wide open, the blood flew everywhere and off he ran home. We were told he had a lot of stitches; he never played with us again. Funny to think about it now, we played that game for many a year and scratches was the worst we ever got.

King of The Hill

This was exactly the same as British Bulldog, the only difference was it was played on a hill covered in grass and we could be as rough as we liked on grass.

Hot Rice

Where these names for these games came from I have no idea. We all stood in a ring with clenched fists, using a tennis ball which was thrown from a clenched fist and caught with a clenched fist. Some people had strong arms and throwing the ball would really hurt. If when thrown to you, you dropped the ball, you were on; as soon as the ball was dropped everyone would run. The person that was on had to throw the ball and try to hit the ones running away; if you were hit it was your turn to be on and you had to throw and try to hit someone with the ball; if you sat on a fence or a gate with your feet off the ground the ball could not be thrown at you. We would lie on the floor with our feet in the air and the thrower would stand poised, waiting for your feet to touch the ground; there was a time limit your feet could be off the ground. I think that's how it went, time is fading the memory somewhat.

Gutter Cricket

With four sticks of wood or lollipop sticks these were placed in the gutter three up right one across the top, same as wickets in cricket. When the ball was thrown if the sticks were knocked down it became the same as hot rice, great fun! It's a shame we had to grow up – ha, ha, my children said I never did.

Famous Stars Initials

This game we played on an old bike we would ride around in circles, say the first letters of the name of the star to the people standing on the pavement who had to guess the name of the star; whoever guessed the name first got on the bike and rode round in circles, they then had to think of a star's name. The most common ones used were D.D. (Donald Duck, or Diana Dors), M.M. (Mandy Miller or Marilyn Monroe), N.W. (Norman Wisdom), W.H. (Will Hay), O.M.R. (Old Mother Riley). We played for hours, boy we had lots of energy, it's not until you look back over your life you realise just how much.

I Wrote a Letter to My Wife

We all stood round in a circle facing inwards, one person stood outside the circle and ran round the outside. The people in the circle would be singing "I wrote a letter to my wife and on the way I dropped it," when the words "drop it" were said, as he or she passed round the outside of the circle, as they passed you, you looked behind you to see if the letter had been dropped by your feet. You weren't allowed to look until the person had passed you. In our case the letter was any item we had at that time, normally it would have been a handkerchief, in our case most times it was a piece of rag. If it had been dropped behind you, you had to pick it up and catch the person that had dropped it before they got back to the space where you had been standing. I loved that game. All the children I grew up with were wonderful. The rhyme we used to sing when we were playing this game was:

I wrote a letter to my wife and on the way I dropped it,

Somebody must have picked it up and put it in their pocket.

Thief, thief, drop it, drop it, thief, thief drop it, drop it.

True Dare Kiss or Promise

I liked this game it was a good laugh. If you said Kiss, then you were told who to kiss, if you refused you had to do a forfeit, the person who was on at that time would tell you to do something really daft: like kiss the floor or take your shoes off and run through a puddle, really daft things that gave everyone a good laugh. Dare of course meant you were dared to do silly things like diving over a high hedge or surprising one of the girls and telling them you loved them. True you were asked something that they knew about you just to see if you would tell the truth, usually they would ask who you were in love with. Promise you were told to make a promise; if you didn't keep it they would think of something horrible to do to you, like get you in trouble with your mom or a neighbour. We really did have some great times playing this game. Oh to be young again.

Football

When we were playing football one day outside Johnny's house I kicked the ball and it came off the side of my foot and smashed a window in Johnny's house. I had to pay 6d (sixpence every week) till I paid for it and I ran errands to save the money up. I was very careful after that.

Playing my favourite game – Football

THINK OF A NUMBER BELOW TEN (DON'T TELL ME WHAT IT IS)

DOUBLE IT, ADD FOUR, HALVE IT, TAKE AWAY THE FIRST NUMBER YOU THOUGHT OF, YOU ARE LEFT WITH NUMBER 2

Do you remember this puzzle? Everyone did these types of puzzles.

DID YOU?

POEM BY THE AUTHOR

Down our street when I was young
we played games all day long.
Hide and seek, tip cat, polly on the mop stick,
lots of games like that.
Football was my favourite game
I played this time and again.
I was poor but that didn't matter
when playing games I forgot the latter.
The only vehicles I used to see were horse-drawn carts,
no others I see.
So playing games in the street was not hard,
nothing ever stopped me not even those carts.
Those open spaces I used to know
were down my street where I still go.

ONE IN THE EYE

One very cold winter's day me and my friends were playing in the horse road, the snow had started to melt but was still sort of frozen – when rolled in the hands it was snow mixed with ice, water would be running through the fingers when rolled as a snowball. We all agreed we wouldn't throw this mixture of snow and ice at each other, only at cans or objects that we stood up in the hedge.

I had been sliding down the hill, and after an hour my feet were soaking so I said, "Lads, I'm going in to dry and warm my feet, I can't feel my toes." "You wimp!" they shouted. "It's all right for you, your feet ain't wet and frozen like mine." So Billy decided to start throwing those icy snowballs at me. "Come on, Billy," we all shouted, "we've agreed we wouldn't throw the ice, it's dangerous." He was laughing, "Come on, you girls, I thought you were tough boys." "Now look, Billy," I was saying, and as I turned round to look at him an ice ball hit me in both eyes. The pain was unbearable, I thought I had lost my sight, all my mates shouted, "Billy you idiot, you've blinded Dave."

Billy was really frightened. I was without my eyesight for about nine days – doctors, hospital – all because Billy couldn't resist throwing snowballs. I was off school for two weeks, could have been three, and when I returned to school I was taken to the headmaster's office, well frog-marched would be the right way to describe it. I was poked and pushed, "why weren't you at school?" I was so scared my mind went blank I just could not think straight. "WELL, WELL ANSWER ME." Because I hesitated he was shouting, "trying to think up a story are we" when I suddenly remembered the icy snowball Billy had thrown at me, "a snowball was thrown at me, Sir, and hit me in the eyes. I went blind for a a few days." "Well that's a good one, did you rehearse that story before you came into my office?" "No, Sir," I replied. "You are a liar." Nothing I said would be believed. "You think I'm stupid don't you, snowballs in your eyes, you were playing truant weren't you?" said the headmaster. "No, Sir," I answered. "Don't you no Sir me, my lad," the head went on. "Go on get out of my office, you are a waste of time," he shouted at me as he pushed me towards the door. It really upset me, I never did have days off school for no reason, I would have but I was more scared of my mom than any teacher. I had really suffered with my eyes. That's one of the reasons I hated going to school. I got in trouble for no good reason from those teachers.

MINE OR YOUR MOM'S

It's hard to imagine these days that a family of six, (four children, two adults) could be living in a house with no food in the house anywhere, not even a crust of bread to eat or any coal or wood to burn to heat the house. That's how we lived for many a year. There were times of course when we would seem to have enough to eat but not often enough, I don't think.

In the 1950s almost everyone got paid on a Friday, but Trevor's dad Fred got paid on a Thursday – he worked in the wholesale fruit market in the centre of Birmingham. Well, my mom used to make me look out of the living room window to tell her when Fred was coming down the road. "He's coming, Mom," I would shout. "Give him five minutes to get into the house then go and ask him if he will lend me 2/6d (that's half a crown)." He always lent my mom money on a Thursday, and after I took the money back to my mom she would send me up the road to the shops for a loaf, potatoes and sometimes Spam (always Spam that was the cheapest meat at that time) from Braggs the cake shop. Some of my relatives worked for Mr Bragg himself during the war, one of them being my Auntie Maggie, being so short of sugar she helped herself and took sugar home in her handbag loose, I was told that by my eldest brother. Mr Bragg went to my granddad's and asked him to have a word with his daughter; he asked him to tell Maggie to stop stealing the sugar. Granddad was none too pleased as he was unaware of what had been going on. My Auntie Maggie was killed during a bombing raid. I would like to have known my Auntie Maggie. My eldest brother passed on all this information to me. The family lived at number 53 Ash Road in Saltley; when they were bombed out they moved to number 20, my Aunty Maggie was killed on the 10th of April 1941 only 34 years of age. The money borrowed off Fred, I did this week after week (poor man), it went to 5/- (five shillings), and then finally it went to 10/- (ten shillings). My mom always made me ask for the money.

It wasn't always doom and gloom, sometimes life seemed wonderful. I think maybe the winters were the hardest times, coal had to be bought, extra gas used and we seemed to eat more in the winter. One Thursday I went to borrow 10/- for my mom and Trevor's dad said, "I'm not sure who owns this 10/-, me or your mother," but as a true friend he never said no. I never knew why Trevor's poverty was as bad as mine because his dad worked very hard, up at four every morning to the market. Maybe his pay was poor. My mom always paid him back his 10/- Friday evenings without fail. My dad got paid on a Friday so some Fridays I was told to go and meet Dad outside his works at 1.00 p.m. dinner time, he would come out and give me a 10/- note and 2d for my bus fare back home and he moaned every time, his cuss words were "Gad blimey". When I got home my mom would send me to the shops up the road to buy some food items. Thinking about it, if I got (10/-) ten shillings the night before from Fred why did I sometimes meet my dad outside his works on a Friday dinner time to get some money off him? Maybe Fred never got paid if his boss didn't go into work that Thursday. I do remember one Thursday I asked if mom could borrow 10/- he told me. "tell your mom I haven't been paid today." It must have been on occasions like that when I had to meet my dad at his works.

THURSDAY PICTURES

Trevor's mom and my mom went to the pictures most Thursday evenings, the cinema was called the Atlas. It was the only couple of hours our moms had on their own, their bit of quality time without kids around them. One Thursday afternoon I had a bright idea, I will scrub the kitchen floor, (they were red quarry tiles) when she sees what I have done she will be delighted and take me to the pictures with her. So I got scrubbing with a big green bar of Fairy soap and a worn-out scrubbing brush. I filled a bucket half full of water and threw the water on to the floor, flooding the kitchen. After I had scrubbed half the floor, right, I thought now I will tell Mom what I am doing and pictures here I come. I went round the house shouting, "Mom, Mom." My sister said, "Mom's gone to the pictures with Trevor's mom." What a shock that was, I was horrified – she had slipped out of the front door and never closed it so I wouldn't know she had gone. I left the kitchen floor swimming in water and ran over the road to see Trevor.

"Trev, Trev," I shouted, "they've gone to the pictures without us knowing, let's run down Audley Road we might get there before they do." We ran non-stop till we reached the picture house and watched two buses go by. "We've missed them, Trev," I said, "that kitchen floor, I left it swimming in water, my sister will go mad at me." "Well don't go back in, Dave, till later," so I stayed out for a couple of hours then I thought I had better go and clean up that mess I left in the kitchen or I will get a good hiding from my mom. When I walked in to my delight Doreen had cleaned up my mess, she was hopping mad, she wasn't very happy with me and I got a good telling off, "I had to clean all that water up after you left," she was screaming at me. I never made that mistake again; I left scrubbing floors to my mom. Mom used to scrub that floor on her hands and knees, and then put newspaper down, we had to jump from one page to another; we dare not step on the floor. This paper was left down until the floor was dry and by this time the paper was all dirty and ripped with us kids running in with our dirty pumps on. If she had enough pennies in the gas meter she would light the oven to dry the floor quicker but that didn't happen too often, as she said with 3d (three pence) she could feed her children so the floor could dry on its own.

COACH TRIP

Trevor came to me one day with what I thought was a brilliant idea. He had seen an advert in our local post office, Bowens a coach company were doing coach trips to a place called Leamington, this town had the whole place lit up, on the advert it said Leamington lights. "Shall we go there, Dave?" Trevor said. "Where is it, Trev?" I asked. "I don't know, Dave, it sounds good though doesn't it." "Yeah," I replied, so off to Bowens to see how much it cost, 3/6 for children I think it was (three shillings and six pence). "Right, Trev, we will have to run lots of errands to get the 7/- (seven shillings) we need." "And we will need some spending money, Dave, we had better start right away," said Trevor. "Yeah OK, Trev," I replied.

We worked really hard; we went back to knocking on doors for old rags and pop bottles, we fetched coal for our moms and neighbours, quarter hundredweight at a time, we never charged our moms, we made 2/- (two shillings) fetching coal. We got up early to fit in all the errands we had agreed to do the day before, and we worked hard for two weeks but we did it. We only had a 1/- (one shilling) each to spend including our 3d (three pence) bus fare back home.

The coach company wasn't far from our houses, only about a mile and a half maybe a little more, so we walked there, it only took twenty minutes or so to walk, that way we saved 3d bus fare. As we walked into the office a very pretty young lady greeted us, I was staring at her she was so pretty, (I'm the same now, anything that looks beautiful to me I stare at no mater what it is) suddenly Trevor gave me a nudge and said, "She's talking to you." "Sorry, lady," I said, "but you are the prettiest lady I have ever seen." With a big smile she thanked me, "Now, boys, can I help you?" "Can we book a coach please to see the lights, at um… where is it, Trev?" "I can't remember, Dave." "It must be Leamington lights you mean, boys." We both said, "Yeah that's it, lady." With a big smile she said, "You can't book a coach, young man, but you can book a seat." "Yeah, that's what I meant, lady, a seat," so we paid her the money. "We want to sit together." she laughed "Yes boys I don't think anyone will want to sit by you." I didn't understand what she meant by saying what she did. "Thank you lady." I replied, "We love sitting together." We were very excited.

We got the coach at 7.00 p.m., I remember that but where it picked us up from for the life of me I can't remember, neither can Trevor. You know not once did anyone ask "where are your parents?" or "who are you with?" I have a good memory but those lights are not very clear in my mind, I do remember looking for a fish and chip shop, after what seemed a long time we found one, after all that walking we were hungry and thirsty. It was a warmish night I remember, that was a blessing as our footwear wasn't the best. Our socks we could not pull up because they were tucked under our feet to keep our feet from getting sore from the pavement. Both Trevor and me only had jumpers on, at that time we did not possess coats. My mom bought all my clothes from the jumble sales and so did Trevor's mom. We weren't the cleanest two little boys in the city but no one passed any comments. The chips we bought were 4d (four pence) a packet. I was very surprised to see the chips, as they were crinkle chips, I had never seen crinkled chips before. We had bought a bottle of pop and shared it. The chips seemed to be hollow inside, I did not like them at all but I ate them because by this time we were both starving.

So we got back on the coach and headed for home and to our surprise we were dropped off in the middle of Birmingham city centre. We had saved 3d for our bus fare home. Town was absolutely deserted, I had never seen it like it, it was like a ghost town. We had no idea it would be so late, we weren't told and as young boys the time never entered our heads, we were just excited to be on our first coach trip. The one thing we had never thought about, because we didn't know we were going to be dropped off in the middle of town, is that after midnight the bus fares doubled. We tried to tell the bus conductor a sad story but he would not have any of it. He told us to clear off. "Please, Mister," I said, "it's a long way home and I only have 3d." He replied, "I told you NO, clear off." He rang the bell and off the bus went with not one passenger on it and we were left there standing. I hope his son gets better treatment from people than he gave to us.

So we had about an eight or nine mile walk. It was creepy, not a soul to be seen anywhere, no traffic at all, We got to the fire station in Gosta Green. It was getting quite chilly at that time of night as we were still in short trousers and no coats, we started to feel cold. As we passed the gun shop called Webley and Scott there were two police officers in the doorway – boy did they have a shock, because we were wearing pumps they didn't hear us coming. A policeman and a policewoman, such a scuffle, the lady police officer was attempting to pull down her skirt and the male officer adjusting his dress. He came from the doorway sounding very cross then he said, "What on earth are you young boys doing out at this time of night?" We explained we had not got enough bus fare to get home and that the conductor would not let us on the bus because after midnight the fares doubled, "so we are having to walk home." "Does your mom know that you are out at this time of night?" "Yes," I replied. I really thought I was going to get a ride in a police car and be taken home (well I was hoping). With a wave of his hand he said, "Hurry up and get home, it's getting late." After saying that he went straight back into the doorway, I had not got a clue what they were doing.

My mom had no idea what time I got in, she knew where I had been. She was never worried about me at all as she knew I could be trusted. She did ask if we enjoyed ourselves. I said, "Yes," but didn't tell her we had walked home from town at midnight. I asked Trevor if his mom knew what time he got in. He said she never missed him

I wonder would you let your children do all the things we did?

HELPING BROTHER

My eldest brother was in the R.E.M.E. as a regular soldier with only six months to demob from the army. He was sent to Korea to fight; he was there eighteen months, when he returned home he was very ill suffering with T.B. and Pleurisy. After coming out of hospital he had to find ways of making extra money because this wonderful country of ours doesn't look after their soldiers once they have done their bit for their country, so he started looking for scrap metal. In those days people used to dump their old cars on any piece of waste ground. Donald used to take the radiators off those old cars because they were made of copper and brass; after fighting for his country that's what he had to do to pay his rent.

At that time the National Assistant Board visited Donald, looked round his newly acquired council house, all he and his wife possessed was a bed, a table and two chairs, and a bed for his little son. The visitor told him he was comfortable and he offered 1/- (one shilling) a week extra on top of his sick pay, which was not even enough to pay his rent. Donald told him what to do with his shilling and ordered him out of his house, as he was too ill to throw him out physically. Thank you, England, that's where I come in. Donald asked me if I collected metal from the tip he would pay me; of course I agreed without any hesitation at all.

Back to the tip looking for metal, scrap metals this time instead of bike parts and the like. I did well out of that tip, Donald gave me a magnet and said, "any metal that doesn't stick to it put in the sack, bring the sack to me and I will give you half a crown" (2/6d) two shillings and six pence; twelve and a half pence in today's money. So I called for Trevor, told him, and he couldn't wait to get started. The tip was the same tip we always went to at the back of the Atlas Cinema; we spent some hours on that tip, talk about Mud Larks, we were the Tip Rats. After taking the filled sack to Donald, "I will weigh it in tomorrow if I feel a little better, so I will pay you then the next day," he said. We were very disappointed to say the least as we had planned to go swimming with the money we thought he was going to pay us.

Each day we went to the tip, there was new rubbish arriving all the time. We did well on the second sack of tat, that day was very good, we filled our sack quite quick so off to brother's with the bag of tat. "Here you are, lads, three shillings for that bag of tat yesterday and half a crown for this sack today. Get me another sack full like this one you brought today and I will give you two shillings and sixpence 2/6d for the next bag."

Trevor and me went swimming the next day, the money was burning a hole in our pockets, we only earned money so we could go swimming and go to the flicks (pictures, cinema). The baths were in Woodcock Street near Birmingham city centre. The very next day we were back on the tip, we had filled one and a half sacks with tat (can you imagine the state our clothes were in, we did give our moms a hard time) when a very rough looking man came over to us and shouted at us and swore. He took our sacks off us and said, "These are mine now, now clear off this is my patch." We had never seen him before, he was rough and dirtier looking than we were. "It's our tat, Mister, we worked hard for it." He tried to kick me but he missed, he terrified us both. "Trev, I'm not letting him steal our tat, I'm going to get it back when he goes down the side of the tip. I'm going to run over there and get our sacks back." As I was stronger than Trevor, I said, "I will grab our two sacks, you grab his sack." When the man went down the side of the tip, we ran over the tip to where our sacks were and grabbed all three sacks; he heard us and tried to get back up from the side of the tip quickly but he kept sliding down. We were running as fast as we could, he was shouting after us, language I had never heard before. Needless to say we never went back to that tip, for a couple of weeks. Doesn't mean we stopped earning money, no way, we came up with all sorts of ideas. We got five shillings for those three bags of tat off my brother.

Donald changed his tactics from tatting to selling door-to-door; he decided to go to a warehouse and buy various items that he thought would sell. Things like American comics, toys, combs, little boy dolls about two inches tall with a rubber dunce's hat on which when filled with water you squeezed the hat the doll weed. Donald asked Trevor and me if we would go door-to-door to sell these items for him, and we were excited at the thought of earning extra money. It was three comics for a shilling (1/-). I remember one of the comics was called Little Sheriff; three combs for a shilling – pink green and blue, I sold dozens of those. I was becoming a proper little salesman and so was Trevor. When I was asked where did you get those from, I said the same thing every time, "I'm selling them for my brother, he's just come back from Korea, he's been fighting in the army and he is very ill with T.B. and PLEURISY." This was the truth, he was very sick for a very long time and I liked helping him and every shilling I made he gave me 2d (two pence) for helping him; people were very kind when it was for a forces man. When he got fed up selling these items from the warehouse he started to buy old cars to cut up and tat in. I must say that selling door-to-door taught me how to deal with the public. I became a salesman not long after I left school.

THE BOYS' BRIGADE

Joining the Boys' Brigade was an organisation I loved being part of. We always met up one evening a week; they had a football team, and at that time in my life all I lived for was football (and earning money of course) so I joined their team. I was asked what position I played, when I said in goal they were overjoyed. When I played in our first game I realised why they were happy to have someone who had a little football skill. They were absolutely useless; we lost every match we played. I saved dozens of what would have seemed cert goals but we always lost, never less than (if my memory serves me right) sixteen nil, normally it was twenty or more. As they thought I was good they made me captain. I'm sure if there was a cup for the worst team in England's history we would have been famous, well we were in the papers as the team that likes losing twenty nil on a regular basis.

I remember one game very well, we were twenty-two to nil down, I got so fed up I came out of my goal, dribbled the ball, got past them all, I got to the goalie, he hadn't touched the ball all through the match, he must have been stiff from having nothing to do. I scored so we lost twenty-two to one. I bet that goalie hated me, the only time he had to make a save he missed, saving only by an inch but he missed, it was more luck than skill on my part. All part of growing up, I really enjoyed being part of the team even though we lost every game.

This Boys' Brigade met in the Lea Village area of Birmingham in a school known as Ridpool Road School. We had to march to church on the last Sunday of the month. I only had part of the uniform, I was the only one that wore pumps as I didn't have any shoes and that was accepted, no one ever said anything I'm glad to say; I would have loved to have worn the same as everyone else but that wasn't to be. However, I was very happy there. Happy times.

SCOUTS

The Scouts was also happy times for me. At the top of my road, across the main road this was Audley Road, to the right was St. Andrews Church and it was in this church where the Boy Scouts held their meetings once a week. I tried to join several times but was always told there was a waiting list of two years.

One evening as I was passing the church I noticed the Scouts were outside recognising different birds and naming them, well I thought I would try my luck, so I went up to the leader and asked him if I could join. "You've tried before haven't you?" he said. "Many times," I replied. "OK," he said to my delight, "fill in this form and I will enrol you. Would you like to stay and join in the activities this evening?" I was asked. "Yes please," I replied. "Right, sit in with that group sitting on the floor, they are being taught how to tie knots," I was told by the Scout leader. I was over the moon with excitement, "Thank you very much," I replied, I was so happy. He shook my hand and said, "Welcome to the Scout movement."

I told Trevor but he didn't want to join so I tried very hard to get some money together to buy part of the uniform. I knew my mom could not afford to spend on items that were not essential, Mom's budget was small to say the least. I ran errands with Trevor, and when I had earned three shillings I went to the Scouts shop in Birmingham city centre; I bought a woggle, the next week I bought the neckerchief, I never did get any other parts of the uniform, a cap or jumper, at that time I was the only one that hadn't got a full uniform. I was asked by one of the boys a few times, "How did you get to join, my friend has been waiting nearly two years to get in to our group?" In the end I told him a little white lie, I said, "I had been waiting over two years to join." I really loved being part of that group. We sometimes went to some woods called Yorkswood, sadly it is now a housing estate. We used to have paper chases, wild animal recognition and tree recognition; these woods were on the border of Shard End area. I loved all that, I was useless at it but I enjoyed it. They held jamborees there, how often I'm not sure. We marched to church the last Sunday in the month as did all those kinds of groups in those days. We were expected to visit church every Sunday and were asked why not if we didn't attend. I loved to march with the band playing, I felt proud to be part of it all, to see the Sea Cadets, the Girl Guides, the Brownies, the Cubs and the Scouts all marching together was for me a wonderful sight.

I was part of that Scout movement for fifteen months or so. It would be nice to see the children marching these days and belonging to a group of one sort or another, of course in those days most of us didn't have a TV and computers were non-existent. After I left the Scout movement I joined the Sea Cadets. Trevor never did join any of these groups with me.

THE SEA CADETS

In the same year I left the Scouts I joined the Sea Cadets. There on the parade ground, all in groups of about thirty, there must have been about one hundred and fifty Cadets, I only stuck it for four weeks, they didn't seem to do much. I never got any part of the uniform plus it just didn't appeal to me. I thought we would be sailing on the reservoir, that seemed rare, so I packed up that group.

I joined the Baptist Church confessed all my sins and became a Born Again Christian. I loved all the people that were part of the Baptist movement, even the girls talked to me; that was a shock, girls normally looked down their noses at me but not those girls they were wonderful. That's the only time in my life that girls treated me nice, mind you it never stopped me hating girls. Till I got older that is, well I… erm… quite like the opposite sex now, ha ha!

I must add when confessing my sins the Preacher was surprised I hadn't sinned at all apart from scrumping apples. Still believing in Our Lord, but do not attend church anymore.

TWO BLACK POODLES

While sitting on my front garden wall one fine sunny morning, wondering what I should do that day to earn some money so I could go swimming, while I was deep in thought, thinking I ran errands yesterday for Mrs R, so she won't want any, when I suddenly nearly left my skin. Trevor had crept round the back of me and shouted down my ear boy that broke my train of thought. He said, "Come on, Dave, let's go to town." "I've no money, Trevor," I replied. "It's OK, I will pay your fare, my dad just gave me some money."

So on the bus we go through Stechford, then the Pelham, Alum Rock, Saltley, Nechells, Gosta Green, then town, Birmingham. It was about thirty-five minutes to get to the terminus, it was known as the old square. Trevor's dad worked in the fruit market, he worked there from a boy; we walked to St. Martins church, where there were barrow boys, Trevor bought us some damsons from him 3d (three pence) a bag but when we opened the bag to eat the damsons they were all rotten. We went back and complained, all the words he used I can't print! They went straight into the bin; 3d to us meant a lot, I could never treat children the way Trevor and me were treated.

We went to the rag market, it was packed. As we were walking round we passed a stall where they sold crockery called Lees when I spotted on the next stall a box containing two black poodles, they were in the begging position with glass eyes, they looked beautiful, they were made of chalk. They were 1/11d (one and eleven pence) for the two. I asked the man if he would save them for me till next week, he said, "Yes," but I didn't think he would for one minute. "Can you make them any cheaper?" I asked him, I will leave his reply to your imagination. Trevor asked me, "What do you want them for, Dave?" I answered him with, "Well, Trev, we were selling all those things for my brother if you remember, I thought we could go all round the houses and raffle them." Trevor's reply was, "Cor, Dave, what a brilliant idea."

So all the next week we ran errands and saved all the money we had earned. I remember not so many of our ladies wanted errands doing that week so we found it hard to get the amount of money together that we needed, we didn't even go swimming. Come Saturday morning we went early to town; we thought the poodles were so good someone might buy them (well we were only children). Trevor said, "Don't ask him for them cheaper, Dave, he might not sell them to us." "Trev, after what he said to me last Saturday I don't think I will." I bought the dogs, "Right, Trev, we need a raffle ticket book now," I told him. We found one on a stall for 3d (three pence), and when we got back home (about one o'clock) we started in Trevor's road. We went down one side, back up the other, selling the tickets for 6d (sixpence) each. Trevor was holding the poodles up so they could see them. We were known to most people because we had sold them comics, dolls, combs, toys. I did all the talking, and when I was asked "who gave you permission to sell door-to-door" I told a little white lie – I said they were being raffled for my brother who was very ill because he had been fighting in the army in Korea and now was in hospital. That was the truth about my brother (well apart from the hospital) but the raffle was for me and Trevor of course. They were happy to buy tickets because they thought they were helping an injured soldier who had been fighting for his country. Well, we were threatened with the police, told to bugger off, called scruffy little urchins, and one or two things I can't repeat. The one that stayed in my mind, a woman threw her arms in the air, went hysterical and shouted, "Get away, get away those are made of chalk, it's unlucky, get away from my house," and slammed the door in our faces. We sold two pounds five shillings' worth of tickets then stopped selling. People did ask how would they know who had won, I told them we would go round and tell everyone. They all put their name and addresses on the stub of the tickets; not one family had a telephone in those days where I lived, we did intend to go round but never did. We got a little lazy when the money was in our pockets.

We sat in my mom's kitchen and I said, "Who shall we give them to, Trev, shall we give them to Mrs G, she is as poor as we are?" Trevor answered, "Yeah, Dave," so off we went. She only lived at the top of my road, we knocked on the door, her son Dicky opened the door and in a very stern voice he said, "Yes?" I told him, "You have won the raffle." His face lit up, "Mother, Mother," he shouted, "We've won the raffle. Thanks, boys." As I walked away I felt good inside, we had made someone happy. People were stopping us for a week afterwards asking who had won and why did you not come and tell us, "we did but no one was in," that's what we told them all who asked us. We could have kept those dogs and no one would have known, well we would have done. We were poor but very honest young boys, keeping them never entered our heads.

Earning our pocket money.
"Buy a raffle ticket, Lady?"

LEAGUE CHAMPIONS

In the juniors school I played football, and at that time it was my life; I played centre forward. 1955 was a magic year for me when we won the League Championship. My teacher Mr Lycehart coached me, I liked this teacher, he was very good to me. I enjoyed my time in the junior school, I was sorry to leave and go into the seniors.

While in the juniors I also used to do high jumping. I was high jump champion all through my school days, juniors and seniors, because I had a good spring in my legs. The teacher, Mr Green, who was my teacher in the seniors, I didn't like him very much, he was my sports teacher. When I was doing my school work he used to hit me across the back of the head, pick me up out of my chair by my hair and sometimes by my ear, that was the worst, by my ear. One afternoon I was trying to write a hundred lines while he was talking to us ('I must not talk in class'). I was at the back of the classroom and I thought he couldn't see me (well as I said before, I wasn't very bright). He called to me to go to him with the piece of paper and as I handed it to him he punched me in the stomach. That took all the wind out of me, I collapsed on to the floor and I was screaming for breath, he kept shouting at me to get up and go back to my seat. I was hopeless at my schoolwork and I was punished for it. I left school not being able to spell or read very well, but in sports I was OK, I could hold my own.

Mr Green thought he would try me in goal, I soon found out that was the position for me, I loved playing in goal. Our team in the seniors wasn't bad but trophies never came our way; we never won a trophy but it was great to play football. Mr Green praised my sporting abilities but slapped me about when it came to my schoolwork. As I said before, to be stood up in the school hall when in assembly and praised by the Headmaster for my achievements in sport for the school, if I'm honest it gave me a big head at times. Well, to be told how useless you are nearly every day it makes you feel good when told you are the best the school has when it comes to sport. When told things like this at times it can give a child a big head.

Author back row, second in from the right.
1955 was a special year for me
Mr Lyceheart, the teacher

The one thing I was good at was high jumping.
I was school champion all through my school days.

Author is second from right in back row, wearing my football shirt, having had my photo taken five minutes before with the football team and told to leave the shirt on for this photo.

BULLYING

I was born with a perforated eardrum; I suffered with itching ears all the time. I had to attend the school clinic once a week and I was accused by the Headmaster of crying wolf. I was a small boy needing treatment and refused because grown-ups know best, but not this time. When my ear started running I was taken to the Headmaster's office to show him. "Please, Sir, may I go to the clinic for treatment." I was waiting for a slap across the head or the cane and to my surprise he looked and said, "So you weren't crying wolf after all? OK, you can go to the clinic." He wrote out a note then handed it to me saying, "and you come straight back to school, my lad."

So off I went, feeling very good because I was getting off school. As I walked into the clinic, brother those nurses were rougher than the teachers. I was ordered about just as though I had been naughty. I never was as a child, I was always afraid of being punished, well I was punished by my teachers all the time because I was stupid (as I was always being told). I just couldn't remember anything I was taught the day before so I was pushed, poked, shook and slapped daily. The nurses had taken lessons from the teachers I reckon. Before I went in to see the doctor they shouted to me to sit in the chair; not knowing which chair, I was frog-marched and pushed (well, thrown) into the chair. When the nurse started poking my ear, rough she couldn't have been any rougher if she had used a shovel. The pain was making me cry. "Shut up, you baby." When it felt like she had cut my ear off, the blood ran down my face. She thrust a tissue into my hand, "Here hold that to your ear, now go and see the doctor," she growled.

As I walked in a very surprised look came over the doctor's face. "And what have you been up to, young man?" "That nurse did it," I said. "Oh," that's all he said. After he stopped the bleeding, drops were put in my ear and a wad of cotton wool pushed hard into my ear, even that was giving me pain. Nothing else was ever done, it was for me to suffer, and children just did not count in those days. It was at that clinic that I found I had been born with a perforated eardrum, and to this day still it troubles me. As I walked out of the doctor's room I passed a nurse ordering some other poor boy about. I never did get a sorry or an apology, nothing, just a "Go on hurry back to school."

Back in school I went straight to my classroom and was greeted with, "Where have you been?" with a slap on the back of my head and ordered to sit down. With my ear giving me pain, now the back of my head had pain, and with cotton wool in my ear my hearing was only functioning at about 40%. Trying to do my writing I didn't hear the teacher shouting at me (well screaming would be a better way of saying it) to pay attention, next thing was the blackboard rubber came flying across the classroom. Just at that moment I looked up because by this time the teacher was screaming at me, I looked up just to see what all the noise was about, the blackboard rubber glanced just off my right eyebrow, right next to my eye, a quarter of an inch nearer it would have damaged my eye. So now I had a bad ear, a headache, and a lump on my right eyebrow. I was ordered to pay attention and to bring back the blackboard rubber to the teacher. On doing this I was slapped again on the back of my head, ordered to go and sit down and pay attention in the future. I wonder if I met that teacher now I'm 65 (at the time of writing), slapped him on the back of his head, grabbed him by his lapels and shook him violently – there wouldn't be any difference would there? He slapped me about when I was defenceless, at his age now I would get locked up, which he should have been for knocking about a defenceless child. I really would like to meet him to tell him what a rotten teacher he was. I was so afraid of him, I just couldn't concentrate on my school work which meant I learnt nothing; in turn this led to being slapped across the back of my head for not knowing how to do any lessons. I left school not knowing the difference between a signature and initials. Which in turn lost me the first job I went for.

DOWN AND OUT

It was one Saturday morning I saw my mate John walking down the path to my house, I was coming back from the shops having done some shopping for my mom. With a very loud voice I shouted to him, "I've been looking for you." He said, "Guess what – na, don't think I should tell you." "Go on, go on, John, what is it?" I said. "I have joined the Morris Commercial boxing club," he replied. "Yo ain't?" I questioned. "I have, honest," he replied, "I went with a boy from my school that was already a member of the boxing club." John is a Catholic, I'm Church of England so we both attended different schools. I hadn't seen John the evening before that's why I disbelieved him, he always told me everything he did so I was very surprised when he told me. "Honest, Dave, I asked the trainer if he would let you join," said John. "Bet he said no," I replied. "Well," said John, with a sad looking face and looking down at the floor, in a soft voice he said, "I was told to bring you along Tuesday evening."

Well I was so excited I jumped up and down and shouted, "Yeah, yeah!" John said, "I thought you would be pleased." "Oh thanks, John, for asking for me, I'll start training right away," I answered with great excitement, so we started to run what we called round the square, that was up my road, along Audley Road, past the row of ten shops then down Swancote Road till we reached my road and repeated it many times over. We were shadow boxing all the time we were running – boy did I have some grand ideas! About the third time around I was going to be world champion; I'm fit and strong, I was telling myself.

After we had stopped running I was by my garden gate, still shadow boxing, I must have looked a right idiot. Trevor came over to me, "What are you doing?" he asked. "I'm training, Trev," I answered. "What for, Dave?" questioned Trevor. "I'm going to be a boxer," the whole time I was talking to him I was shadow boxing, "John has joined the boxing club down Alum Rock and he has got me in, I will ask for you Trev," I told him. "Na, I don't want to box, our Tony went there some time ago," Trevor said. So I went with Trevor to talk with his brother Tony, he said he liked it but just stopped going, "Try it, Dave, you will like it," he said.

So come Tuesday evening, I think that was the night, might have been Thursday evening, any road up I started at the boxing club. I was training with a medicine ball, after that we all did roadwork, that's running round the streets. I felt good; my ideas of becoming a champion grew even stronger. I did all this for a few weeks even did some sparing in the ring with older boys. I held my own, mind you they weren't hitting to hurt, only getting me used to the feel of the ring. After a few months I had my first bout; a visiting team came, it was only a friendly so we could gain more experience – my turn came, three rounds, three minutes each round, out I came for the first round I was quicker than my opponent, I jabbed with my left, I only threw my right once, I remember he never laid a glove on me. Yeah, I thought, this is easy; I am going to win this fight, end of round one. The trainer was well pleased with me, he said, "Just keep doing what you are doing, it's in the bag." Round two, out I went really cocky if I'm honest, my opponent came out, hit me with a left hook and knocked me out with one punch, I'm ashamed to say. I was out for nearly three hours, not knocked out completely but not able to stand on my own two feet. That day was the end of my boxing career. Some champion eh?

101… 102… 103… I don’t think he wants to play any more.

OUR PARK

Glebe Farm park is in Birmingham, I spent many hours in that park. The River Cole runs through that park, and on the edge of the park there is an alleyway that runs the whole of the length of it; the front cover of my book PUMPS WITH HOLES IN is loosely based on that alleyway or pathway that runs alongside the River Cole. At one end of that pathway there is a road called Colehall Lane, at the other end is Bushberry Road, half way up the pathway is a very big tree. I have no idea what type of tree it is, it probably was an oak tree, we used to have rope tied to that tree and swing across the river, most of the boys that lived around Glebe Farm and Shard End used to play by the river. One dry day we were playing on the swing, my friend Trevor and me, when a bully boy came up to us and told us to get off the swing as he was now going to use it. He wasn't a school boy, I reckon he was in his twenties. Me and Trevor weren't bullies at our young age, well at any age, I suppose you could call us cowards, well to be very honest at that time in our lives we were cowards, yes for sure we were. The bully got hold of the rope, ran in a circle, went sailing through the air shouting, "Yeah, yeah, this is great I haven't done this in a long time." He was very well dressed, he had on what looked like a new suit, well in those days everyone seemed well dressed to Trevor and me. He went across the river two times, on the third time as he was coming back across the river the rope snapped; the river was quite deep at that time, and he disappeared under the water, which looked very dirty. We stood on the bank laughing and shouting abuse at him, only because we felt safe where we were and knew he wouldn't be in the mood to chase us, well I did say we were cowards. We shouted as we were running away, "We are glad you went into the water," Trevor said, "Ay, Dave, I hope we don't bump into him again." "Cor and I do, Trev, I'm staying away for a while, Trev," I said. "Yeah me too, Dave," Trevor agreed.

We never did see him again, that bullyboy. A long time after that we did go to that tree where we all played swinging across the river, this time we were with our other friends Billy, Johnny and Eddy, but Dougie wasn't with us that day. As we approached the big tree with the swing, there were lots of lads from our school playing on it, and just as one boy went to swing across the river the rope snapped. Fortunately he didn't go into the river; as he clung to the side of the riverbank to save himself from falling in he shouted, "Has anybody got a decent rope?" Billy suddenly shouted, "Yes I've got a rope, it's a great big thick one, it's that thick it will carry ten men, but I want it back when you've finished with it." They all shouted, "Go on, Bill, get it now." We never lived very far from the park.

Billy asked me if I'd go home with him to get the rope, he needed help to carry it; he told me it was his dad's rope. It was a black tar rope and very thick. "Wow!" all the boys gasped when they saw the rope that would hold ten men. Up the tree Billy went, the taller boys were throwing the rope to Billy, it took a while before he caught the rope, and by this time there were about sixteen lads all wanting to be first. Alan Blackwell's brother (whose name I can't recall) won first go by picking the shortest straw. He took a good run and swung across the river, when the rope snapped on his way back and into the river he fell, he scrambled out dripping wet. All he said as he walked off home was, "Ten men," and he disappeared across the park. He didn't have very far to walk as his house and garden backed onto the park.

I was pushed into the river at that same spot a couple of times, we never learn, well I didn't that's for sure. I went to that same spot to collect grass with a boy named Reg. I never ever played with him, as he was about three years older than me, so I was surprised one day when he asked me to help him pick grass for his rabbits. Near the river where the swing used to be there were spiked railings right up to the river's edge, the reason that those railings were there was because there was an outlet pipe there where the sewage went into the river, yes untreated sewage. I might tell you we used to swim in that river. Inside those railings there was long lush green grass; we climbed over the railings, we then picked quite a big bagful of grass. Reg suddenly threw the bag over the fence and shouted, “Dave, come on quick, get over the railings.” I became very frightened seeing the look on his face, and his hurried actions. I got over those railings much quicker than when I went in I can tell you. Reg ran much faster than me, as he was about three years older. When we reached the road puffing, panting and our lungs screaming for air, I finally got my words out and asked him what the matter was. What he told me worried me for a long time afterwards; he said there was a man creeping up on us on his belly. It took me a long time to go back to that place again and to this very day I have no idea if he was telling the truth or playing me up.

When we played on those rope swings they of course got worn out very quickly and eventually would break. We never knew where all those ropes came from but I will for sure remember that thick black tar rope of Billy’s the most. To this day it brings a smile to my face whenever I think about it.

CYCLING

Going to Kenilworth Castle on our bikes, we did this many times but one occasion stands out in my mind far more than any other. Once again it was a warm sunny morning, I'm sitting on my front garden gate when Johnny came down the road from the shops, he had run an errand for someone. He shouted very loudly, "Hi Pross," he was always very loud, one of those boys you could hear and pick out in a crowd and know exactly where he was, but he was a great mate of mine. He asked, "What you doing today?" "Nunk," I answered. I always used that common word "nunk", meaning of course "nothing". Thinking about it, all or nearly all my speech was in common Brummie slang, I had quite forgotten about it. Words such as nunk, nowt, spondulucks, akers, 2/6 two and a kick, 2/6d half a dolla, 5/- a dolla, 10/- ten shillings half a bar, 10/- ten shillings half a sheet, 1£ a sheet, £1 a wonna, 6d a tanner, 1/- a bob, ain't, wunt, gob bin yow sharnt – gosh so many of us boys had our own language and many more slang words like bin means been, gooing means going, I think I would need another lifetime to write them all down. Well another book anyway. Thinking about it, I am writing a book with the way we talked. It's called JUST A BRUMMIE. IF YOU READ IT AND CAN UNDERSTAND IT YOU WILL HAVE BECOME A BRUMMIE, WELL ALLMOST!

"I thought we could go to Kenilworth Castle," Johnny said. "I'm game," so off we went to call on our other mates Trevor, Billy and Eddie (Dougie stopped going around with us, I think he had to make sure the pigs were all right); all agreed, we set off half an hour later. None of us had any money or food or water to take with us we never did, we lived like this all the time. We looked after each other; we did whatever we could to survive. From Glebe Farm, to Kenilworth Castle seemed a very long way, I drive it now in the car and I always say the same thing, how on earth as young lads on bikes with no food or water did we do a long run like this and we did it many times.

I remember going across Stonebridge one late morning, on the way to Kenilworth, it was just a country lane then, now a major road. All riding together, if we saw blackberries we would pick some, damsons, apples, swedes, carrots from the farmer's field, we only took what we could eat, no more, never destroyed anything and of course it depended on the time of year what we ate. It usually took us about an hour and a half to two hours to reach the Castle depending on how many stops we made.

The Castle was wrapped up in scaffolding the one time we went there. We walked with our bikes round the outside of the Castle and always picked a spot where we could climb over the wall; we did this every time, well we couldn't pay to go in as none of us had a penny to our name. First place we headed for was the water tap, thinking back now I can't remember where it was situated, what I do remember was whoever was drinking the ones waiting for a drink would be saying, "Come on, hurry up we all want a drink." When we were all watered (I would like to say and fed but alas water was all we had), we would climb and investigate the ruins. Billy who was very daring, very skinny and wiry, decided to climb to the top of the scaffolding, he got right to the top. We were saying to each other "where is Billy?" None of us had a clue, Billy suddenly appeared from the back of the castle, he looked in a very bad state, it turned out he had slipped off the top scaffold bar and hit every bar on the way down. Those bars being rough were like rubbing sandpaper on one's skin, every bar he hit took skin off some part of his body because of the concrete that was on them. He hit the ground with a thud. It took five minutes for him to come round. He told us he could hear us asking about him and where he was as he approached us. He was moaning and groaning with the pain, he was in a state. Fortunately he hadn't any broken bones, so we all climbed back over the wall where we had left our bikes and walked back to the road. By now Billy had recovered some of his senses but was badly bruised, battered, skinless and very sore. He was just about to get on his bike when two cyclists stopped, the lady asked, "What happened to you?" We all told her, she was very sympathetic took out her first aid kit and cleaned him up, she was very thoughtful, what kindness she showed. We returned to Kenilworth Castle a few times after that, but none of us ever climbed on the scaffolding, especially not Billy.

My friends and I at Kenilworth Castle

PAPER BOY

When I was 13 years old I got a paper round, 13/- (thirteen shillings) a week. I went to Hunts Radio Shop where they also sold bikes and records and my mom signed for me to buy a bike on H.P. (hire purchase) which I paid for out of my paper round money. My mom had to sign for it of course, as I was too young to take out hire purchase agreements. It was a Raleigh bicycle.

I adored a girl named Carol who was in my school, I suppose it was puppy love at the age of 14 years. This girl lived in the road opposite the paper shop that I delivered papers for. On the way home from school we took a short cut through an alleyway, this alleyway ran through a field known as the home guard field. It was in this field I had my first kiss and cuddle, it was very passionate or so it seemed at that time, but at that time she wasn't my girlfriend.

The next day at school I plucked up the courage to ask her to be my girl and go out with me, she smiled and said, "Yes." All my nerves jumped I was so excited, nothing in my young life had made me feel like I did the moment she said yes. Every day I walked her to her road, she was adopted and her adoptive father forbade her to have anything to do with lads.

After walking her to her road one day as I was on my way to the paper shop, I stood talking to Carol at the top of her road, when a gaze of total fear came into her eyes, "It's my dad," she said trembling. He was a little white-haired man, slightly bent forward in a raging temper. I was slightly nervous, I just waited there to say hello to him, just to prove to him everything was OK because I knew how over-protective he was as Carol had previously told me. Just as I was about to say hello, without a word his right hand came round and gave me one almighty slap around the face, which hurt my ear. Instinctively I swung my right fist at him, fortunately I missed, as he walked away slapping Carol round the head, in a hurt rage I shouted, "If you touch me again I will kill you." I laugh when I think about it now, as a skinny 14-year-old I couldn't have slapped him, never mind killed him.

Next day at school I was summoned to the headmaster's office and told in no uncertain terms I must never talk to Carol again. It turned out her dad had been up to the school that morning and told the headmaster that under no circumstances must Carol talk to any boys. In a mixed school that was impossible especially as she was a rebel and her dad didn't know, it made the whole episode a joke, so I had been given a smack round the ear for nothing. The laughable thing about the situation is on the day she said she would be my girl on that very evening she also arranged to go out with someone else. I learned of this about a week later from a lad who was in the same class as me and also lived in my road, at this time I was really hurt seeing as it was my first real puppy love. It turned out she loved the attention she got from the boys and the boys were only to willing to pay her attention, strange thing she never ever told me she was going out with another boy. Funny thing was I never got angry about it and I talked to her every day even though I wasn't supposed to.

MORNING DEW

My friend Duggie had two cousins, girl cousins who he said were jolly and liked a good laugh; they lived in a village called Polesworth, in Staffordshire. I just couldn't wait to meet them, for some reason and I can't remember why we never did meet those girls, We all went there on our bikes to look round the place, it was very nice, and on the way back we stopped at Tamworth where there was an open-air swimming pool in the park, we all liked that, swimming in the open air. Some time later my other friend John suggested that we go to Polesworth camping for a few nights. John brought a loaf of bread and a block of butter. I got a jar of jam, packet of tea and a bag of sugar just for the two of us. John brought the primus stove saucepan and a frying pan. There was one little draw back, we hadn't got a tent! What I had was a towel, Johnny had a mac nothing else, to say we were not prepared is an understatement. It was a very warm summer that year so we assumed it would be all right and the nights would be warm as well, so on our bikes and off we went. With the blessings from our mothers, never dads, they never missed us no matter how long we were away.

It was great fun cycling to Polesworth. Before we went through Tamworth we stopped for a piece of bread and jam as we sat looking at the castle, so off again and cycled to our destination and found a nice spot where some of the local lads swam known as the basin. As we got into the water a few of the local boys turned up for a swim we got very paly with them, we were asked many times, "Do you come from Brum?" (in those days they didn't see many Brummies). Polsworth is now awash with Brummies, the days I'm writing about it was a beautiful little village. One boy said, "Are you camping here?" "Yes," we replied. "Watch out for the farmer, he doesn't like people on his land, we always swim here in the basin, he catches us sometimes and gives us a clip round the ear," he then said, "Where is your tent? You will be cold by the river." "We will be OK, I'll light a fire," I replied.

“Don’t forget about the farmer, if he catches you with a fire you really will be for it – is that all the food you have?” he asked. “We’ve eaten half the loaf, so we still have half the loaf left and butter, we will be OK,” we said to him.” “You can’t survive on just that,” he commented, and then John reminded me we had jam as well. “That’s still not enough, would you like me to bring you some eggs back later?” He shouted as he walked away, “I’ll be back in about an hour.” “We have no money,” I shouted to him. “You don’t need any, I know where they are free range, I know where the chickens lay them,” he shouted.

About an hour and a half later he returned with four eggs, how wonderful to live in the countryside and get free food like that, one would never go hungry. We thanked him and said how kind he was, “I’ll see you tomorrow,” he said. “If you want any more eggs I’ll get them for you.” He shouted “bye” as he crossed the field. We gathered up as much firewood as we could to light the fire and got a real good fire going. Out came the frying pan, and with butter melted in the pan I cooked two of the eggs. I felt really good, and with two pieces of butter we made egg sandwiches. We felt really good, “this is the life ain’t it, John. We will have to come camping again,” I said. “Yeah,” replied John, “this is great ain’t it, Dave?” “You know what, John, I’m going to live outdoors when I grow up.” “Good idea, Dave, we could travel the world together.” What a dream, well the thought was good or so we thought at that moment in time. I carefully placed the other two eggs in with the rest of the bread so they wouldn’t get broken. “We’ll have the other two eggs for breakfast,” John said, so we saved those two eggs even though we were still hungry.

We decided to have a swim in the river after we had eaten, and we had a great time swimming with the local boys; they all were skinny dipping as they put it, I had never heard that saying before. Me and John wore trunks. After swimming and drying ourselves on the towel it was so wet we lay it by the fire in the hope it would dry enough to put over us when night time came, but it never dried, it was far too wet. We tried to put the mac over both of us and the wet towel on top of the mac. Fire going, all seemed good at that moment in time, we fell asleep, then the worst of the nightmares started, I woke up shivering, wet and very cold, the fire had gone out; we didn't know mist from the river would soak everything. Trying to light the fire was almost impossible, everything was so wet. We finally got the fire going again and as we got warm we fell asleep. Early in the morning a white mist was everywhere, the sun started to shine, all seemed good to us, it was beautiful to see the white mist rising from the river and the sun shining through the trees. John said, "I'm going in for a swim." I lit the camping stove and made two cups of tea with water from the river. As the water boiled the scum that came to the top of the water looked liked green slime with other colours mixed in with it; I never gave it a thought if there were poisons in it. I just scraped it out and made the tea. I drank my tea but Jonny left his to cool down. "I will cook those two eggs after I've had a swim," I said to Johnny. We were enjoying ourselves so much we didn't notice what was going on around us. Johnny suddenly said, "I'm hungry, I'll cook those two eggs, Dave," and put the kettle on. "OK, John," I said, "give me a shout when you've cooked them." As he climbed up the bank he gave out an almighty shout, "OH NO! Dave, come and look at this, the cows have eaten all our food and trodden all over our cooking equipment." I laughed, "Oh yeah," I said, "pull the other one." "No, Dave, it's true – come and have a look." To my surprise he was right, they had eaten all our food, they had trodden on the frying pan, ruined the primus stove, so we had no food or equipment. Johnny was so angry he threw everything into the river, so the great outdoor explorers were beaten after only one night. We cycled to Tamworth Park to the open-air pool, another very warm day. We lay on the grass and dozed off for a short while as the sun shone on us and made us feel very comfortable. We woke up feeling very relaxed and just lay there for about another thirty minutes or so, reminiscing about our great outdoor adventure and agreed we would do it every year but with all the right equipment, we never did of course. We then cycled home. My bed was such a wonderful and welcome sight. I slept like a log, next morning back to normal. So if ever you go camping by a river, don't be stupid like we were. Take a tent, better still stay in a hotel, but we never had any money so we made the best of what we had, but what I do have I have all these wonderful memories.

Enjoying the great outdoors without a tent

MY DAD

My dad worked at the Metropolitan Carriage And Wagon Works. That factory was situated in the area of Saltley in Birmingham. He worked there all through the war years. Every night when he walked in from work he smelled of suds (suds was a liquid soap that was used to cool down the drills when going through thick metal that Dad was drilling). All his clothes became very shiny. His flat cap was that shiny I could have skated on it. He wore that same cap until the day he retired. It hung in the hallway with his waistcoat and overcoat. Those items of clothing were retired the same day as Dad retired. They hung there until the day he no longer needed them.

When he was a workingman he drank very heavily. Before he went to bed he would count all his cigarettes that were left in the packet. He would count all his change and put it in separate piles of copper and silver. He even counted the nubs in his waistcoat pocket that he hung in the hallway. No matter how drunk he was he did this every time he took himself to bed.

I started to smoke at the age of thirteen; (I stopped smoking when I was 38) I took a nub out of his waistcoat pocket. When he got up he told me he knew I'd had a nub out of his pocket.

One Sunday afternoon he really was the worse for drink (more than he normally was) and he took himself to bed. I waited until he dropped off into a deep sleep then I woke him and asked him if I could have next week's pocket money (in our house we never got pocket money all the time). He said, "Take a shilling off the shelf," which was over the gas fire in the bedroom.

So the next Saturday afternoon I thought I would try the same trick again. He again was the worse for drink, but not as bad as the week before. I waited until I thought he'd got into a deep sleep. I shook him and was shouting down his ear, "Dad, Dad, can I have my next week's pocket money this week and I won't have my pocket money for next week?" To my surprise he jumped out of bed and said, "You think I'm stupid, you came that last week," and he threw me out of the bedroom and said, "don't you ever wake me again when I'm asleep!" No matter how drunk he was, when it came to his money and cigarettes he always knew exactly how much money he had and how many cigarettes.

PAWN SHOP

Once a week my mom took whatever she could to the pawnshop, sometimes she would get 2/6d sometimes 1/6d, sometimes only 6d. Once or twice when I took some items of clothing they wouldn't give me anything on them. This pawnshop was in Wyndhurst Road, Stechford, by the Atlas picture house (that cinema has since been demolished and the pawn shop has gone). I hated going to that pawnshop, it smelt funny, it was dark and dismal. My mom had to pawn her wedding ring one day, they gave her 10/6 on it; she told me that years later that broke her heart, she never ever got it back. Many years later she bought herself a new wedding ring, my wife Irene got it for her out of her cataloguc. If it wasn't for that pawn shop I would have gone hungry more than once, so I suppose I mustn't knock it too much, they even later on in my life laid on a special bus to take people to that pawn shop. It isn't there any more but I'm sure people still need them. It was always called nunkies in our house, never the pawn shop; why nunkies I have no idea, I believe pawn shops were known as uncles maybe nunkies was said instead of uncle.

As I was approaching the age of 14 years, I bought a lovely blue suit on the "glad and sorry" – I paid 1/6 every week, I earned this money by running errands. My mom of course had to make believe she was buying it for me. It was the first suit I had ever owned, and I only wore it on special occasions. As I didn't have a wardrobe in my bedroom, I had a picture rail running all around the room about eighteen inches from the ceiling and I used to hang my suit with a coat hanger on the picture rail. I loved that suit. One afternoon I went to put it on (for what occasion I can't remember), only to find it wasn't there. Mother had been not very well off that month, she had pawned my suit two weeks before and, can you believe it, I hadn't missed it hanging on the wall and all that was in my bedroom was a bed. It's sad to say I never got that suit back one of the times it was pawned, money was always very short in our house.

MOM'S CAKE STAND

Off our kitchen was a walk-in pantry, in there was a concrete slab over the gas meter which was called a cold slab, the purpose of this was to keep the meat and various foods cold as we didn't possess a fridge in those days, but there again not many people did, well not where we lived anyway. On the right-hand wall was the electric meter, on the left-hand wall were three wooden shelves one above the other. On the top shelf was a glass with Mom's false teeth in; there they stayed until she no longer needed them, even though she hadn't worn them for over forty years she would not throw them away. On the other end of the top shelf was a cream cake stand that was purchased from Woolworths for 6d (six pence) long before the day I was born. It was used rarely in our house but it was used every Christmas Day and put on the table in the living room at teatime. Mom told me that when she bought that cake stand that all the items that Woolworths sold at that time cost 6d (six pence). This cake stand was Mom's pride and joy, I do remember her lending that cake stand out a couple of times to her friend Lizzie for birthday parties. It did get chipped on the underside, which upset Mom quite a bit, none of us children were ever allowed to wash or carry that cake stand. (I am very proud to say I now own that very cake stand.) I walked into the living one afternoon after school had ended for the day. To my surprise the table was laid with fruit, sandwiches, jelly and Mom's wonderful cake stand in the middle of the table with a cake on it. I was excited I can tell you, I hadn't a clue what was going on, not a soul to be seen, then in walked my sister Doreen with her fella or as Doreen put it "her chap", my mom and other people as well. It turned out Doreen had been up to Birmingham Register Office in the city centre and got herself married. I was glad she was married; it meant I was going to eat all those nice things on the table, it was a rare treat. I knew nothing about the wedding until that very afternoon. It was a lovely surprise. Lenny that's Doreen's husband told me Trevor's mom Lizzie had laid out that table for them, what a wonderful lady.

MY MOM'S DEAR FRIEND RITA HILL

A very close friend of my mother's was Rita Hill, and I'm pleased to say still to this day a friend of mine, her sister Ann, was a friend of my sister Janet. Rita lived in Swancote Road, we lived in Plowden Road, and our house was just across the road from Rita's house. Rita was still at school at that time, when she was supposed to be there she would sneak back and go to our house, walk in the back kitchen and shout, "I've come to wash up for you, Pross." She always called Mom "Pross". Mom loved Rita and always referred to her as "our Rita" like she was her daughter.

Rita, like myself, loves the past, and from our childhood days she has one memory that I think she could do without, our chicken Lonesome, yes it chased her up the line post, Rita was shouting, "Pross, Pross, the chicken's biting me." We were reminiscing about this on the 6th of August 2009; we were having a laugh about those days. She told me all these things which is how I come to know about them. As well as her sister, Ann, she also has a brother named Barry and we all played together from time to time. Happy days, eh Rita. I'm glad you are still my friend.

SHOPS REMEMBERED

My first recollection I have of our fish and chip shop was paying 3d (three pence), for a bag of chips then 4d, then they went to 6d and stayed that price for a very long time. I can still see in my mind's eye those fryers, they were in the style that they had in the 1930s, Art Deco style. The mirrors on the back of the fryers which were situated against the back wall, opposite the counter where they served the customers, they had a chrome edge all around them, they looked like an opened fan; the outer mirrors were plain green, the middle mirror was green with a picture of an old sailing ship with sails on it. I remember it so well because I admired it so much, I used to stare at it and study the art form while I waited to be served, I just loved the shape of the whole fryer. The owner always asked if you had brought your own newspaper to wrap your fish and chips in. I've seen those chips put straight on to the newspaper, I've even taken piles of newspaper to him myself, it never hurt us, in fact it was a pleasure to eat fish and chips straight out of the newspaper. As I walked down the road, I've eaten my share of newspaper ink. I wonder how many germs we ate from those old newspapers, they never knew how clean the people were that gave them those newspapers.

Wrensons was the shop that is most vivid in my mind only because of the bacon slicer. That slicer used to fascinate me, the big wheel they turned to make the bed of the slicer move backwards and forwards. I stood and watched that machine doing its work while my mom was being served on so many occasions, that machine to me seemed to be dancing, I just loved that movement. On a white marble slab was a cheese cutter that really was fascinating to watch, a piece of wire was placed on top of a big block of cheese, and the manager (whose name was Oakley) would say to whoever he was serving the cheese, "Is that too big or is it all right?" If it was OK he pushed down on the wire with no effort at all, the wire did a perfect cut; it was then wrapped

Note all the men in collar and ties and white aprons. I bought vegetables many times from this shop. Brown's Fruit and Veg Shop on Glebe Farm Road, Glebe Farm, Stechford, Birmingham 33.

Looking at the egg board rationing was on, maybe it's still war time (Second World War 1939-1945). It's possibly Christmas time in greaseproof paper, very neatly wrapped. I wonder now how clean was that wire, it would have only been wiped of with a damp rag I bet. Presentation in those days showed pride and respect for their customers; slabs of butter were wrapped up in the same way as the cheese. When Mom bought 2oz of tea it was put in a blue cone-shaped bag; the sugar was also weighed and put in a blue bag and they folded the bags very expertly so the contents would not fall out. I remember going to that shop for 2oz of sugar, it was put in a blue cone-shaped bag; yes very small amounts could be purchased in those days for they knew how hard-up most people were in that area. The front window of the shop was big with two handles at each side at the bottom of it so the window could be slid upwards. Behind the window was a large marble slab; bacon was laid on it in rows. In the summer when it was warm that window was opened – talk about health and safety, can you imagine all the dust and the flies landing on that bacon and who knows what else. Trouble was in those times there weren't any fridges, it's hard to imagine now. My mom told me one sunny day when she was passing that shop with my brother Kenny the window was open displaying bacon in neat rows. Kenny slapped every pile of bacon as he walked past, which led to Mom having an argument with Mr Oakley because he shouted at Mom to keep her kids in order. Mom was laughing when she was telling me this story; she did tell it to me many times that's how I remember it. She also told me she had a go at Mr Okley and told him "I raise children up not kids." "Well tell your children to leave my bacon alone," he shouted after her from his doorway as she carried on walking away.

In our two rows of shops were Stockton the newsagent, Holidays the butchers, and next to the butchers was a children's clothes shop, The Walkin, which was originally a fancy goods shop, Braggs cake bread and cooked meats shop, Wrensons groceries, Tranters hairdressers, Wilkes a grocery shop, Goldings Chemist, the Post Office, Browns the greengrocers then the Co-op Butchers and Co-op Groceries. On the opposite side of the road was Lathems haberdashery, the butchers, Hunts radio and bicycle shop, Saxons men's clothes shop, Paynes shoe repairers, fish and chip shop, Turners seed merchants, Carmichaels faggot and peas shop, Suches hardware shop and The Glebe public house (or the boozer as we all called it). Sadly now demolished.

Across the main road there were several more shops whose names do not come to mind apart from Ted Haynes, Stanley James, Vernons Gowns, Taberers newsagents, a shoe shop, a butchers and an outdoor (a boy from my school, his parents ran that outdoor).

DISRESPECTFUL CHILDREN

As I grew up with my three sisters there was a word I learned to use that was used very frequently used in our house, I must admit if I could change it I surely would and that word was "rotten".

As the girls came home from school at dinner time, when they walked in the house from the backyard into the kitchen if what they saw for dinner was not to their liking they would say something like, "What's this rotten stuff? I don't want it, I don't rotten like it, we had this rotten stuff last week, I told you I didn't like this rotten stuff last rotten time." Mother would say, "Stop using that word rotten." Their reply would be, "Well you know I don't rotten like it." As I got older I automatically started to use it, it became normal speech in our house going something like this, "What's for dinner, Mom, not rotten stew I hope?" We rarely had puddings in the week; I would ask after dinner, "Is there any pudding?" When I heard the word "yes" I got excited, "Cor, what is it, Mom?" "Ball sago pudding," she would reply. "I hate that rotten stuff!" (and I still do!). "Well bloody well go without then," she would reply, and I did. My sisters loved it, I had to watch them eat it. I would be saying, "It's not rotten fair, they got rotten pudding." Mom would say, "Well serves you right, they have had your share." All I would be saying was, "It's not rotten fair, it's not rotten fair."

Mom I think got a little used to us talking like we did. The one time that really sticks in my mind I was in my teens, I think I was fourteen at the time, and Mom must have had a bad day that day. I had been playing football in the horse road as Mom called it, she called me in for my tea, it was 4.30 p.m. I remember, as I walked in I took one look at the dinner and said, "Stew! I'm rotten fed up of rotten stew." Mom shouted at me saying, "And I'm rotten fed up of you saying rotten, now it's got stop, if you say rotten one more time I will put this rotten plate of dinner over your bloody head." For some reason (I can't remember now why) I turned to look at the fire or to throw something in it (we still had a coal fire in those days), while I was doing whatever it was, I said, in a very cheeky manner, "Oh yeah," and as I turned back towards the table, Mom had picked up the plate of stew, tipped it over my head, keeping her hand firmly pressing the plate to my head. It ran down the back off my head and down my neck over my face and all down the front of my shirt. She looked me square in the eyes and with a fierce look on her face she said, "Well?" I was so shocked at what she had done I remember saying, "It's better on the plate, Mom." "Let that be the last time you talk to me like that, you hear?" "Yes, Mom, I'm sorry," I replied. I had to have a wash down as there was not enough pennies to put in the gas meter to heat the water for a bath. I also had to wash my shirt and dry it as it was the only shirt I possessed, and in cold water. Well done, Mother, I needed that discipline, who knows how I would have turned out if I had not been kept in check by you, thank you.

That was the last time if my memory serves me right I ever said that to my mom. My younger brother John told me he tried saying rotten to Mom because he had heard me say it, he said she gave him such a smack round his ear and told him she would not allow it anymore so he never did again. I never did that's for sure. We were very cheeky to you, Mother, but every one of your children loved you very much.

MISDEMEANOURS

Fare dodging we did on the West Midlands buses and trains, we worked out a plan. When we got on the bus we stayed downstairs, when the conductor came to collect the fare we would get up from our seat and as the conductor was taking a fare we would walk past him. (We never ever tried it when a lady conductor was on duty, they never seem to forget who's paid and who hasn't, men on the other hand didn't seem to be as dedicated.) Then as though we were getting off the bus they would take no notice who was walking past them, so upstairs we would run, they had to concentrate on giving the correct change as you did not have to have the correct fare to pay as you do nowadays. The one thing I always did was to put bus tickets from past journeys into my top pocket and then the dodge we used was to take the appropriate coloured ticket from my pocket, hold it in my hand with my face pressed up the window, Trevor doing the same, with the ticket in full view so as the conductor walked up the aisle shouting, "Any more fares please," it looked like we were looking out of the window innocently with our hand on the sill, as he walked past it looked like we had paid. We did this many times and we were never caught, as we were looking out of the window I would be saying things like, "That's the shop we went to," I could never think of anything else to say. Well it worked every time, we always had enough money to pay the fare just in case we were caught out by the inspector, we could never fool them.

Trevor and I used to chew lots of chewing gum. There was a machine on our Post Office wall that gave out a free packet every fourth turn of the knob. We tried many times to fiddle that machine by putting chewing gum on the back of the penny to make it stick so the penny would not go into the machine, but it never worked. Every packet had four pieces of sugar-coated gum inside it, if we only had one penny between us we would buy a packet and have two pieces each. We always shared and looked after each other, we never ever fell out that I can remember. That same Post Office had a cigarette machine outside of the shop and a milk machine; the milk machine held what was then new cardboard cartons with a pint of milk inside them. When we put our sixpence in we found if we kicked the front of the machine really hard we got two cartons of milk instead of one; after a few months that machine was so damaged it was taken away. In those days if a shop stayed open after five o'clock you were very lucky, that milk machine would have been a godsend to people working late. The cigarette machine suffered the same fate as the milk machine, both were taken away.

In those days the phone boxes had A and B buttons; if you couldn't get through to whoever you were calling, you pressed button B to get your money refunded. We found that by pushing a piece of rag up the return coin tray in the telephone box, when people would press button B to get their money back no coins would fall; punching, kicking and shaking and also putting their finger up the return tray compartment to see if the coins had got stuck, they would eventually give up. After they had gone we would go in with a piece of wire with a hook on the end, push it up the return slot, hook the rag pull it down and out would come the coins; myself I only did that once. I preferred to make my money the honest way by running errands for the neighbours. The rewards for doing errands were more satisfying and of course honesty is the best policy. I think at times I was easily led but I knew it was wrong so I'm making up no excuses for my bad behaviour. That was the only bad thing I can remember doing but I'm sure there must be other times I went off the rails as the saying goes.

This is the juniors playground. The wooden buildings in the background are classrooms. The window facing was the Headmaster's office, Mr Taylor. The brick building on the right is an air raid shelter, and next to that was a wooden building that was the boys and girls toilets.

AUDLEY ROAD SECONDARY SCHOOL

Showing the infants playground where I played on my first day at school. The wooden building was divided into two classrooms; on the right was the infants at that time in 1948, on the left was the juniors. I was taught in both classrooms. That building has since been demolished.

AUDLEY ROAD SECONDARY MODERN SCHOOL

The low brick buildings shown were air raid shelters built in the Second World War. Entrances were bricked up and they too have now been demolished. Me and my friends used to climb in them after school. They were at the far end of the juniors school playground. The grass is where we practised our football sometimes, but most times it was on the concrete playground. I played centre forward for the Juniors Football Team. Happy days!

BECOMING AN ADULT

In 1958 there were three terms for leaving school, EASTER, SUMMER AND CHRISTMAS. All my friends that I grew up with left in the Easter and summer of 1958 and were working. I didn't leave till the Christmas 1958.

I found my last six-week school holidays very lonely, as this was the first time in my young life that I had no friends to be with. Day after day I struggled to think of things to do on my own. I still had three months of schooling left to do, this not only meant my friends would be at work but that they were no longer interested in playing out in the evenings in the street. Youths at work wouldn't dream of playing in the street like they did a week or so before they started work. They were now young working adults. Me, still a child at school, meant I hadn't grown up at that age like they were, one week you are a child, the next week you become a young working adult.

Being on my own for those last three months after being with my friends from the age of five, doing so many things together for so many years, I found that very traumatic. I still wanted to play, but day after day I was alone. I went to the park just like I did when with my friends, sat by the river, went cycling to the places we all went to. I wanted to play football just like I had done for so many years but I had no friends to play games with anymore; it wasn't the same now; I was lonely and lost, with only the memories of the things we all did together. Even running errands lost its magic for me. Eddy, Billy, Dougie, Johnny, Trevor; they now just wished to act like grown-ups.

It's a shame to lose one's childhood overnight, when one leaves school that's exactly what happens.

So now it's Christmas 1958. I've left school, I'm now classed as a working man. Now I've become a lodger, expected to start and pay my way in life. That was the hardest step in my life I think that I ever had to take, the transition from boy to working man. (Man indeed.)

CITY OF BIRMINGHAM EDUCATION COMMITTEE

SCHOLAR'S LEAVING CERTIFICATE

THIS IS TO CERTIFY

that

David Prosser. Class 4.3

has attended

Audley Sec. Mod. Mixed School

and is legally exempt from attendance at School, having ceased to be of compulsory school age as defined by Sections 35 and 38 of the Education Act, 1944

General Remarks

A boy of reasonable intelligence, but unfortunately does not always use it fully. Can produce good work given proper supervision. Represented the school at soccer, hockey and athletics. Attendance and punctuality very good.

4th yr 3rd Division

S.A. Bradbury
Head Teacher

N. Russell
Chief Education Officer

Date 19th Dec 1958.

P50416

I was very happy the day I was given this certificate, little did I know I was about to start learning all over again. The headmaster wrote nice words, yet when I left school I could hardly read or write.

City of Birmingham Education Committee

SCHOLAR'S LEAVING CERTIFICATE

1. NAME David Prosser
2. ADDRESS 38 Plowden Road. B'ham 33

BOYS AND GIRLS 15 to 18

EMPLOYMENT:

Boys and Girls who want employment or advice about employment are invited to come to the YOUTH EMPLOYMENT DEPARTMENT, EDUCATION OFFICE, MARGARET STREET, BIRMINGHAM, 3. The Department is open Monday to Thursday 8.45 a.m.–5.15 p.m., Friday 8.45 a.m.–7.0 p.m., Saturday (for National Insurance purposes) 9.0 a.m.–12 noon

In addition to the Education Office, the following District Offices are open at the times stated:

District Office	Hours & Days.
Selly Oak Institute, 646, Bristol Road, Selly Oak.	Same as Margaret St. (see above)
Sparkhill Methodist Church, Warwick Road, Sparkhill.	Tuesday, Thursday & Saturday, 9–12 noon.
Garretts Green Technical College, Garretts Green Lane, Sheldon.	Tuesday & Thursday, 2–4.30 p.m.
215, Birchfield Road, Perry Barr.	Tuesday, Thursday & Saturday, 9–12 noon.
Brooklyn Farm Technical College, Aldridge Road, Great Barr.	Monday & Wednesday, 2–4.30 p.m.

NATIONAL INSURANCE:

Boys or Girls must obtain a National Insurance Card immediately they secure paid work after they have left their day school.

This should be obtained by personal application to the Youth Employment Department, or at one of the District Offices. The Birth Certificate bearing full names must be produced at the time of application.

RECREATIONAL ACTIVITIES:

Boys and Girls who would like advice or information about clubs and other forms of recreation are advised to enquire in the Youth Employment Department.

REMEMBER TWO THINGS:

1. **If you want employment, or if you desire to change your work come to the YOUTH EMPLOYMENT DEPARTMENT.**
2. **If you are in work you must have a National Insurance Card.**

A29960 8/57

This is the envelope my leaving certificate was in.

MY LATER YEARS

EMPLOYMENT CARDS ALSO KNOWN AS INSURANCE CARDS

When one became 15 in 1958, you were given the address of the insurance office near Birmingham City centre, known as – Youth Employment Department, Education Office, Margaret Street, Birmingham 3.

When inside the – what I thought was a very dismal – office I was given a set of insurance cards, those cards were given to the firm or office or shop or the building firm you were going to work for. Every week an office worker would stick a stamp on the insurance cards of every person that worked at that firm. When one handed in one's notice to leave, on the evening of leaving that employer you were given your insurance cards with one stamp on them for every week you worked for that employer. It was important to count the amount of stamps on the cards as it was not uncommon for the office person to miss one of the stamps off, especially the last week's stamp. If at the end of the year you were missing any stamps you were made to pay for the stamps that were missing. The (National Assistance Board) now known as Social Security were the organisation that made you pay for missing stamps. If, however, you didn't pay the missing amount, it affected your old age pension.

When any employer upset me I would say my favourite saying - Lick-em-on-I'm-off. Meaning, of course, the stamps.

INTRODUCTION

STARTING IN THE WORLD OF WORKING ADULTS

When it came to my time in December 1958 to leave school, jobs were plentiful as England was still being rebuilt. I could walk out of one job, walk across the road and get another, which I did many times through the years of my working life. Then came the depression in the 1980s when one had to think twice about leaving one's employment. We all thought it wouldn't happen again, and here we are in the 21st century – another depression.

I met my wife, Irene Yvonne Parker, of 132 Timberley Lane, Shard End, on Sunday 13th March 1960 at the Castle Cinema, which was situated in the Castle Bromwich area of Birmingham – I was 16 years of age. We married on 23rd December 1961 at All Saints Church, Shard End. We had three children, Anthony, Wendy and Matthew.

A POEM FOR MY WIFE

13TH of March is when we met

At the Castle Cinema, a meeting I will never regret.

First real love I ever knew

It was real love for me that I knew

I stroked your hair, I kissed your lips

I walked you home, my heart was mixed

Mixed up it was, I knew not why

You were my first love

My mind did fly

I was scared excited too

My heart it went from me to you

It never died just faded a bit

You were strong and kept hold of it

You knew when all the years had passed

Our love was strong and would always last.

The photograph opposite (David with Irene) was taken outside my then girlfriend's house, 132 Timberley Lane, Shardend Birmingham 34. We were both at the tender age of sixteen and very much in love. We had only known each other for fourteen days; it was the Sunday 27th of March 1960 when the photograph was taken. She was so pretty I could not believe I would ever be so blessed. That time in my life was certainly heaven sent.

MY FIRST JOB

I left school in December 1958, at the tender age of fifteen. I'm a working man now I've left school, I thought to myself. Man indeed; I wasn't even an old 15, still very much a child. Life has a habit of taking away the boy, and then hits one with what we call manhood. How did I find out I was still a boy? When I went for a job at the Metropolitan Camel Carriage Works I was asked to sign my signature. I was horrified, I never knew what the difference was between a signature and initials; what do I do now? I was terrified, so I put my initials; the foreman looked and said, "No son, your signature." I knew then at that moment what the difference was. I've never forgotten that moment; I was so frightened my throat was dry, my speech had gone and I was shaking – I needed the toilet and fast.

I realised at that moment in time I was virtually unemployable; I couldn't read or write very well, I could just about write my name – maths were non-starters. I was fifteen and nearly totally illiterate. Well I never got that job; I did some time later. I walked homeward feeling very much the failure I was, I headed for the park as I did so many times before with my friends as a school boy. I was alone and very low in my self esteem, asking myself what am I to do? What can I do? I'm nothing, I know nothing. Adults could not see or understand a boy screaming inside himself, please someone help me. No one could, that was down to me, so life had just started for me. I must work out how to get started, I was telling myself. I sat on that bank by the river for nearly half a day, my head was all over the place; I got up and headed homewards.

My mom was always kind to me. "Hello, son," she said as I walked into the kitchen via our back door, "did you get a job?"

"I filled in an ap... ap..."

"You mean an application form, son."

"Yes, Mom, that's it."

"Well, keep trying," she replied.

I was drained of energy so I went and I sat on my bed, to be honest I was close to tears, I was lost in a world of adults. I sat on my bed just as I did on the river bank, clueless, I had no brains. Some of my friends' parents took their children to have interviews, but I never wanted my parents to take me around to all the factories, I just needed some advice and guidance. I was screaming inside myself please someone help me, why oh why won't someone help me? I was keyed up, so exhausted from all the torment that I fell asleep.

Mom woke me from my sleep asking if I was all right as I looked very pale. "I'm OK, Mom," I told her.

I could not face my friends that evening, so I went to bed at 7pm only to be shaken the next morning by my dad. "Come on, son," said Dad, "you have got to find a job today." It was 6.45a.m. "Early start, son, beat the others to it. Welcome to the working classes." Thanks Dad, I thought.

Getting up early in the mornings was not one of the things in life I liked doing. With no money to my name and no food in my belly, well a piece of toast, I started to walk the streets to find employment. It was a cold day, no underwear, no overcoat and still I had pumps with holes in, (that's living, eh?) the crotch of my trousers was ripped; more air vents in my clothes than there was material, even my coat was too small for me, so I couldn't fasten it up, it was one my mom got for me from a jumble sale just before I left school – it cost the sum of 4d four pence.

Any road up, I kept walking and found myself almost in town, (Birmingham city that is) when I saw a factory that restored and, I think, made guns. I walked into the reception area, it was dark looking, not very well lit, very quiet, even a little bit creepy, with dark oak panels and a smell I had never smelt before. There was a beautiful counter, very long and very wide and very dark in colour, and glass cases on every wall displaying guns, bullets, tools and all sorts of wonderful looking items. I was captivated; it was so silent I could hear myself breathing. Silently staring at all those wonderful cases, when the silence was broken by a very soft and feminine voice saying, "Can I help you?" She said with a smile, "You should have rung the bell."

"Erm... erm..." What do I say? I was asking myself. My nerves were shot once again; no one had ever told me how to approach an employer.

"Well, young man, how can I help you?" she asked again.

I blurted out, "Got any jobs?" Well a shocked look appeared on her very pretty face.

"I beg your pardon, that's no way to find employment."

I said sorry with a bowed head and her face changed to a soft smile again as instantly she saw a little boy that was worried to death and didn't know what he was doing. "You sit there," she told me, pointing to an old leather chair – I could have been back in the Dickensian era. A couple of minutes passed when a very large man appeared, his face was round, red in colour with little round wire framed glasses on the end of his nose. With a deep but posh voice he asked, "So you are looking for employment are you?"

"Yes sir," I replied.

"Where have you worked before, what experience have you?"

"I've just left school," I replied, very nervously.

"Oh, I see," he said with doubt in his voice. "All right, can you start in the morning?"

"Yes sir," I replied with a surprised tone to my voice.

"We will show you what the job is all about and how we work tomorrow. Your wages will start at two pounds ten shillings a week."

"Thank you, sir," I replied.

"We start at 7.45am sharp; I will see you tomorrow," the man told me.

The lady I saw when I first entered the building gave me a beautiful smile. "See you tomorrow," she said.

"Thank you lady." I was feeling very good at that moment in time. I've got a job, I'm a working man – I was full of the joys of spring. My mom will be pleased, I thought, as I walked up the road to head for home. I kept saying to myself, I've got a job, I've got a job! I couldn't remember what the name of that firm was, but I did remember it was in Loveday Street.

As I reached the main road where the buses ran, I saw an old school mate of mine with his mom, waiting at the bus stop, "Hiya," I shouted, "where have you been?"

"My mom took me to the co-op bakery employment department for a job delivering bread. I did an I.Q. test but I failed it," he told me.

"Where have you been?" asked his mother.

With my chest out I replied, "I've just got a job at a gunsmith's."

"What that gunsmith's in Loveday Street, over there?" she said, pointing to the road.

"Yes," I replied.

"Well I would not let him work in an old fashioned place like that," she said, pointing to her son. "I would not allow him to mess about with guns. They would take anybody there, that's why you got the job," she said to me. I felt so deflated, even hurt, all my excitement vanished with the blink of an eye. She was upset because her son failed to get his job. I was really hurting at that moment, and then she asked me, "Where are you going now, David?"

"Home," I replied.

"Oh I see, so you will be getting on the bus with us then."

"No," I replied, "I haven't any money."

"It's a long walk, David, it will take you ages; it must be seven to ten miles."

Just as she said that, a bus pulled up. She smiled as she got on the bus and said, "Bye, David, enjoy your walk."

"Bye," I shouted as the bus pulled away. I wonder why she wouldn't lend me the three pence, I thought. As she sat down and looked out of the window she gave a big smile and waved. It did take me ages to get home, how long I'm not sure.

As I walked through the back door into the kitchen, Mom asked how I had got on. I very proudly said, "I start work tomorrow." She was so pleased it made me feel good. I ate my tea very quickly; mind you I usually did anyway.

I went to see my mate Trevor to tell him the good news. He thought it was great and congratulated me. "I'm very happy for you Dave." I felt quite relaxed at that moment, being with my mate who I had grown up with and had done so much with as a child.

Next morning up very early, I tucked my collar into my shirt to wash my neck as I had done all my young days, then I dried myself on a wet towel as usual as we still only had one, and using the family comb that we all used that was always on the windowsill next to the sink in the kitchen, I combed my hair.

There was Kathleen, Doreen, Janet, me, John, Mom, Dad and Doreen's husband, and we all washed in the kitchen, dried ourselves on the same towel, and used the same comb. The kitchen sink was the only sink in the house in those times. A sink wasn't fitted in the bathroom when the house was built but one was fitted at a later date. The comb was a blue nylon one and it was used for many, many years – no money was wasted in our house, I can tell you. So I ate my one piece of toast, drank my cup of tea and put my two pieces of bread and butter in my pocket, which was my lunch for dinnertime. Dad had the meat on his sandwiches; well the men were always given the most as they were the bread winners as the saying goes. Mom gave me sixpence for my bus fare, three pence there and three pence back – that was a child's fare. I walked from the bus to the factory, which was only a few strides from the bus stop. I walked into the factory through the entrance, the men's entrance, the other entrance was marked 'Girls Entrance' above the door, I think carved in sand stone. I was shaking with nerves as I walked in.

I was greeted by a little man wearing a cow gown that looked bigger than him, it looked like his head was trying to hide inside it, and it almost touched the floor – it looked really funny on him. "Have you brought your cards with you?" he asked, looking me up and down as he spoke. I gave him my cards. "Follow me," he said in a frightening voice. He showed me to a bench where there was what seemed like a pile of rifles. "I will show you how to strip these rifles, so pay attention." By this time I was terrified. "When you have stripped one with this sanding block," he was showing me, "I want you to sand the butt of the rifle till all the varnish has gone." Still he looked me up and down, muttering something.

"Sorry," I said, "I didn't hear what you just said."

"It doesn't matter now, get on with your work, I want a good job doing of those butts."

It took me ages to do the first one; my arm was really aching so I stopped to rest it. The little man came from nowhere. "Come on you lazy idiot, you will have to buck your ideas up. I don't think you will be any good here."

I had only been there two hours; he growled at me, every time he said anything to me. When I came to strip another rifle I had forgotten how to do it and now I was really panicking, I was afraid to ask. In the end I had to. "I've shown you once," he snarled, "you must pay attention." So I did four butts.

"Where is the toilet?" I asked a boy who I think was a teenager, and off I went. When I came back the little man was waiting for me, his face was like thunder.

"Where have you been to?"

"The toilet," I replied.

"Already? Well don't let me catch you going again till this evening." He was really growling at me, his face was all screwed up with anger. I will show him, I thought. I will work really hard and get all these rifles done before dinner. I must have been standing funny, my legs were really aching, so I sat on the bench still doing my work, when a very loud voice from the back of me screamed "Do you want a cushion?" as I was being dragged off the bench. "Don't you ever sit on the bench!"(I'm not sure, but I don't think he liked me very much!). Well it was dinnertime and I was ready for it. "I asked, "Where do I get a cup of tea from?"

"You have to bring your own," I was told, so I ate my two bread and butter sandwiches, had a drink from the tap in the toilet and off I went outside to have a cigarette to calm my nerves. I sat on the wall; it was cold so I went back in to the factory, only to find no one was talking to me. I was finding things a little stressful by this time. Back to work, just as I reached my bench the little man came to me again snarling at me. "Did I see you smoking?"

"Yes, I smoke; my dad gave me three cigarettes this morning," I told him.

"How dare you smoke around me! You are not old enough to smoke; don't let me catch you smoking again." It was worse than being at school.

After about ten minutes he came to me and told me to go to the office and get a box, they were expecting me. The box contained sticks about two feet long, half inch thick and pointed at one end. I was shown downstairs where there were many machines. It was a very big room there must have been twenty or so machines down there, no one worked on them, they were there and used only when needed, so I was shown how to put the sticks in the machine which was a lathe. With emery cloth I was told to sand them. This is easy, I thought, I will work hard then the little man will be pleased with me. When I had done what was in the box, I took them back to the office and got another box off them – what they were for I have no idea. I did five boxes altogether. The lady in the office said, "Well done, you have worked hard." That was very pleasing to hear, it made me feel good. "Have you enjoyed your first day?" she asked.

"Yes," I said; I was lying, I didn't really, that little man made me nervous and worried me; I was a bag of nerves when he was around.

First day done, I ran out of that factory as fast as I could and got on my bus. I went upstairs, you could smoke upstairs on buses in those days, I got my cigarette out but before I lit it I looked around to see if the little man was watching, he had got me in a state. I was glad to get home that evening.

The next morning I arrived on time. I was saying good morning but no one spoke to me. I went up to the teenager and said, "That job I had yesterday, I liked it, do you do them all the time?"

"We don't have those very often, all the ones you did weren't good enough, I worked over last night and did them all again."

I felt terrible and I thought I had done a good job, why didn't they show me what I was doing wrong, I was thinking.

The little man came up to me and said, "Carry on doing those butts you did yesterday."

Well, I thought, he seems better today; I will do a good job, he might start to be nice to me. So I started sanding the butts. It was almost dinner time and the little man had not been near me so I started to feel relaxed. This is not so bad today, I thought. It was about half an hour to dinner time when a lad came up to me very smartly dressed, he even wore a tie, I had never owned a tie. "Have you just started?" I asked him.

"Yes," he said to me. "How long have you worked here?"

"I only started yesterday," I replied. He then went to talk to the other people that worked there.

Dinner time came; I ate my two pieces of toast, and went to the toilet for a drink of water. As I came out I noticed the new boy having a cup of tea. I looked at him dressed in clothes that would have been my Sunday best, that's a laugh I never had Sunday best since the day I was born! Next to that boy I looked like a tramp.

After lunch the little man was talking to the new boy really nice, why didn't he talk to me nicely like he is talking to the new boy? He came to my bench and said, "Stand away a minute, I'm going to show this lad how to do this job." He even gave him an apron – he never ever mentioned an apron to me. "Ok son, you carry on with those," he said to him.

I wonder what he is going to ask me to do now, I was thinking. "Right," he said as he turned towards me, "the boss wants a word with you in the main office."

As I knocked on the door I was a little nervous. He called me in, it was more like being in the Dickensian era than the office area, it was dark oak panelling floor to ceiling, with old portraits all-around the walls and very old looking leather chairs. As I was looking at the portraits I almost forgot where I was. "They are my ancestors," he said. "Look son, I have bad news for you. I've taken on too many staff, I put all the names in a hat and yours came out." And I believed him. He handed me my cards and said, "I have paid you a little more than you have earned, one pound seven shillings." He handed me the money in cash in my hand, no wage packet, he then said, "Don't go back into the factory; I want you to leave the premises straight away." One and a half days and I was sacked, fired, kicked out, given the boot. I was still wet behind the ears, had seen nothing, done nothing, been nowhere in life and I wasn't given a chance. Welcome to the world of working life, I said to myself, that little man saw how poor I looked and took a dislike to me, well maybe I was a bad worker and I didn't know it, all I can say is that I hope any offspring of that little man receive better treatment than he dished out to me.

I have taken on too many staff – your name came out of the hat, don't go back into the work shop, leave the premises now.

VARIETY IS THE SPICE OF LIFE

I worked on the Chelmsley Wood Estate, for the building firm known as Bryant's, driving a dumper truck taking compo to the bricklayers, who were building a blue brick wall; it has since been rendered in pebble dash, it's in a road known as Moorend Avenue. I only stayed at that job for six weeks, now there's a surprise. I worked casual for lots of different firms – I drove a lorry for an Irish man for a month, when the motorway M42 was being constructed in the Castle Bromwich area.

I worked casual for a firm cleaning rust off machines that was caused by flood damage earlier that year; I worked in the main fortnight's holiday, the last week in July and the first week in August, most big factories closed down in those two weeks, so they set to getting all the necessary cleaning and repairs done. I worked all over the country working casual inside factories in those main two holiday weeks. Yes I would do any job for a short time; I most certainly had the variety and the spice of life.

I worked on farms all over the country. I did nearly all the jobs a farmer would do: vegetable farming, cattle farming, even milking, and I worked on the railway delivering to farms all around Warwickshire, Staffordshire and Leicestershire. In those days those farms were isolated, quiet and tranquil; it was a real pleasure in the summer, not quite so good in the winter. I did sink down to the axle on one occasion, which cost the railways, and I got a good telling off for that – I never did it again.

I even joined the army when I was twenty-nine; I did seven years in the pioneers, I went all over the continent driving, and a few years later I joined the H. S. F. Home Service Forces, commonly known as Dad's Army. I did seven years training, so for the defence of England I trained for fourteen years and I loved every minute of it I would love to be part of it today but they don't like slow old men in the armed forces.

CLARKS

My sister Janet worked at Clarks, in the Nechells area of Birmingham, St Clements Road I think it was in, a couple of hundred yards from the Saltley gasworks. They produced all sorts of cables for motor bikes, cars, push bikes and many others. I went there for a job after I had the sack from the gunsmiths. I had an interview and was asked how I had heard about this factory, and how did I know there was a vacancy going there. "My sister works here," I explained, and told them who she was and where she worked in the factory.

"She is a good worker; I hope you are as good. Ok you can start tomorrow and bring your cards with you," I was told. My mom was very pleased.

Next morning, same old routine, tucked my shirt collar in to wash my face and neck, dried myself on the wet towel and used the old nylon blue comb after getting all the hair out of it. Mom had made me egg sandwiches – well I had taken some money home from the gunsmith's! That's why I got eggs instead of just toast.

What a wonderful atmosphere! Everyone was kind, I was even given a cigarette; I loved it. When dinnertime came the foreman came to me. "Have you any tea, Dave?"

"No," I replied.

"Come with me; you can share with us till you sort out with the others – they put a shilling a week into a kitty, and that pays for the tea, milk and sugar. Have you brought any sandwiches with you?"

"Yes, thank you," I said to him.

"Good," he replied, "I would have bought you one from the café; you could have paid me back out of your first week's wages." What a difference from the gunsmith's, I was happy, so I got a cup from home and had tea at work. So all firms ain't like that gunsmith's and like that little man that was buried inside his cow gown, I thought to myself, this firm was friendly.

I was shown in detail how to do all the different jobs. When I was putting the ferrules on the end of the cables, I didn't do them quite right, I was worried to death and afraid to ask the foreman to show me again, but I had to. When I went to him, he said, "You look worried sick, whatever is the matter?"

I explained to him my problem. With his hand on my shoulder he said, "It's all right, Dave, don't worry, you will soon get the hang of it."

I was so relieved. There was a wonderful family atmosphere every day in that factory; it was a pleasure to go to work. There were a few people that worked there from where I lived in Glebe Farm, Stechford. My next door neighbour Beryl worked there. Everything was going good, £3-10-0 a week and not a soul screaming or growling at me. I was given a job soldering the ends of the cables, putting what they called barrels on the end of them, then with a bunch of them I very slowly put the ends of the cables with the barrels on the end of them into a big bowl of melted hot solder, this operation welded the barrels firmly to the cable – it was a very satisfying job. After that I was asked to put the cables into the outer cases, those were for motor bikes. It was a little tricky at first but I got quite fast at it.

My sister Janet worked alongside a girl that lived just around the corner from the factory; she was so pretty, I just couldn't stop staring at her. My sister used to go to her house for lunch, and I went with her on a few occasions. As I sat looking at her with all the desires of youth, I was thinking I wish you would go out with me; of course it never happened. The first time I walked into her house I was shocked, it was a little back to back house. I lived in poverty and knew hard times, but that house looked like it needed knocking down – her upbringing was even lower than mine. She was always well dressed and very polite; I on the other hand suited that house very well, course and common. Any road up, I worked at Clarks for four months. I was getting bored by this time, I had learned how to do all the jobs, I wanted a new challenge, and so I handed in my notice. The foreman asked me to reconsider as he liked the way I worked, he said, "You are a good worker it's a shame to lose you."

I said, "No, I'm leaving."

"Well, if you ever want to come back, I will give you your job back," the foreman told me. So I left. I have fond memories of that firm; the kindness, the friendliness and the family atmosphere. Yes, time to move on to pastures new, I thought.

An elderly gentleman once said to me, "Son, variety is the spice of life; do as many different things in life as you can." Yes, I have certainly done that, as you will see as you go through my life with me in this book.

METROPOLITAN CARRIAGE WORKS

The second time I tried to get a job at the carriage works, I got a job working in the rivet shop. The day I started I was very happy, as I loved the railways; it felt really good to be part of them. I was a very tiny cog in a massive machine – well a tooth on a cog would be more like it. It was based in the Saltley area of Birmingham, and my dad worked there for many years; he worked there through the war years.

He was a radial driller, and he did his share of fire watching, well most of the time, he sometimes paid a man to do his fire watching. If he did that, he went into the tote, that was a club on the Alum Rock Road, just up the road from his firm. He told my mom he had been fire watching – typical male. He told me his wages were £25 a week, and all he gave my mom was £4 to keep six children at that time. I never knew how he made that sort of money in those days, but my uncle Bob was the manager there, maybe that had something to do with it.

As I walked through the different shops, as the different departments were called, I was staggered at the size of the place and the amount of people that worked there. I was taken to the foreman who showed me my job. There was a frame of what looked like a box with two thick cables going to it, and a foot pedal. When this was pushed down with the foot it opened a jaw with a pair of tongs. A rivet was picked out of a sack, there were a few sacks of different size rivets for use on different jobs, and the rivet was placed between the jaws when the foot was taken off the pedal. The rivet started to heat up – it went cherry red to white hot, that was the moment it had to be taken out or it melted, so with rivet in the tongs I had to throw it to wherever the men were working; sometimes I threw it a few yards, sometimes only a couple of feet. The machine was at the end of the gangways, not many people walked down those gangways, when the rivets were being thrown. The rivets had to be used before they went red, but many a time they were not hot enough, as they tried to ball the ends over – boy did they swear when that happened, and getting them back out could sometimes be a problem. They even had a man check them and if he found one or two were not tight enough he would tell them to replace them, and the bad language started again. When I threw them, sometimes one would bounce over his boot, boy did that annoy them, they used to threaten to do all sorts to me; of course I played the innocence, I would say, "sorry mate, was that too hard? I'm trying to get the distance right." By that time the rivet wasn't hot enough. What annoyed them was they got paid for the amount of work they did.

After a couple of months they were short of manpower in the saw mill. I was transferred to the mill, and I was very happy in there, I love the smell of wood. That mill was the most laid back workshop I have ever worked in. The most work I ever did was about two hours a day; I swept and cleaned the machine just for something to do. My job there was to stand at the back of the machine and take whatever was cut and stack it on a trolley; I was forever picking up the off cuts of timber and smelling it, I loved the aroma. I think it was pitch pine, I'm not certain, it was pine anyway.

We only cut timber for carriages. In the compound out the back of the saw mill were thousands of pounds worth of timber being seasoned in the fullness of time, some piles were dated war time, what I didn't know was any newcomer to the saw mill was chased round and round the timber piles till one was really sweaty, then they threw you into the sawdust pit under the machine – that was very uncomfortable I can tell you, as you calmed down and stopped sweating, you had to strip off, or itch all afternoon. Machinists mate, that was what I was, and had to make the tea for the machinists mornings, dinnertime and afternoon. Each of the lads had so many men to look after; I had nine Billy cans, nine machinists to look after, I got to know every little thing about each man and just how they liked their tea. I used to put the tea and sugar in each can; carrying nine Billy cans full of hot tea was a little tricky at times when walking back trying not to spill them. The cans were not marked, but I got to know each one like it was my own. It was about thirty or forty yards to walk from where the boiling urn was. One dinnertime an office girl was running fast down the gangway, and she ran into me and knocked all the cans out of my hands; she never stopped to pick them up, she just shouted sorry and carried on. At that time I had only been doing the cans a couple of weeks so I guessed what tea and sugar they had in them. Of course I got it all wrong; boy did they moan! Afternoon tea was ok though, when the cans got too stained with the tea all the lads used ashes to clean them. One of my men asked, "How do you get the can so clean?"

I told him, "With ash."

He had a fit. "Don't do mine anymore like that." That news went around the shop floor like fire, all the men told their tea boys not to clean them that way, and we said we wouldn't any more – of course we did, but they never knew. Me and my big mouth!

We got a shilling a week off each of our men we made tea for, that 9 shillings came in very handy at the end of the week. When the shift was over, every boy in that mill had to clean down the machine and use the air lines to blow the sawdust down the pit; sometimes it was easier with a broom. Some dinnertimes I went and sat with my dad in the machine shop – it wasn't ever so clean. Dad did the drilling of the axle boxes and the wagon chasses. He had six machines on the go because the chasses were very long so six holes at a time made the job easier. One dinnertime I knocked dad's Billy can over, he wasn't very happy; I never sat with him again after that.

I liked the smell of suds; it's a milky looking liquid that runs over the drills as they are cutting through the metal, it kept them from getting hot.

As I mentioned before, uncle Bob was a manager there; he never once came to say hello, in fact I only saw him twice that I remember all through my life. I remember those two times because he bought me an ice cream, 6d they were, we only got 3d ones usually and that was on very rare occasions, mind you it made it a special treat.

After three months I was starting to get bored again, yes bored, so I handed in my notice. Is it boredom or am I lazy? I'm not sure, well new adventure here I come, I used to say to myself. It's strange you know, all the places I worked at I used to look around to try and remember what certain walls looked like and the washrooms and the inside of certain rooms, and think I won't be seeing any of this again after today, and for a reason I can't explain I felt sad. I've had that many jobs I can't remember most of them, inside that is, but I can a few.

As I left this firm it was the start of the industrial holidays, this was when the factories closed down and the industrial cleaners and maintenance workers went into the factories to clean or do any repairs that needed to be done. I was glad I had left because this was when my friends asked me to go with them to Upton on Severn camping.

UPTON-ON-SEVERN

Seven months after leaving school in the July of 1959, two of my friends, Maurice and Johnny asked me if I wanted to go to Upton on Severn camping, only for a week. It was in the main two weeks holiday when all the factories closed down – the last week in July and the first week in August, that was how it was then. The camp site was right on the river's edge, and we could go swimming every day, which we all loved, so I agreed to go. That was on the Friday evening, and we all went the next morning.

None of us had much money; we did what we had always done, did everything with nothing, well almost. That evening Trevor and me went to the Beaufort Cinema along with my younger brother John, but unknown to us he had a water pistol with him. Trevor started to chat up two girls that that were sitting in front of us when they suddenly jumped up with a sort of a quiet scream – my brother John was squirting his water pistol under the seat onto their legs and they couldn't understand what was going on. John sat up and made believe he knew nothing about it, well not until they caught him doing it that is. Well we went on the bus with them to take them home; John got off and went home, Trevor and me stayed with the girls on the bus, and we all got off at the Mackadown, Tile Cross. The two girls lived about twenty yards from the bus stop; we talked for about three quarters of an hour I suppose it was. "Can I see you again?" I asked one of them.

"Yes please, I would like that, tomorrow," she replied.

"Oh I can't," I told her, "I've agreed to go camping with my mates, to Upton on Severn for the week."

"Don't go," she said with a sad look on her face, "I want to see you tomorrow."

I was so tempted; I really wanted to see her again. "I will meet you here tomorrow night, at seven o'clock," I told her.

"Yes," she said, "I would like that." So we said goodnight – I never even attempted to kiss her, (I never did have any brains or guts) and we parted. I'm not sure if Trevor turned up the following evening, I've never asked him, thinking about it, so me and Trevor walked home . I never did see that girl again; I can't even remember what she looked like or even her name.

Yes I went camping to Upton on Severn near Worcester, as I said none of us had enough money for a week's holiday, not even enough to feed ourselves let alone pay for anything extra. We took a primus stove, a loaf, some tinned beans, butter and two tins of soup, that was it. Three growing hungry lads were about to experience weight loss without wanting to. We cycled to Upton on Severn, pitched our tent, and had bread and butter and a plate of beans on a lovely sunny afternoon. Moored on the river where we were was a boat that had been dragged off the bottom of the riverbed, it was in a right old state, so we used it for our diving board. We had great fun. When we had had enough, we dried ourselves on our hand towels, yes hand towels, we draped them over our tent to dry, which you would, that was the only place to dry them anyway.

That evening we explored the town hoping to find a couple of beauties, but no luck, any road up we had breakfast next morning, soup and bread and butter, and that was us – skint. On our site there were lots of tents and caravans, and the smell of bacon cooking was more than flesh and blood could stand, especially for young teenagers who just lived to eat. Well, as you can imagine, us three growing lads were starving. Next to the site was an orchard of egg plums, we lived on them for four whole days, and no, we never did get stomach ache.

A very observant lady who was caravanning a few yards from our tent came over to us and asked, "Why do you boys keep eating those plums?"

"We ain't got any food or money left to buy any food," we told her. Nearly an hour later she came over to us with a tray, it must have been three foot long by eighteen inches wide, and on it were sixteen sausages and they were swimming in tinned tomatoes, not in the tins I might add, just the tomatoes, she even gave us a loaf of bread – we shared it equally. It was like a feast we had never had or so it seemed, to three starving boys. We had a few hours swim, and after that we were in top form. When night time came and we were back on the egg plums we decided to call it a day and head back home. The next morning we did just that. I love these memories; if only I had that sort of energy now! Still, it was great to be young. Happy days.

COOKS FOR CLOCKS

When I started at Cooks, the clock face makers, they were situated in the Bulls Head area in Stechford. It was known as the Bulls Head because the pub was called the Bulls Head; it was a lovely building, but sadly it's now been demolished. Lots of women and young girls worked at Cooks, it was a family firm and it had a very friendly atmosphere. I worked in the degreasing room; my job was to put sheets of metal into a vat that had a liquid in the bottom of it, this was known as Trykoethylene, I think that's the right way to spell it; we always referred to it as Trike. The liquid created a mist which very slowly rose and covered the metal sheets, taking off any grease that was on them. I wore gloves as the sheets could not be touched by human flesh, as this made the metal greasy. I had a timer to set, I think it was for three minutes, when the bell rang I then waited for the Trike to evaporate. I had to very slowly take out the sheets of metal – if removed too quick it left streaky marks on the sheets, this created a problem for the ladies who before they could spin the clock circles on them, had to use a powder called Fullers Earth with a soft rag, this would rub off every streak; they got very annoyed with me when I messed up. Mind you, sometimes I did it on purpose, and used to say to them, " Well it gives you something to do," boy did that get them going – I had to move fast to avoid flying objects! After the circles were finished and the silver was put on them, they then went to a young fella to guillotine them to the sizes required.

I was in the darts team, we played every dinner time. One evening we had a darts match in the Bulls Head pub opposite the factory. Every one of our team won, all except me that is, I lost on my double. No shame; my opponent got to his double first and hit it, one of our players tried to embarrass me saying sarky things, he knew I didn't drink. "Come on, Dave, I will play you for a pint."

"Ok, let's do it," I said. We played 301, and I beat him easily.

"That was a fluke; let's play again."

"Ok, for another pint?" I asked.

"Yes, of course. I want to win my pint back," he said. Well I left him standing. I'm no good at darts; it just went right that evening.

"Another game?" I said cockily.

"No, you got lady luck on your side tonight." I gave the two pints away.

We saved every week for the Christmas party. Inside the factory a week before the party someone stole the money, the party funds. Everyone was very shocked and very hurt. The ladies took it the hardest – we all thought we were friends, yet one of us was a horrible, despicable thief. They said they knew who it was but just could not prove it. The ladies, God bless em, did what ladies always do, and they saved the day. They made cakes, trifles, sandwiches and put all the trimmings up as well; wonderful ladies, wonderful memories.

Not long after the Christmas holiday in the middle of February, I fancied a change of scenery, so I handed in my notice. I've no staying power – four and a half months it seems is about all I can manage. My longest job was at Coca Cola, most was four months. To be honest I hated going to work, but one has to earn a living.

Degreasing the metal sheets ready for the clock faces to be put on them.

The Bull's Head public house
Sadly now demolished

DOING A RUNNER

Me and my friend Johnny, who I grew up with and now worked with, always had a game of snooker every Friday after work. We were hopeless at it but we enjoyed playing – we worked at Cooks the clock face makers at that time. As we walked through the front doors of the snooker hall, along a passage, through two other doors and into the main hall, we said the same thing, we sounded like a stuck record: "Any tables free?"

He shocked us this one Friday evening by replying, "Sorry lads, I'm fully booked up, but seeing how you are regulars I will open the upstairs up for you."

It was creepy, dead quiet, with only the light on over the table. We played for an hour, and then went downstairs for a cup of tea and a packet of Cadburys short bread chocolate biscuits. When we played on the tables downstairs, it was always lights out after an hour; we would either pay for another hour or go home, but because we were upstairs on our own the light never went out. The man behind the bar switched them off by hand when we were downstairs, so we got carried away. Three and a half hours later, John said, "Dave we've been playing for three and a half hours." I was horrified; we couldn't pay for the table.

"We will have to do a runner, John," I told him. So we very quietly crept down the concrete stairs and into the street and we ran like the wind away from that hall. "We will have to stay away for a few weeks, Dave," John suggested to me, and I agreed – the boys who ran that hall were a rough bunch.

The next Friday we forgot all about doing a runner the Friday before. In we marched. "Any tables free? we were just about to ask when he got hold of us.

"I've been waiting for you pair; you owe me for three and a half hours for last Friday."

We both said together, "It wasn't us, mister, honest." I told him I hadn't been to work all that week.

"I never went out of the house till this Monday, Johnny said, "We come here all the time, we wouldn't do that to you, you always look after us,"

"I know it was you," he shouted.

"Honest, mister, we didn't come in last week," I told him.

"Right, I'm putting you on this first table next to me, you try doing a runner from here."

We had confused him enough to put a little doubt in his mind; if he had been sure, we would have been taken round to the back of the hall and given the beatings of our lives. We were never allowed upstairs again, I felt terrible for running but it was a good beating up or risk getting away with it – we were very lucky.

After I left Cooks I got a job on the Co-op bakery as a rounds boy delivering bread. Me and Johnny didn't meet up again for a very long time, and it was many years later before I went in to that snooker hall again.

ROUNDS BOY CO-OP BAKERY

It was a sunny Monday morning; I was sitting at the table eating my usual piece of toast when for a reason I can't explain, I was thinking about my first job and how much that little man disliked me for reasons I have never known. Then my thoughts went to that bus stop where I met an old school chum and his mother – not a nice memory. I thought to myself, right, I will go up town to the Birmingham city centre, and see if I can get a job at that Co-op bakery. I remembered my school chum saying he failed to get a job there.

I arrived in town via a number 14 bus. I remember the Co-op well because my mom took me there as a small boy a few times to see Father Christmas, well to see the grotto not Father Christmas, as Mom could rarely afford to let me see Father Christmas. I went to the personnel office to ask the young lady if there were any jobs going. I remembered my mistake from my first job, not to blurt out "got any jobs", so all confident, no nerves at all, I enquired, "Have you any vacancies please?"

"What are you looking for?" I was asked.

"Anything," I replied.

"We are looking for rounds boys to deliver bread in the Stechford area. Would that be too far away for you?"

I could not believe my luck! "I live in Stechford," I replied.

"You will have to take an IQ test."

Those words scared the life out of me. It was a simpleton's test, well no trouble there, I thought, there is no one simpler than me. I was shown into a room, given a sheet of paper and to my surprise it was easy; it had things like apple, orange, stone – which is the odd one out? And what is the capital of England? When I had finished I took the sheet to the reception. The young lady put a card with holes all over it on top of the sheet, looked up at me, smiled and said, "You have got the job."

I felt so good. I've passed a test! To be honest I felt a little proud, it was such an achievement for me.

Artist impression of the Co-op bakery in Manor Road, Stechford

I had to report to a Mr Starky at the Manor Road bakery in the Stechford area, with a note, that afternoon saying I would be starting work there the day after tomorrow. I was so excited I went to see my old school chum to tell him my good news, you know, the one I met at the bus stop with his mother. His mother said, "Oh, they are short staffed at the moment, they are taking anybody on, that is why you got the job." Well that burst my bubble of excitement, I can tell you, but at least I got the job. That was the second time she insulted me.

I had to go back to the main office in town the next day. There was a room full of people, and we were given a talk on the Co-op, how it started, what they did and sold and a film show on hygiene and the dos and don'ts when working for the co-op. The one thing that stuck in my mind was a man sneezing and seeing in slow motion how far the spray from his mouth travelled as he sneezed. I enjoyed that talk, funny really, I hated the word 'classroom', it meant learning; not being very bright, it was always traumatic for me especially when asked questions in front of a room full of people – that always scared me.

The bakery wasn't far from my house so I hadn't any bus fares to find, I walked there. As I walked down the hill of Manor Road towards the bakery, the smell of baking bread travelling up the hill on the wind was pure nectar to me. Every morning I would take deep lungs full of air to take in that wonderful smell.

On my arrival I was taken to the stores and given two cow gowns, this made me very happy because it covered up my bad attire – I was desperate for a new pair of shoes and trousers because the crutch of my trousers was ripped from the flies to the rear, and my pumps still had holes in. After the first day my feet were very sore as the cardboard in my pumps soon wore out. I can't remember what my wages were for sure, £3-3/- seems to ring a few bells.

My round was all around the Stechford area. Malcolm Brown was the rounds man I worked with; he had worked for the Co-op since he was fourteen. We loaded the electric van from the deck alongside many other vans. It was a long deck, and it was loaded the same way every morning. On the right hand side on the top runners we put the uncut bread, the next two runners down were the thick and thin sliced, waxed paper wrapped bread on the floor under the trays of bread that were on wire trays. We slid two wooden trays containing the cakes and biscuits on the left and right of the van, and on the left runners we put sliced bread and the two runners below we put the cottage loaves, milk rolls, bloomers and brown Hovis loaves. Bread was always put on wire trays. We had a long pole with a hook on the end to pull the trays out as these were too far back to reach by hand. Thinking about it now, how we got the cakes and biscuits seems very old fashioned. In the corner of the yard was a brick built building about the size of two 8x6 sheds, where two men worked. One was an elderly gentleman who had worked there forever. We had to stand in line out in the open. If it rained all the confectionery got wet, so we ran to the van as quick as we could. What was really surprising was we would say just what we wanted, for example, six packets of rich tea biscuits, two lemon cakes, six steam puddings and so on, and as the old fellow placed the items asked for on a wooden tray, on a piece of paper he wrote down the prices of each item. What amazed me was he would run up and down the list of prices adding up all the money, he was so fast, if he made a mistake and under charged the rounds man, it was a gain to the rounds man. A slip was given and added to the cost of the bread when we cashed up on Saturday afternoon for the week's goods and handed over the money. All the time I was there, I never knew that man to make a mistake when adding up for the confectionary.

Off we go. To my delight our first stop was the Jolly Tea Pot café, situated in Stechford lane. That was the start of our round in that lane. We had two slices of toast and a cup of tea every morning, and the rounds man always paid. It was a very pleasant job in the summer, not so good in the winter when it rained, trying to keep the bread dry.

I found I had a flair for selling. The more cakes and biscuits we sold, the more bonus we got. Malcolm said his wages had never been so good. I loved selling. By the time I had done one month, we were getting four wooden trays of confectionery every Monday, and we added more items to them through the week. Malcolm thanked me. I was called into the office and praised for my endeavours and given a raise of a shilling. Ok, only a shilling, but it was worth that for the praise I got, as that was a rare event in my life.

I was eventually taken off that round and put with a man called Mr Pratt; his rounds boy had passed out as a rounds man and got his own round. He whispered to me, "I bet you don't last the week with Pratt." He was right, I lasted three days; nothing I did suited him. I tried selling and pushing the confectionery, as I did on my other round, but he told me not to do it as his customers knew what they wanted. Plus, he didn't like my attire. All the rounds boys had a little book in which we put down what we had given each customer – he didn't like that, he wanted me to remember what they had had without writing it down. He got verbally very aggressive. He said, "You work on my round now, not on Malcolm's round." Every hour seemed like a week, he was a horrible man.

On Saturday when the rounds man was collecting the money, all the rounds boys had to deliver to every customer. The rounds man never touched a loaf on that day, he moaned at me nonstop. I never knew all my customers, never mind his; I had only done three days on his round. I went into work late on the Monday morning to make sure he had left the yard; I went to see the manager,

"May I go back to my old round, please? I can't work with Mr Pratt."

"Yes, ok son, I know what he is like, he gives all the rounds boys a hard time. His customers love him – they sing his praises, so we put up with him. Well, all the vans are out now so you can work on the deck today," the manager told me, so I swept up the deck and arranged all the cradles in the bays ready for the returning vans to unload any bread that they hadn't sold. I liked working on the deck. When the vans had all returned and unloaded I saw what I didn't like to see, a man backed up to the deck and threw all the returned bread into the back of his lorry, so I asked him what he did with the bread. He told me each loaf cost him a penny, yes one penny, and this was fed to the pigs as it wasn't allowed to be sold to the public a day later.

I asked Mr Starkey if I could do the job on the deck permanent, but I was refused because it wasn't classed as a job. Mr Pratt's old rounds boy backed onto the deck to unload the returned bread ready for the pig man to collect. After he'd unloaded he turned, saw me, smiled and said, "Told you you wouldn't last the week with Mr Pratt."

I worked there for eight months. Part of my job was to plug the van into the electric ready to be charged up for the next day. Each van had two very big batteries, one each side, underneath they were the length of the van.

As usual I got fed up and handed in my notice. This type of behaviour became the norm for me throughout the rest of my life.

A few years later I went back to the Co-op and became a rounds man. Nothing had changed, the only difference was that I was in charge of and responsible for the money. I much preferred being a rounds boy – no responsibility.

Manor Road Bakery, Stechford, showing the lorries backed on to the deck. The van far right is where I used to plug in the electrics for the batteries to be charged over night.

DONOVANS

Early one morning I had the idea I would go all around the local building sites, so I sat for a while and worked out a route I would take, starting with the nearest first, in the hope I wouldn't have to walk too far. I got to a place called the Atlas, well that's what we called that area because the cinema there was named the Atlas, and the area was Stechford. About a quarter of a mile from my house was a café on the corner of Albert Road, I can't remember the name of it, it was there for years, it's gone now like all the things we wish were still around. I went in there and had three tomato dips, that's bread dipped in the juice of the tomatoes, they were only 2d each, two pence, 6d in total; sixpence, that's all I could afford – all my mates had tomato dips when short of money. With a little food in my stomach, off I set. Just behind the café was a grove of factories. As I was passing them, I thought, could I be locked away all day working in one of those? I pondered on it for a while and thought, well it might be all right; it won't hurt to give it a go. These factories were in Northcote Road, and at the bottom of the grove was a firm that made items out off concrete. I thought I'd try at Stuarts granolithic, but as I passed a factory called Donovans, for reasons I can't explain, I walked into their office and asked if they had any vacancies. The ladies had only just taken off their coats, and I was asked to wait ten minutes. I filled in an application form, and then a foreman whose name was Johnson came to me and asked what type of work I was looking for. "Anything," I replied.

"Are you ok at maths?"

"Not too bad," I replied. Good at maths? I could hardly read; well, all they could do was sack me. I always took chances like that; normally they would just put you on a different job if you weren't any good on the one they employed you for. I was shown all over the factory and shown what they made, which was electric boxes, well all the wiring that went inside them, from six foot tall cabinets to little on off switches, the type with a lever on the side that you pushed up for 'off' and down for 'on', these items were for factories. It was a family firm, a wonderful atmosphere.

They used thick copper wire bent into shape with a pair of pliers, they used a sheet with all the shapes on it, so they knew the shape was correct, and then it was placed in the cabinet with a nut and a washer, and was fixed into place. The job I was given was a checker; the foreman said I was in charge of seeing the girls and ladies had enough work in their trays so they didn't need to stop working. They were all on piecework. Using hand presses, they punched out all sorts of electric parts. I had to collect the trays when full, weigh them, write down the amount they had done, put it in my book then hand it to the manager so the ladies money could be worked out. The ladies kept a record of what they did so they could make sure their pay was correct. Working around all those ladies and girls this is, I was thinking to myself, heaven, yes sir, heaven.

The foreman asked, "Are you interested in taking the job?"

"Yes," I replied.

So I now had a title – Checker. Can you believe it, me with a responsible job? I felt important at that moment in time, I can tell you. This was a learning curve for me; I was what was known at that time as dim, yes, very dim. There were sixteen ladies to look after.

"Start at eight in the morning and bring your cards with you."

"I have them with me," I replied.

"Ok, I will take you to the office and you can do the necessary there." He told me his name and said I will see you in the morning.

The next morning I started rather nervous, in fact very nervous. I had a little office, well a corner with my scales, note book and pencils. I swept up, got a rag and cleaned down the scales and tided up all around what I called my office space – boy I felt important!

The foreman brought Mr Donovan down to show him what I had done; they were well pleased. I had to eat my lunch in my little bit of heaven.

Across the gangway from my scales were all the presses. The lady who worked closest to me was named Valerie; she was a large lady, like my mom was, and I got on so well with her. I explained to her, rather embarrassingly, that I did not know how to weigh and calculate the scales. She looked amazed, "Do you know how many there are in a gross?" she asked me.

"No," I replied. She said she would take me under her wing and very quietly would tell me what to do and how to use the scales properly.

"Don't worry, Dave, I won't tell anyone," she very kindly said. "Dinnertime I will write all the amounts down for you, and if you get stuck just come and see me and I will put you right." I was so relieved.

After a week I was ok, I picked it up and knew how to do the job properly, so I really looked after Val, making out she had done more than she had. If we fiddled too much she would make a note of the work she didn't want paying for that week, and put it down for the next week, which meant she could have an easier week and not have to work so hard. Valerie had a free day every week because I said in the book that she had done that day's quota – well one good turn and all that. It also meant if she had a day off she never lost any money.

I joined the football team; my position was right half. We played every dinnertime at the back of the factory – we were called the Donovan F.C., makes sense I suppose. We played on a Saturday morning. We won the league that year 1960, Mr Donovan was well pleased.

Well, time to move on. I did well there – I lasted about four months. When I left that company outside the sun was shining. I felt I needed to work out in the fresh air instead of a stuffy, dark factory. I was asked if I would still play football for them, which I agreed to do.

STUARTS GRANOLITHICS

This firm was situated in Northcote road off Albert road in the Stechford area of Birmingham, the same road that Donovans was in. I left Donovans to start work with Stuarts, and I was told the firm were moving to Coleshill in six months' time, after their new factory had finished being built. The day I went to ask if they had any vacancies, they had just started building their new factory that very week; the new factory was in Station road Coleshill, in the county of Warwickshire, and they made various items of concrete for the housing market. I walked into the office and asked the manager if they had any vacancies.

"We are looking for a strong young man to do some labouring on our new building site at Coleshill," he said.

"That's ok," I told him, the personnel manager that is.

"Right son, start tomorrow eight thirty," he told me.

"How do I get there?" I asked him.

"By bus son, we will be putting on transport to pick the men up but not for another week, we have only been on the site for three days getting ready for the building to start, which we have done today," he told me.

The buses were every hour but they didn't run to Coleshill from where I lived, so I walked to that site in Coleshill. It took me over an hour and a half, and it was winter time but the days were quite warm – well, they were to me as I didn't feel the cold like most people did – and it had rained the night before. On the first morning I started I didn't do very much work, I was asked to level out a large pile of rubble, well it was called hard core and was crushed up old house bricks, but that was all I did that morning. By lunch time I felt really rough – I had the flu coming on. I had my lunch with the men in the shanty, which is the wooden hut used by the workers to hang up their coats and have their breaks in. I started back on the site after my lunch break, but by this time I was feeling really ill, and after about an hour, maybe a little more, I just could not carry on – it got so bad I couldn't even lift the shovel. I went to see the boss in his office, I knocked on the door and a voice shouted 'enter,' and to my surprise the boss had his trousers around his knees and he was adjusting his pants. There were two other men in there with him and they were laughing – I had no idea why at that time.

"I'm sorry boss, I will have to go home, I – " but before I could finish what I was saying he interrupted me.

"I don't know why they employ people like you, your type shouldn't work around men." I was getting worse by the minute and had no idea at that time what he was trying to say to me – I just wanted to go home. "You are not the type to work for me so I'm letting you go, you can come and collect your wages and your cards at the office on Friday."

I was devastated but far too ill to argue or defend myself, and as I left the site I realised what he meant: he thought I was queer, or should I say gay these days. Gay meaning happy, I wasn't very happy and I can tell you no way am I gay, I love the ladies too much. As I started on the long walk home it started to pour with rain, and I was wearing a coat that was too small for me and I couldn't button it up, so I just felt like I was going to die – not that I know what dying is like, but I'm sure you know what I mean. Walking down that country lane where they were building their new factory, there were lots of puddles quite deep all down the lane from all the rain the night before, and they were being made worse because as I walked the rain got really heavy.

What made me feel even worse was a lorry coming towards me just as I got near a very deep puddle – I turned to run away but my legs just wouldn't move fast enough. I felt so weak and the driver in the lorry thought he would have a bit of fun and put his foot down, steered his lorry closer to me and hit that puddle so fast the water rose into the air and came down over me like a tidal wave. Talk about being wet, if I had jumped into a river I would not have been any wetter. I was shivering, my whole body was shaking and I had a terrible headache. It was really hurting me to even walk by this time and I still had about an eight or ten mile walk to reach home. I just wanted to lie down and sleep, and as I walked – more like staggered – I came across a fallen tree. I sat down and tried to regain some of my strength but I was getting worse, and still it poured with rain. I forced myself off the tree and headed for home. I shivered and shook with every step I took and as I reached my house I wasn't sure if I was alive or dead.

As I walked into the back kitchen my mom said, "My word son you look dreadful, get yourself off to bed I will wash those wet clothes." I took off my clothes and just left them where they fell on the bedroom floor. I never even dried myself, I just got straight into bed, and fell asleep as soon as my head touched the pillow. I was asleep for two days and not once did I wake up – my mom said she was thinking of getting the doctor to me as she was very worried. When I finally woke up, boy was I weak, and my mum made me a big fry up for breakfast. It was over a week before I ventured out again. There is one thing I would like to do, and that is see that Forman again and tell him how wrong he was about me, and say it was because I had the flu not because I was queer, bent, gay or whatever…well, that will never happen now.

DONOVANS FOR THE SECOND TIME

So I was sacked from Stuarts Granolithics and the time came for me to be a little cheeky. So with a nice smile I walked into the office of Donovans and knocked on the personnel office window. It slid open, and the office girl recognised me. "Hello David, how are you? How can I help you?"

"Would you ask Mr Johnson if I can have my job back please?" Well if you don't ask, as the saying goes.

It was a good ten minutes before he came out to see me. As he walked through the door I held out my hand with a smile, and said, "Hello, Mr Johnson, how are you?"

"So you want your job back do you?"

"Yes please," I replied.

He smiled and very sarcastically said, "So your sandcastles fell down, did they?"

I laughed, hoping it would keep him in a good mood. I told a white lie, I said I missed working there {truth is I don't like working anywhere, well there was one job I did love working at, that was Kunzles).

"I can't offer you your old job back, would you like to work on the big cabinets?"

"I would love to do that, Mr Johnson," and I meant it, I even thought to myself, I'm going to stay here till I retire (I'm not sure who was the biggest fool – me or my mind!).

I started the next day. The section was on the other side of the factory from the ladies on the presses. The big cabinets had a printed panel already fixed inside them, with a pair of pliers, I bent the copper wire to the shape printed on the board and placed it on the bolts sticking out of the panel; with a nut and a washer I bolted it in place. The charge hand over that section kept an eye on me for a short time.

"I see you have the hang of it, now you will be ok," he said at the end of the first week – I was well into it.

I found in life if you have a go it might turn out all right, nothing lost if it doesn't. When all the copper wire was in situ it looked really nice, seeing all the electric circuits together to me looked like a piece of art. I always imagined it in a beautiful gold frame as a piece of art.

As usual I started to get bored, and I was late a few times. One time I was late I went to the office, that's what you had to do when you were late. One of the office staff went to Mr Johnson, told him I was late and asked if I could start work. The answer I received was, "Tell Mr P to have the rest of the day off," so I wasn't allowed in that day.

I got a telling off the next day. I said, "Better late than never," and he replied, "Better never late." I've never forgotten that. I tried to overcome the boredom but it got the better of me, so I handed in my notice.

The one thing I did really miss was my girlfriend. She left her job at Barrows Stores in town and got a job in the office at Donovans to be near me; I never knew she did that till one Monday dinnertime when she came and sat with me; I was shocked, I can tell you, what a lovely thing for a person to do. We got married on the 23rd December 1961, aged eighteen (poor girl). Wonderful memories.

F- LINE AND CO

When I started at this factory I was so surprised at how old fashioned it was; it was situated near the Birmingham city centre, in Staniforth Street. The methods used there were so old fashioned it opened one's eyes to think in these days of modern technology, or should I say in those days, these machines were still being used, mind you even when I was young I loved the past, that's what I do, live in the past. Any road up, the machines were being driven by leather belts. It was a very interesting building, cubby holes, passage ways, hidey holes everywhere; honestly if I hadn't known better I could have thought I was working in the Dickensian times. Brick walls, whitewashed, hanging in dust and cobwebs, nails knocked in the joints between the bricks with all sorts of things hanging on them, some of those items hanging on those nails looked like they had been there five hundred years or more. I used to grease the pulleys that drove the leather belts that made the machines work. I was taught how to repair the belts when they broke, it was fascinating to me, learning the old fashioned way of working and repairing items that had been used since the year dot, well the early eighteen hundreds I would imagine. It was much harder than it looked getting things level, and make do and mend, nothing at that firm was wasted, they were very frugal. I thought they were mean at that time when I worked for them, I can see now I'm older that every penny counted.

The room that really fascinated me was the degreasing room; this room had sacks of sawdust in there, which was put in wooden barrels which were turning at an angle with the items to be degreased in them, usually spanners or wheels for roller skates, all metal wheels. This method worked very well but it made a deafening noise as the barrels turned and the metal objects hit each other. Whatever was put in the barrels came out very shiny, it was amazing. The trouble was when working in the degreasing room it turned out the sawdust affected my eyes, I started to suffer with sties on my eyes. My doctor told me not to work in the sawdust, and I took a note from the doctor explaining the problem. I felt like a little school boy taking a note from my mommy. The boss was ok about it; he asked me if I wanted to be a tool setter. "Very much, thank you, sir." I always said 'sir' when I was creeping.

I really enjoyed learning something new. I was shown how to sharpen drills, set presses, how to grind down a press punch when it went blunt. He was so pleased with my work he put me in charge of six presses. That was funny; the six ladies always wanted the best jobs that brought them better wages, and I tried to be fair, but as they say, you can't please them all. One lady started to bring me sweets, one lady fruit, and one, well let's say she tried to touch where the sweets and fruit never touched. It got so I was worried about walking past her. Today she wouldn't be so lucky – I'm not so innocent now.

One day I was setting up a press for punching out blanks for spanners, the shape that came out looked like dogs bones. "Ok Ann, you can go on this press now." I'm not sure why I remember her name. After about eight or ten minutes of her working on the press I heard such a bang, I ran to see what had happened. Poor Ann was in tears, I calmed her down and told to go and have a cup of tea. I had forgotten to tighten the bed down, what a terrible mistake it was, a new punch and it had a chunk out of it. I very quickly put it on the grinder and sharpened it back up. I must have ground five years worth of work off it, I set it up as quickly as I could and the boss never knew it had happened. I put Ann back on it and told her it was an old bed and it had a crack in it so I had replaced it with a new one. She was ok, and then I booked her extra work so she didn't lose any money. I never did make a mistake like that again, I checked twice every time I set up a press.

Next day I was talking to the boss and he said, "I like your time keeping and your work is good. About six weeks after that I handed in my notice; new horizons here I come. I have to say, it was bad news for any firm to take me on.

Putting the metal stamped out shapes into the barrels with sawdust shovelled into them all the grease was removed, they came out really shiny.

KUNZLES

It was one of those days I didn't care if I got a job or not, I suppose it was because I wasn't responsible enough, I don't know. I was walking down Garrets Green Lane, hands in pockets, not a care in the world, you would have thought not caring that I was rich or I had lots of money, no way, I hadn't a penny to my name. When I saw the Kunzles factory, I thought, well it won't hurt to try; I will ask if there are any jobs going. Just as I was about to walk down the slope a gentleman standing at the foot of it said to me, "Are you looking for a job, son?"

"Yeah," I said, thinking he was a worker there.

He said, "If they say there are no vacancies, tell them they want a worker in the warehouse in Tyseley."

So I knocked on the sliding glass window and asked if they had any vacancies. I was told no. I told them what the man at the top of the slope had said, that there was one at Tyseley. Well, out came the personnel officer, who said I could have the job as a warehouse hand. The wages were £8 per week and I was to wait at the top of the slope for him and he would take me in his car, show me the way and the job. As I approached the gentleman who was still standing at the top of the slope, he said "Did you get it?"

"Yes, sir." He smiled and I thanked him. He turned out to be Mr Kunzle junior himself.

The warehouse was on the side of the canal. I thought, yes this looks ok. Only four men worked there; one did all the export packing, his name was Michael, he had worked there a few years; the other three, Howard the boss, and Bill and Phillip the warehouse hands, all had worked for Kunzles since they were fourteen it turned out. I was told Mr Kunzle created that position for me – I must have looked very down to him; what a kind thing to do. The warehouse was rented off the British Waterways, it was off the road called Wharfdale road. I was taken back to the office and filled in all the forms; I felt good at that

Ladies packing marshmallows

The export department. I'm packing chocolates in foil with plastic coating and sealing it before I pack it in wooden cases moment in time, funny really, I didn't care before if I got a job or not, now I felt pleased.

The next morning I caught two buses to get there. As I walked from the bus I was lost, I just could not remember where the warehouse was. I had my lunch in a paper carrier, it was raining, I still only owned a coat that was too small for me so I couldn't fasten it up, or hide my lunch under it. The carrier fell apart and to be honest so did I. I threw my lunch in a rubbish bin and thought, that's it, to hell with the job; I'm going home – I was very wet by this time. As I turned to walk to the bus stop I noticed a phone box; I rang the operator, got Kunzles phone number, asked them where the warehouse was, and explained the problem – they were very understanding.

When I arrived the men told me to take it easy and to dry my coat by the heater. Come dinnertime they shared their food with me. I liked that day; after all, my job was to load all the lorries that came in with bundles of cardboard boxes, and of course to unload them. The printed boxes that they put the cakes into for the shops were for their famous cakes called showboats, a chocolate case filled with cream and decorated. I have a very sweet tooth but I just could not eat those cakes. The cardboard boxes had codes on them so we knew what size to send back to the factory – ax ½ ax and many more funny codes like that.

When it was quiet they put me to work in the export department, I loved it in there. I had to use silver foil with a film of plastic coating on it, this I used to wrap up boxes of chocolates, then with a soldering iron, I sealed all the folds I had made. I can smell that melting plastic now as I type. Then with the right size wooden crate, I lined it with tar paper, placed the tin foil wrapped chocolates in the crate, I then put wood shavings or wood wool as we called it, all around the parcel for further protection. I then nailed on the lid and with a stencil I stencilled on the name and the destination. I then put four steel bands around the case so no one could lift the lid. Those chocolates went all around the world, I loved that job.

After a few months of working there I got married on the 23rd December 1961, it was going to be the week before, but Irene's dad asked if we would change it to the week after as his two sons and Irene's young sister were booked at his firm's Christmas party on the 16th. That week leading up to the 16th I got a throat infection, I could not even swallow or say a word, so if Irene's dad hadn't have asked us to change the date I could not have got married, I could not have said I will. The good Lord smiled on us that year that's for sure. It was a very bitter cold day; on the 23rd December 1961 I was warm with love though.

On my return to work after Christmas it was still very cold and icy. I repaired the bike I had made up from the tip all those years before but my then wife didn't want me to go to work on my bike. "Don't worry," I said, "I will be fine; anyway we can't afford the bus fares." We had five shillings, that's all we had, 5/- between us – nothing in the bank. I had never had a bank book at that time in my life, sounds like I'm old, I was only eighteen. Any road up, I cycled through Shard End, Lea village, through the Mackadown. When I got to the Meadway I cut through the housing estate I did a right hand turn – the bike went right, I went left, and my bike stopped in the middle of the road. As I tried to get up I kept slipping back down, the road was a sheet of ice and it was on a hill. A car turned the corner, all his windows were iced up, and all he had to see out of was a little round circle. His face was pressed up to the windscreen so he could see where he was going. He spotted my bike, and skidded all over the place. That's it, I thought, he will squash my bike. He stopped about two inches from it, so I avoided that road till all the snow and frost had gone.

As I was now married and only earning £8 it wasn't enough for us to live on. I had done one year and I loved the job, I never had a day off all the time I was there – when the day ended I never wanted to go home, it was a fantastic place to work for, but we needed money to live so I got a job just around the corner at a bed factory called Slumberland. My wages were doubled, £16 per week, so very reluctantly I left. I never felt that way ever again about any of the jobs I had, and as you will see, I had many.

SLUMBERLAND

After leaving Kunzles, now that job I loved but the pay was low, I started working for a bed company known as Slumberland. At Kunzles my wages were eight pounds a week, but I had just got married so I needed more money. Slumberland started me on at sixteen pounds a week, which doubled my wages from my last job. In those days you didn't get full wages until you were twenty one, they considered that to be the coming of age.

Slumberland was just around the corner from the warehouse that I worked in for Kunzles, that was Wharfdale Road, Tyseley; Slumberland was in Kings Road, Tyseley. I told my then wife I had got a new job with double the money, but she wasn't surprised, I had had a few jobs, even at the tender age of eighteen. I rode that old bike that I had made up from the tip to work, so I never had to pay out any bus fares.

I reported to a Mr Beddows, he had the right name to work at a bed factory; well it amused me at the time. I hadn't a clue what job they were going to give to me; I was taken all around the factory and shown all the different departments. "Well, young man, I think seeing how you are a big fellow I will put you loading the lorries with the bed springs." Oh, good, I thought, I will be working outside. Just inside the bay was a big vertical machine; twelve completed mattress springs were placed in that machine and squeezed together, then with pieces of wire threaded through them and twisted the springs were easier to move as one lot. My job then was with another helper, we would wheel them to the lorry then with hooks we dragged them on to the lorry – it was very heavy work, by the time we had loaded the lorry we knew we had done it. I think those springs were sold to other companies because they hadn't the machinery to make the springs. When the lorry pulled away we had sometimes a little breathing space. I used to go all round the different departments, it was fascinating to watch the different operations, plus I used to help myself to the different size screws, in those days screws were expensive. I loved to learn about different things in life, maybe that's why I've had so many jobs. When no lorries were expected I had to sweep up the yard and drive a forklift truck. I didn't drive till I was twenty but I picked up driving that forklift with no bother, another string to my bow I thought at that time. (I've thrown that bloody bow away now, ha, ha!)

If you worked over, the wages officer always went round asking the reason why and you had to explain, overtime was a rare happening in the week but one was expected to work Saturday mornings. One evening I was messing with my push bike doing a puncture, so I thought I would be clever and clock out at fifteen minutes after five, the next afternoon the wages officer came to me and hit the roof! I was accused of fraud, threatened with the sack and court, and all for fifteen minutes. The foreman was called and I explained about the bike and said I forgot about clocking out. The foreman was asked if I was any good or should I be sacked; he stuck up for me so I was told never to let it happen again – as if I would after all that!

Saturday came; it was my first anniversary so I asked Mr Beddows if I could go early so I could go up town to get my wife a silver bracelet she had asked for specially. It was all hearts joined together; it cost thirteen shillings and sixpence 13/6. "Yes, ok, seeing how it's your anniversary. I will clock you out at twelve midday." So that was done. It was H.Samuel's last one as well. Every year after that I bought a silver charm for our anniversary, which she put on the bracelet.

While I worked there I got a new cot mattress for my new son at only a third of the price.

One day out of the blue, and it wasn't planned, I handed in my notice. Well I got fed up. You are irresponsible, I hear you say; yes, I was, I would have to agree with you there; to be honest I think I still am.

CONCENTRIC

This firm was based in the Erdington area of Birmingham, on the Tyburn Road, just up the road from where Spaghetti Junction is now. They made transmission parts for cars. If that firm was around today they would be had up by the health and safety body.

I was on a milling machine, milling parts that were obsolete, for old cars, classics they call them now. Talk about going back in time, if you were seen talking to anyone the foreman told you off, and you even had to tell them when you needed the loo; it was like being back at school.

One afternoon I was told to go upstairs to work, to go on a drilling machine. There were lots of machines and lots of women working up there – now that I didn't mind. As you got to the top of the stairs the room was filled with oil mist from floor to ceiling. "Ain't that bad for you?" I asked the foreman.

"It ain't done me any harm, as it? I've been here for years."

I was breathing that oil mist in all afternoon; I only worked in there that once I'm glad to say. I wonder if those ladies health suffered in later years. They no longer use that building, I wonder if they moved somewhere else or if they went bust. I only lasted a couple of months there, now there is a surprise, eh?

On the machine opposite mine worked an old school chum, his name was Michael and he was telling me he had a moped for sale and would I be interested in buying it as he knew I had no transport. As I was talking to him the foreman spotted us and shouted, "Stop talking and get back to your machine." I'm a married man with a child, I thought to myself, I'm not at school now; I will not be spoken to like a child. A few days after, I did buy the moped and travelled to work on it. One lunch time I thought I would go out for a ride on this lovely new toy, I got a bit carried away and ended up at my cousin's house in Aston. Needless to say, that afternoon I did not return to work. Next morning I was asked what had happened to me the previous afternoon. I told the foreman a lie, that I had got lost and couldn't find my way back, to which the foreman said," Aston is only down the road."

"I know," I said to him, "but I don't know this area that well."

He just kept moaning at me, so I told him to, "Lick em on – I'm off."

So my dear wife once again went short of money. Writing this I can see just how much of an idiot I was, yes, and truly irresponsible, I can see it now, I couldn't then.

TWO BUILDING FIRMS

On A very cold and frosty morning I went to the then closed down Castle Bromwich aerodrome; they had just about started what we now know as the Castle Vale housing estate; Bryant's, if my memory serves me right were the builders. I went to the site agent's office and made enquiries about a job.

"I need a few labourers, are you interested in that?" the foreman asked me.

"Oh yes," I replied.

"Have you got your cards with you?"

"Yes," I replied.

"Oh good, that makes a change. I've been told not to start anyone on without their cards; hand them in to the office then see the store man."

Office? It was a little shed. I did what was asked of me and went to the stores, and I was given a second hand pair of wellies, a pick and a shovel. Did you know every time a building firm set up a new site whoever started on that site got a pair of Wellingtons that some other person had worn before – three or four different people could have worn those same Wellingtons, many hours of people's sweaty feet in them, and now I was wearing them. What I did was to say they were leaking. I did that till I got a new pair; mind you that didn't work every time. Any road up, all building sites in those days did that, I wonder if they still do. So I was taken to the very first foundation being dug out by hand, yes by hand, we have come along a bit since then, they now have mechanical diggers. I went into the hole where six Irish men were swinging their pick axes to loosen the soil then shovel it out. As I said, it was a very cold frost bitten morning. I swung my pick at what I thought was a powerful swing, but on contact with the soil it made a little dent in the ground. Right, I thought, I will show you who the master is. I swung that pick with every ounce of strength I had and to my surprise another little dent. There was a Polish ganger walking round this trench, well foundation, shouting come on, come on we have to get this done today! I never liked working under those conditions. I was working on the first foundation to be dug out on the Castle Vale estate. I picked up my shovel, threw it out of that hole, the pick followed it, and I followed them both. "What do you think you are doing?" I heard a voice shout after me.

Turning around I just shouted, "I'm off!" I handed my wellies, pick and shovel back to the store man, then into the office I went. "I've packed it in."

The young man looked at his watch and in a shocked voice he said, "What's the matter?"

I told him, "I don't like people shouting out orders."

"I don't know how much to pay you," the surprised looking pay clerk said.

"Don't worry about that," I replied, "just give me my cards back."

So that was that. I walked across the road to another building firm known as Wimpey's, I was told this means we import more paddies every year – an Irishman told me that; I've never known if he was joking or not, I've never ever tried to find out. This building firm Wimpey's was on the Chester Road, it was their main office. I went to the reception and asked if there were any vacancies. I was taken to the yard foreman.

"Yes I could do with a lad to work in the yard, would that be ok for you?"

"Yes sir," I replied with enthusiasm.

"Right, go to the stores, get a donkey jacket and a pair of gloves and a scraper then report back to me."

I did what he asked. He said, "See those two silos, go and scrape all the concrete off them, sand them down then go to the stores and get a gallon tin of yellow paint and paint them."

Silos are filled with cement, when a lever is pulled it releases a measured amount of cement to be used in the concrete. It was a great job, easy, not like digging holes, and I had a nice warm donkey jacket to wear. I worked hard and the foreman was very pleased with me.

I was the only Brummie there in that yard at that time. I was driving the dumpers moving items, all sorts of things, it was great. I was alone, the men only talked to me if they had to. One morning a boy straight from Ireland was put to work along side of me, he was very nice, well brought up, excellent manners, he put me to shame. We got on so well I was asked to look after him. Every now and again he took out his rosary beads. His name was Michael. Once he found his feet he got in with the other Irish men and he started to work alongside them, so once again I was alone.

Three and a half months passed and I went to see the foreman – he was a very nice man, very easy to talk to and he treated me very well.

"I wish to hand in my notice," I told him.

"Oh dear, are you sure, Dave?" he said. "Now the weather is better it will be much easier in the yard from here on in."

"Thank you," I said, "but I want a change."

"Ok, son, if you ever decide to come back you, can have your job back."

Well, on my travels once again; it was always an adventure to me to start a new job.

MARSH AND BAXTER'S

Marsh and Baxter's, now this was a different type of job altogether. I was taken on for two weeks; this trial period was to see if I was any good. I was taken all around the factory by the supervisor to see all the different operations from slaughtering the pigs, to the curing of bacon and making lard – it was a fascinating and wonderful experience, so different to what I had ever done. I found the slaughtering of the pigs a little disturbing being an animal lover, so I kept well away from that department.

I was shown into the lard room. "This is where you will be working; what do you think?"

"Yes I would like to work in here," I told the supervisor.

"That's fine, we start at six am. I know it's early but we have had to do it that way because of the car factory down the road, it was chaos when we knocked off at the same time as them so we start early and finish early." That was a body blow to me; I found getting up in the mornings a real problem, plus I hated going to work. "Are you still wanting the job, son, you look a little doubtful?"

"No I'm ok with it. I look forward to learning all about this side of life, it's all new to me," I told him.

"That's what we like to hear at Marsh and Baxter's," he said. "Right, see you in the morning then."

The next morning I was given a pair of white Wellingtons, two white coats and an apron, and a little cap – the cap of course was to prevent hair getting into the lard. They had a room to get changed in. No matches, cigarettes or food of any kind was allowed in the abattoir – or slaughter house to anyone who is like me and had never heard the word abattoir – well anywhere inside the factory. The changing room was across the yard from the factory. I was taken to see the foreman of the lard room, a quiet spoken man, nice to work with, John was his name. The vat where the lard was refined was sunk on a lower floor; it was two levels, top floor then down six steps to the bottom floor. The vat was round and six foot across and five foot deep. The top of the vat was level with the top floor; there was a rail right across the top floor, when leaning over it the boiling lard could be viewed. It got to twice the heat of boiling point, so I was told. My job was to fetch the trolleys full of the pig skins with lots of fat on them, throw them in to a very big mincer that was fixed over the vat, and then fill the vat with water that was very hot. Then the foreman turned on the steam pipe which heated the vat to twice the heat of boiling point; this melted the fat off the skin, which turned to lard – there was a big paddle turning all the time it was boiling. The foreman set a timer so he knew when to turn off the steam, and we piped the lard into tins which were already in the fridge, one pound tins that customers bought after it had been delivered to the shops, and six pounds tins which some shop keepers had delivered like this and then they would cut, weigh and wrap the amount the customer had asked for.

First thing every morning when the vat was full and rendering, me and the other lad would get the tins from the fridge that we had filled the day before, bang them upside down on a steel table, then wrap them in the greaseproof paper. We had a trolley with a wheel on each corner, the sides were two foot deep and six foot long made of aluminium, and very light. The trays could be taken off the wheels, they were stackable, and we always had two trays. When we had filled the top tray with the lard we had just wrapped – we always timed it so the deck foreman went to have his breakfast, this left the deck and the fridge deserted – we would empty the top tin fast as the bottom one never had anything in it, and we could hide whatever we wanted in the bottom one – we always had a frozen chicken – when back in the lard room we tied a piece of string to the chicken, put it in the vat and it cooked in no time flat; we did that every day and it tasted good. One day it fell off the string and got rendered down with the lard. When the vat was emptied it left the scratchings, we shovelled them in to sacks, and they were then sold to a firm who salted them and put them in little bags, the type you always see in pubs (public houses).

One day I pushed a trolley load of skins that had been left or forgotten about, and as I was throwing it into the mincer I was looking at the end

Burning the hairs off the pigs then scrubbing them clean before they are dipped in boiling water

Taking the warpped lard to the deck fridge so it can be put on the lorries to be delivered to the shops for sale seeing all the strings of meat coming out, the patterns fascinated me. When I looked into the trolley, to see how much skin was left to throw in, I could not believe what I was looking at – thousands of maggots! I had been mincing up maggots by the thousands, how long that trolley of skin had been there I have no idea. When I say thousands that is no exaggeration, I had minced over half the trolley load, so I went to the hygiene man who looked and said, "I will take a sample out of the vat when it's at its top heat." So I was told not to put anymore in to the vat but we poured it into the tins as normal. Next morning we wrapped it and it went to the shops as normal. Two days later the hygiene man came up to me and said, "That sample I took hasn't bred any bacteria."

"It's a bit late now," I said, "it's gone to the shops and sold by now."

So I told my wife, "Don't buy any Marsh and Baxter's lard, it's rendered down maggots." They say what the eyes don't see – how true that is.

When we cleaned down we used a very hot steam gun, it made the room spotless. It was like a skating rink, with a push off the walls we could slide right across the room with no trouble.

As per usual, after three months I handed in my notice, time to move on. Mind you, I did go to see the boss and said, "I have changed my mind; can I stay?"

"All right," he said. But the next morning I was half an hour late and he told me he had changed his mind and said I wasn't wanted any more. Do you know I was shocked he made me leave, I thought at the time, what a cheek, he doesn't deserve to have me work for him anyway. He did that firm a favour did he not?

REMPLOY

Remploy, in Garrets Green Lane, is a firm mostly for the disabled; why not, I thought it might be an interesting job. So into the office I went. A very pretty young lady slid back a glass window, I always remember a pretty young lady. "Can I help you young man?" she asked.

"Have you any vacancies please?" I asked, half hoping she would reply with those words I loved to hear, 'no sorry'. I hated working, especially inside a factory. "Please wait a moment, I will ask the personnel manager," she replied.

A very smartly dressed gentleman came out and said, "Are you looking for employment?"

"Yes sir," I replied.

"We need a charge hand, would you be interested?"

"Yes sir, what are the wages."

I can't remember what he told me but I do remember it was fantastic money for a youngster. "Are you interested?" he asked again.

"Oh yes," I told him.

"Ok, good," he said to me, "could you start tomorrow?"

"Yes, no problem," I replied.

"Good. Wait there, I will tell Mr (I can't remember his name) he is the boss; he will bring the forms to you for you to fill in."

This is too good to be true, I was thinking to myself, and so it was. In walked the boss and he took one look at me and said, "I'm sorry, son, I can't offer you the job Roy offered you, he gets carried away sometimes, I can offer you a job as a checker, checking the work that the workers produce and weighing items they are pressing out on the hand presses, but the wages are less than half of the wages that were offered you in the first place. However, you can get advancements if you prove your worth." What the wages were I can't remember, but I accepted the job and started the next day.

I had no idea what any of the items I was weighing were for, and I wasn't really interested. The building was full of disabled workers but I do remember a lad who wasn't disabled who just constantly chatted up the young girls and the older ladies. I tried hard to like that job, but after a few days I hated it so much; I was bored stiff. So after only two and a half weeks I handed in my notice and it was back on the building sites for me...

HUMPHREYS AND GLASGOW

Humphreys and Glasgow was a firm that were based in the north of the country, Yorkshire or Lancashire, I really can't remember. I was earning thirty pounds a week when most people were only earning twelve to fifteen pounds a week. This company's main role was boiler work.

I started work with this firm on a Monday morning, and travelled by coach with my brother in-law, Thomas White, who had got me the job. We caught the coach every morning at 7.15 to Hams Hall Power Station where I was labouring for this company. It was the easiest job I've ever had. We were carrying fire bricks, and those bricks weighed nothing at all. We also mixed the fire clay, which was really easy. I got there a little early each morning to load up the boilers with the fire bricks and the fire clay, and the rest of the day was really easy; about every two hours I would take a few bricks and some clay up to the brickies and then I just dossed about. Sometimes I would get on a dumper and race the regular dumper driver around the site – it's a wonder we weren't sacked!

One afternoon the ganger called me and said, "Come with me Dave, I've got a nice easy job for you." There had been a load of insulation rolls delivered, and he asked me to take them into a shed and stack them. They were made from fibre glass wool, I had never heard of this wool before. I made that job last all afternoon, this is money for old rope, I thought to myself – then the itching started. I did all that throwing around without a mask, which as we all know now, fibre glass can be lethal to our lungs; I wonder if it will affect my lungs when I'm old, ha ha, I'm 67 years old now. I know I am old; mind you, I'm still very active; well I'm slowing down a little nowadays...

When the cement lorry arrived with a few hundred bags of cement, the work force disappeared; the bags in those days weighed one hundred weight each; you knew you had earned your money when the lorry was empty.

The first morning I started work for that company, as we arrived in the coach it was like a bombed building site – someone in the night had set fire to all the shanties, or should I say large sheds. All the workers made a claim for a pair of wellies, a donkey jacket, coats, shoes, boots and many other items. I was standing by the site foreman, he was laughing and he said, "Those shanties wouldn't hold that amount of gear!" In groups they were taken to the town and they picked up the items they said they had lost in the fire, it really was the best paid job ever.

The boss asked me to stay on and travel around the country with the firm; all the regular work force lived in caravans with their families and travelled with the firm – that was their lives. I declined his offer even though he offered me a new caravan and a lorry to tow it with. A week later I handed in my notice; he tried to talk me out of leaving but I left anyway. Why I get bored so quickly I have no idea.

REDCROFTS TIMBERYARD

This firm is situated in the Castle Bromwich area of Birmingham where it still is to this very day. They sold and delivered all types of building materials, and I visited this yard to purchase one hundred weight of sand when I spotted the notice for a driver. Why not, I thought, if I need any materials for my house I would get employees discount, so I saw Mrs Phillips who was the owner along with her husband; they hadn't been trading long. I was shown around the yard and the saw mill by Mr Phillips.

The manager at that time was a man named Terry; I didn't like him at all. Well, I got the job. I was delivering all around Birmingham; the areas I mostly delivered to were Tile Cross, Castle Bromwich, Lea Village, Shard End, Coleshill and Coventry, in fact anywhere that I was told to go to. It was an easy job most of the time; I used to shovel the sand onto the lorry, seven shovels to the hundred weight. Yes it was all shovel work in those days, that has always stuck in my mind, seven shovels for one hundred weight. When two tons of sand was ordered that was a lot of shovelling. The bags of cement were in hundred weights, that weight wasn't a problem for me at the time; it would be a different story now I might tell you. I think it was all the bags of coal I carried as a child that built up my muscles, well it earned me pocket money, carrying coal I mean, not driving a lorry. (Oh I don't know though ha, ha!) Mind you, those 3x2 paving slabs gave me a problem.

One day I hadn't any deliveries to make so I was asked if I would work in the sawmill, I was delighted – I love wood and the smell of it. The pitch pine when cut was my favourite wood, when cut it gave off a perfume second to none; I used to sniff the off cuts like I was addicted to it, I even cut the off cuts up in to fire wood just so I could smell the wonderful aroma it gave off. I worked on all the machines, but the planing machine I liked the best; I was even allowed to serve

Redcrofts Timer and Building Materials Yard

customers from time to time – what's so special about that? I hear you say. If you left school as illiterate as I was, you would understand, every little step in life, like serving a customer, to me was a great achievement; it didn't come easy, I really had to workhard at life to make things work.

I worked alongside a young lad who had just started there, he was fresh out of school, Malcolm was his name and to this very day he is still there, he now is the manager of that sawmill. I just can't imagine working in the same place for all those years, that ain't me, that's for sure.

Next to Redcrofts was a club called The Rob Roy where many stars stayed, such as Cliff Richard, on their way to venues; previous to this it was run as a nursing home for many years. The owner of Redcrofts ran this as a club. I remember seeing Cliff Richard's photo on the wall. I asked Mr Phillips if I could help to knock the wall down. I helped to put in an R.S.J. but for the life of me I can't remember what they used that club for after it was finished, but what I do remember was when Barrows store closed down Mr Phillips bought all the carpets that were in their restaurant, I went and took it up, and the stair carpet. I have no idea where he used it in the club; I would imagine it was put in the main club room it was a sad day to see Barrows in such a mess with people tearing things apart. When I first met my wife who was my girlfriend at that time, she worked there as a junior clerk for a lady named Miss Lycett, who had worked there forever. I sat in that restaurant a few times while waiting for my lovely girlfriend, but it always seemed too posh for me. I drove back to the yard with all the carpets and I carried them into that Rob Roy club because it was empty, then back to my deliveries. After the Rob Roy club the name was changed to the Bel Air then the Chesterfield Night Club and the Westbank Club and it was demolished around 1977 and purchased by M.F.I. which has since been sold and is now owned by Aldi and Halfords.

The yard manager, Terry, I just could not get on with at all, so I knew I wouldn't last there. Saturdays I worked in the saw mill till I had a delivery to make. I made some terrible errors when cutting the timber. One error I remember was a customer asked for a piece of pine six feet long by two inches wide and a half inch thick. I got a long plank of pine, cut a strip off it, planed it to size, then cut it to two foot in length, I have no idea why I did that, I covered up that mistake and cut another piece. I did learn a lot about timber and the building trade while I worked there though.

There was one incident I must tell you about. A customer phoned up complaining they hadn't had their delivery – it had been forgotten by the manager so Mrs Phillips asked me to do three deliveries after closing time. I agreed; they were C.O. D. cash on delivery, I did the deliveries, when I got back I knocked on the then bungalow (it's been demolished now and made into a car park) and Mr Phillips came to the door. I gave him the delivery notes and the money, and he pushed a ten shilling note in my top pocket and said, "There you are, Dave, have a drink on me." I thanked him and went home.

The next morning Mrs Phillips told me in a stern voice, "I was ten shillings short in the money." I explained that Mr Phillips had given me the ten shillings and said have a drink on me. She shouted at me and said I shouldn't have taken it and I was not to take any money off him again. I heard her telling him off as well; she was the boss and the driving force in that business. I must add though, a good boss to work for.

No matter how hard you worked it was never good enough for the yard manager. He had no idea how to run a team, so one day I told him to lick em on – I'm off. Not long after that he was sacked. Over the years I have used that firm to buy many items of building materials. Actually I do now from time to time.

M. I. C.

M. I. C. – Midland Industrial Cleaning. I worked casual for this firm many times at different factories all around Birmingham over the years. The work varied quite a lot; this firm stripped, cleaned and polished floors, even polished office furniture, swept up roads, cleaned out acid pits, you name it, if it needed cleaning they would do it, it was a fascinating job.

My younger brother, John, had his cards in with them for a while, but I worked for them cash in hand on a daily basis; if the job was for a couple of weeks or so, they paid me weekly.

One time I worked at King Street in Hockley at the Lucas factory. It was in a room that was air pressured, and as you opened the door there was a very strong wind that came at you. The reason for this was to keep out the dust as they did the sealed head lamps in there for the cars, so no dust could be allowed to get into those lamps. I used Kex mops; I constantly pushed that dry mop around that floor, I wasn't allowed to lift it, it had to be kept flat on the floor. Those mops were about three foot long and about ten to twelve inches wide.

It was only ladies working in that room, and they just loved to embarrass me and make me blush, they were quite naughty at times, one or two were even very rude. I wish it was these days, at my age I would surely make them follow through with their comments – shame I was so young, ha, ha. After working in that room we went outside, my brother John, his co worker and I, and we swept the roads all round that factory.

Some time later I went to Shirley, Lucas's had a works there where they painted the starter motors bodies and other items mostly black. Me and John cleaned the spray paint booths. I worked all the weekend for five pounds and was grateful for that little extra money.

Across the road were the laboratories for Lucas; we worked in there cleaning the stairs, which was such a waste of time as we were cleaning them with liquid polish. There were dozens of people walking up and down every minute of the day; how were we supposed to polish stairs while this was going on? Trouble was we weren't allowed to go in there at night. The windows were cleaned inside and outside from cradles; they had a special team for that job, I would have done it if I had been asked.

At one stage I was given a van to pick up all the men in the mornings; I used it to run my family around, well it was a perk as the saying goes. We all had some cleaning items to take home, with the boss's permission, of course. I did so many different jobs for that company, always cash in hand, and I really enjoyed the variety of jobs and travelling all over the country. I was asked many times if I would go on the cards for them, I always refused, if I had been on the cards I wouldn't have been able to take as many liberties as I did; they say variety is the spice of life – I certainly had a lot of that spice.

BRYANTS

Working on a Bryant's site in the Birmingham area that was once a horse racing course known as Bromford Racing Course (which is now a housing estate) I was a general dogsbody driving the dumpers, running the hoist on the twenty story block of flats, taking all the materials such as bricks, mortar and timber. The hoist was driven by a diesel engine known as a Lister; the drawback to driving that hoist was there were no telephones or bells to let me know when one of the many workers wanted to use the hoist, so to attract my attention they would throw certain items to hit my hard hat – it was very dangerous, if I looked at the wrong moment I could have lost an eye. I did complain to the site agent about the dangers but nothing was ever done to change how that hoist was operated; in those days they got away with health and safety regulations.

There is one time I remember well. I had sent the hoist up to the ninth floor so one of the lads could put a barrow full of rubbish onto it. I thought I heard him shout "OK, Dave," but it wasn't him shouting, it was someone fooling about, so I started to lower the hoist. Unfortunately he had only pushed the wheelbarrow half way onto the hoist, but luck was on his side as he managed to jump back onto the scaffolding, one hand holding on to a scaffold bar and one leg dangling in mid air. The wheelbarrow fell backwards down the gap at the back of the hoist and fell to earth at what seemed like a hundred miles an hour! House bricks, dust, pieces of timber, even lumps of concrete came raining down hitting the scaffolding on its way down, forcing it to fly about twenty yards across the site. I shouted "Take cover!" as I tried to escape the flying debris. The wheelbarrow hit the ground and it seemed to be following me as I was running to avoid getting hurt. The site agent saw what had happened, came over to me and started to shout; I soon put him in his place. I told him where to stick his hoist, and with a red face he got off his soap box and in a calm voice he asked me if I wouldn't mind going around the site with a wheelbarrow and picking up all the rubbish – he even said please! I had to do this with a new wheelbarrow, I might add, the barrow that had fallen was unrecognisable as a wheelbarrow.

It was coming up to dinnertime, about five to one, when I was stopped by a little Irish man, it turned out he was the scaffolding foreman. "I have seen the site agent about you," he said to me. "I told him I want you to work for me scaffolding, and if you agree I will give you scaffolder's rate of pay."

"Yes, I agree," I said to him with no hesitation. Those words, more pay, was music to my ears.

"OK, start after dinner." Well to be honest I got a little big headed, well I was still young.

The foreman handed me a belt with all the tools hanging off it. I swaggered to the hut (known to building site workers as shanty) for my dinner with my brother in law Tom, who worked on the same site. The look on Tom's face when he saw me walk into the shanty with my belt of tools! "What are you doing with that belt of tools Dave?" he enquired.

Chest out, I proudly replied, "I'm a scaffolder now." With a smile and a chuckle from Tom no more was said, we ate our lunch then back to work. I was really looking forward to learning a new skill.

The scaffolding foreman showed me how to set up the start of the scaffolding around a new block of flats that had the first floor finished so the builders could start on the second floor. As the days and weeks went by I was doing each lift on my own, and all was fine till I got to the eighth floor, it was then I realised I wasn't keen on heights. I was getting very nervous with one foot on the outside scaffold bar and the other foot on the bar going into the building and no safety harness, and nothing between me and God's green earth. I was attempting to put in an upright to start the lift for the ninth floor, when a gust of wind rocked me; I dropped the scaffold bar and fell but just managed to grab the bar I was standing on. The bad language that was shouted at me from the workers below me I can't print but it was very bad, I can tell you! My heart was pounding and I was shaking with fright so I crawled off that scaffolding, I ran down the stairs to the ground floor, I found the little Irish scaffolding foreman and said my favourite saying when I wanted out of a job, "Lick em on – I'm off."

The foreman was very softly spoken and very much a gentleman. He smiled and said "I understand, Dave, you would get used to it in time, I was the same as you when I first started. I don't want you to leave, you are strong and a good worker." he said to me. My mind was made up; my nerves were still dancing. "Well if you decide to come back and give it another try you can have your job back," he told me. I thanked him and that was the last time I ever saw him, or did any scaffolding.

That evening I walked into my house and said to my wife, "I've told em to lick em on."

With a painful look on her face my wife replied, "Not again!"

I was very irresponsible in those days (well nothing has changed to this day).

PARKINSON COWEN

Parkinson Cowen were based in the Stechford area of Birmingham, 33, Iron Lane was the entrance to their personnel office. They made gas stoves, or as my mom put it, gas ovens. As I walked in to that office I remember thinking how quiet it was, mind you, nearly all personnel offices were like that and I've walked in to so many it could be in *The Guinness Book of Records*! Any road up I had my interview, all went well and I was told to start the next afternoon as they did a three shift system. I hated shifts as much as I hated being locked up in a factory, mind you, I hated work, as I have said before, I really did hate working, being told what to do so they could make money out of me. I was put on the back end of the ovens where all the panels that had been painted were baked. As they very slowly went along on the conveyer belt, my job was to take them off the conveyer and place them on a trolley that had separate compartments to keep them from getting scratched – they were very hot as you can imagine. When the trolley was full the heat was overbearing; I then pushed them to a cooling down area.

The foreman was Polish and not a very nice man, he was always moaning, nothing suited him. I did one shift on afternoons and one night shift, but on my last night I was so fed up with that foreman I told him to, "Lick em on – I'm off." Well there is a surprise. I worked with the maintenance men in this shop shown when it was being changed around. I was working for Clyde Hopkins then.

Showing inside the factory.

Parkinson Cowen factory.
Again sadly demolished.

POTATO PICKING

My younger brother John and me, we used to go potato picking on the farms around the Warwickshire and Staffordshire counties when we were between jobs, which was nearly all the time, well for me it was. I used to pick him up in my car early in the morning, and travel all around the countryside looking for jobs on the farms. It was usually wet and cold but we loved it, we used to have such laughs. John had a very infectious laugh, and when I was driving and we were telling jokes or saying something that made him laugh, he would start me off – I laughed till I had tears running down my face. So many times I had to stop the car because the tears would blur my vision.

We were very careful when going onto farms as they all had dogs; we were chased many times and John would split his sides laughing at me running to the car terrified. One time we went to a farm in Tamworth, a man named Kingslake owned it, we were led to believe he was the richest man in Tamworth at that time, and was the head of the organisation in that area known as The Round Table, they did a lot of good work for charity. Any road up, we went on to his farm or small holding as it was, and there were piles of hard core so we went to the barn where there was a man working; he gave us the job of levelling out the hard core, and stamping it down. It took a couple of days doing that job; we were paid one pound ten shillings a day and we were very happy with that. I asked, "Have you any other work?"

"Have you ever picked potatoes?" he asked.

"Yes, we both have," I replied, "many times, but we ain't as fast as the ladies," I explained.

"Can you drive a lorry?" he enquired.

"Yes, no problem," I told him.

"Oh good; in the morning you pick up the ladies from here and take them to the field. I will show you where, you follow me."

I did that every morning and it was fun; this potato picking was different from the norm, he had a trailer on the back of the tractor. It was a new machine; we all stood both sides of the trailer, and as the spuds came up on the conveyer belt we had to pick out the spuds which were put on a different belt to a shoot and into a trailer that was running alongside of our trailer, both being pulled by a tractor, it was really much easier than bending down and dragging a sack behind you and picking up the potatoes from the ground – that was back breaking.

We left that farm as the work dwindled and went to another farm that was very short on labour. We started working, picking potatoes at eight a.m., the ladies came at nine a.m. and by ten a.m. they passed us – they made us look like children. The boss asked me to get the tractor and trailer and load up all the bags of potatoes that we and the women had picked; that was a relief, I can tell you, I wasn't any good at picking potatoes, men cannot pick like the women can. When the trailer was loaded with the sacks of spuds, my brother and me took them to the barn and emptied each bag onto a conveyer and they were added to a mountain of spuds already there. After lunch as I was driving the lorry on to the field there was a black bag in the mud, I ran over it, it turned out to be one of the ladies lunch bags with her flask in it, she went barmy, said her husband would beat me up! He didn't, I'm glad to say.

When we went to another farm the next year, it was in the Tamworth area, next to a pub called the Jolly Sailor; I went with my brother in-law, Len. The farmer was John, and he showed us how to clamp up potatoes in the field, the way the Victorians did it. First we dug a trench, lined it with straw then piled up the potatoes in the shape of a tent, then put straw in thick layers all over the potatoes, then we put a tube in the middle of the pile on the top, that was to let the heat out, then we covered it completely with soil, all by hand, a shovel full at a time, that's what is known as clamping up. Those spuds lasted all through the winter, and when they were needed the end of the clamp was opened up, they took out the amount of spuds that were needed, and then closed it up again – the mice loved it, it kept them warm in the cold winter months.

Working in the country side potato picking

There was a time when John and I worked on different farms because they had a position for only one of us. John worked on a farm that was run by two brothers, I worked across the road on another farm, Blackgreaves Farm it was called. I was driving a tractor and loading the trailer with the sacks of spuds, John was picking spuds. I finished at five thirty, jumped in my car and went to the farm where John was but they were all behind, lots of sacks still in the field waiting to be loaded up on to the trailer. John said, "I can't leave, Dave." So rather than leave him, I offered to load the sacks onto the trailer. By this time it was pouring with rain and I hadn't any rain wear, neither had John, but we worked till seven o'clock. We were like drowned rats and covered in mud – strange thing was we enjoyed it! The farmer gave me ten shillings, so that made me happy, I thought I was doing it for nothing to help my brother out to get him finished and get home. The farmers liked the way I worked so they gave me a job. We both worked there till all the fields had been picked – working on the land gave me much satisfaction. Again cash in hand. All the farms we worked on did more or less the same work, well we did anyway. I enjoyed my brother John's company, and we always worked well together.

RAILWAY

I loved the railways from my very early childhood. The railway goods yard that was in Rupert Street in the Nechells area, that is where I worked for British Rail; I was trained up to drive the three-wheeled scammels known as the Iron Horse. I loved the training; in that yard we had to back the trailers in the tightest of gaps, and I wasn't allowed to touch the sides of anything at all with the trailer. When backing it between two parked trailers, there was only half an inch either side, and you weren't allowed to touch the sides of the other trailers parked there. I practised and practised every day, it seemed it was never going to happen. Then one day it changed, it all fell into place, and then with no effort at all I did it every time. It was the same for all trainees, I've watched them many times, one day they are struggling, then the next day something clicks and it all falls into place.

The next step was taking the cab and trailer (some call the trailer a drag and the cab a unit) on a test. The railway, the L. M. S., that is, had their own examiners, government trained I was told. Onto the road I went. The one thing I was taught when learning to drive a car was never let go of the steering wheel; with an artic you have to do just that, so down the hill I went, and when the examiner shouted "Now!" I hit the foot brake, put on the hand brake and kept one hand on the wheel. "No," he said, "your driving is first class but in order to make sure you don't jack knife, and you didn't that time you kept it straight, I want to see you let go of the steering wheel, hit the foot brake and pull on the trailer brake and the hand brake together, if you don't do it I will fail you." So down the hill I went again. When he shouted, "Now!" I left my hand on the steering wheel. "Right," he said, "yes it was straight, you didn't jack knife. Right, switch off the engine and take a deep breath and relax for one minute. Your driving is excellent, your reversing between the trailers was perfect, in fact it was so good

I thought it was a fluke, that's why I got you to do it again, it was just as good the second time but you have to let go of the steering wheel, so I'm going to let you do it again, but I will fail you this time if you don't do as I ask."

So down the hill I went, saying to myself, let the wheel go, let the wheel go, over and over I said it. "Now!" he shouted. I hit all the brakes. "There you go, I knew you could do it," he told me, and made me do it again. I had no trouble at all the third time, and he wrote out my licence there and then.

After he had gone I practised doing it on my own, I did it every time, no problem at all, but to be honest when I had to do it one day for real, I kept my hand on the wheel and I didn't jack-knife. I asked a few drivers and they all said they kept one hand on the wheel. I was so pleased when I passed my test, the one thing I haven't told you is when being trained to drive those three wheelers, it always made one sweat and no one knew why, it just did, it happened to everyone and I was no exception; when backing the trailer up to the deck you had an audience of the drivers that had gone through it themselves, they stood along the wall and laughed, they had it done to them and so did I.

This is exactly how it went, when starting to back the trailer on to the deck the steering wheel would be gripped far too tight, you could see the knuckles going white and the cab would swing from left to right because the steering wheel was moved too much, then the cab would hit the trailer so the wheel was swung in the other direction, which completely ruined the whole exercise and the sweating got worse – being watched of course made it worse. I did my share of laughing at them then, they did it to the raw recruits.

I did most of my driving around the Hockley area of Birmingham. It was tight going around Hockley, that's the jewellery quarter and the parking around there was horrendous. Vehicles parked both sides of the road and down the centre. I worked over every night and did collections from the jewellery quarter to make my wages worth picking up. The sheets that I received from the customers were about a foot square and there was a dozen all joined together, this happened with every collection I did. By the time I did my last collection I had what looked like a mountain of paper; it filled the passenger side of the cab. As we entered the yard just by the entrance, there was a little brick built hut, we gave all the paper work to the man who put it through a copy machine, I then took it to the main yard office but before that I would run into the yard, swing the vehicle round and back it to the deck. I was supposed to put the trailer brake on first but we drivers never did that because there was a slope, only slight but it was enough to stop the trailer from rolling away from the deck. The far end of the deck you couldn't do it as there was no slope to the deck. I didn't know this at first, so I backed up the deck, pulled the trailer release lever which dropped the trailer legs, and as I pulled away all the drivers were laughing – the deck hands had to run after the trailer as it rolled across the yard! I got a good telling off for that; well I never did it again, not at the far end of the deck anyway.

One morning I was told to go to Lawley Street depot, which was a really big railway yard. A young lad about the same age as myself came over to me and said, "Are you from Rupert Street?"

"Yes," I replied.

"Oh good, I've been waiting for you, I want you to deliver house to house with catalogue goods." He told me to back up to a deck where all the parcels were piled high, and lots had fallen into the bay where I was told to back up.

"There are parcels on the floor; I can't back into there," I told him.

"Don't worry," he said, "just run over them." So I did. I could hear the crunching as the parcels got run over. It's no wonder the railways were losing money, I thought to myself. At Rupert Street that never happened, that yard was kept very clean and tidy.

The following day I was sent to Curzon Street railway yard, with twelve rolls of carpet underlay. I roped it up but was too lazy to sheet it, and when I arrived at Curzon Street, to my horror I had lost a roll – I never even noticed it dropping off! I immediately dropped the trailer and run all over the route I had taken. I never found that roll. When I got back to the yard two railway police were waiting for me, and I was questioned for two and three quarter hours – I was being accused of stealing it! It all came to nothing in the end, but I was more careful after that.

So I was put back on delivering empty wooden cases and tea chests all around the jewellery quarter. There was a small firm there that asked me for empty cases with no names on them – I got 3d, three pence, for every case I took to them, and that paid for my breakfast most mornings. The rail company just wanted them gone. At the end of each day I parked my cab in the old stable block right at the bottom of the yard. I worked there almost twelve months! One morning I turned up for work as normal and for reasons I cannot explain I handed in my notice. I was given a form to fill in, on it they asked reason for leaving, but I just didn't know what to say so I put 'fed up' I did miss doing that job for a while but I soon found something different to do.

I drove these three wheeled Scammels in 1963

To be carried in, but not attached to, the Statutory Driving Licence

BRITISH RAILWAYS

B.R. 14114

L/M REGION

MOTOR DRIVER'S DOMESTIC LICENCE

Name (*in full*) D.A.PROSSER

Station ASTON Dept. GOODS

Groups of Vehicles authorised to drive	Examiner's Signature	Date
Group 1. Rigid vehicles up to and including 3 tons capacity	[illegible]	15-11-63
Group 2. Articulated vehicles up to and including 3 tons capacity		
Group 3 Rigid vehicles exceeding 3 tons capacity ...		
Group 4. Articulated vehicles exceeding 3 tons capacity		
Group 5. Tractors including articulated tractive units when used for hauling drawbar trailers		
Group 6. Road Motor Horse Boxes		
Group 7.		

The holder of this licence is not authorised to drive any type of British Transport Commission vehicle other than stated above and is not authorised to drive on the Highway unless he holds a Statutory driving licence.

My licence for driving British Railway vehicles

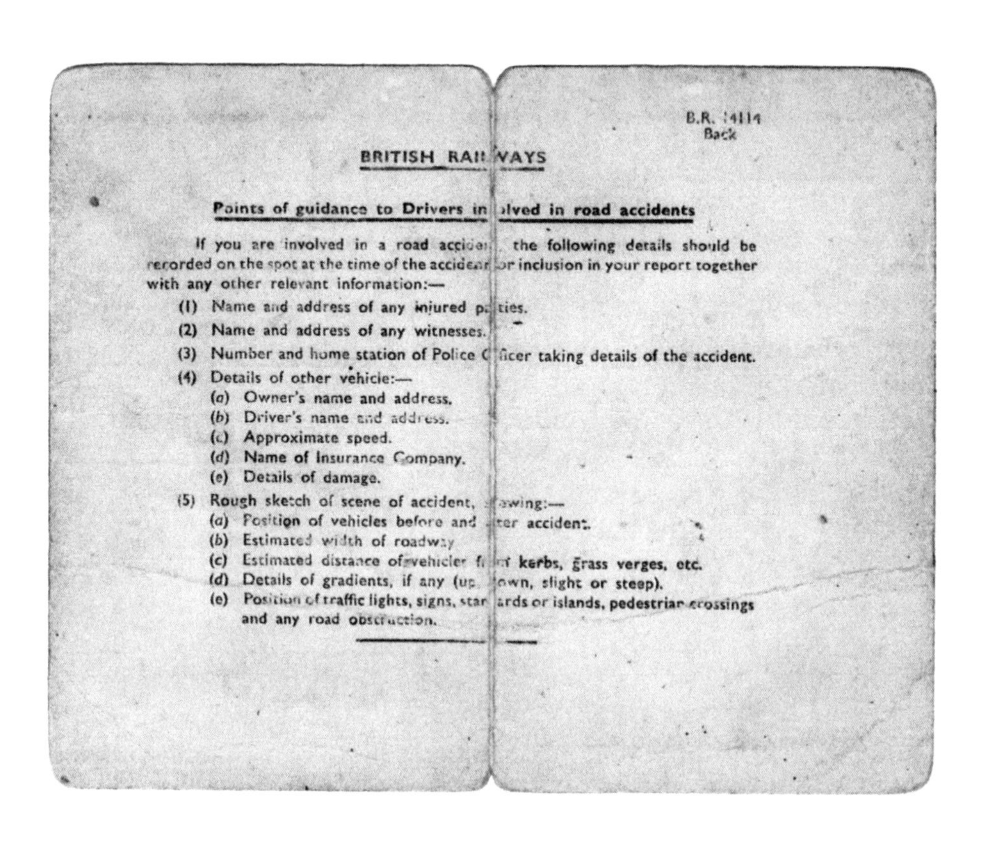

B.R. 14114
Back

BRITISH RAILWAYS

Points of guidance to Drivers involved in road accidents

If you are involved in a road accident, the following details should be recorded on the spot at the time of the accident for inclusion in your report together with any other relevant information:—

(1) Name and address of any injured parties.

(2) Name and address of any witnesses.

(3) Number and home station of Police Officer taking details of the accident.

(4) Details of other vehicle:—
   (*a*) Owner's name and address.
   (*b*) Driver's name and address.
   (*c*) Approximate speed.
   (*d*) Name of Insurance Company.
   (*e*) Details of damage.

(5) Rough sketch of scene of accident, showing:—
   (*a*) Position of vehicles before and after accident.
   (*b*) Estimated width of roadway
   (*c*) Estimated distance of vehicles from kerbs, grass verges, etc.
   (*d*) Details of gradients, if any (up, down, slight or steep).
   (*e*) Position of traffic lights, signs, standards or islands, pedestrian crossings and any road obstruction.

My licence for driving British Railway vehicles

ALBERT HALL

After leaving the railway I went to a builder's type yard. The builder contracted to the council doing pavement and curb stone laying. The owner had three tipper lorries and five gangs doing the laying of the pavements – tarmacing mostly, they were doing away with paving slabs at that time. Any road up, this firm was in Cooks Lane, Tile Cross. The builder asked me where I had been working and what I had driven. "A three-wheeled railway scammel."

He looked a little shocked. "So have you ever driven a tipper, young man?"

"No, but they must be easier to drive than an artic lorry," I replied. "If it's got wheels, I can drive it."

He looked at me funny. "OK, there is the lorry, go to Kelynmead Road. There is a gang tarmacing, go and shovel up all the rubbish they have created onto the lorry and come back here with it."

So I did as I was asked. I pulled into the yard a couple of hours later. "You managed that all right then. OK, take it to the rubbish tip in Meriden." He gave me the directions; I did that, and got back to the yard. "Good," he said, "you can have the job; start tomorrow."

The next morning the JCB loaded the lorry to capacity with broken slabs. I was given the address, it was a private house. I remember that day well only for the reason it was a very cold day. The boss sat in a shed that was his office, opposite the door which was wide open, and all he wore was a vest – everyone else had donkey jackets on and gloves. The area I was given to take the load of slabs to was Sheldon, near the Birmingham airport. I knocked on the door. "Good morning, sir," I said to the man of the house in a cheerful voice and shivering at the same time. "Broken slabs."

"Great; tip them on the garden for me please."

"No problem, sir."

So I did as he had asked. When he saw the amount, he had a fit. “I only ordered five tons!” I’d tipped about twenty tons. “What the hell am I going to do with all this?” he asked, rubbing his head with both hands.

“Sell it to your neighbours,” I told him.

“Ah, that’s a good idea, I will do just that,” he said.

Some weeks later I went down that road and it seemed nearly every garden had broken slabs in them. Not much different went on there, every day the same, delivering slabs and curb stones to the gangs and shovelling rubbish on to the lorry and tipping it at the tip. Guess what? Yes, three and a half months later I handed in my notice.

BOOTHS

Booths are an aluminium company in the Kitts Green area of Birmingham, making tin foil for wrapping food up and also making many other items from aluminium.

I went into the office and asked as I usually did, "Have you any vacancies?" To my surprise they said, "Yes, we are looking for an overhead crane driver."

"I've never done that before," I told the personnel officer.

"That's OK," he replied, "we will train you." Great, I thought, another string to my bow. "Do you mind having a medical now?" he asked me.

"What, right now?" I asked.

"Yes, we have our own surgery, and a doctor."

So off I went to a very clean surgery. All was well until I was told, "You need glasses, son." I was shocked and disappointed. I had never been in an overhead crane, I've driven cranes, I've used overhead cranes, looking up at it with a hand control, but I've never sat in one. I'm retired now and I've no wish to sit in one. Any road up, I got my glasses and went back to Booths with them. I was told they didn't need an overhead crane driver any longer as that vacancy had been filled, so they offered me a job running a machine. It was a rolling machine, rolling out square blocks of aluminium; these were about three feet square and a foot thick. It rolled it backwards and forwards till it became tin foil. It was a very clean work shop. When I was interviewed for the job by the foreman he asked me, "Now are you sure there isn't a better job out there that you would prefer to do, before I set you on?"

I told him there wasn't. It was a three shift system; I started on mornings, then one week afternoons, then the night shift for five nights. It was summer and I longed for the great outdoors, not to be locked in a horrible factory, so on the last night shift being a Friday, I handed in my notice. The foreman wasn't very happy with me, he said, "I asked you if there was a better job out there, didn't I?"

I got my wages and started a new job on the Monday, delivering bread door to door for the Co-op bakery. Their bakery was in Stechford, the same bakery I had worked at as a boy and as a rounds man; it's a wonder they took me back. I wasn't there long; as usual I got bored and left after a few months.

CARS

After leaving the Co-op bakery I signed on the dole. I hung around the garage where my two eldest brothers had started up their own business doing car repairs in Orphanage Road, Erdington, Birmingham. It was a very large wooden building with enough space to house, or should I say park, four cars. I was just sixteen at the time, so I watched and tried to learn as much as I could for when the day came that I would own a car. I picked up a few tips. I passed my test when I was twenty, by that time my brother Donald had bought a shop in Booth Street, Handsworth, and altered the back yard into a car repair work shop. They sprayed cars, did de-cokes on car engines, and under-sealed cars. They dug a pit – it was a good work shop.

They had converted the shop premises into flats; I had a downstairs flat there after I got married. I used to help fetching spares for the cars that were being fitted with new parts, and I did a little spraying. Sometimes I did a few de-cokes and regrinding in the valves. I was taught a lot by my eldest brother Donald, in fact it was him that taught me to drive. I passed my test after my ninth lesson – twelve hours of driving then I passed my test! Donald taught many to drive. When I passed my test my brother sold me a ten hundred weight van for fifty pounds, of which I paid twenty five pounds back and that took nearly six months to pay that, so he let me off with the rest of the payments because I was always helping him. I travelled all over England in that van; it had windows put in the sides and two seats in the back. It started to burn oil so I took out all the necessary bolts, stood on the wings, and with a rope round the engine and around my neck I lifted that engine out, rested it on the wing, with my wife steadying it till I got off the van, then I put my arms around the engine lifted it off the van and placed it on the ground. No way could I have done that with today's engines. I remembered what my brother had taught me, so I striped the engine down, put in new rings and new big end shells, (those are on the ends of the pistons) that's what most people did that were not well off – poor is a better word.

My car driving licence, 1963

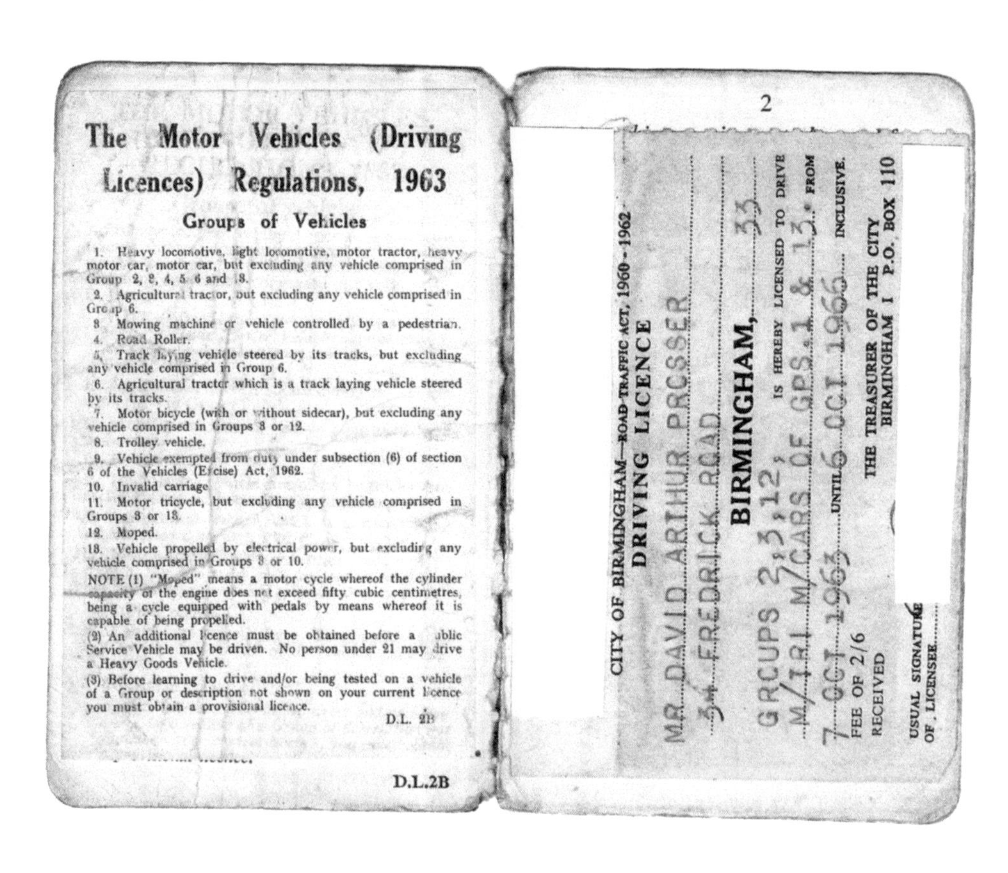

The Motor Vehicles (Driving Licences) Regulations, 1963

Groups of Vehicles

1. Heavy locomotive, light locomotive, motor tractor, heavy motor car, motor car, but excluding any vehicle comprised in Group 2, 3, 4, 5, 6 and 13.
2. Agricultural tractor, but excluding any vehicle comprised in Group 6.
3. Mowing machine or vehicle controlled by a pedestrian.
4. Road Roller.
5. Track laying vehicle steered by its tracks, but excluding any vehicle comprised in Group 6.
6. Agricultural tractor which is a track laying vehicle steered by its tracks.
7. Motor bicycle (with or without sidecar), but excluding any vehicle comprised in Groups 3 or 12.
8. Trolley vehicle.
9. Vehicle exempted from duty under subsection (6) of section 6 of the Vehicles (Excise) Act, 1962.
10. Invalid carriage.
11. Motor tricycle, but excluding any vehicle comprised in Groups 3 or 13.
12. Moped.
13. Vehicle propelled by electrical power, but excluding any vehicle comprised in Groups 3 or 10.

NOTE (1) "Moped" means a motor cycle whereof the cylinder capacity of the engine does not exceed fifty cubic centimetres, being a cycle equipped with pedals by means whereof it is capable of being propelled.
(2) An additional licence must be obtained before a Public Service Vehicle may be driven. No person under 21 may drive a Heavy Goods Vehicle.
(3) Before learning to drive and/or being tested on a vehicle of a Group or description not shown on your current licence you must obtain a provisional licence.

D.L. 2B

D.L.2B

2

CITY OF BIRMINGHAM—ROAD TRAFFIC ACT, 1960-1962
DRIVING LICENCE
MR DAVID ARTHUR PROSSER
34 FREDRICK ROAD
BIRMINGHAM, 33
IS HEREBY LICENSED TO DRIVE
GROUPS 2,3,12, M/TRI M/CARS OF GPS 1 & 13, FROM
7 OCT 1963 UNTIL 6 OCT 1966 INCLUSIVE.
FEE OF 2/6 RECEIVED
THE TREASURER OF THE CITY
BIRMINGHAM 1 P.O. BOX 110
USUAL SIGNATURE OF LICENSEE

My car driving licence, 1963

CLYDE HOPKINS

This firm was situated just down the road from where I lived at that time in the Stechford area, just across the road from the Atlas cinema, where I used to stand outside with my friend Trevor asking the people if they would take us in to the cinema. They had an office next to the snooker hall where me and my other friend Johnny used to waste a few hours every Friday after knocking off for the weekend from Cooks the clock face makers.

Clyde Hopkins was a maintenance firm; I did all sorts of jobs for this firm and worked for them on and off a few times. This one time they gave me a job on nights at the Lucas factory in Great Kings street in the Hockley area, and I was assigned to the maintenance department. I worked with a Scotsman, who was working making all sorts of things out of sheet metal. He was a very soft spoken man who would only make things that were perfect, he was a perfectionist and very skilled. I learned a lot from him; he taught me how to make a tool box to put my spanners in, in fact I made two, one for me and one for my brother Donald, I also made a pair of car stands for Donald.

There were six men that worked in that department; they all got their heads down at midnight on makeshift beds in the office – the daytime foreman's office. All those men had worked on nights for years; one had done thirty five years, the youngest had done nineteen. Anyway, one night after midnight when I was quietly making one of the tool boxes, I was told I was being too noisy and had to get my head down come midnight or he would get me sacked. So I was sent to bed, ha, ha – it's true, I was. It would have been easy for him to do that as well, as I didn't work for Lucas's direct, I was supplied labour, it was an easy way of earning a living, it's no wonder firms went broke. Why I was there I had no idea, I did nothing for Lucas's that would have made the slightest of difference me being there or not, all I did was to make things out of metal for myself. Mind you, I was useful once, yes, only once. The maintenance man from the main factory who had nothing to do with this side of the firm needed a hand to fix a conveyer belt that had broken in the main building. So I was woken up at one thirty (yes, one thirty, what a nerve, eh?), it was an overhead conveyer, so I was close to the ceiling, it was hot and I sweated like a pig, (do pigs sweat?) it was so uncomfortable – it was very high up. I was taking out bolts by the dozens, it was steel rollers with a rubber belt running over them and the belt had broken. It was repaired then put back; it was harder putting it back trying to line up all the holes to re-bolt it all back together.

After working there I was transferred to a steel mill in the Black Country. I can't remember the name of it, but what I do remember is it was like going back once again to the Dickensian times – braziers glowing with red hot coke, and the fumes from coke was awful; it brought back the memories of my childhood when my mom burnt coke because it was cheaper than coal. The taste in one's mouth was awful (did you like that, *one's* mouth, that's not me talking – in my gob I would have said as a youngster). There were boxes surrounding each of the braziers for the men to sit on for their breaks. The factory was cladded in corrugated tin panels, there were more holes in the roof and the walls than in the braziers, and it was plain to see why they had braziers all around the factory floor.

I worked nights at that factory, and I was given the job of looking after a machine that looked like it could have been used in the *Doctor Who* films. I have no idea what the machine did or was used for, all I know is every now and then it would throw out a blue green crystal; there were long plastic pipes all around the top of the machine and they came down the outside of it and attached in the middle of the machine. It was round, about ten foot high and the round plastic tubes were about two inches across. Air went through them and every now and again a tube would come off at the top of the machine and made a loud hissing noise, so I had to push it back on. When there was a small pile of crystals I shovelled them into a wheel barrow, took them outside and shovelled them onto a mountain of crystals – what they did with them I have no idea.

There was a similar machine next to the one that I was looking after, and it was attended to by an elderly man, well he looked old to me, I suppose he was worn out by that time, working in those conditions. About four feet away from those two machines was a brazier with an armchair – that was the old fella's – a couple of boxes and a bench. I asked the old fella if I could use the bench. "That's OK," he said. "The armchair is mine." So I pushed on a tube that had come off, shovelled the few crystals that were there and threw them on the outside pile. It was now twelve midnight.

I said to the old fella, "I'm getting my head down for an hour, OK?," He pulled a face, and shrugged his shoulders, so I rolled up my coat, put it under my head for a pillow, lay on that bench and fell asleep.

I woke up with a start, it was a quarter to six in the morning and I knocked off at six. All the tubes were off the machine hissing like mad and there was a very large pile of crystals around the machine. I pushed all the tubes back on, and it took three barrow loads of crystals to clear the machine, it was now just after six. I was putting on my coat when the day shift man who looked after the machine came in. "Was everything OK with the machine through the night?" he asked me.

"Yeah, no problems," I told him.

"That makes a change," he replied. I never went back there again so I have no idea if that machine with its pipes off all night did any damage to whatever it was making. The next afternoon I phoned up the office and handed in my notice, telling them I didn't like working nights – me work; now there is a laugh for you.

A WORKSHOP IN HANDSWORTH

My brother Donald asked me to help him for a short while in his new car repair shop; he was in partnership with some of his work mates at that time, they all worked at Fisher and Ludlow's, later to be renamed B.M.C. Apart from making the tea, running errands and fetching paint to spray the cars with, Donald taught me how to strip an engine and do a de-coke at his old garage as well. We had fish and chips every Saturday dinnertime.

I even towed cars in from wherever they broke down, but well before that Donald was teaching me how to drive. He was a very good instructor. I had nine lessons; seven were for two hundred yards up the road to the pub, the Lea Village Tavern. It was on that car park where it all clicked into place. He went inside the pub to get a pint, and as I sat in the van, I thought to myself, if I let the clutch out slowly, when I start to move, if I dip it I will stop. So I started to drive backwards and forwards. That's easy, I thought. Donald's brother in-law, Gordon, was sitting on the wall watching me. As Donald came out with Gordon's pint in his hand, Gordon said, "It's just clicked, Don."

"About time," he replied.

So seven lessons, then the other two were four hours long. One day he asked me how many lessons I'd had.

"Don't know," I replied.

"It's seven. I know this Dave because every time you back off my driveway you take a paling off the gate." So I counted them and sure enough there were seven palings on the floor behind the gate. As we went down the road, I told him he didn't need to shout. "Is that so?" he said. "OK I won't shout anymore. So he quietly said, "Stop here." I carried on. "OK," he said, "stop by that tree." I still went past the tree, so he screamed, "Stop!" I hit the brakes and stopped dead. "There you are, see, I asked you to stop twice and you didn't; when I shouted stop, you did. You are stubborn, Dave, that's why I shout at you – you only obey my instructions when I shout. So now I want you to change up and down the box from this corner to that one and see how many times you can do it."

Well I got to third gear when I reached the corner. "You can only do one up the box before you reach the corner," I told him, so he got in the driver's seat. He went up and down that box a lot of times.

"Now believe what I tell you." so I did. I failed my first test, but I passed on the second one, so all in all I had eleven driving lessons, that's counting the two tests. Since then I passed a test for my H.G.V. Class Two, and advanced driving tests for the army to carry chemicals, poisons and hazardous materials. I've also drove a coach, troop carrier, a crane and many other different small vehicles. Driving changed the way I could earn a living. Variety, yes, I had that, when in between jobs I helped my brother in his garage. Thinking about it, I was always between jobs.

PONDSFORDS

Pondsfords was a maintenance firm based in Handsworth, Birmingham. They contracted out their labour force to any firm that needed any and all types of machinery moving or transporting anywhere in the country. They did all kinds of steel erections for machinery to stand on, and staging as well. My job was a fitter's mate, known now as a semi skilled engineer. I travelled all round the country; I liked the freedom of this job.

One firm I remember well was Pirelli Tyres, it was very noisy. There was a young girl in a very long room with machines that looked to me like very large sewing machines. The room was spotlessly clean. There were lots of those machines in rows and that young lady looked after them on her own, and all day long she sang at the top off her voice. She always seemed very happy.

After that I went to many different factories, I even went to a power station called Hams Hall. Why we went there I have no idea; we did ten minutes of welding on the first day, the rest of the week we did nothing. What confused me was they had their own maintenance work force that did all the welding themselves. They weren't very nice to us I remember; I don't think they wanted us there. When we walked in on the morning and said, "Good morning," we never got a reply. Were they trying to tell us something? Yes, I think they were.

As per usual I got fed up, handed in my notice, and got a job at Factory Plant Removals doing the same type of work, but as a driver as well. This firm was in the Handsworth area of Birmingham at that time.

FACTORY PLANT REMOVALS

I lived at number 78, Downing Street, Handsworth in Birmingham. The rent was fifteen shillings a week (15/-) but it went down to fourteen shillings and ten pence (14/10d) when the area changed to Smethwick. The house was directly on to the pavement. All the houses at the back which would have been up the entry into a yard had been demolished, and my house had a demolition order on it. I got a job just around the corner in Brearly Street, with a firm known as Factory Plant Removals. They moved heavy machinery anywhere in the country to whatever factory or site they were asked to move it to or from; they worked out of town quite a lot.

Not long after I started work there I was sent to Blackpool for a week. We took heavy machines to a factory there and bolted them in place. I cannot for the life of me remember the name of that factory, but I enjoyed the experience, it was the first time I had bolted down a machine. The machines were something to do with glass fibre, as the firm made car bodies in glass fibre – they would be wouldn't they? I do say daft things at times, ha, ha. It was in the middle of winter, it was raining all the time I was there, and the winds were so strong it was hard to walk; very tiring.

After the first week the boss asked me if I would go back with him, as he needed a driver for another job. I drove back in a Commer van, I had to work the wipers by hand because the electric motor had burnt out, and the steering was all over the place. I drove one-handed all the way back from Blackpool to West Bromwich, then off the M6 to the yard in Handsworth. I would get locked up these days for driving such a bad unroadworthy vehicle – that van should have been driven to the scrap yard.

When I arrived back at the yard I picked up a Guy lorry, it was a seven man crew cab, it had a big jib on the back of it, and the wheels were as tall as me, the same type as Pickfords used at that time. I hooked up a low loader trailer and went to Salters factory in West Bromwich, they were moving to new premises, I think it was in Willenhall; anyway it was in the Black Country. I had to stand up to drive that vehicle; if I sat down I could only just about see over the steering wheel.

I worked all the weekend at that Salters factory getting those machines out, we used metal tubes as rollers. As the machine went forward I would take the back roller and put it in the front of the machine. It worked well till we hit uneven ground, then with six feet long solid steel crow bars we bared the machine along till it came in contact with the rollers again. I really enjoyed the physical side of that job, it kept me fit and strong and sometimes knackered, fit for nothing; that type of employment was defiantly no good for weaklings. When we got those machines outside we put chains around them, hooked them up to the crane, or jib as we called it, which was on the back of the wagon, then slowly moved to the trailer and loaded it on to the trailer. Those trailers are known as low loaders. We got four machines on at a time, with heavy duty chains they were safely held in place, all seven men got into the cab and I drove it to Salters new factory. As I had passed my test on those railway three-wheel Scammels I was ok reversing, mind you low loaders are a different ball game as the saying goes. Well I backed it into the yard perfectly, but on the second load I made a complete mess of it, I just couldn't do it, so I asked the other driver if he would back it in. "No problem, Dave." He never took the mick, he just did it for me; he was a nice man to work with.

On the Sunday there were no buses running to West Bromwich, so I had to use my car, well in those days that area was a ghost town on a Sunday, no cars running, nothing. I hadn't any road tax on my car, but I thought it, will be all right; I will hide it round the side road behind the foreman's car. I had only been working for twenty minutes when the foreman shouted, "Dave, there's a copper wants a word." I explained my predicament to the officer but he would have none of it – he only looked about fourteen,

I asked him how long he had been an officer. Two days on the beat, it's no wonder he wouldn't let me off, he was earning his brownie points. I got a fine of twenty five pounds; all that hard work

I did went to paying that fine. I was allowed to pay a pound a week, which was a lot out of my wages every week, I mean, my rent then was only fourteen shillings and ten pence a week, so it hurt to pay a pound for my fine. I know I should have taxed my car; I was saving up for it, that's why I was working all the hours God sent, as the saying goes.

The next job we went to was in the Aldridge area, at a factory called Crabtree, they were doing the new tableware called Melamine, I was told it was a new material on the market at that time. We did to be honest borrow one or two items of that new tableware to take home. We were installing a brand new lathe into their redesigned work shop, I wasn't the driver that day, an Irishman named Billy was. He picked up the lathe off the trailer and I asked him if he was going to put the hydraulic legs down and put the skates under them, as those skates allowed the cab to move forward away from the trailer. "It will be OK," he replied, "it's not that heavy." As he moved away from the trailer, the weight of the lathe tipped up the cab; it hit the ground hard and broke some of the casting off one corner of the lathe. Billy had to let the cables from the crane down to lower the cab to the ground. A little red-faced he said, "I didn't think it was that heavy." The boss blew a gasket, well both bosses, theirs and ours. Billy nearly lost his job; he was one of those people that thought he knew it all. Then to make matters worse the machine wouldn't go through the door so I took the door off, I had done that so many times on other jobs, it was the norm, and we did what was needed to do to get the job done. We had the machine halfway through the door; it was going through just right with the door off, when we noticed all the workers at the factory were in the yard. We all thought there must be a fire or it was a fire drill, when a loud mouthed man came up to us and demanded to know who had taken the door off. "I did," I told him, "but I will put it back on as soon as the machine is clear of the door." He had called a strike because of little old me.

"I want you all off the premises," he was saying in a very loud voice.

"Why?" I asked.

"Why? Why?" he bellowed. "We have a carpenter and that's his job. You are not a qualified carpenter are you?"

"No, but we always do things like take out windows and remove doors." I was apologizing, almost kissing his feet.

"People like you can put skilled men out of work!" He went on and on. The management was trying to calm him down, he really did go over the top; talk about power mad, he kept insisting he wanted us off the premises. It took one and a half hours to get him to understand we put that machine in place but we never bolted it down, we were told to leave it. The boss told me some time later that the company claimed off my boss's insurance, and they got a brand new machine. We didn't fit it; I assume they got another contractor to fit their new machine as we never went back there, nor was I allowed to put that door back on.

The next Monday we went to the Aston University to erect a very big ariel mast on the top of it. We had to winch up four twenty feet long tubes, the circumference must have been something like eighteen inches, one at a time. With two cables bolted to the anchor points used by the window cleaners, we used two winches with long handles on them. By pushing the handle backwards and forwards the cable went though the winches one inch at a time. There were four of us, three Irishmen and this little old Brummie, me, we took it in turns to winch up those tubes, it was quite tiring. When at the top, we man handled them to the other side of the roof, and as we got the second one to the roof top, the tall fella shouted as he tried to lift it on his own, "Come on you idiots, this is heavy!"

Little Billy put his hand around the throat of the tall fella till he almost passed out. He was a violent man, little or nothing or anyone scared him, and the tall fella was his mate. He said, "Don't you ever shout like that again or call me an idiot." The tall fella never said a word. I just can't remember his name, the tall fella that is. It took a few minutes for Billy to calm down.

When it was dinnertime we went down in the lift as there were no stairs. I sat in my car to eat my lunch, and just before dinner break was over the boss turned up. "You got two tubes up I see; well done."

"I reckon we could pull those two up together," I said to him, "that would save us time."

Me and my big mouth – when the others came back the boss said, "You carry on up, and I will sling the tubes."

As we were winching up the tubes the tall man said, "This is bloody hard, I bet Norman has put both tubes on, he thinks we are donkeys." (Norman was the boss's name.) All three of them were getting very angry.

We finally got them to the top, and I said, "Well at least we can go home early, it wasn't that bad," hoping they would think, that's true, we can knock off early. I was hoping the boss wouldn't come to see us but he did. As he got out of the lift they ran up to him and started shouting abuse at him. "What the hell do you think we are, donkeys? Why did you put the two tubes on, don't you think we work hard enough?" I could see the boss was getting worried even a little frightened, and by this time I felt very nervous.

The boss said, "Someone told me to." I stood behind the big fella hoping the boss wouldn't see me. "He told me to," he said pointing to me. As they turned to have a go at me, the boss ran to the lift and disappeared, so there I was stuck on the highest roof of the university, no lift because the boss had taken it, and no other way down! The three Irishmen knew how to get me off that roof, but I couldn't fly! I was now very nervous but I thought, I mustn't show it, the three Irishmen were out for blood, mine to be exact. The one man known as Pat had only been in England a week or so. I'm not sure, but I don't think he could read or write, but his farming skills were first class the other two told me.

Pat said pointing to me, "He is going over the edge." They were all so angry I couldn't talk to them as they approached me.

"You're going over," the tall one said, so I ran to the edge of the building, I was dying inside – there is a time in life when a man has to stand and be counted, that time had come for me.

I stood on the edge of that building and said in a calm voice, "I have a grip like iron and I guarantee two of you will go over with me."

They stopped dead in their tracks and the toughest one of them said, "He ain't worth it, come on lets go down."

I was so scared I nearly wet myself. What do I do now? There is only one lift and no stairs. Oh well, I thought, if I get a good beating up in the lift that will be better than going over the edge. As I approached the lift, I said, "Sorry lads, at least we go home early."

I was shaking inside. As we entered the lift Pat, the man that had only been in this country a week, took the fire extinguisher off the wall of the lift and was hitting the top of it pointing it at me. When Billy asked him what he was doing, he replied, "I'm going to spray him with it," meaning me of course.

"Put it back," Billy told him, "leave him alone." He had calmed down by this time. "He is right, we have finished early." But he wouldn't listen; he just kept on hitting the top hoping it would work; what he didn't know (thank God) was he had to take off the cap, and then strike the plunger on the top. It felt like a lifetime waiting for that lift to stop! As the doors opened I shot out of that lift so fast my shoes melted, well you know what I mean! I got into my car, my heart was pounding, I was shaking, and that's as close to death as I ever want to be.

The next morning I went to see the boss in his office – I had a real go at him. "You can sack me if you like; you nearly got me killed yesterday! Why did you tell them it was me? You could have said you couldn't remember?"

"I know, Dave," he said, "I'm sorry but they scared me so I left thinking the situation might calm down without me around."

"Well I ain't working with them again," I told him.

"OK, Dave, you can drive for the other gang." Great, I thought, all Brummies.

One morning a couple of weeks later, I walked into the yard and there stood a man all six feet three of him, looking like he had never had a wash. He was unshaven and he wore the oldest overcoat I had ever seen. He looked poorer than me. He was as broad as he was tall – a real tough looking character. I smoked in those days, I had three cigarettes to last me all day. I lit one up. "Give me a ciggy," he said in an angry voice.

"I've only got two to last me all day," I told him.

He took his hands out of his pockets. "I said, give me a ciggy." He

Getting steel tubes on the roof of the university for an arial scared me to death so I gave him one. Here we go again, I thought, I'm going to hand in my notice. Those types of firms always employed those types of men. When I got home I was thinking, I will hand in my notice in the morning.

The next morning I went to see the boss and said I was thinking of handing in my notice. That same morning that angry man wasn't around. Good, I hope he has packed up, I was thinking.

On that evening I parked up my wagon and the boss called me and said, "That rough looking fella that made you give him a fag, he has been done for murder. When he got home last night his wife was in her friend's house and he wanted his tea, so he knocked on the friend's door, the man of the house came out and said, "She ain't coming out, I'm keeping her here." So the angry man went home, got a big knife and went back to the friend's house. He knocked on the door, and when the fella opened it, the angry man stabbed him to death."

"I've had it here boss. Lick em on – I'm off," and off I went. That's one firm I never missed working for.

WELLMAN INCANDESCENT

Wellman Incandescent was a good firm to work for, based in Cornwall Street in the Handsworth area of Birmingham. When I went for my interview I was asked, "What type of work are you looking for?"

"Anything," I replied, "I can do many things."

"Can you drive a crane or have you had anything to do with cranes? We are looking for a mobile crane driver," the personnel officer said in a doubtful tone.

"No problem," I replied. "If it's got wheels I can do it." I'd learned that by being confident it gave a good impression, so long as you didn't come across cocky or cheeky.

"What did you say?" he asked.

"If it's got wheels I can drive it."

He laughed. "Well for your cheek, come with me." We walked to the bottom of the yard, and he pointed to the oldest crane I have ever seen – it was just steel girders with a jib on the top, a cast iron seat, three wheels, two at the front and one in the centre at the rear, and solid rubber tyres. Boy it was old. Smiling, he asked, "Well, what do you think? He could see the shocked look on my face.

"Yes," I replied, "no problem."

"OK, start tomorrow and bring your P-45 with you and your insurance cards." On the card were stamps. The firm you worked for had to put a stamp on the card, one every week for the whole year, these were for insurance covering you if you were off sick from work and towards your pension when you retire. (Sick notes from the doctor were charged at a shilling (1/-) in those days.)

I started next morning, another string to my bow of life, I thought. Well, I had a shock coming. I drove into one of the workshops, they made lampposts at this firm, and the shock I had when I put my foot on the brake and nothing happened! I gripped the steering wheel

Putting tubes in the works shop to be turned into lampposts.

and pressed down with my foot with every ounce of strength I could muster. I just managed to stop in time as I was about to go through the back wall which was corrugated iron sheets. What have I let myself in for, I thought to myself. The yard foreman laughed and said, "Now you know why the last driver left."

Without road tax I used to take it on the road about once every fortnight. The steering was all over the place – the steering wheel shook from left to right, it was all I could do to keep it something like straight; the engine sounded like a load of nuts and bolts going round in a tin drum, and when it rained I got wet, no cab, no cover whatsoever.

I lived just around the corner from the firm so I went home to dinner. My wife asked me how I got on. She couldn't believe that such vehicles were still being used, actually neither could I. When I first started to drive it, because the brakes were so inefficient I used to slam it in reverse, this was the most efficient way of stopping it. Trouble was, by doing it that way, eventually it stripped the gears. Whenever I wanted to get out of working I did that reverse stunt and it went into the workshop for three days at a time. The maintenance men used to go mad and the language they shouted at me would make your hair curl; I was threatened with annihilation more times than I could shake a stick at.

There was another crane, a modern iron fairy – the driver sat in that crane in his heated cab reading a book. He moved to do a lift about twice, and then it was for only ten minutes. Some days, he didn't move at all, and there was me not a moment to myself most days. Still, he had worked there forever so he had earned that cushy job. One thing I'm sure of, that crane I drove belonged in a museum. Well at least when having conversations with the older seniors about work, I can say if they talk about cranes, I've been there, done that. Yes, it was another string to my bow of life, even though I only did it for three months. Only three months, I hear you say, well that was normally all I could do any job for.

As I was walking home one dinnertime, an elderly gentleman asked me, "Have you been working at Wellman's long?"

"No," I replied, "only a couple of months."

"Do you like it?" he asked.

"It's OK," I replied. "To be honest, I don't like work," I told him.

"I've worked at Wellman's since I was thirteen, I don't know anything else. Don't you make that mistake, do as many things as you can, son, variety is the spice of life." I had already had lots of different jobs, so I was having my variety. Then to my surprise he said, "I suppose you are going home to get your leg over."

"I hope so," I replied, knowing full well I wouldn't.

"Yes," he said, "I can remember when I was like you, son, I used to rush home, I just couldn't wait to get her knickers off." Then with a laugh he said, "I could sit and watch her knit a pair now." That's one conversation I will never forget.

CO-OP BAKERY HANDSWORTH

After leaving Wellman Incandescent I got a job at the Co-op bakery in Handsworth, I doubled up with a rounds man who had worked there from a boy; that's what they used to do, start you on as a boy, then when you became eighteen they trained you up to become a rounds man, then you had to learn how to order the bread and cakes, calculate if the money was correct, then once you got all the items required, how to fill in the rounds book at every call. It seemed hard at first but like everything in life, when you got used to it you could do it blindfold as the saying goes. When the rounds man gave the bosses the OK, if there was a round going it was offered to you, if no round was available they made you work on the deck. I liked that job working on the deck, or if a rounds boy had a day off they doubled you up on that round.

One Monday morning I was asked to do a round as the rounds man was off sick. They gave me a boy that was lazier than me, he was useless. I told him, "Under no circumstances do you drive the van."

"It's only electric," he replied, "I can drive these, they are easy."

"Well, easy or not, you do not drive this electric van," I repeated. Those vans had two very large batteries underneath, one each side of the van almost the length of it. I was delivering all around the Ladywood area of Birmingham, and nineteen per cent of that round was flats. I was delivering to one block of flats, and as I got to the third floor, I looked over the balcony just in time to see the lad getting into the van to drive it. I shouted to him very loudly not to drive it, but he pretended not to hear me. Next to the block of flats was a row of terraced houses, the type with no front gardens. The front door opened onto the pavement, just like the house I lived in at that time, and I watched in horror as he drove up the hill. Suddenly he turned left, mounted the pavement and drove straight into the front door of the house, smashing it open. I ran to him in case he was hurt, but when I saw he was OK I gave him a telling off he will never in his life forget. He was shaking. The front of the van was smashed but I was still able to finish the round. I phoned the bosses who arranged to get the door of the house replaced. The lad kept saying, "Please don't get me the sack; say you did it."

"No way," I told him, "I have a family to support; I'm not getting the sack for your stupidity."

When the bosses asked me if he was any good, I said, "He will be an asset to the company in the future." I was lying, he was useless.

Any road up, almost at the end of that round I knocked on the door of a customer, and a very pretty lady opened the door. "Good afternoon, madam, would you like any nice cakes or biscuits, I have a good selection on the van today?" (I got commission on the confectionery.)

"You must be joking," she said to me, "I've got seven kids."

I laughed. "You haven't, you ain't old enough to have seven kids." (I really thought she wasn't.)

"Oh what a lovely thing to say; you can take me to bed tomorrow, I will show you what real sex is," she told me. I went as red as a beetroot. She laughed at my red face. "I will look out for you tomorrow. What time will you be here?" she asked me.

"About this time," I replied.

She gave a shudder and said, "I will look forward to it."

Well I wasn't sure if I was excited or scared to death. So back at the yard the van went into the work shop. When I got home I told the wife about my day, had my tea, and settled down to watch the television.

A couple of days later I was put on a round in the Kingstanding area, that rounds man was on holiday. It turned out he was the shop steward for the rounds men. The rounds boy was very well dressed and nicely spoken; he was also very cocky and very cheeky. How it worked on a round was like this: he had a little book and he served half the customers; he wrote down what each customer had that day, and on a Friday and a Saturday he delivered to all the customers, while I collected the money. The way I worked was that at the end of every third road I would ask the lad who was my rounds boy, to tell me what each of his customers had, and I entered it into my book. So at the end of the third road I asked him to tell me what his customers had had. He replied, "I'm not telling you and you can't make me."

"it's my money you are playing with here," I told him.

He laughed, "Your money? It's the Co-op's money, not yours."

"If I'm short, it comes out of my wages. If I lose money on this round I will make sure it comes out of your wages, not mine."

"My rounds man is the shop steward, I know what I can do and can't do."

"I'm your rounds man now, and you will do what I tell you," I told the lad. "We always enter all the transactions at the end of the round."

"My shop steward knows how to do this job properly," the lad was telling me.

"You really are trying my patience," I told him.

"I don't care," he said. "I know how this round works, not you."

So I drove to the next road – he was grinning like a Cheshire cat – he thought, I got him, I've won. I was going to get him the sack when we got back to the yard.

In the next road he disappeared for twenty minutes. "Where the hell have you been?" I asked him.

"Having a cup of tea with a customer."

That was it, the end of the line for me. I got out of the van, shut the rear doors, put on the padlock, got back in the van and started off down the road.

"What are you doing?" he asked me, "we haven't finished the round."

"You have, son, I have just sacked you. I'm taking you back to the yard; I've had it with you. When I tell the boss just how cheeky you are and the rude comments you made and refusing to tell me what your customers have had, that's instant dismissal. I bet your shop steward never told you that, did he? And I am going to ask them to hold back your wages in case I come up short."

He went white. "I'm sorry, Dave, I'm sorry, honest I am. Let's finish the round please; I will do all you ask, and tell you what my customers have had when you ask me to. So I turned the van around and finished the round. For the next two weeks he turned out to be the best rounds boy I had ever worked with. Why he thought he could behave like that I will never know – it wasn't his nature, so me shocking him the way I did bring him to his senses.

What's that I hear you asking? Did I have sex with that pretty lady who had seven kids? Well the very next day the checker came out with me asking all the customers if they were happy with the service they were getting, and if the quality of the goods were to their liking. I knocked on the door of the lady with seven kids. "I've been waiting for you; I've got it all ready to give you the time of your life." Then she noticed the boss was with me. "Is that the boss?"
"Yes," I told her.

"Damn, and I was really looking forward to today. OK, I will wait for you tomorrow," she said. "Trust me, you are going to have the time of your life."

The next day I was taken off that round and put to work on the deck because the rounds man had returned to work. Would I have? Well, we will never know.

I went to work for the Raleigh bicycle company for a short while after this job.

I got a new house in Chelmsley Wood, so I left Handsworth and handed in my notice at the bakery, well that's no surprise is it? Some time later I got a job at the Co-op bakery in Stechford, the same bakery I was at as a boy. I was only there two months, so I haven't written about it, nothing to write about that job really.

PITCH AND TOSS

Along the Chester Road in the area now known as Smiths Wood, Bryant's the builders had their compound. There, me and my brother John got a job. We were given a pair of Wellingtons, and a shovel to clean up the site. To start with we dug out drives and levelled out the shale for the pathways. There were no fancy diggers in those days, all the fetching carrying and levelling was done by hand. When the cement lorry and the brick lorry came in, they were unloaded by hand. The house bricks were the worst to unload, none of the labourers liked that job; we used to try to hide so we wouldn't be picked to unload it, but the site foreman knew this, and he knew when the lorry was coming in so he used to round us up before it got to the site. In those days the driver would climb onto the back of his trailer and throw the bricks to us, three at a time. Brick dust went in our eyes and that made one's eyes very sore for a good few days, sometimes even worse than that, the ends of our fingers used to get skinned and bleed, it was like getting an electric shock every time you touched anything. The firm never supplied gloves, no one would ask for any because the other workers would laugh at the person asking. It took about two hours to unload those brick lorries, sometimes even longer. I think that was the worst job to do on any building site.

Any road up, one afternoon we were in a house, me my brother and two other lads, and we started to play pitch and toss – one of us pitched a penny towards the wall, then the others would toss a penny to see if they could cover the penny or land on it, and the one that did land on it would be the winner. He would then claim the coins that had missed. If none of the coins was touching the first coin that had been pitched, we just kept tossing coins till one did land on the first one. Well, we got carried away; we were supposed to be working and the site foreman had been looking for us. When he caught us playing pitch and toss he sacked the four of us. The whole site heard about us and our little game – we were famous for a while.

RALEIGH BICYCLES

Just up the road from my house in Downing Street (no, not number 10, number 78) in Handsworth, was a well known firm called Raleigh, and they made bicycles. Well I went into their personnel department and said my famous speech, it's almost like I invented it I said it that often: "Have you got any vacancies please?"

"We have a position going in the maintenance department," I was told.

"That will do," I said to the young lady.

So out came the foreman, "So you are looking for employment, are you? And where have you worked before, and why have you chosen this firm?"

I hate those stupid questions, they were always looking for silly, clever answers, and I always refused to do that, so I always said, "There is nothing unique about me, I'm just a common person but you will not be disappointed with my work." I remember only twice being refused a job because I wouldn't give clever answers.

"Can you weld?"

"No," I replied.

"Would you like to learn?"

"Yes, I would," I told him.

So he took me to the maintenance shop, and introduced me to the welder. He told him I was starting in the morning, and asked him if he would train me up. He agreed so no problem there. I was shown all over the factory. "Are you happy to start in the morning?"

"Yes."

"Good, I will see you tomorrow then."

My wife was happy; she thought, well, we might get some money coming in for a few weeks.

Well I started, got my leather apron, goggles and face shield. The welder had worked there for ten years, he was good. "The hardest welding is gas welding, arc welding is easy," he told me. So he showed me how to set up for ark and gas welding. "Let's see how good you are? I want you to do some gas welding around eight inch steel tubes, this is the hardest of it all to do." so he did some to start me off, and then I welded that tube all the way round. "Well that's as good as I can do."

Pointing to some other tubes he said, "Those two tubes, let's see if it was a fluke." I did those as well as the first one. "You are a natural at gas welding," he said, and he showed me vertical gas welding, that's a little tricky but I was ok. "Well, arc welding you will do with no trouble at all." I found I couldn't do it, I kept getting the rod stuck. "I don't believe it, gas is the hardest to master, yet you took to it no bother, ark is easier and you can't do it, I'm amazed," he said to me. "Keep practicing, it will come to you," but it never did. I went all over that factory with my gas bottles, never the ark welder.

One day in the maintenance department I overheard the welder talking about his wages, I was shocked; I was getting the same money as he was and he was training me, I knew nothing. It was good for me, but not fair on him. I can't remember what my wages were, I remember lots of what was said to me and what I did when at each job but for some unknown reason I can't remember figures like the wages, I've tried, but I just can't remember. I started to get bored after two months so I handed in my notice. Well the forman had a go at me about my time-keeping so yes, I said "Lick 'em on – I'm off!" and off I went.

MORRIS COMMERCIAL CARS

Morris Commercial Cars made the Morris Minor car and the van. This factory was situated in an area known as Bromford. Just across the road from this factory is Ward End Park where my dad fished for many years and I played as a child, and went to as a teenager on a Sunday in the summer in the hope of meeting my dream girl. I never did (ah). The Morris Minor was a wonderful and sturdy little vehicle.

I started at the Morris as a labourer sweeping up (money for old rope as the saying goes) all around the tracks. I watched with interest how things were done and put together, and when no one was about I had a go at doing the different jobs. I tried to get involved talking to the men, asking if I could have a go on the assembly line.

I was helping one day to lower the chassis onto the track, because I was a labourer I wasn't rushed like the men on the track. When any of the men needed the toilet I would say, "You go, I will carry on for you." If the boss or the shop steward had seen me doing what they classed as a skilled job, there would have been hell to pay – strange saying that, isn't it, hell to pay.

I asked the person who was putting in the two little back windows in the rear doors of the Morris van, "Can I have a go?"

"More than my job is worth," he replied.

"Go on, let's have a go."

"Oh go on then, but do it slowly, and be careful not to scratch the door," he told me. So I did a window. "Well done; that was very good," he said to me.

Every now and again I put windows in for him while he sneaked out for a smoke. This is easy, I said to myself, I'm getting good at this. But I got too big headed for my own good; I slipped one afternoon and put a scratch from the end of the window right to the top of the door. Needless to say, he wouldn't let me do any more, and I cannot print what he called me.

At the end of the track there were men called snaggers, they put right any mistakes that were made. When they saw the scratch they went, well...they were annoyed. It meant they had to move themselves and do some work and they did not like that.

I was transferred to the press shop, that part of the factory was called Nuffields. I was a labourer in that shop as well. I had a little electric truck that had bins on wheels towing behind it, those were for the scrap that came off the presses. When a bin at the side of the press was full I changed it for an empty one, then I took all the bins outside and tipped them out into a large bin that was taken away every so often to a foundry to be melted down. All the men on the presses were old hands, nobody left there unless they died.

One day four of us men were offered jobs on the presses, they had a large rush order so they created four new jobs, which meant four more jobs were available, so four men could get a job labouring. This is how it worked, on the presses, one man pushing a button, two men putting the metal sheet on the press, one taking off the scrap, while the two who put the sheet of metal on took off whatever had been pressed out. On some presses there were two putting metal on the press, two taking off the pressed out item on the other side of the press, and one pushing the button – pushing the button was the best job, the old hands always did that job, it was piece work, so no hanging about.

All the presses had a counter clock, this told the bosses how many times the press had gone up and down. If they never reached the quota and the boss wasn't around they would operate the machine without anything in it, in other words they were fiddling. Some of the clock counters had glass missing or broken, this helped the men to fiddle – with a pointed piece of metal they could change the number on it, showing more than they had done. When they did that, the men would stand on each corner of the machine to keep an eye out for the boss, if caught fiddling it meant instant dismissal, the union could not help under those circumstances.

I went on a machine one day and I asked one of the old hands to put me one hundred on the clock. It was a one man press. Unfortunately after about eighteen minutes the boss came to me and said, I need you on a big press." When he went to write down the amount I had done he scratched his head, called the head boss over and said, " Look at this, the machine does one hundred an hour, he hasn't been on it for half an hour, it's impossible to have that many on the clock."

I'm in trouble now I thought. I was thinking of all the excuses I could put my tongue to, when the head boss said to the other boss, "You must have forgotten to clear the clock."

"I didn't," he said. "I didn't, I know I didn't."

I just kept quiet, that made a change for me.

I had to work nights at Nuffield's, I did not like that at all. Thinking about it, I didn't like days either, ha, ha! I never went to work on a Monday because I was earning big money – I remember that wage, thirty two pounds a week when I worked nights; I always knocked Monday night off as well.

I was called into the office and the manager said, "You know what your trouble is, son? You are earning too much money."

"Too much?" I said, with a cheeky smile.

"If you knock any more nights off I will sack you."

Well that was a red rag to a bull was that. "Oh yeah?" I said, pulling a nasty looking face, don't bother yourself; lick em on – I'm off."

Talk about cutting your nose off to spite your face. When I got home I said to the wife, "I told em to lick em on.

"Not again, Dave!" she said.

I sat drinking my cup of tea and I thought to myself, well, if brains were made of dynamite I wouldn't have enough to blow my nose. Ain't that the truth!

CHELMSLEY HOSPITAL

I lived just across the road from Chelmsley Mental Hospital as it was known locally then, I got a job there working in the maintenance department as a fitter's mate. My role was to follow the fitter like I was a little puppy carrying his bag of tools. My title was known as a fitter's mate (fitter's get) get me this, get me that, whatever I was asked for by the fitter. Then one day my title changed from fitter's mate, to semi-skilled engineer, so incline your head, you are now talking to a man with a title – same job, same money, nothing changed only on paper. The job that was allocated to me was unblocking toilets on a daily basis, (well toilet attendant would have been a more appropriate title at that hospital) they always told me to unblock the toilets and that was continuously.

The boss came to me one day and said, "I want to see how good you are, I want you to go all around the wards and fix wire cages over the radiators, the rads get very hot and I don't want the patients burning themselves."

Strange, I thought, cages around the rads now when there has been nothing around them since the place was built in the 1930s, I believe, so I placed wire cages around every rad in every ward, it took me a long time; I didn't rush because I wanted to stay away from those toilets.

Another afternoon the boss came up to see how I was getting on. "Well done, David," he said in his posh voice (anyone that ain't a Brummie to me talked in a posh voice). He then asked me if I would like to learn about boiler houses.

"Oh yes," I replied; I wasn't the least bit interested really, I was just humouring him.

"Good, David, I'm very glad to hear that. With an attitude like that you will go far." Far? I thought, I'm only a fitter's mate, (oops, sorry, a semi-skilled engineer, don't you know). "Follow me," he said."

At the front of the hospital we went down a flight of steps into a boiler room. "There you are, two boilers. I would like you to clean them."

Well now that's how to learn about boilers, I don't think, I was thinking to myself.

"When the dirt is removed you can see what they look like."

As if I didn't know what a boiler looked like! OK, I thought, this will last a very long time, weeks in fact. I very quickly cleaned the brass and copper items so when he looked in to see how I was getting on it looked like I was working hard at my job.

"Oh splendid, splendid job, super, keep it up!" He was a very intelligent man; I was skiving and taking him for a fool and I thought I was being clever. Three weeks I was in that boiler house, sometimes I sneaked out and went home and had a three hour dinner break; well, all good things come to an end, so did that boiler job.

Then it was toilets to repair or unblock. When one afternoon we ran out of gasket paper which was used to repair steam pipes – when I say repair I mean it went inbetween the joints to stop them leaking steam – I went with the fitter to the maternity hospital next door; both hospital were only divided by a high wooden fence running the full length of the grounds. We entered the maintenance department to scrounge some gasket paper, and I started to talk to the fitter, Tommy. "How are you getting on with Pipey?" that was my fitter's nickname, his real name was Jack.

"Oh Jacks' OK, it's the job I don't like. All I seem to do is unblock and repair toilets."

He laughed, "Why don't you have a word with our engineer, I need a mate to work with me."

"What's his name?" I asked.

"Bob."

So I walked around the maternity hospital, and after ten minutes I found the boss, Bob. I explained to him the situation – that I couldn't stand cleaning and repairing toilets anymore. "I don't blame you, I couldn't stand doing that either," he told me. "OK, look, don't say anything to anyone, just report here on Monday morning and I will square it with head office, but if your engineer gets wind of it, he will try to block it."

Come Monday I started working around the pregnant population of Birmingham – it was like coming off a tip to a holiday camp. The engineer did get wind of my transfer and tried to block it, unsuccessfully I'm glad to say.

MARSTON GREEN MATERITY HOSPITAL

I transferred from the Chelmsley Hospital on the morning I started working at the Marston Green Maternity Hospital. I found the atmosphere very calm and peaceful. My role at both hospitals was to carry the tools for the fitter, I was known as the fitter's mate, just the same as before (well semi skilled engineer).

All the wards at this hospital were surrounded by a corridor in such a way that it was in the shape of a horseshoe, so it was always referred to as the horseshoe. My job was to go all around that horseshoe every morning and put oil in the pumps that supplied the hot water to that particular ward. Every ward had its own pumping system for the central heating and hot water. On the roof of the laboratories was a huge extractor fan, I used to grease that fan after I had oiled all the pumps in the horseshoe, after that I had to work with whichever tradesman needed a hand. I worked with the electrician, the carpenter, the plumber, the builder, and of course the fitter and I learned a great deal from each one of those tradesmen.

All the steam pipes that fed the wards were old and prone to leaks; I was fascinated to see how those leaks were stopped. Whenever we saw steam puffing out of the pipes we would get what they called lead wool, bearing in mind those steam pipes were very hot, I would put some of the lead wool into the spot where the steam was escaping – I had a glove on of course, then with a screw driver I would ram the lead wool in place, then with a little hammer and a very small chisel I would tap it in till it was really rammed in, that is how we stopped steam leaks.

One afternoon I was working with the plumber – the main stop cock was leaking in a wards kitchen, it was fed by a lead pipe. That day I learned an operation I have never forgotten. It's not possible to lead wipe a joint when water is present, so with a nail the plumber put a hole a little away, underneath from the stop cock, this allowed a jet of water to escape out of that hole that stopped the water from reaching the stopcock, which allowed the plumber to lead wipe the joint using his blow lamp putting in some Talla fat to clean the joint. Then he melted the lead into the joint making it water tight, with a leather pad he smoothed the lead, that was known as lead wiping a joint. What really fascinated me was then with a match stick placed in the hole he had made with the nail, he placed a screw driver over the top of the hole, he taped down forcing some of the lead from the pipe to cover the matchstick and to my surprise the leak was stopped, that's how to lead wipe a leaking joint.

I bought two cottages in a little village. I had central heating put in, and I watched the plumber do exactly the same operation. When he found my stop cock had a leak I told him the plumber at the hospital did exactly the same thing. "Yes, that's how it is done," he replied.

"Have you ever had a leak from where you put in the matchstick?" I asked him.

"Never," he replied. "That will never leak as long as you are alive," he told me.

At the hospital, I was working with the carpenter, he was known as Clem because he looked just like an old Prime Minister, Clement Atlee, I did many jobs with him. He told me that originally the maternity hospital was built and used for the Canadian servicemen (women?) in the war, and the ballroom floor which was maple wood was supplied and fitted by the Canadians, as wood in this country was in short supply at that time.

One thing that may make you smile: there was an engineer that worked at the maternity hospital and he was a real snob. One afternoon he was telling me and the two men that worked in the stores, "A man walked past my house last night and he was scruffy," his face screwed up as he repeated himself, "yes, really scruffy and he walked past my house."

We all laughed and the Scottish store man said as he was holding his stomach while laughing and trying to get his breath, "If air was on ration he wouldn't let you anywhere near him."

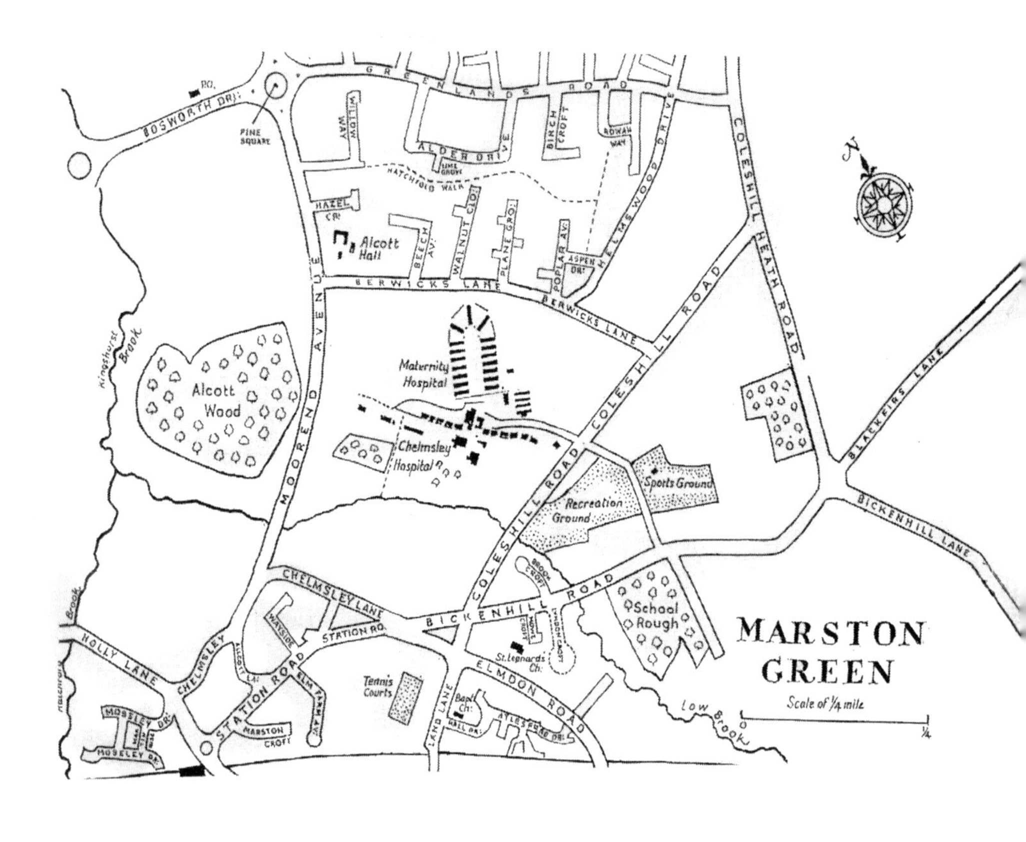

Marston Green Maternity Hospital
This map is showing the maternity wards, they were on both sides of what was known as the 'horse shoe' because of its shape. The map also shows the Chelmsley Hospital next door.
I worked in both these hospitals as a semi-skilled engineer

Well, the engineer could not understand why we weren't agreeing with him. "Well you wouldn't like a scruffy man walking past your house would you?" He said as he walked away.

There was a tradition that was adhered to at that hospital: when a child was born there and it was time for mother and baby to go home, a nurse always carried the baby out of the ward to the awaiting transport, and then wished mother and baby good luck. My son and my four grandchildren were born at the Marston Green Hospital and that was a really nice tradition.

All Marston Green Hospital and most of Chelmsley Hospital next door have both since been demolished but part of Chelmsley Hospital is now Brooklands, and also there is an NHS crèche and some new houses have been built on the site. A lot of the buildings were saved and altered into dwellings and some into offices and it is known as Pinewood Business Park. The original chapel is still standing on that site.

MOTHER'S PRIDE

I went to work for Mothers Pride Bread, because it was a job working outside – I didn't want the job really, but it was three weeks before Christmas. I doubled up with another man till Christmas was over as he was leaving and I was taking over the round; the round was in the Studley area.

On Christmas Eve, just as we were approaching the depot at the end of the day the driver said, "I can drop you off here if you want so you can go home to your family – I will see to the van and the returns." The returns were the bread and cakes that were unsold. So I got into my van and went home. Great, I thought, spend more time with my family, when I suddenly remembered I hadn't picked up my wages – how can anyone forget to pick up their wages? I did. So I went all the way back from Chelmsley Wood to Bordesley Green where the bakery was situated near the city centre.

The supervisor smiled at me and said, "I thought I was going to have a great Christmas on you!"

I never opened that wage packet till after Christmas so I needn't have gone back for it.

When I started to deliver on my first week I was offered sex from a customer – no I didn't, I refused, I made them pay their bread bill!

After I had worked for Mothers Pride for one month, I was told to have a medical. It was a Thursday, I remember, pay day. When the doctor looked at my ears he asked, "How long have you had a perforated ear drum?"

"I was born with it," I replied. He dismissed me on the spot – well I didn't have to say, lick em on – I'm off, they did it first.

Two weeks before on a Monday I had an armful of bread and cakes to take home, and went to the car park only to find someone had stolen my van. A week later I went to a sweet shop just up the road from the bakery and I was telling the lady that someone had stolen my grey van. She in informed me there had been a grey van parked in the road at the side of her sweet shop. I went to have a look to see if it was my van, and to my surprise it was! I was wondering what had been stolen from it, but there was nothing missing, in fact it had been filled up with petrol, what's more I had been passing my van all the week travelling on the bus to work and back. Since then I have often wondered if they intended to use it for a robbery as it had stood there all week and was full of petrol.

Anyway, there I was – jobless again.

STEWARTS AND LLOYDS

This firm was based in the Bromford Bridge area of Birmingham. On the front of the building was a very long tube, this was facing the road so people passing could see it, it had a plaque above it saying, the longest tube in the world, or words something like that. They made all sorts of tubes, from lampposts to injection needles.

The firm on the other side of the road facing Stewarts was Rollason wire rolling mills, where Barry Farrington worked, he was my next-door neighbour when I was living with my parents, before I was married.

Stewarts was a little different from other firms I worked for in as much as they insisted on the first day of your new job you had to do an introduction course. I found this to be a total waste of the firm's money, a drain on the firm's resources. There was about eight of us freshmen, plus two men taking the class that had worked there since they left school at the age of thirteen and fourteen, plus two young apprentices that were also employed there. We were given a talk on how and where the firm started and what they produced, and when that was over we had our dinner break. After dinner we were taken around the factory by the apprentices, we were given a hard hat and a pair of goggles and told when to put them on and take them off. It's got to be the most pathetic thing that's ever happened in my life. As we walked into one part of the factory we were told to put on our hard hats and goggles as there were men cutting steel and sparks were flying. So in we went, all looking like bandits, only to see that none of the men working in that department were wearing any kind of safety equipment – we found this throughout the factory.

Next day I was put working with two men rolling round long lengths of steel, twenty feet long and about eight inches in circumference. A man on the night shift had put a cut in these with a gas torch to the length required (most bars had four nicks in them). With six-feet round steel crow bars, two of us would bar one of those lengths of steel into a trough, then all three of us would put our crow bars as far under the long length of steel as possible and with a sort of rowing action we walked that length of steel along the trough under the machine, with the nick in the steel facing downwards, and a sort of arm would come down with a flat piece of metal, with the bottom of it shaped like a V –it looked like the blade of a bolster chisel. As it touched the steel with slow pressure and putting a few tons of pressure pushing downwards, the steel rose into the air; I bet it lifted three feet into the air, and when it snapped at the point where the nick was it fell back into the trough with a bang. We had to stand well away because sometimes it would bounce out of the trough and spin round. The trough was made of steel, very thick steel.

The other strange thing about that firm was there were more holes in the sides and the roof than you could shake a stick at. When the wind was blowing hard the rain or the snow, whichever was about at the time, made it very uncomfortable to work in those conditions, and to help you to not freeze altogether the firm in their infinite wisdom put braziers around the work shop with a pile of coke – just like that firm did in the Black Country – in really bad conditions they were as much use as a teapot with no bottom in it. Any road up, one afternoon as I was barring one of those steel rolls towards the trough, because the floor was uneven the steel roll was slightly rising over a lump in the floor so instead of going over, it came back so all the weight rolled on to my crow bar. Pushing it down to the ground, with my hand underneath that crow bar, boy was it painful! The man who was barring with me had his bar wrenched from his hand as the weight of the steel roll went onto it; he very quickly got another crowbar to bar the steel roll off my hand. That was only in the 1960s; once again it was like working in the Dickensian era. I was off sick with my hand, and never got compensated for that accident. I handed in my notice while I was on the sick, so it was off to pastures new once again.

WONDERLOAF

Wonderloaf was a bakery company based in Wolverhampton and they rented a yard in Blake Lane in the Bordsley Green area of Birmingham. What that company were hoping to do was to break into the Birmingham area bread trade, of course that was impossible with the well established bread companies like the Co-op, Mothers Pride, Hawley's, Harding's, Wimbushes and Scribbens, plus many smaller companies like Braggs.

I started to work for Wonderloaf on a Wednesday, and I was immediately put on a round all around the Northfield and the Lickey Hills area. After a couple of weeks they had a competition selling Hovis. Out of one hundred and fifty calls, I got one hundred and fifty customers buying a Hovis loaf for a whole week. One by one they cancelled the Hovis orders till I was only selling two Hovis loaves a week. I came second but I could never find out who had won or how many loaves they sold. I went to Wolverhampton and I was asking all the rounds men if they knew who had won but no one would tell me, not even the head office; as I was an outsider I had my nose pushed out – I think I won that competition. Still, I got a boxed set of Parker pens which my wife loved.

Wonderloaf never got going in Birmingham, I for one stopped trying; to be honest I was putting the customers off – I lost a few. The calls were so spread out it was costing more in petrol and wages than the amount of goods I was selling; the wages were poor anyway.

One morning I noticed a tray of twenty four blackcurrant fresh cream cakes on my van, I hated those cakes, the boss said, "I've put those on your van because you never order any, that's because you don't like blackcurrant do you?"

"Nobody does, do they? Well when I bring them back unsold don't blame me," I told him. I sold them all in my first two roads, so after that he kept on putting fresh cream items on the van – trifles, cakes and sponges. The customers got fed up with them, and I started to take them back. He accused me of not trying; I even ate a few myself.

One day I had a dozen fresh cream trifles on, I was driving too fast, I hit a bump, and every trifle went into the air and turned upside down! I sold them at a quarter of their price that came out of my pocket.

I got really fed up with that job so I went off sick, but when I went back a week later I was called into the office by the boss and was told, "I'm letting you go, I don't think you want to offer any more of your time to the company; I think you have lost interest." He was so right. The daft thing was, a boy my wife knew through his mom-in-law (I didn't know him but I had put in a good word for him) worked on the side lines and they took him on and got rid of me. Oh well, I thought, new horizons here I come. That company only lasted a few months longer in Birmingham; they gave up the fight and went back to where they belonged, Wolverhampton. I don't think there are any firms now delivering bread and cakes door to door these days.

COCA-COLA

When I started at Coca Cola I had driven artics, three wheeled scammels for the railways, lorries of all sizes and weights, and an ordinary car licence was all one needed to drive lorries at that time. When I went to Coca Cola by this time the law had changed. If there were two axles on the rear of the lorry, you needed an HGV, heavy goods vehicle licence, class two. One axle and you had to have a class three licence. So the Coca Cola Company put me through a driving test for a class two licence. Their retail lorries at that time were only three tons max weight. So a class three was all one needed to drive their retail lorries.

On my interview for the job of salesman driver, a driver put his head around the door – he had just come from having his driving test – and the man interviewing me, Mr Frank Bunce, asked him how he had got on. "I've failed," he said. "He won't pass," he said pointing at me. He didn't know me; I was annoyed because I was on my interview, but he was upset because he had failed.

Frank knew, he said, "Don't worry about that." He asked if I had an HGV.

"No," I replied.

"That's all right; I will put you in for your HGV test."

Great, a heavy goods licence and I won't have to pay for it, I was thinking.

I started the next day. I was used as a rounds boy for the first week, I didn't even drive the lorry, they said they wanted me to get used to the job to see if I wanted to stay. I was working with a supervisor, his name was John. I did do some of the paper work, working out the bills for the customers, but the job was very hard and it carried a lot of responsibility – a lorry, lots of cash, a lorry load of pop, plus a rounds boy, and all my wages were at that time was £25.23p a week. I was delivering down alleyways, up and down cellars, up flights of stairs.

Some of the cinemas were the hardest, three flights of stairs with two crates of pop in each hand, yes, very hard.

I went out one week with a driver, his round was different to all the others, he carried one gallon jars of concentrated Coca Cola, Fanta Orange and Fanta Lemon, and these were for the machines that were on the counters of cafes, restaurants and pubs. They were the type of machines where you put your cardboard cup against a lever. The syrup of Coca Cola would be mixed with soda water to give it the fizz, and when the cylinders needed filling, I would let the gas out of the cylinder, take off the lid and pour the syrup in. Those cylinders were stainless steel and held four gallons of the syrup; if my memory serves me right they were always under the counter, directly under the machine on the counter. I liked that round; they called it 'post mix'.

I went on many different rounds just to get used to all the different areas. I was working on a round in the Solihull and Shirley areas, the salesman was off sick. One morning I got the lorry loaded and went into the office to get the rounds book, those books had all the days of the week in them, the name of the shop and every customer on the individual day – on average there were thirty customers to serve a day, we called once a week to each customer. The summer was a different ball game, as the saying goes, that job became very hard. On very hot days the customers sold out very quickly so they would phone the office for an extra delivery. On those types of days there were never enough hours in the day to do the job, and some customers were never satisfied, no matter how good you were to them. The winter was really easy, some customers had only one delivery in six weeks, and then only two cases. There were twenty four small bottles of coke in each case, and with the post mix most customers in most cases had only one jar every four to eight weeks, when snow was about even longer. The wages were poor in the winter, and our bonus was very low.

One Monday morning I went to get the rounds book. Frank Bunce, the sales manager said, "Are you looking for the rounds book, Dave?"

"Yes."

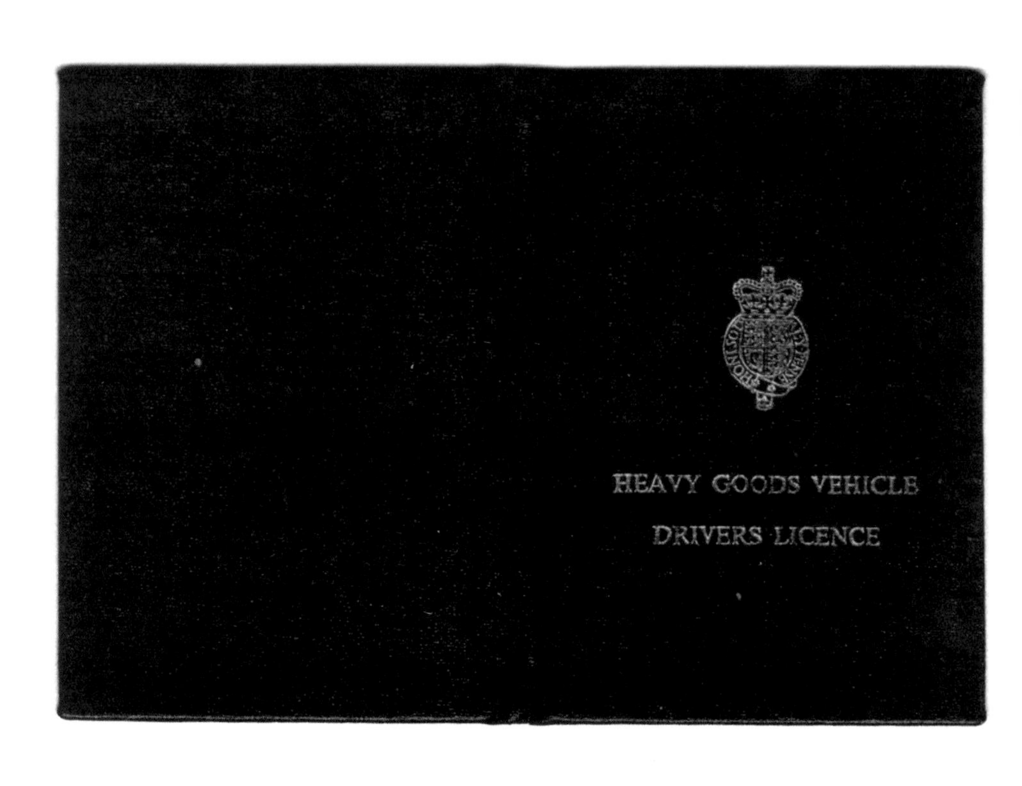

My H.G.V. Licence
Heavy goods vehicle
1972

CLASSES OF HEAVY GOODS VEHICLES

1 Articulated vehicle, not fitted with automatic transmission, other than a vehicle coming within Class 4.

1A Articulated vehicle, fitted with automatic transmission, other than a vehicle coming within Class 4A.

2 Heavy goods vehicle, not fitted with automatic transmission, other than an articulated vehicle, designed and constructed to have more than four wheels in contact with the road surface.

2A Heavy goods vehicle, fitted with automatic transmission, other than an articulated vehicle, designed and constructed to have more than four wheels in contact with the road surface.

3 Heavy goods vehicle, not fitted with automatic transmission, other than an articulated vehicle, designed and constructed to have not more than four wheels in contact with the road surface.

3A Heavy goods vehicle, fitted with automatic transmission, other than an articulated vehicle, designed and constructed to have not more than four wheels in contact with the road surface.

4 Articulated vehicle, not fitted with automatic transmission, the tractive unit of which does not exceed two tons unladen weight.

4A Articulated vehicle, fitted with automatic transmission, the tractive unit of which does not exceed two tons unladen weight.

1

Issued by the Licensing Authority for the West Midland Traffic Area.

DAVID ARTHUR PROSSER
56, BERNICKS LANE
CHELMSLEY WOOD
BIRMINGHAM.

is hereby authorised to drive heavy goods vehicles of Classes

1, 1A, 2, 2A, 3, 3A, 4 and 4A.

subject to the conditions prescribed in Regulation 9 of the Heavy Goods Vehicle (Drivers' Licences) Regulations, 1969.

from 5-4-72 until 4-10-72 inclusive

Usual signature of licensee

51—0019 C.M.R.C.P.

My H.G.V. Licence
Heavy goods vehicle
1972

"The supervisor is doing the round; you are having two days driving tuition. You are booked in for your test on Wednesday; I never told you Friday, I didn't want to spoil your weekend."Now that's what I call a boss.

Frank was a nice man, he worked his way up from a delivery driver, and he did well for himself. Coca Cola is a very nice firm to work for.

I was waiting in the sales room for my instructor when Frank came in and told me my lorry had been checked over. "It's all ok, so it's ready for your tuition."

I drove it to the front of the building, and a little man got in and introduced himself to me. "I'm from the British School of Motoring B S.M, he said, then laid out on the seat all his licences and certificates. "These are to show you I'm very qualified and I know what I am talking about. I've taken all the vehicle tests and advanced tests that are going, OK?"

"Yes," I replied.

"Good, now start off, go to the end of the road, turn left and head for Stratford upon Avon; only turn left or right when I tell you to." Just before we got into Stratford upon Avon, he said, "Pull into the left by that lamppost and switch off, this is where we have breakfast."

Two hours later he decided I was going to get some tuition. We went to a disused airfield known as Long Marston, where there was a long run of concrete that used to be the runway. There were lots of cones already set out; it appeared that all lorry drivers used it when being given tuition. He reset the cones for different manoeuvres. I zigzagged in and out of the cones, and backed into a bay where the cones were set out in a sort of square to represent backing into a bay. He showed me the right way to do it; he drew a line. I was travelling at thirty miles an hour when he shouted, "Stop!" I hit my brakes. He got out and looked to see if I had stopped on the line. "Perfect, just do everything I've showed you and you will be OK on your test." So four times I did all the manoeuvres that he had shown me, and he was very happy. We then went back to the café and sat in there for three more long hours – I was bored sick.

The following morning the driving instructor strolled up nearly an hour late. "Are you all right, driver?" he asked.

"I'm fine, thank you."

Doing a delivery of Coca Cola

"Good, come on then we are running a little late." We set off. "Drive to the café, driver, we will have breakfast." We sat in that café all day, never moved – brother was I bored, even more bored than the day before.

"Am I having any tuition today?" I asked him.

"No you don't need any."

I laughed. "You won't say that if I fail tomorrow," I told him.

"Look, if you needed it, I would take you out and give you some. Remember I told you I was qualified – and don't question me." So I apologized, I think I had upset him. "I have never had a driver fail yet." Yes, I had upset him. I hope I'm not the first to let him down, I thought.

Next morning I was feeling very nervous as we went to the testing station at Garrets Green. The examiner was a little bald round-faced man, with round wire framed specs, and he was wearing trousers that were too short for him – they came past the top of his boots. Oh no, I thought, he looks horrible. I did the test pad just like I had been shown, did the reverse zigzag, thirty mile an hour emergency stop, all OK. I was told to look in my mirrors every seven seconds so all over my test I was counting to seven, then left mirror, then right mirror, on to the road we go, throat dry, nerves all over the place.

"Pull over to your left please driver and stop." He looked at me and said, "Well."

"I'm sorry, I didn't hear what you said," I said to him.

"I didn't say anything; cancel your indicator."

That's it, I thought, he will fail me for that, so I took a deep breath and thought to hell with it, if I fail, I fail, he knew I was nervous. I was told to pull away so I drove like he wasn't there. "Turn only when I tell you to, driver." Well I drove and drove, I went through Stratford, I glanced at him a couple of times, I'm sure he is asleep, I was thinking, by this time I had been driving for nearly an hour, so I coughed loudly and his head came up with a jerk. "Oh, erm...take the next right, please, driver," he said. By the time I got back I had been on that test just over two hours, and I felt drained. He looked at me, smiled and said, "That was a beautiful drive, thank you, driver."

Then questions on the highway code followed. "I'm pleased to say you have passed."

"Would you like six bottles of coke?" I asked him. "I wouldn't ask you before in case you thought I was trying to bribe you." He shoved them in his briefcase like he was scared I would take them back. I shook his hand and off he went. I don't like Coca Cola myself but I opened one and it went down so sweet – I needed it, my throat was so dry.

My tutor came up to me, congratulated me on my pass then said, "Where the hell have you been, you should have been back over an hour ago?" I explained I thought he had gone to sleep. He laughed, "See, I told you you were a good driver." Easy to say that after the event isn't it?

I got that round selling the gallon jars of coke (you know the post mix I was telling you about); I loved that round. I delivered to the Shakespeare Theatre in Stratford upon Avon, and Winston Churchill's place of birth, Blenheim Palace. I went to all the main towns, Oxford, Banbury, Leicester, Stratford, Birmingham, Leamington, Rugby and many more.

Every year come Christmas we had the chance to win a hamper, it was a team effort. All the roundsmen were involved, including the management. There were spirits of all kinds, big tins of ham, tins of fruit and a thirteen pound turkey. We won the top hamper every year, every salesman got one – the turkey only just fitted in our oven!

The insurance cover that Coca Cola gave to all their staff was second to none; if I died while in there employ for whatever reason at home or at work, my funeral would be all paid for by the company and my wife would receive a few thousand pounds, so I was told, who it was I can't remember.

When I joined the Territorial Army I was paid full wages, plus bonuses no matter how long I was away, wonderful company, plus I got paid by the Army as well. I left that company because they went to telephone sales so I became a delivery driver, no longer a salesman. Want a shock? I worked there for three and a half years and never lost any time, and then I went to a firm called Goverbrook Loft Conversions. I must say a big thank you to France Bunce for his kindess, he helped me so much by giving me the opportunity to get my HGV licence. Thank you Frank.

GOVERBROOK

Goverbrook was a firm that did loft conversions. I went to see Bill, the owner, in my Coca Cola lorry; this lorry was a 25tonner, one big old fashioned lorry, wooden cab, no power assistance, horrible to drive. The boss of Goverbrook came out to look at it. "Good God, I never knew they still had lorries like this on the road." It was definitely a museum vehicle in my opinion.

"I heard you were looking for a driver." he looked surprised as I said it.

"How did you find that out?" he asked.

"You have a relation working at Coca Cola, I told him. I know the foreman here; he worked at Coke alongside me.

"Oh you mean Friar Tuck – we call him that because of his size."

I laughed, "We called him Polly because he never stopped talking."

"You can start Monday if you want to," the boss said.

"I have to give a fortnight's notice," I told him.

Bill agreed. "OK, that's all right, see you in a fortnight."

So after my delivery that day, I gave in my two week's notice. When Friday afternoon came, I got back to the yard, loaded the wagon for Monday, handed in my sheets, and the sales manager said, "I've paid you a fortnight's money in lieu, plus bonuses, holiday pay and what they owe you – over £400." So I had a nice week off before I started work for Goverbrook.

I started on the Monday; it felt very strange working with timber after carrying crates of pop for three and a half years. This job was easy, all I had to do was load up the timber, take it to the customer's house, and unload it – it was always put in the garden. I carried a large roll of plastic, which I cut to the length of the timber covering it all so it wouldn't get wet.

I was very interested to learn how to construct a loft conversion, and I asked questions all the time. I got to know about all the different materials needed to convert a loft. This is easy, I thought. I built a garage on the side of my house, and I got all the timber from work nice and cheap. The brother of a lad I went to school with was a bricklayer, and he laid the bricks and helped to put the roof on the garage; he taught me a lot. He got me all the bricks from a job he was doing. The carpenter at work made the door frame for my up and over metal door.

I worked a lot around Stoke on Trent; I delivered many loads of timber around Stoke and Bristol, Tamworth, Coventry, many, many places. Worcester was a favourite run for me. After a few months our boss was going broke. He sent me to Telford to pick up a cheque. "Be as quick as you can, Dave," he said, "so I can get it in the bank so I can pay your wages." I got nicked for speeding. "Don't worry, Dave, I will pay the fine for you, thanks for being quick," Bill assured me – too right I was quick, I wanted my wages. It did make me wonder just how broke he was, if he needed a cheque that badly. It turned out he was desperate, he had six teams, two men to each team.

The following Friday as I was loading up my wagon, a team of two men walked in. "Is Bill in his office?" they asked me.

"Yeah, he has just walked in, well ten minutes ago." They looked very angry. "What's up?" I asked.

"What's up? The cheque he gave us for our wages has bounced," they told me.

Oh my God, it's worse than I feared, I was thinking. I heard the boss say, "Morning lads," as though there wasn't anything wrong. I heard lots of shouting; they were saying, "We ain't doing another stroke on the loft we are waiting here till we get our money."

"I will pay you this afternoon, lads," Bill told them both.

"Yeah, and we want cash, not a cheque," the both men were demanding. So off they went.

The boss called me into his office. "Take the lorry Dave to Bristol Street Motors in Perry Bar for a service; tell them you will wait for it."

I walked in."Hi, I'm from Goverbrook, I've brought the lorry for a service."

"Park it there," said the boss of Bristol Street Motors, pointing to a corner, "and give me the keys." I gave him the keys. "Right," he said, "that lorry is going nowhere till your boss pays us what he owes us."

Not again, I thought, so I phoned up the boss. "Bill, they won't give me the lorry back till you pay the bill."

I handed the phone to the boss. I heard Bill shouting, "I've got money, how dare you hold my lorry!"

"Well, just get down here and pay the bill."

With that, Bill came to the garage and paid them with a cheque. Things were getting really bad. The lady in the office told me to find another job as the firm had no money. That was the last time I saw her, she left. I got my wages in a packet as normal, it was a cheque, and yes, it bounced. I was very angry. I went in to the office and had a go at him. "Sorry, Dave, here you are, my personnel cheque."

"I want cash, Bill, not a cheque."

"It's OK, Dave, it will cash, it's out of my own account."

That bounced as well, so in the office I went. "I know Dave, here is another cheque made out to cash."

"It had better cash, Bill, it's nearly two weeks since I had any money and I have two children."

"It's OK, Dave, honest it will cash." So I took it straight home to my wife, she took it to the bank, and yes, it cashed.

I went in on the next Monday and Bill said, "Dave we are now called Dormer Construction, Goverbrook has gone into liquidation. So Goverbrook had finally got taken over by a timber firm in Dudley. They owed lots of money to that firm I never heard how much, I have no idea. So I teamed up with a carpenter named Barry who was a loft converter. I did a few lofts with him all over the country. We slept in the back of his van on the hard floor in a sleeping bag. It was winter and very cold; when I woke up in the morning the inside of the van was white with frost. I opened my flask and drank an ice-cold cup of tea. What the hell am I doing this for? I asked myself. I was working very hard carrying all the timber, plasterboards and eight by two floor chipboard up a ladder, never Barry, always me. I had no money, so I took a loaf and butter and jam; Barry had some of my bread, so half way through the week I wasn't eating at all. I found carrying the materials up the ladder getting harder by the hour, as I got weaker and my head was aching and I had no pain killers. Barry said, "I have only enough money to buy my meals," so I sat every evening watching him eat a roast dinner. They had a shower in the place he ate at, and I asked him to lend me ten pence for the shower. "I ain't got ten pence, Dave," he said. "I wanted a shower and I can't have one either."

So I went back and sat in the van. Barry came back. "I see you had a shower then, Barry, I thought you hadn't any money left."

"Oh I found ten pence in my pocket," he said.

"Well you ate my bread and jam and left me with nothing. Well I'm finished with you when this loft is finished, you ain't a nice person to work with – we are supposed to look after each other." I said to him. Barry only thought about himself.

By the way, that fine – Bill never paid it; one Saturday morning I was got out of bed by a police officer and arrested and taken to the police station. I was bailed, and I told Bill on the Monday. He laughed, said it was still in his drawer – he had forgotten all about it! He did pay it that same day.

GOING ABROAD

I remember this journey to Italy very well because a few funny but scary things happened to us on the way back.

Andrew, who I went all over Italy with before, came to me one Friday afternoon and asked me if I would go to Italy with him and share the driving. In Chelmsley Wood there lived an Italian man who was married to an English lady; they had been living in Italy for a long time and decided to come and live in England. Andrew was asked if he would hire a furniture van and collect all the items of furniture from a flat in Milan. The couple travelled that Friday back to Italy so they were there before we arrived. Andrew knew I wouldn't refuse a free trip so it was all agreed before he asked me to go. I got a date with a lady, of course I didn't go with her, I did tell her.

On and off the ferry, no problems, through France I was driving great, I thought. As we approached the start to the Alps I shook Andrew who was asleep at the time. "What are all those signs meaning?" I asked him.

"I don't know," he replied, "just carry on up over the mountain road." The road looked like it was super glued to the side of the mountain. Well it was getting dark, I drove and drove till it got light, and then we came to a lodge, which turned out to be the border control. Not a soul was in sight; there were a lot of barriers across the road and round the buildings – it turned out there had been a rock fall and the mountain road leading into Italy was closed for repairs, so all the way back down we went, it was one hell of a drop from that road to the ground. We wasted a lot of diesel that day just because the sign wasn't in English, as well as French, I was glad to get off that mountain road.

Any road up we made it to the destination and loaded up the lorry. "May I have a shower?" I asked, the man whose furniture we were collecting. The shower was turned on for me, but it went bitter cold, the water that is. After I got dressed I told them the water was freezing.

"Oh no," the man said, he couldn't apologize enough, "you know that lady who lives in the bottom flat, she is not nice, she thinks she owns the place. I bet she has turned off the hot water in the basement." And that is exactly what she had done.

Andrew had his shower, and he started to play me up, saying, "That was a lovely hot shower I had."

The young man, whose name I can't remember, took us to a restaurant to try proper Italian spaghetti, it was very nice.

It was about four in the afternoon, if my memory serves me right, maybe a little earlier, when we started back for England. It turned out we didn't know our vehicle was over three tons, lorries over three tons were not allowed on the roads at weekends. When we reached the Swiss border we were asked by the border guard, "What are you carrying?" We told him furniture and showed him the list. "Is he an Italian that is moving to England?"

"Yes," we told him. He pulled a face and asked, "For goodness sake, why?"

"For work," we explained, "for a better living than he can get in his own country." We were being sarcastic.

"You have to pay taxes of one hundred pounds now, or I will take the lorry off you," we were told by the guard.

Andrew was having a fit, he explained to me, "We will only just about have enough for our meals and the toll roads if I have to give him one hundred pounds, we might even be short!"

"It's OK Andrew, I've got fifty quid on me," I told him.

So as he turned towards me, away from the border guard, he slipped some notes under the seat, and with a fifty pound note and a couple of tens and some fivers, he fanned the money in his left hand, turned to the border guard and said, "This is all I've got and we have to pay the tolls."

The border guard reached in, snatched the fifty pound note and said, "That will do." He went into his shed and brought out a receipt, went to the back of the lorry and put a seal on it so we couldn't open up the back of the lorry, then he told us, "Over three tons, no travel on roads till Monday morning, so go round the corner and park up."

We had to get back to England or the lorry hire would cost us more money. As we turned the corner I said, “I will drive on Andrew, we will say we are only just three tons in weight if stopped.”

The roads were almost deserted. As we passed the occasional motorist we got some funny looks. Just before we got to the next border I took the wrong turning, and I went through I think it was the Belgium border. I did a sharp turn about and put my foot down. The guard came running out with his pistol in his hand – that was a scary moment. We are very lucky to live in England.

We got to the next Swiss border as they were just changing the night shift to the day shift. Well the look on their faces, it was too early for them to want to bother with us, the guard only asked how heavy we were. I told him, “Three tons.”

He waved his hands, he wasn’t interested in our paper work, “Go, go” he was saying, “Go, go,” and go we did – very fast, well as fast as we could. We sighed a sigh of relief! In France you can drive to the ferry, but not from the ferry on weekends if you are a commercial vehicle. All went well from then till we got home; it was quite an adventure, I enjoyed it.

MAXIPOPS

Maxipops was a mineral water wholesale company, based in the Chelmsley Wood area of Solihull, near the N.E.C. Only wholesale companies were allowed to purchase their product. I absolutely hated working for this company. Most of the workforce came from the firm Corona, I believe Corona went into liquidation, but I'm not altogether sure about that. Their pop was, I thought, the best on the market, any road up, my job was to deliver to the shops around the Coventry area. Trying to work out their road system in Coventry was a day's work in itself. I had a rep working with me; he was good at his job.

We decided one day as it was coming up to Christmas, we would go all out, push the sales to make our wages better, as we were aware that after Christmas all we would be doing was picking up empties, and not such good wage packets. Off our own backs we were doing deals – if they only wanted one case, we would say, if you buy ten we will only charge you for nine, or buy ten cases we will give you one free; if they took fifty cases we gave them six cases free. The firm had an incentive scheme where we were allowed to give two free cases away, but not the amount we gave away. How the rep worked it, I have no idea, all I know is we sold thousands of cases in that three weeks, and our wages were very good for Christmas. We even swapped bottles of pop for bags of nuts and tins of sweets. After Christmas all we did was pick up empties, the bosses were none too pleased.

One very foggy morning I filled up the diesel tank and started towards Coventry. As I was going down a hill towards Stone Bridge Island, that's just down the road from the N.E.C. and the Birmingham Airport, a lorry had been dropping scrap metal onto the road. I saw it at the last minute because of the fog; I tried to avoid running over it, but the shape of the metal was boomerang, and I caught it with the inside of my tyre. It made a lot of noise as it hit the underside of my lorry. I turned to the rep and said, "That metal will cause an accident if it's not picked up." Visibility was only about ten yards so I couldn't stop to pick it up. As all drivers know it takes a lot of concentration when driving in fog. When I got to my first call I was facing uphill, and as I jumped out of the cab I saw diesel running down the hill from under my lorry. On close inspection I noticed a hole in one side of the tank and a hole on the other side of it. To say we were gobsmacked would be an understatement, but we were, that piece of metal I had hit had spun, gone through my diesel tank and out of the other side. Diesel is like ice when on the road so we phoned the fire brigade who came out about an hour later. In the meantime we had phoned the depot, told them the problem, and they sent out a mechanic with a new tank and twenty gallons of diesel. On arriving he told me that on the road where the diesel had come out of the tank because the metal had ruptured it, there had been a massive pile up – lorries and cars all skidding down the hill till they all met at the bottom. Among the vehicles, in his week old car was Sir Robert McAlpine. His car was squashed between two lorries. The mechanic said, "No one knows it was you that spilt that diesel."

"Well I'm phoning the police," I told him. "The firm is insured and those people have a right to compensation." I gave them the facts on how it happened, and then went about my business delivering the pop. On that Friday evening, on returning to the depot a little late, all the office staff had gone home so I couldn't hand in my log book.

On returning back to the depot on the Monday evening, I felt really rough with the flu. Just as I was about to enter the road where my depot was, I was stopped by a police car. "Let's have a look at your log book, you buggers never bother with them half the time," he remarked."

A lady police officer that was with him remarked how ill I looked. "I just want to go home to bed," I told her.

"You will go when I'm finished with you," the male officer said to me. He booked me for not handing in my log book Friday evening. I told him the offices were locked when I got back Friday so I was about to hand them in as soon as I got in that evening. I hadn't signed that day's sheet, so he booked me for not signing that day's log and not handing in last week's log sheets. I pointed out on the back of the log sheets that it states, if you are not able to hand in your log sheets do it at the next earliest possible convenience, but he wasn't interested, he still booked me. I wrote to the courts and explained what it said on the back of the log book and they weren't interested either – I got fined ninety pounds. A couple of weeks after that I handed in my notice; again I joined the ranks of the unemployed.

Nearly twelve months later a solicitor came to my house and asked if I would go to court as a witness about the accident. He explained they had offered a quarter of a million pounds to all the people who had their vehicles damaged, but Sir Robert McAlpine had refused, said it wasn't enough to pay for all the damage that had been done to all the vehicles involved in the crash. I didn't have to appear, but I was told, "We can't win without you."

So into court I went and sat and listened to all the owners of the smashed up vehicles. The barristers with white wigs and black gowns on truthfully were making me very nervous; I had to stand in front of them. After lunch the rep and the young lad that was with us at the time had a slap up lunch, I wasn't allowed to talk to them. I hadn't any money on me, so I sat on my own with one piece of toast and a cup of tea. As I walked into the dock I was grilled by their barrister. I'm not having this, I thought, so with a deep breath I piped up and said, "Excuse me, your honour, I'm only a common person, I just don't understand the big words the gentleman is saying to me, would you please ask him to talk to me in common English," which he did. After I had explained that if I hadn't have phoned the police no one would have known it was my lorry whose diesel tank had split, the case was dismissed. That insurance never paid out a penny.

I went into the solicitor's office; he shook my hand and said, "You were brilliant, you saved our company a lot of money."

"How much do I get?" I asked him.

His reply to me was, "Nothing, that would be against the law," and he gave me my bus fare home. If I had known then, what I know now, if they weren't going to pay me at least a day's wages, I would have refused to testify on their behalf – they really should have paid up to those people whose cars were damaged; that's why we have insurance.

WG.440.

WEST MIDLANDS POLICE

Our Ref : L1670/79

Your Ref :

Dated : 22 April 1980

From :

Mr. D. A. Prosser
102 Orton Road
Warton
TAMWORTH
Staffordshire

Superintendent
Eastern Traffic Sub-Division
Homer Road
Solihull B91 3QL

Dear Sir

I am directed by the Chief Constable to say it has been reported to him that

on Tuesday, 20 November 1979, you deposited diesel on the A452 Chester Road, without lawful authority or excuse.

It is not proposed to take any further action on this occasion.

Yours faithfully,

Chief Superintendent.

A letter I got from the police after the accident on my way to Coventry in my lorry to deliver Maxi Pop to the shops. They made it sound like I went with a can and poured diesel all over the road. I did smile when I received it.

COUNCIL

Working for the council made me wonder why the bosses were not stricter with the workforce – one could get away with such a lot. I used to dodge the bosses to get out of working; don't get me wrong, the bosses were a very nice bunch of men. How I came to be working for the council was, one day I walked into the unemployment office in Chelmsley Wood and asked if any new jobs had come in that weren't yet on the board. "Would you do any type of work?" I was asked. "We have a temporary job with the Solihull council."

"Yes, no problem."

"The council are very short staffed at the moment, what with sick leave and holidays. I see you are a lorry driver HGV class two."

Yes, I am," I replied.

"Here is a letter, take it to a Mr Lightfoot at Moat Lane, Solihull."

As usual I wasn't concentrating (That's always been a problem of mine). I went to the council yard in Coleshill, well, no good being thick and not showing it, and handed in my letter. "This is fine; can you start in the morning?"

"Yeah, no trouble."

He knew I had gone to the wrong council so he took advantage of it because he was short staffed as well.

"We start at six a.m," the boss told me. Six a.m! I hate getting up in the mornings.

Well, I got there, only just, I might add, and I was introduced to a gang of men. "You will be working with these men."

"What am I driving?" I asked.

"No, you are not driving; you will be working on the refuse lorry emptying the bins." A dustman, I thought, no way – I came to drive lorries. I did go with the gang though, We went to Kingshurst, to pick up a man, and he strolled out like he was the boss. The driver had only been with the council a week, and I found that the four men sat in the back of the cab had taken a dislike to him. I had no idea why, they laughed and took the micky out of him behind his back. We were emptying bins all around the Marston Green area that day, and I was talking to the driver, he seemed OK to me. The crew were running around like wild things, I asked the driver," Why are they running around like wild things?"

"To get finished," he replied.

"What happens then?" I asked him,

"Nothing, we sit around till gone three, and we can then go back to the yard."

"But why run around like idiots, when it could be done almost as quick by walking fast?"

"I know that, try telling them. We would only take about an hour longer," he said. "I asked them that when I started last week, they said 'Toe the line and don't try to change things.'"

I asked, "How come we picked that fellow up this morning, why doesn't he come to the yard like the rest of us?"

"I'm not sure, he seems to tell the bosses what to do," he told me.

Next morning, same again, only this time we waited almost twenty minutes for the man to come out of his house. He said, "Morning lads, I got up late."

I thought I'm not having this, this will be my last day, I don't like this job and the bins smell something awful. One bin, I remember, had lots of waste food in it, and was crawling with maggots, thousands of them – I don't think they had emptied it for a long time. They missed bins, dropped rubbish all the time and never picked it up, they really were a law unto themselves. I don't know what hold they had over the bosses but they seemed to do just what they liked. We finished at eleven thirty that day and hung about.

When we did finally get back to the yard, I clocked out and shot over to Moat Lane depot where I should have gone in the first place. I went to see the boss, Mr Lightfoot, and there was another boss there named Sam, I can't remember his surname. I explained the mix up. "I'm not doing those bins anymore; have you a driving job or do I leave?" I said to him, Mr Lightfoot that is.

"I have a driving job for you – that boss at Coleshill, he should have sent you to me; he tried to keep you because like us he is short staffed. I will phone him and tell him you have transferred over to me, and I will sort your money out for you. The driving job I have is emptying the cess pits."

My God, I thought, out of the frying pan and into the fire! "Yes, that will be fine," I told him.

"Good, I'm desperate for drivers; all the customers are overdue for emptying."

It was expected that you empty six cesspits a day; I had a driver's mate, Dougie, working alongside of me. It was most certainly different to anything else I had ever done. The sewage farm was situated in Friday Lane, Barston, near Balsall Common. Come dinnertime I said to Dougie, "Where do you go for dinner?"

"We stay at the sewage farm where we empty our loads."

"Go on, you are kidding me, ain't ya?"

"No, what makes you think that?"

"Eat my sarnies with this smell around us?"

"What smell?" he asked me. "What do you mean? What smell, are you having me on?"

We were emptying our load as I was talking to him. I pointed to the sewage that was passing us at about thirty miles an hour. "That smell that comes from that," I said to him.

He put his head under the railings with his nose about two and a half feet from the sewage, took a really good sniff, looked at me and said, "I can't smell anything."

With a rubber hammer we uncoupled the pipes, put them away on the side of the tanker, sat in the cab and ate our sarnies. Dougie opened his sarnies, held one in his mouth while he poured out his tea from a flask, put his feet on the dash board, opened his newspaper and never uttered a word for the whole of our lunch break. I was feeling a little sick at the thought of eating my lunch in a dirty cab in a sewage farm, I tried, but I couldn't face it, so I drank my tea. I thought the dust carts were bad enough, but this!

I worked there a few months, I even enjoyed doing it after a couple of days, and yes, I ate my lunch at the same spot every day, where at first I couldn't, and believe it or not after a couple of weeks I too could not smell that sewage – they say you get used to anything in time, that is so true.

Apart from going around to little villages, we went to some beautiful little cottages that stood in little gardens on their own. To my surprise they had an outside toilet, you know the type, they had a plank with a hole in it with a bucket under the plank – those cottages didn't have a cess pit. I had to carry the bucket to the tanker and pour it into an aperture that was designed especially for that operation. At the back of the tanker I turned on a valve that would suck up all the waste that was put in it, it then entered the main body of waste in the tanker. I then replaced the bucket back in the correct position, that was one operation I defiantly did not get used to. When I returned to the back of the tanker there was a little hose pipe fixed by the aperture, and when the pump was turned on there came a strong jet of water from the hose, which allowed me to wash away any waste that was clinging to the sides. People that lived in the countryside in those days were subsidised till it changed overnight. The charges went from fifteen shillings a load, to seven pounds a load – they were angry, I can tell you; a lot of them let their cess pit overflow and soak away through the soil. One man I was talking to was throwing in a bucket attached to a rope, and when he retrieved it he watered his vegetable garden with it. I declined the offer of free veg from him. I don't think it's legal to use sewage to water the garden, and anyway, I wouldn't recommend it. I was asked many times if I would do a load half price with no ticket, of course I refused (I didn't have many friends when I did that job, ha ha); talk about Dickensian times, and that was in the 1970s when I was emptying buckets of waste.

SOLIHULL COUNCIL

When I was working temporary for this council helping out in the bin lorry, I was asked if I would work for them permanent, driving a new road sweeper. Why not, I thought. It was very small and it sounded like a jet engine when it was put into the sweep mode – I had to wear ear defenders it was so noisy. I was asked to go around the Solihull area to try it out, so I went into a grove where there were lots of leaves on the road and they were damp, but it would not pick up wet leaves. As I was running up and down that grove a lady came over to me and started to bang on the door of my sweeper – she asked me if I would go away as her husband was very ill, that tells you how noisy it was. So I tried other roads, but it was the same, I made more mess than there was there before. Back to the yard I went and explained it was a useless tool. It turned out it was made to sweep around shopping precincts for dust and bits of paper, not roads. It was broken down more than it was used, so I doubled up with a crew going around, sweeping the streets for a short time.

The winter came, and I was driving a snow plough at night, and gritting the icy roads, and in the day time I even drove a lorry with a gang of men cleaning up the town centres of different areas. I drove the cesspit lorries in the Meriden area of Warwickshire countryside, emptying the cesspits and taking them to the sewage farm in Barston lane, Solihull, that is mentioned in another chapter in this book. I even worked in the yard at times.

One day I took the team out to sweep the roads up by hand, I then returned to the yard. I wanted to leave early as it was my anniversary, but the boss was in a bad mood that day, for what reason I have no idea. He started to have a go at me, saying no one cared enough about their jobs enough. That was it, I said, "Lick em on – I'm off." That was the last time I worked for that council.

EAST BIRMINGHAM HOSPITAL

My wife, Irene, worked at this hospital, so did my sister, Doreen, they both worked there for some years. I got a job there as a driver-porter, and I remember that interview very well. I was asked if I could drive their little three-wheel artics. "Yes, I have a licence from the railway to drive those," I told them.

I was taken to a quiet spot where there was a large concrete pad. There were two doors in the building, about five feet apart, and the head porter got into the cab and reversed it up to one of the doors, parking it across the doors, then he asked me to drive away, then back it up to the same door, as he had done. So I did it perfectly. I thought, after all these years I still have the knowhow.

He laughed and said, "That was great, and dead straight – I can see you have done it before." My chest came out, I felt good. He said, "Trouble is, you backed up to the wrong door." I felt such an idiot. Still laughing, he said, "It doesn't matter, you have got the job."

I had to work shifts, weekends as well. Every dinnertime when the kitchens had leftovers from the restaurant, us porters were given them; needless to say I ate very well while I worked there and piled on the pounds.

One of my duties was to go around all the wards collecting drugs and specimens. Another duty was to collect the dirty laundry, boy some of those bags stunk – those nurses deserve medals. Another duty was to take bodies to the mortuary, or Rose Cottage as it was known, we also had to take dinners to the wards, then collect the dirty dishes, if that wasn't enough we were used as security guards as well! We were taught to do cardiac massage, but I'm glad to say I never had to do any of that for real. I also changed oxygen cylinders and delivered them to the wards; it's a very worthwhile job but it wasn't for me (what was I wonder?).

EAST BIRMINGHAM HOSPITAL

MR. D PROSSER.

This is to certify that the above named has been authorised to drive Hospital Vehicles of the following types:
ALL TYPES

Drivers Signature ....

Authorised by : ....

Expiry Date :........31.12.78

MR 107

My East Birmingham Hospital Driving Licence
(now known as Heartlands Hospital)
My Mom always called it Little Bromwich Hospital.

I had to go in on Christmas day, and I missed my two children opening their presents; I missed seeing the excitement on their faces as they tore open the presents – that hurt.

I transferred to the maintenance department, and I was literally all over the hospital then, seeing to pumps, attending to leaking steam pipes, even plumbing. I spent most of my time hiding and skiving – no walkie-talkies or mobiles in those days – when the boss was looking for me, he hadn't a chance of finding me. When he said he'd been looking for me and mentioned different places in the hospital, I would say, "Oh, by that time I was somewhere else, doing something else." It was easy to lie and get away with it. Nowadays it wouldn't happen, not with mobiles on the scene.

"Oh, never mind," the boss would say.

All the maintenance men did it, I bet there is still a way of hiding, there always is.

New adventures calling, I handed in my notice; I'd done about five months. Hospitals – definitely not my cup of tea, mind you, no job ever was.

D AND G SUPPLIES

When I left East Birmingham hospital (many years ago it was known as the fever hospital) I got a job driving a Luton van for a firm known as D and G Supplies. They sold plumbing materials, bathrooms and kitchens.

After a very short time I was asked to sell bathroom suites on Saturdays, I enjoyed that, it was a challenge. I tried to excel as a salesman. I'm ashamed to admit when a customer was looking around the sales room, I would very slowly walk up to them and say, "Is there any one bathroom suite you like more than the others?" I got to tell which customers were really interested. I did get it wrong a few times, but in the main I won the day. I was not on a bonus or any extra wages, I just really enjoyed helping out the customers. I got a kick out of it when I got a good sale, the only little white lie I told them was, whatever bathroom suite they picked, I would say, "How strange is that? I've just bought that same one, I had it fitted last week; it looks lovely in situ." I would steer them away from the cheap, rubbish one. The one thing I do remember was the name, Sherrington; we had a cheap one and a dearer one – one was ten ml. thick and the other was only eight ml. thick, but they looked identical, so I always told the customer how to tell the difference.

One Saturday afternoon a lady went to the owner, my boss, and said to him, "Your salesman, Dave, is the most polite and well mannered salesman I have ever come across." That was my third Saturday as a salesman with that company. Another Saturday I was talking to a couple who had their two children with them, why I remember how many of them there were, I have no idea, the only thing I can think of was it was because of the man. How it worked at that time was, I would sell the goods, hand the paperwork over to the boss, and he would work out the discounts and the total cost. This particular day we were very busy, that family spent over a thousand pounds, and I took the paperwork to the boss.

"Dave," he said, "you do it, I'm very busy."

So I sat down and filled out the bill, did the discounts and costed it all out. As I looked up the man was looking really concerned. "Everything OK, sir?" I asked him.

"Well," he replied, "you working that out in your head..."

His wife interrupted him, "It's all right." she looked at him with daggers.

"Would you like me to use a calculator, sir?" I asked.

His wife, again going red, said, "No it's all right."

"Yes," he replied, so I went to get the calculator. As I was walking away I heard her having a right go at him. So I did it on the machine – I had my toes, legs and fingers crossed – please let it be right, I was saying to myself. It came out to the penny, exactly as I had worked it out. I kept showing him the calculator, and his wife kept apologizing; he didn't care, he was happy to know he hadn't been fiddled. I helped them load up the van, I never got a tip, and as they got into their van she was still having a go at him. Next customer here I come.

At the end of that day the boss came up to me and pushed a five-pound note into my top pocket. "Thanks, Dave, you did a great job today, you are the best salesman I've ever had."

The manager said, "What does he think the rest of us have been doing, sitting on our backsides?"

All the other staff were annoyed. It was a bad move on his part, because they all said, "Right, we won't try anymore." They were the sales team; I was only the delivery driver.

The only trouble with selling a lot of bathroom suites on a Saturday was it meant a lot of deliveries in the week. Come Monday morning we loaded the van only to find I had two deliveries in Hall Green and a delivery in Stechford and one in Chelmsley Wood. Trouble was, they were all for dinnertime, twelve noon. Of course I got it in the neck from all the customers, I was late getting to them. I think the sales team were getting their own back and all because the boss gave me a fiver in front of them. When I got back I asked them why they put the delivery times at the same time, and with a smile they said, "Oh dear, you shouldn't have sold so many, should you?" as they walked away from me. That fiver gave me a very hard time and the boss lost sales because of it.

After that I went into the shower room selling the showers on a Saturday; that was an interesting job. All the sales were down and the boss never knew why. They all gave up trying, mind you, it made my job easier – a lot less deliveries, more time to myself. I got fed up, the sales staff weren't happy, and the customers were moaning.

One Wednesday afternoon when I was serving, the boss said, "Dave, the till was down yesterday, so will you not go on it anymore; leave all the money side to Derrick." He always worked behind the counter selling the plumbing items. Well as you can imagine, I hit the roof and told him to, "lick em on," there and then, and I walked out. That was me back in the unemployment queue.

THE JOB I NEVER GOT

When we sold our house, number 56, Berwicks Lane, Chelmsley Wood, we moved to Warton in north Warwickshire, on the edge of the countryside, number 102-104 Orton Road. I was jobless once again.

For the first time in our lives we received from our solicitor a cheque for £2,000. We were advised to apply for a grant from the council to renovate the cottages we had just bought. The council approved a grant of £2,000, but only as the work progressed. In the meantime I found a warehouse that sold cane and basket ware, you know the type, raffia and dried grasses, it was all the rage at the time so I bought mountains of it, so much I couldn't get it all in the car. It was very cheap, so I sold it cheap. I had bought hanging baskets, hammocks, picnic baskets macramé, raffia, fly swatters, corn dollies and many, many more items of that nature. We did house parties at night.

My then wife worked as a dental nurse in Marston Green and Chelmsley Wood in Birmingham. I stayed at home ripping apart the two cottages we had just bought. I had signed on the dole, as at that time there were almost four million unemployed in the country. I used to take my wife to work in the mornings, go back home, work on the house until it was time to pick her up in the evenings, then back home I would start working again on the cottages. I knocked the two cottages into one, ripped out the ceilings in one and dug up the floors. I took out the stairs, knocked the plaster off the walls and stripped out the wiring of one house while we lived in the other one. Then repeated it all over again in the other cottage. After we had our dinner we would get changed and sell our basket ware in people's houses. To start the ball rolling I would wrap up an ornament that cost only 75p and sell strips of raffle tickets for 50p, I made as much as £10 on some occasions. I did that at every house party, sometimes I only made £3. I used to buy sand and cement, plaster and gravel with the raffle money.

Not far from our two cottages was a working coal mine and I had the idea I would become a miner – I know it's a joke, and I know it's on me! As my money was running out I needed to earn and with the lack of employment I thought I would try the coalmines. So one Monday morning on the way back from taking Irene to work, I popped into the personnel office of the coalmine to enquire about their vacancy. A round-faced little man came out to see me. "You are enquiring about the vacancy we have are you?" he asked me.

"Yes, sir." I always said sir when I was creeping to get a job.

"Where are you working at present?" he questioned.

"I'm unemployed at the moment," I told him, and his mouth opened and his eyes went wide, well that happened after I had explained I handed in my notice and left my job as the travelling was too much – it was 17 miles there and 17 miles back, 34 miles round trip and I just couldn't afford it.

"Well surely you knew that when you came to live in this area," he exclaimed.

"Well, yes I did," I explained. "I was hoping to get a job here in this village."

"And you just packed your job up – just gave it up." He started to stammer, "You, you ju... just pa... pa... packed it up so you don... don't earn any wages at... at all, just packed it up!"

I was smiling, it was then I realised no one did such things in that industry. "We have men here that... that started as very young boys, their dads and their granddads worked here, whole families, generation after generation – no one leaves, only to retire and we have to push 'em to do that. I'm sorry, son, I could not employ you." As he turned and started to walk away he was muttering to himself, "Just packed his job up." He was still muttering as he disappeared through the door. I thought it was funny; it was a normal occurrence for me to hand in my notice. So I never became a miner – that was one job I never got, to be very honest I only wanted that job so I could say "I've been a miner" as well. I might even have lasted a couple of weeks. Since then that mine has shut down. (Not because of me, I must add).

WORKING AWAY

When me and my brother John were between jobs, (I was between jobs much more than John was, he was more steadfast than I ever was) we were in our mom's back garden one afternoon when the lad who lived next door climbed up his ladders to fix his guttering. We started to have a conversation with him; his name was Stuart, he had been unemployed for a short while, and he told us he was a floor layer, well floor screeding. He was telling us he had been in touch with a firm and was waiting for the boss of the firm to tell him if he had acquired a contract that was in Wales. He asked would we be interested in working out of town, casual, cash in hand, as the job needed two labourers and a floor layer.

He did get the contract – the job was in a town named Haverfordwest in Wales, not far from St. David's. We went in my car as I was the only one with a vehicle at that time, and booked into a pub – for the life of me I can't remember the name of it, but we were on the top floor of that pub.

Next day we went to the site for a look to see what was what. It was a lovely setting. They were building an indoor market, it went about the quarter way across a river and boats were going under that building, it really was in a beautiful area. They were building walls and walkways in beautiful stone boulders, but the only drawback for me and John was to get to the top of that building with our barrow loads of floor screed. They had erected a ramp that went up a slope to a small square landing, then up another slope to a square, the same again, three slopes. Brother, that was hard work to begin with till our muscles got built up, then we enjoyed it.

We had dinner cooked for us every night, well she wasn't a cook, all we got was chips all the time, and we asked for a cooked roast dinner but never got it. Every night they had late night drinking that sometimes went on till the early hours of the morning.

One Tuesday evening we were getting ready to go for a walk around the town to see if there was a restaurant where we could get a nice meal, when we heard what seemed like a thousand women's voices. It turned out, every Tuesday was disco night, and the floor below our floor was where the ladies toilet was, and as we sat on our beds listening to the conversations of those ladies we were a little shocked I can tell you – I thought only men talked like that. Well I was a lot younger then and innocent, well younger anyway. We were away doing that job for three weeks; I loved it, happy memories.

MY SHOP

It was the one thing I wanted to do as a youngster was to have my own shop, well we all have a dream of one sort or another, but mostly we never realise our dream do we? I always fancied opening a hardware shop, I used to love the smell of them, and when seeing them on films they always looked better than they actually were in real life. As a child I was sent to the hardware shop for a ball of white and a blue, this was used to whitewash the coalhouse (yes, sounds a bit mad when I think about it now). The smell of paraffin and soaps, straw, timber, all those smells mixed together, I loved it, makes me feel very nostalgic thinking about it, and yes, I have my rose coloured glasses on as the saying goes.

I saw a shop across the road from the snooker hall I used as a youth in Stechford, the same one me and Johnny did a runner from, this shop was a very well used grocery shop in those days when I worked for Donovans, but by this time it was a second hand clothes shop. It was up for rent at twenty pounds a week. I went to the council, signed all the necessary documents and paid a month's rent in advance. The lady who had been running the shop was really glad to leave, she wanted out, but me, I was full of enthusiasm, I had this dream of a string of shops, Prossers, a string of shops all over Birmingham (well OK I can dream, can I not? It was a very short lived dream I can tell you).

I loved making models so I opened up as a hobby shop, Family Hobbies we called it (my wife begged me not to have a shop; I wish I had listened to her. I can sell and make money for anyone, but not for myself it would appear). I sold fur fabric, eyes for furry animals, matchstick kits, all sorts of things for the hobbyist, trouble was, I was still living in the forties and it was the 1980s and I thought everybody was like me, but I soon found out different; it was a disaster, it wasn't working at all.

My nephew came to see me; he had been made redundant from the Co-op where he had been a manager in the delicatessen department. "Dave, why don't you turn your shop into a delicatessen shop? If these hobbies ain t doing any good, I can teach you all there is to know about selling cooked meats – how to slice them up, even how to slice up half a pig and all the different cuts and how to slice up the bacon." Sounds good I thought, can't be worse than these hobbies.

So I sorted everything out with the council and the health and safety people. I bought tiles and did all the walls in tiles top to bottom, fitted in a sink, I bought fridges, scales, counters and knives, even cooler counters, all second hand from the Co-op warehouse. They stored all the fridges and counters from shops that they had closed down and I bought them for next to nothing, fifty pounds in fact. I even got scales from there at a fiver; this manager was really good to me.

My nephew Kevin, that's my sister Doreen's son, he taught me well, he knew all the right contacts to buy the meats from. I found a firm in Perry Bar called Warwick Meats, and I bought my sausages from them, 300 pounds in weight of sausage every week. We did sandwiches at dinnertime, and all the factory people would queue outside the shop for them. I ran a raffle on my first week of opening, £20 worth of free meat to one of my lucky customers for shopping at my shop. We were getting known and were doing well. We called the shop W. P. Cooked Meats. Then one Monday morning not a customer came in. Strange, I thought, OK, I will do some boning and slice up my bacon. Come dinnertime I was ready for the crowd of office workers who bought lots of sandwiches from me, but not a soul. I stood outside my shop and it was a ghost town, I just could not understand what was going on, no one had said anything to me.

On that same evening, a lady that worked in the office across the road from my shop for a haulage company, and always came into my shop, walked in. "You are my first customer today," I told her, "it's been absolutely dead, have you any idea what's going on?"

"Have you not heard, Dave? All the factories across the road there," she was pointing to factories, "have closed down and the entire workforce has been made redundant. Didn't anyone tell you last week?" she asked.

My hobbies shop

My hobbies shop changed to a cooked meats shop, W.P. Cooked Meats

"Not a word from anyone," I told her.

That was the start of my downfall. What do I do now, I thought, I haven't recovered all of my money yet. I was thinking, OK, I will weather the storm, but it got worse and worse.

One Monday morning I opened up, filled all the counters with the cooked meats, black puddings, bacon and cheese, I made a really good display. I cleaned everywhere, I was proud of that shop, it looked good, but still no customers. After an hour I closed the shop, weighed and wrapped up all the meats in quarter, half and one pound packages, ready to go around to all my family and friends that evening and sell it all. I phoned up a company that bought second hand machines, counters and the like, told them how much I wanted, and they came the next day, took out the shop window and emptied the shop and replaced the window. I phoned the council to say I had ceased trading and was putting it up for sale. It took a few weeks to sell that shop, by which time I was in arrears – I hadn't a penny to my name. We were eating toast for Sunday lunch, I couldn't feed my two children, that hurt me the most. I sold the shop, my life's savings had gone and I had to sell my two cottages that I had worked on for three years knocking the two into one. I sold them, or should I say *it,* as it was now one dwelling and not two, and I paid off all the debts I had acquired through the shop from the sale of the cottage, and bought a cheap council house. I had cleared all my debts; I owed no one anything, and I bought the council house for cash – I had no mortgage, not a penny in the bank or in my pocket. My wife worked part time, that's how we ate, because of her, so after all that hard work at the age of forty, we were back to how we were, well we had a house.

Since then we worked hard, sold that council house, bought and sold houses and did them up as we went along. I started to collect antiques toys, which I have now sold to fund the books I have written, including this one. We now own two houses and have got a little sum of money in the bank. We are now retired and enjoying the freedom of life.

This photograph was taken in March 1955.
The shop on the far right became my shop in July 1979.
It was situated in Station Road, Steachford, Birmingham. At first I had it as a hobbies shop called Family Hobbies, then I changed it into a delicatessen shop called W-P Cooked Meats. It has now been demolished. The factory on the right called Parkinson Cowen made gas stoves has also been demolished.

WORKING WITH BOOKS

As I was looking through the jobs that were on the boards in the job centre (known as the labour exchange) there were many, but as normal when jobs were in that place the wages offered were always very poor. As I scanned the rows of vacancies I came across what looked a very interesting job, it was a job I had never thought of doing. On the card it read: *Temporary H.G.V. driver required for six weeks only, to drive a coach converted into a mobile library.* Well I've never driven a coach, I thought to myself, nor have I ever worked with books, but I took the card to a lady sitting waiting for a fool like me to take on a low paid temporary job like this one. I was quite excited to be honest with you, I loved doing different things and seeing how things worked. I had never worked with books or driven a coach before but I really wanted the job. The lady explained to me that the regular driver was off sick, that's why the job was for such a short time. How they knew he would only be off sick for six weeks I have no idea.

I went for the interview in a little town known as Atherstone, in Warwickshire. The library wasn't a large one; I was interviewed by the Head Librarian, a very nice gentleman, very smart and quietly spoken, I bet that's because working around books they never raised their voices, well it's a thought. Any road up, after I had had the job explained to me he took me to see the vehicle, the mobile library coach. I always fancied driving a coach but you had to have a special licence called a P.S.V. (public service vehicle) for driving passengers, and as I didn't have such a licence and I only needed a class two, driving that coach really appealed to me, and I could drive it on my licence. I can now proudly say I've driven a coach. As I walked into the coach the librarian told me to sit in the driver's seat to see if I liked it. "It's OK," I said, "I don't need to sit in it, I know it's all right." But he insisted so I sat in the seat.

"How does that feel?" he enquired.

"It's fine, sir." (I always said 'sir' when I was grovelling.)

"Do you want the job?" he then asked me.

"Yes, sir," I replied.

"Good. Can you start in the morning at 9am?"

"Yes, sir."

"Good; follow me, I will introduce you to the two ladies who you will be working with." Now that really excited me, two ladies – I wonder if my luck will change, I was thinking to myself (I know I'm a married man, well men always hope if they are truthful. I wouldn't have chatted them up it's just wishful thinking). It just got better and better when I saw how beautiful the ladies were.

The next morning I got to the library an hour before my time. I was a little apprehensive because I'm not the brightest pin in the box, so I did what I always do in those circumstances, I kept quiet (I know that made a change for me) till I had some idea about what was being asked of me. As far as chatting up the ladies that was a definite no, no all they were interested in was books, oh well you can't win them all can you? It made such a nice change to work with nice educated quietly spoken people (and they talked with a posh voice), never a word was said out of place by them, nor me if it comes to that, life for me was very pleasant at that time. I loved driving around the country lanes.

We were about half way round the route when one of the ladies left us, I think she must have been there just to make sure I was OK. The other lady told me to drive to a cottage where the driver who was off sick lived, he was doing lunch for us, he only charged five shillings – he lived on his own. His cottage was in a little village known as Wood End. I parked right outside his front gate; there was no footpath. It was a beautiful little cottage, the type I wished I lived in now in this year of 2011. As the door of the cottage opened a four foot nothing man stood there, he was as fat as two matchsticks tied together! How on earth do you drive the mobile library coach, I was thinking to myself. The inside of the cottage was a dream, I felt so at home there, low polished beamed ceilings, an inglenook fire place, polished beams surrounding it. There was an Aga cooker with a steaming kettle on it, and cast-iron saucepans simmering next to it with potatoes and vegetables in them and the smell of beef cooking (I can smell it now, and as I write I can still see the inside of that beautiful little cottage). It was winter so it was a little dark so the wall lights were on; having red shades on them they gave a very nice red glow to the white walls and the dark oak

Delivering books all around the countryside

polished beams. With the flickering flames from the Aga dancing on the ceiling for a moment I was a boy again remembering how our fire at home flickered images on the walls and ceiling. I felt so much at peace I could have been in heaven. The table and chairs were dark oak, and the table was laid with a red cloth with white plates and tureens that matched with serving ladles, and bone handled knives and forks. Yes, my friends, I was in heaven. As he opened the Aga cooker oven door there was a large earthenware dish which he pulled out and placed on the top of the Aga. He turned and said "I hope you like beef?"

"Yes," we both replied together.

"I've also made an apple pie and custard for you."

My mouth was watering as he put the veggies in the tureens and the steam came floating out; again it reminded me of home as a boy. He put the beef on a large meat dish and placed it on the table and carved it up. We handed him our plates and he was very generous with the portions; we helped ourselves to the vegetables. It was all cooked to perfection – the beef melted in one's mouth and his apple pie was to die for, as the saying goes. What a gentleman; a first class host and to top all that, a wonderful cook.

After we had eaten we chatted for half an hour. It turned out he had joined the library at the tender age of fourteen. He was called up to do his National Service in the army and he went to war for the defence of our wonderful country. He came home after being demobbed, and got his old job back at the library. I never found out why he was off sick, I never asked. He looked well to me, but looks can be deceiving, can't they? I paid him my five shillings and shook his hand. We had lunch not every day, but twice a week, and I will never forget that wonderful English gentleman, his kindness, and his wonderful cooking. His way of living is what we all dream about but never get. The first time I left that little cottage to return back to work, I turned to the young lady I worked with and said "I want that cottage and that life style."

"Me too," she replied with a smile. He was a working class man but he had all that life can offer anyone.

Off we went to rich and poor alike, cottages, manor houses, farms, I loved every moment of that job and I was very sorry when it ended. Now there was a job I would never have said "Lick em on – I'm off" to.

CLEANING UP THE ESTATE

The second time I started working for the Solihull Council I was asked if I minded cleaning toilets for a short time, a couple of weeks or so. Cleaning toilets is a job I swore I would never do – one should never say never! Well I did start to clean the toilets in the Chelmsley Wood area and I hated every second I was doing that job.

The toilets around Chelmsley Wood were vandalised on a daily basis. I was asked by the foreman if I would nail up the doors of the cubicles on one particular toilet block because the pans had been smashed and were dangerous to the public, as china when broken is extremely sharp. So with lengths of timber, six feet long by three inches wide by one inch thick, and six inch nails, I nailed up all the doors to each cubicle from the inside. I climbed back over the partitions (I was fit in those days) and assumed that all would be OK from there on in. The next morning, to my surprise, the lads from that estate had worked very hard to open those doors, they had kicked and bashed them till they could no longer be called doors, they were in pieces. The noise they made must have been immense; why the neighbours living close by never did anything about it I will never understand. I went straight back to the depot and made out my report. A team went out and locked up the toilet block, and it was never used again, so the older folk of that area had a long walk to the town centre if they needed to use a toilet. That toilet block has since been demolished. I hope those mindless idiots when they become elderly, find when they are taken short that the toilets they wish to use are closed down or have been demolished.

I was taken off the toilets (I'm glad to say) and given a little tipper van to drive. My new job was going all around the Chelmsley Wood Estate emptying the concrete rubbish bins at the end of every walk way. They were all full of garden rubbish, and as soon as I emptied them they were filled up by the next morning. One morning as I was removing clods of turf, house bricks, boulders, metal objects, from one of those bins, a gentleman came out of his house and said, "These bins cause more trouble than they are worth, if they weren't here I'm sure the area would be cleaner." So I told my foreman what had been said.

"OK, Dave," he replied, "go to the stores and get a sledge hammer and start to knock them all down, but I haven't told you to do it, you will have to say you know nothing about it."

So back to the bins I went and over a couple of weeks I demolished dozens of them – no one from the council ever noticed that they no longer existed.

I went around that area for a few weeks and it was always clean, which meant I was having a really easy job, I was getting paid for doing nothing. When the foreman finally realised I was doing nothing, he put me driving the gully emptying lorry (that's the drains in the road). Those drain covers were very heavy, mind you I was quite strong in my youth. They were hard to move at times because of the traffic running over them all the time, and with the dirt going down the sides of them they became wedged. So with a sledge hammer I hit one corner of the drain cover and that always worked, it made it loose so I could then lift it off to suck all the rubbish out with the long vacuum hose into the tank on the back of the lorry.

In between driving the gully emptier, I drove a little lorry; I used that lorry like it was my own. For two weeks I went to my brother's house that he had just purchased, and I worked pulling down the ceilings. I filled the lorry up every day with the rubbish from those ceilings and took it to the tip. When the foreman asked where I had been working I told him the name of a road, and he would say, I looked for you there, I would then say, well after that I went to such a road, and he would reply, I went there as well, we must have been passing each other all the time. I got away with it for weeks. I was moving rubbish for myself and for my friends all the time; it's no wonder the council struggle for money, for I was not alone doing my own thing in work's time. I liked that job but the jobs one liked doing were always low pay.

One morning the boss was in a bad mood and he started to have a go at me, so, yes, my favourite saying was used, lick em on – I'm off.

S. G. B.

Scaffolding, Great Britain – this firm is based next to Birmingham airport. I got the job from the job centre in Chelmsley Wood; it was only temporary, eight weeks in total, not a bad job.

I worked in a shed with no doors; my job was to sand down the shuttering boards that had been returned from the building sites all around the country. Any holes and deep scratches had to be filled in with car body filler; I think it was called Tetrasill. Mixing the paste with the hardener, which came in small tubes, it went hard in seconds, then with an electric drill gun with a sanding disc fitted in the chuck, the whole board was sanded till all the concrete and body filler was smooth, then the boards were put in piles awaiting the fork lift to take them into the yard. They were then put on top of many other boards ready for the next building site that would be concreting new walls. When the walls were finished those shuttering boards were returned to the SGB yard where I worked, and the sanding process started all over again. The boss liked the way I worked and said I was a hard worker and would I like a permanent job with a rise in pay. I refused; I wanted to try to get a job I had never done before. I had no staying power at all, so I left and was again unemployed and I signed on the dole. The only excuse I can give in my defence is once I had mastered a job, I got bored, the challenge had gone – maybe I was lazy as well. When in a new job, I loved the challenge of mastering it. What's that I hear you say? I was irresponsible? I was, and that's the truth.

SECURITY GUARD

I worked a few times as a security guard, but I wasn't keen on this job, it was the kind of a job not many people liked doing. It was always cash in hand, and I worked sometimes in department stores. The young lads I found to be the worst, always trying to prove themselves, especially when they were with young girls – some of the shops deserved to get robbed. I know it's wrong to steal, but when you don't know where your next meal is coming from it makes one change from the way one normally acts. I know, I've been down and out; OK, I had a house, but no food or money, nothing coming in, and no one to turn to. Yes, I've been there. I might add it was all my own doing. I never was tempted to steal.

I worked nights in London in the Next shops. Their stores were having all the floors sanded and resealed; all the doors had to be open as the fumes from the sealant were overpowering. The finish was superb. I caught one of the workers going through the shoes; he soon stopped when he saw me. Mind you, me a security guard, that's a joke, while the floor sealant was drying we all got our heads down. I went fast asleep and one of the workers had a hard time waking me up. He remarked, "Boy, when you sleep you die, I had a real job waking you up!" They could have stolen lots of items, I'm sure they did. Did I care? No, not at all. I was getting two pounds fifty pence an hour cash in hand, no tax; slave labour wages, so I was only there for the money.

After all the Next shops had been done, I was sent to a place called Corby, Northamptonshire to a Woolworth store. The youths there were bad; it seemed nearly all of them there were banned from that store, the girls as well as the boys. They tested me all day long. I escorted many of them out of the store. They would try to see how weak I was; when I grabbed one of them by the arm he soon realised he was no match for me, so he stood outside the store shouting abuse at me, showing off in front of his mates and the girls – I think he was hiding his embarrassment at being thrown out of the store.

The manageress came up to me one day and said, “Watch that man there.” She pointed to a man that looked ok to me; shows you can never tell. “He carries a knife and he steals.” So I made sure he was aware of me. I did see him put a cassette tape in his pocket and then walk out of the store and I let him, I wasn’t about to get stabbed for two pounds fifty pence an hour, well for any amount of money if it comes to that.

A woman came up to me and introduced herself as the store detective – her nose looked like she had been ten rounds with a heavyweight boxer. She told me her nose had been punched so many times over the years, that’s why it looked like it did. I asked why she did such a job, and with a surprised look, said, “I love this work, don’t you?”

I very quickly replied, “No.” I was just filling in, I normally worked nights in the security game. I’m a peaceful loving fella, and I like the countryside. Chasing thieves and throwing people out of places is not me, I told her. I’m only here for the money; store security was a big no no for me. That Woolworths was the last store I worked in as a security guard. New horizons here I come.

GOVERNMENT SCHEME

This was the first government scheme I went on. I was working in peoples' gardens in the Atherstone area of Warwickshire; I worked two days one week and three the next week. I don't think I had a title, I did all sorts of jobs from digging over gardens, hedge cutting, sweeping up grass, seeding, even taking up lawns from the front of a house and relaying it in the back garden. The idea was to help the senior citizens that couldn't do the gardens themselves. We started to do young ladies gardens, and when I questioned them about this I was told to mind my own business. Just as I thought; the charge hand was taking back-handers, and not sharing it with us, his four workers, so I refused to do any gardens unless they were senior citizens.

As the weeks passed and the winter set in and the days became frost bitten, I asked the management if we were going to get a shanty to have our lunch in. "No," was the reply, "go to the nearest pub."

"That's not possible," I explained, "we are doing gardens in the country lanes at isolated cottages and there isn't a pub for miles. The foreman goes home in his car for dinner, so we are stranded." (It was agreed that any foreman taking on the job would use his car to transport the workforce to and from the job wherever it may be.) On one occasion we had to sit in a greenhouse, the wind was howling, everywhere was white with frost. It was colder inside that greenhouse than it was outside of it, so we sat at the back of the greenhouse outside to shelter from the wind to eat our lunch. Two of us went to the office to complain about the conditions, and we were told to get on with it and to stop complaining. We invited the two persons working in the office to join us for lunch in the greenhouse; of course they refused and accused us of being moaners, as they sat in their very hot office.

So they transferred me to the Coleshill group of gardeners. I was close to home with that group, and I had my car then on the road, funny thing was I never went home. The foreman was a much nicer person than the one on the other scheme, his name was Les, and we had a laugh with him. We did more playing around than we did gardening, mind you, when we did a garden it looked really good when we had finished it. I even as a favour to the foreman plumbed a tap in his outside garden toilet for him.

They gave them the title of foreman but like us they were just labourers. He was full time but only for a twelve month period. I did my two days one week and three the other, and at the end of the twelve months I was back on the dole. When those schemes finished, all that were employed went back on the dole. One thing I did notice among the youth that worked on those schemes was that it was soul destroying for them; they felt useless when thrown back on the unemployment system. Me I did OK, I knew how to survive one way or the other. I had taught myself many different trades – you know Jack of all trades, master of none.

B.V.S.C

This was a firm, well a scheme, which was started up in the 1980s by the government in the depression; it was a way for the government to get young people working. It was a scheme where the young generation of the country worked two days one week and three the next, just the same really, as the previous chapter. What the job was really, was to clean up the country. These jobs were advertised in the job centres as trainee gardeners, if you can call cleaning a waste piece of ground up on street corners and erecting a little wooden barrier up and raking over the soil without weeding, then throwing grass seed over it, gardening. OK – they were training as gardeners. All the lads moaned all the time saying, "We are just labouring, we wanted to be trained as gardeners."

We worked in the Aston Cross, Lozells, Perry Barr, Selly Oak, Small Heath, Tyseley, Acocks Green, and Handsworth, and my job was driving a lorry. I had two lads to do the labouring for me, there was about one hundred and fifty youngsters working there, they were in groups of eight plus the driver who had the privilege of being called the charge hand. The vehicle was a thirty-five hundred weight van. The youths had to sit on the wooden boxes along both sides of the van, that's where all the tools were kept and I might add padlocked up – there were a few vans. I was full time but the scheme only allowed me twelve months employment, then back on the dole. My job was to drive around to all the different sites where the teams were and load any rubbish they had accumulated, throw it into the lorry then off to the tip. I soon found out how unfair that job was. On some jobs where there was a load of earth that had been cleared from a site and left in a big pile by a team of eight or ten youths, it was expected that my two lads would load it on to the lorry. I soon put a stop to that. I used to get the team plus my two lads in a line and told them to do two shovelfuls each, that way my two lads were not worked to death, as the saying goes. On a good note, those two lads loved working with me; I would take them home early and clock them out or drop them off in the middle of town. I treated that lorry like it was my own and the job likewise. I would go joyriding in it round the country lanes, and use it to do jobs that were nothing to do with the firm, and get paid. I gave the lads any money we earned from the jobs we did – I always shared it out equally between them, well they were poorly paid so any extra was a Godsend to them.

Every morning was a trip to a café before we started work. Every Monday morning I used to go to the Birmingham rag market, and there was always an antiques fair on. I used to park outside the market, leave the two lads in the lorry and tell them to say I was inside looking for a Mr Jones, I had to pick up some rubbish, just in case a traffic warden tried to book me for illegal parking. I got away with that for a whole twelve months! That was my last job with my insurance cards placed in with a firm, the end of my working life – I hurt my neck and back, and became riddled with arthritis. I hated work anyway.

STUBBINS

I worked on Stubbins sites, but I didn't work for Stubbins direct, I worked for a carpenter, cash in hand. The site agent asked the carpenter why I always turned up at nine and not eight like he did; he told him I had to take my little boy to school. The agent thought I was a carpenter.

I was working on a roof one day fixing the rafters, and as I turned round I noticed the site agent was watching me, he never said a word, he was satisfied I was a carpenter and never bothered me again. Me a carpenter, that's a laugh! I'm what's known in the trade as a butcher of wood, mind you I have seen carpenters that weren't as good as me and I'm no good. I did it all with that carpenter, first and second fix, first fix being joists, roof timbers etc. and second fix being architrave, skirting boards and doors etc, on those houses. Stubbins paid the best wages of all the well-known builders. That company no longer exists, they went broke, and no – it wasn't because of me! Well it might have been – most of the places I worked for or at have ceased trading or their premises have been demolished. Would you like me to work for you?

APPENDICES

ROOMS AND HOUSES

I was born two years before the end of World War II, in October 1943. I was born and grew up at 38, Plowden Road, Glebe Farm, Stechford, Birmingham 33, and that's where I lived till I was eighteen.

My friends and I used to go to the pictures (cinema) every Saturday evening to find a tart, that's what we called young girls in those days; nowadays the lads call them birds, even totty. The picture houses we used in the forties and fifties were the Atlas, Beaufort and the Capital. There was a place, or should I say area, not far from where I lived called Shard End, next to an area known as Castle Bromwich, and there was a picture house there called the Castle Cinema. One Saturday morning my friend Trevor Kendall told me Cliff Richard was showing at the Castle Cinema – the film was called *Espresso Bongo*, so for the first time in my life I went to the Castle Cinema that evening, not to see the film but to see if I could get a tart. We had no luck that Saturday evening. "Well, that was a waste of time," I said to Trevor.

"It's OK, Dave, we can try next week."

"Yeah, that's true, Trev," I replied. So we decided to go to that cinema the next Sunday evening to find a couple of tarts.

We did what we did in every cinema we visited, we walked up and down the aisles trying to see if there were any girls sitting on their own, all the boys did that in those days, looking and hoping to find the girl of their dreams. Just to have a girl talk to me would have made me very happy, girls didn't go for me in those days. We changed our minds and went to the Atlas cinema on the Saturday evening; we went to the Castle Cinema on the Sunday evening instead. Any road up, as we were walking up and down the aisles, Trevor caught hold of my arm. "In here, Dave, there's a couple of tarts."

I looked but I could see only darkness so we sat down. When my eyes came used to the dark, I noticed a couple of girls sitting in front of us. "Trev, Trev," I said shaking his arm, "girls in front."

"I know," he said, "why do you think I said sit here?"

The film showing was *The Last of the Hunt*. That evening was to change the rest of my life; a whole new way of life lay ahead for me. Trevor being Trevor started to touch the girls' hair, they turned and smiled at him. The girl in front of me had a duffle coat, charcoal grey with white fur lining. Trevor said, "Look at her coat, Dave, they ain't half expensive."

The girl turned and said something to Trevor, I can't remember what now, but I made a comment and stroked her hair. I was shaking, waiting for the normal response of being told to get lost, but that never happened so I started to run my fingers up and down her face. To my unexpected surprise she allowed it! I was, to say the least, very excited. Trevor and another friend were chatting up her friend. I got really daring; I leant over her seat and kissed her, and I knew at that very moment what the opposite sex did for a man's insides, or at that time boy's – what boys say to impress the girls and our actions, are at the very least bizarre. As we walked the girls home my two mates were, how can I put it? – when birds dance and show their feathers, and Rhinos show their strength – my two mates were doing just that. Brother, did they look and sound stupid, and it was at that very moment I realised just how pathetic I had been in the past when trying to impress the opposite sex. It's something boys have to do as they are growing up; girls never seem to have to do such silly things. I smile now when I see and hear the young lads trying to impress the young girls, mind you when it works there isn't a feeling in the world like it! I was locked in the arms of the girl that bowled me over while Trevor and Michael were still trying to impress Susan Godden. The girl I was kissing was Irene Parker; she wore white slip-on shoes with a big white button in the middle of them, the skirt and top were lilac and white check that she had made herself, and with the duffle coat she looked to me a million dollars, and she was.

I was wearing (and I thought I looked great) black slip-on shoes, white socks, black trousers, orange shirt, light green jumper with an orange v neck, and a grey coat with black and white dots; the white was mixed in with the black dots, not separate, with locks over the pockets, I say locks, they were pieces of material with a buttonhole at the bottom of them and they buttoned up over the pocket. I had bought all my clothes on HP (hire purchase) a couple of weeks before. I must have looked like a clown. I met Irene inside the Castle cinema at approx 7.45pm on the thirteenth of March, 1960 (poor girl). We got married at All Saints Church, Shard End, Birmingham, because where your young lady lived that's where you had to get married. On the evening of our wedding day, we slept on a mattress on the floor of Irene's parents' living room; I smoked at that time. The day I got married, I hadn't a cigarette, not a penny piece to my name, no bank account, no nothing, I suppose really we should not have got married but she was three months pregnant. Irene had five shillings – that was our wealth. Well, we had each other and that's all that mattered at that moment in time, so apart from five shillings we had nothing.

When I met Irene on the 13th of March 1960, she worked at Barrows stores in the Birmingham city centre as a wages clerk, and I worked as a rounds boy for the CO-OP bakery Manor Road in Stechford, Birmingham. The day we got married Irene worked for a firm called Donovans, who I used to work for but I left. I used to play for Donovans' football team; we won the league that year. My new job was at Kunzles. Donovans made electric interiors for mains electric cabinets to go in factories or very large buildings, Kunzles made cakes.

Our lives changed as they do when one gets married. The day before I got married I moved all my belongings from my mom's house to Irene's parents' house; I had a bike that I had bought out of my paper round money and three Kunzles paper carrier bags, yes all my worldly possessions were in three Kunzles paper carrier bags, but I was very happy. As Irene became more pregnant she left Donovans and worked part time for a lady who ran a sweet shop just up the road from where we lived, the shop was called Keens. We only stayed at Irene's parents' home for a short time, trouble was I was really common and her dad couldn't stand the sight of me, he would have done anything to have got me away from Irene. Looking back now at the young me, if my daughter had met someone like me, I too would have worried like Irene's dad did.

Irene's parents lived at 132, Timberley Lane, Shard End. My first son was born there in 1962, we named him Anthony. Just before he was born I papered and painted the bedroom so it looked nice for my wife and when all her family and friends called to see her with our new son. The trouble was there were stripes in the paper and I got them slightly on the slope, everyone thought it was great but I think people were just being kind. The paper was white with tiny lilac flowers, the doors were lilac and the paintwork white. I was very proud of my first painting and decorating job, Irene said she loved it and was very proud of me (I wonder if she would say that nowadays, yeah, I think she would).

In July 1962, as I could not get on with Irene's dad, we found rooms in a big old house in Birmingham, an area known as Erdington. The house was in Mason road, I think it was number 2; it had been turned into flats. It was quite run down but we moved in. In July 1962, the rent was £2/15/-0d a week. We took the flat on the second floor, it had two more flats up in the attic, and we lived there for only four weeks. After the first week I walked into the house from work, and as I started to climb the stairs my wife popped her head out from the flat on the ground floor. She told me the landlord had asked if we would move to the ground floor flat, as we had a young baby and it would be easier to get the pram in and out of the house, plus it was a nice view out of the French windows onto the garden. The interior was worn and dirty, and as my son was only six weeks old then I was concerned for his health. One evening as I was plugging in the iron, into the light socket, the light fitting fell off and left the bare wires hanging from the ceiling. On closer examination I found the fitting was held in by matchsticks! Just thinking about that now makes me angry; that was a very dangerous thing to do – and my son at times in his pram would have been asleep under that light fitting!

One Saturday afternoon a young lady appeared with a man and a baby; it turned out she had left her husband and was outcast by her family as she had had an affair, got pregnant and bought shame on the family. She was a twin and came from a wealthy family. We helped her and gave her things as she had nothing. We ourselves had only one knife and fork each and two spoons, even our baby clothes were hand me downs. We tried hard to clean up the place but it was a job too far at that time, so my wife, Irene, asked her dad if we could go back to his house for a short time. The rent on the flat was paid up to date, but the landlord said we had to give two weeks' notice and find him another tenant, so Irene's dad came late afternoon to move us out, but the tenant in the other flat was a friend of the landlord's and she phoned and told him we were moving out. He didn't live far away because he came around to see us before we had got everything in the car, and what we had would have hardly filled a car boot. Well the landlord was red-faced and very angry shouting and waving his arms about. "You are not leaving," he shouted, and then he grabbed the father-in-law's suitcase that we had just filled, saying, "Well, I'm going to have this," and he ran out of the door and attempted to go up the stairs. My father-in-law chased after him, caught hold of the suitcase, and as he did the handle broke.

"That's it now," Irene's dad said to him, "I will sue you for damages."

"You are not leaving," the landlord kept shouting, so I slipped out and called the police. When the police arrived they tried in vain to calm down the landlord, but it was hopeless, he kept saying, "My brother is a policeman."

"Where is he?" he was asked time and again. After the police officer had asked a few more times, the landlord said, "In Dublin, Ireland."

"That's it," the police officer said, as he shoved him out into the hallway and into the kitchen, "now stay away from these people and let them leave."

Irene got into the car with my son Anthony. I only had two suitcases left to put into the car, so her dad started the engine. I ran as fast as I could with the suitcases, threw them into the boot of the car, and we newlyweds were driven away from what then was a terrifying ordeal. Welcome to the world of married life, I thought. Even though Irene's dad didn't like me, he was there to help his daughter as any good father should be.

Back at Irene's parents' house once more in Timberly Lane, we had the little small bedroom that my son Anthony was born in, the one I had decorated. We were there for only three weeks when Irene found rooms in a house in Shard End, not far from her parents house, this house was in Priestland Road. I moved all our belongings on a pram, mind you all we had was a cot, a borrowed suit case and a few clothes, and in just over half an hour we had moved.

We set up the bedroom and left some bags in the dining room. We had rented the dining room and the bedroom and shared the kitchen, but it was never going to work, the woman only wanted the money, she never wanted us there at all, she lived on her own with her little dog and her tins of snuff.

After the first night, she said, "Would you move all that rubbish out of the dining room?" I explained it wasn't rubbish, it was our clothes and we had rented the dining room. She was a very funny little lady, we laughed because every night she took her little dog to bed, and her tin of snuff. The house smelt of snuff, we only stayed there for three weeks; we couldn't stand it any longer; that was September1962.

I went and asked my mom if we could live with her. "I will ask your father," she said; she always said that, even if he said no, mom would say yes, dad had no say in the matter; he wouldn't go against my mom. Any road up, we moved again. I moved all our belongings on our pram, as many people did in those days, it was not unusual to see those type of happenings. It felt really good to be back home, and everything went well for a while – of course my mom always let Irene know whose house it was, dad on the other hand didn't care so long as his meals were on the table. He was never keen on the nappies hanging all around the fireguard and hanging in the kitchen, mind you he never moaned much about it – to be honest, I hated to see those nappies everywhere, never mind my dad. It was good for me living at home, but not so good for Irene.

One evening in December 1962, Irene told me her dad had agreed to let us stay with them at their new semi-detached house, so we left my mom's house again, on our pram. Their new house was in West Avenue, Castle Bromwich, and at that time that area came under the Meriden County Council, Warwickshire. I thought, what a posh house; it had a long back garden and a proper shed – I refurbished a baby walker in that shed, it felt really good, when I was in there it was my den. I thought, I'm going to get a shed when I get a house of my own (I know what you are thinking, and you are right), it was however many years later before I lived that dream. Living with Irene's parents for the second time did not improve from the first time, well not for me anyway.

Trevor Kendall and his wife Patricia came to visit us one afternoon, and I did what all good mannered Brummies do, I asked them if they would like a cup of tea, so I went into the kitchen and put the kettle on. Irene's dad walked in and asked me "What do you think you are doing?" I explained that our friends had come to see us and I was making a cup of tea for them. "Oh no you are not," he replied, and turned off the kettle. Going back in to see my friends and telling them I couldn't give them a cup of tea was I think the most embarrassing thing I have ever done in my life; Irene was more embarrassed than I was because it was her parents' home. I was never accepted by Irene's dad, he spoke to me only when and if he had to.

Some weekends I would help my eldest brother Donald, he had a car repair shed in Orphanage road, Erdington. I was trying to learn as much as I could about cars. It was a fruitful exercise; it helped me a great deal in later years of my life.

When it became more difficult to live with Irene's parents we moved. Irene found more rooms for us to look at, they were in the Strechford area of Birmingham, in Fredrick road, right by Stechford railway station – that was in February 1963. I loved that station, and the house backed on to the railway lines. Again it was a big old Victorian house that had been turned into flats, it was just like all the others we had looked at, run down and dirty, but still it was ours and we would be on our own. We had a sitting room on the second floor and a bedroom in the attic. In the attic newspaper was pushed in the cracks all around the window, it was a sash window, and on very hot days that bedroom became airless, we couldn't sleep at night, it was unbearable. In our living room we had a sink and it started to leak. I knew nothing in those days about plumbing, so we put bowls under the leak but as it got worse it filled the bowl much quicker than was good for the couple down below. We shared the kitchen which was on the same landing as our living room; originally it would have been the small bedroom. The stop tap was under the sink in the kitchen, this turned off all the water to the whole of the second floor. I explained to the couple on our floor about the leak and would they be kind enough to turn off the stopcock whenever they used the kitchen sink, but not once did they turn off that stopcock, I asked them many times but they just didn't care. I never can understand why people are so horrible; I always go out of my way to help people. Irene is a gentle soul and always helped anyone that needed help, it really hurt her when the couple did what they did, or really what they didn't do. We never knew what to expect when we got back to the flat, it must have ruined the ceiling of the flat down below us, the landlady just didn't seem to care, and it took over a week to have that leak fixed.

There was a Scottish older lady a lovely jovial person in a bedsit, and in other rooms a very friendly couple who were really nice living downstairs, and between us all we tidied up the back garden and cut the hedge to have a nice place to sit and chat. Many of those types of houses in the 1960s were turned into flats and they were always dirty looking. We did our best to clean them up when we had them but they needed more than a lick of paint. We left those premises in October 1963, and went back to live at my mom's at 38 Plowden Road, as my sister had just got married and mom had a spare room. It was nice for me to be back home again, me being a typical mommy's boy, that's what Irene kept telling me.

Any road up, we stripped that bedroom's wallpaper, we laid new lino that we purchased from Stanley James, that was our local hardware shop, we papered and painted – a yellow paper with little flowers on it with blue stripes, the woodwork was blue doors, with white skirting and window frames and architrave. I fixed a broom stale across the recess, wall to wall, and hung a green plastic curtain and used it as a wardrobe, it was great, I could now hang my one and only coat up instead of hanging it on the bedroom door. There wasn't any bedroom furniture in my mom's house, just a bed, well mom had a wardrobe, no rugs or carpets anywhere in those bedrooms, but mom did have a peg rug that she had made out of old coats in the living room, it felt very nice to sit on when there was a fire.

Irene had a little trouble with my mom, she tried very hard to please her but alas, Mom didn't allow it to work – understandable I suppose two females in the same kitchen, that's a non starter. Mother and daughter no problem, daughter-in-law, now that's a different ball game. One evening Irene put a saucepan of potatoes on the gas stove ready for my tea when I got home from work; my mom had taken the saucepan off the stove and put her saucepan on but never told Irene. Well that really upset Irene. As I walked into the kitchen via the back door Irene with tears in her eyes said, "I'm ever so sorry, Dave, your tea will be late tonight."

"That's alright," I told her after she had explained what my mom had done.

One day my mom even said to Irene that our son Anthony was hers. My sister Doreen said, "My God, Mother, she did give birth to him!" Mom must have thought me being her son, my son was hers as well. Well time passed, it was forgotten, well, put to one side anyway.

One Sunday evening, Dad was sitting at the table, so was Mom, Irene was sitting by the fire, and I was sitting on the other side, when Anthony came running up to me all excited with a small piece bread in his hand. I thought he had picked it up off the floor, I took it off him and said, "It's dirty, son," and threw it in the fire. Well Anthony cried his little heart out. My dad swore at me and called me all sorts of names and Mom shouted at me; it turned out my dad had given that piece of bread to Anthony. I tried to explain I thought he had picked it from off the floor, but they said I was lying, I was just being spiteful. Irene picked up Anthony and ran upstairs (if I could change anything in my life it would be those few seconds, it hurts me just thinking about that time). The next morning my mom told me she wanted us out of the house that day, we were no longer wanted there, and all over a little mistake – that was on the 13th of June 1964.

Irene had a friend named Brenda Benbow that she went to school with. We had been invited to tea there as Irene's parents now lived in Wales, and as it was Irene's 21st birthday Brenda's mom thought it would be nice for Irene. Brenda still lived at home with her parents; they lived in Hall Hayes Road, Shard End, Birmingham. Brenda's mom could see how upset Irene was so she insisted on us staying the night at her house; we slept on the bed settee in the living room.

The next morning we went to the council office in Broad Street, Birmingham city centre, to declare ourselves homeless. They put Irene and the baby in a home for homeless mothers, and they told me to go and fend for myself. I have no recollection where I stayed that night, none at all, probably in my van.

Irene's nanny Parker had a friend named Tom who had a house in Ward End in Sladefield Road, at the back of the Capital picture house. He said we could stay at his house but only for four weeks because Irene's cousin Diane had been promised the rooms and Diane and her husband to be were getting married in four weeks time. Irene worked hard at finding us rooms, she found rooms in Highfield Road, Alum Rock, Saltley (that's the area my mom was born in, she came from Ash road); that was in August 1964. Again we had the rooms on the second floor. Irene and her friend Carol scrubbed that flat top to bottom and I decorated it, again blue and white, my favourite colours. Irene worked part time with Carol at a post office in Bordesley Green, next to East Birmingham Hospital, it now known as Heartlands, when my mom used to take me there it was called little Bromwich. My mom never called that hospital by any other name, it was always Little Bromwich.

My son Anthony had a scooter for Christmas. As Irene turned her back for a few seconds Anthony had followed her into the kitchen on his scooter. He fell, put out his arm as one does, but there was a three inch gap between the kitchen units and the flex of the electric kettle was always hung down inside that gap. Anthony's arm went down the gap and he caught the flex and tipped over the kettle which had just boiled, (this is heart breaking to write) and it took the skin off his face, neck and shoulder. I was outside at the time trying to get my van started, but when I got back to the flat I was given the news about my son. I'm going to leave it there – I just can't face thinking about it anymore. We left that flat; again we had trouble with the landlord;

he wanted two weeks rent in advance and for us to find a new tenant for him or we couldn't leave – that was February 1965. My eldest brother Donald said we could have one of his flats; he had converted a shop into flats and built a car repair garage at the rear, that was in Booth Street, Handsworth, so with his van he came to move us out of Highfield Road. The lady that had rented the ground floor flat left a few days before we intended to move. Any road up, on the evening we intended to move out the landlord started to work on the ground floor flat, so I phoned my brother from a phone box and explained about the landlord and for him to come late. The landlord worked till nine thirty, so we did a very late night move – our rent was paid up so we weren't doing anything wrong. The landlords in those days, from what I experienced, were horrible, well to me and mine they were anyway, and we always played the game, so at my brother's flat we felt secure. We had the ground floor living room, the bedroom was upstairs where there were two flats, and the trouble was our bedroom was next to the toilet. We had to share it with two other couples, but they were nice people.

My daughter Wendy was born in that bedroom on the 5th of August 1965, I was there at the birth, what a wonderful moment! She was born with ginger hair and the midwife said, "Ginger hair, you have some explaining to do young lady." I was a very jealous man in those days, that comment could have caused very serious problems as my wife and I had brown hair. The midwife couldn't understand the change in the hair. My sister's two children had ginger hair, and both parents had brown hair, also Irene's great aunt had ginger hair and other cousins, so I wasn't surprised my daughter had ginger hair.

I did that flat up; I even separated the kitchen from the living room with a partition wall, which I got paid for by my brother. One nice day we were offered a council house in Downing Street, number 78, just off Booth Street, it was about three hundred yards away from my brother's flats. It was a one up and one down with a kitchen that was four feet wide, and six feet long, with a Belfast sink and one cold water tap. It was a one up, but the council put up a partition across the bedroom to make it into two bedrooms, with a door that opened straight onto the stairs, but being so dangerous we never used that room. The living room had a fire grate, very small, it was a grey tiled fireplace, and a door that shut off the stairs. The toilets were in the middle of a field which was supposed to be the gardens, and there were three toilets in a block shared by all the tenants, six couples and their children in all; it was a newly built block of toilets. The reason the toilets were in a field was all the back houses had been knocked down, our row of terraced houses all six were on the front facing the road with an entry in the middle of the block, and we were on the end of the block. There were houses joined to our house at one time, but they had been demolished, so from our house to the pub on the corner known as the Phoenix, it was now a field, well, overgrown land where once stood houses. We were happy; Wendy was two months old and Anthony was three by this time. It was our first rent book; we were told we would be there for only six months as there was a demolition order on the houses, but it was two years and six months in all.

I made a garden and planted it up; I put up a little fence with a path up the middle. We loved our little house, and I decorated it top to bottom – all the other tenants said we were barmy as the houses were being demolished; why bother? "It's our home," I told them, "we love our little home." All those tenants had been there for a long time. We had a rent man call every week for the rent in those days, 15/- fifteen shillings, the boundary changed from Birmingham to Smethwick and our rent went down to fourteen and ten pence, 14/10d.

The rent man said, "It's nice to see a person take pride in where they live, so I'm going to help you get a house."

He got us a house in Chelmsley Wood, Birmingham (that move changed our lives forever, thanks to that rent man, and all because we had pride in where we lived). The day we were moving the neighbours came out saying, "How come you have got a house and you were last in this block?"

I just said, "I don't know." They were angry. That was in January 1968.

We walked in to our new home and it was heaven. We hadn't much furniture, and no carpets – the house looked empty, but it was ours now

My wife Irene in 1966, standing in a field that was once an area of back-to-back council houses. Just to the right of her is a block of three toilets; these were also in the middle of the field. One of those toilets was ours, we shared it with the family next door to us – not nice having to use the toilet in the middle of the night, or when it rained, and even worse when it snowed having to walk through the wet grass.

Our house was in a block of six that was on the front. Our front door opened onto the pavement. Those six were the last ones standing. There was an entrance in the middle of our block that gave us access to our back doors. It used to also be the access for the back houses that had been demolished. We were told our block was to be demolished in six months, that's why we took it.

We were living there for two and a half years. It was a one up and one down house. We had two small children at that time. It was our first council house, our first rent book.

to build a new life for my family. The house had been decorated and painted throughout, it had a modern kitchen, and would you believe it a box of twelve, thirteen amp plugs given free with every house. Then the milkman, Midland Counties, said if we took them on as our milkman we would receive six egg cups free – we were in shock, all this was now ours, we were so grateful and we took nothing for granted. And to top all that we had central heating. We were happy, very happy, we came from slums at 14/10d a week fourteen shillings and ten pence, now we had a brand new palace at £5-1-0 a week, five pounds one shilling. That house was in Brickhill Drive, and we lived there from January 1968 to December 1968.

We asked the rent man if we could move to an end house on the edge of the estate with a bigger garden, as we had been good tenants. We were offered a house in Berwicks Lane, still on the Chelmsley Wood Estate, number 56; it was still being built when we first saw it, we couldn't believe our luck, a double fronted house. The back garden was very private; it had the gable end of a house at the end of the garden so we weren't overlooked. At the side of the house was a wide piece of ground that had been planted with bushes so that made our garden even more private. We moved into that house on the 14th of December 1968. I was happy; I had my wonderful wife Irene, and my wonderful two children Anthony and Wendy. Irene worked really hard for her family (and still does). We decorated that house top to bottom. After we had been there quiet awhile, as just like the house in Brickhill drive it had been papered and painted throughout. I landscaped the garden back and front with my wife Irene; she could turn her hand to anything, she even made me a suit one day to go to a wedding as I hadn't any decent clothes to my name. We were always short of money because of me always packing up my jobs.

After we had lived in the house for six years we were allowed to buy it from the council, leasehold, at a cost of three thousand eight hundred pounds £3,800 or freehold for four thousand three hundred pounds, £4,300, so we bought it on a mortgage freehold. I asked the man in charge of the houses at that time if I could buy the piece of land at the side of the house so I could build a garage. "If you promise to build a little wall and put up a six foot fence all around that plot of land

I will give it to you free of charge, and I will add it to your plans and deeds after twelve years," he said.

I did everything that was asked of me, and the man was delighted with the finished product, and so were we. Irene dug holes for that fence (it's still there to this very day thirty five years later). That piece of ground was eighteen feet wide and thirty six feet long. I dug out the foundations for my new garage and made it twenty three feet long and eight feet wide, with an up and over door at the front and a normal door leading to the back garden. I had it plastered, and put skirting boards in, and it was more like a study than a garage. It was a dream come true for me; it was my domain, my sanctuary, my shed, my playhouse. It's what all little boys dream of – it was my Den.

My job at that time was doing loft conversions all over the country. I drove a small Mercedes lorry; I used it like it was my car – I took it home and parked it on my drive all the time, and I never used my car at all, it was parked up in the garage. I even took Irene shopping in it, and we went for drives in the countryside on a Sunday. I sold my car and bought a Cedar conservatory from a firm called Kenkast and built it on the back of my house, we loved it. We built a wall all around the front garden out of those concrete bricks that were all the rage in the sixties and seventies. It was fifty feet long and three feet high. I had them delivered, and while I was at work, to my surprise when I got home from work Irene had carried every brick from the pavement to the back garden – that really pleased me, she is such a grafter is our Irene. The one thing that does make me smile, when we decorated the hall stairs and landing, which in my humble opinion is the worst place in the house to decorate, we were so pleased with it we sat on the top step of the stairs for what must have been an hour, may have even been more, that's youth for you.

As time passed, we found it hard to pay our mortgage, so after a very long discussion over many weeks in fact, we decided to sell our beautiful home. We went riding around the countryside; it was snowing and very cold, but we were on a mission so no snow or cold weather was going to stop us from finding our dream home. I had big ideas, trouble was I only had ten thousand pounds from the sale of our house, which at the time I thought was a fortune. We came across two cottages in Orton Road, Little Warton near Twycross Zoo in Warwickshire; they were numbered 102 and 104. They were two up and two down, no inside toilets, they were in a block outside, just like the one we had in Handsworth. They were the last two cottages in the village, and the views we thought were stunning. They where owned by an elderly couple who lived a couple of doors away. As we were looking, the old fella who owned them saw us and he asked if we would like to look over them. Of course we said yes. They were well run down! It was the old tin bath job in those cottages. Out the back belonging to the cottages was a large piece of land for growing vegetables, it was known as the man's garden and would you believe it women weren't allowed down anywhere near those gardens. The ladies had to shout to their men folk when it was dinner or tea time or one of the children would be sent to tell them. That was a shock to me, I can tell you. I was told this by a gentleman who was born in one of those cottages, his family were fourteen strong and next door were sixteen. Those poor women!

So after looking round, being young and foolish we both fell in love with them, and agreed we would buy them off him at a very large sum of seven thousand pounds. We shook his hand, and he agreed they were ours. We went into Atherstone to the agent and told him we were buying them, and the next day we went to our solicitors and started the ball rolling, as the saying goes. When all was signed sealed, we moved in. We got fourteen thousand five hundred pounds for Berwick's Lane house, that was May 1979, and we had two thousand pounds left after all the expenses were taken out. We had no idea what we had taken on – we bought with our hearts instead of our brains.

Irene and I were good labourers but our building skills were limited. We were given a grant from the council of two thousand pounds, and I pulled down the ceilings in the one house and lived in the other. On the landing I knocked through to the next cottage and did an arch, it looked great. I fitted a bathroom, got a plumber to fit central heating, that was solid fuel heating, dug up the floors and re-laid them with six inches of concrete – that was the regulations at that time. My eldest brother

My wife and I bought these two cottages. They were two up and two down. A gentleman who was born at number 104 told me that in one house there were 12 children, with parents that made 14. In the other cottage there were 10 people – at one time 24 people lived in these two cottages.

They were in an area know as Warton and were situated in a road called Orton Road. At the time of purchase they were 102 and 104. We made one dwelling out of the two. It then became 102. It was surrounded by countryside and oh so peaceful.

helped me to trowel up the floors, my younger brother helped me with bricklaying and rendering the house outside, and a carpenter showed me how to make ledger and brace doors – I even made a stable door leading from the dining room to the kitchen. I bought all the wrought iron door fittings for every door in the house. I fitted a kitchen, and I landscaped the front and back gardens.

I found a timber yard that sold reclaimed timber. They had twelve pitch pine lengths of timber fourteen feet long; I purchased them; they had come out of an old Chapel. How old they were I've no idea. They were eight inches deep, and six inches wide. It took me two weeks to strip all the old paint off them, and then I stained them with Jacobean stain, then I yacht varnished them – they looked beautiful. When I cut them to length one could smell the pitch pine, it's such a wonderful perfume, I kept picking it up and smelling it. With all the bricks I had knocked down inside the house I built an eight foot wall at the bottom of the garden. I made arches, four in all, that looked just like church windows. I also made an inglenook fire place in the living room with Ibstock smiling bricks, with a foot square oak beam, again in Jacobean stain and varnished.

I made the back door opening bigger and fitted a French window. I had to fit two seven by four RS Js, eight feet long, over the French windows first of course. I fitted those at night in the dark with the wind blowing, I had a sixty watt light bulb hanging on the wall and it was swinging in the wind. As I had two front doors, I bricked them up and put a new front door in the middle of the house, yes, that's what I had ended up with, a really big three bedroomed house. I had even converted the loft and put in a window in the gable end. During all this work I had a terrible chest infection and I was giving up smoking but because it was wintertime the work had to be done otherwise we would have all frozen to death.

In between all this I opened a shop in Stechford, plus running Irene to work and it took its toll on our marriage. People that lived in the village, whom I had never met, came knocking on my door asking if they could look round my house. It wasn't long before we were the talk of the village. We heard them saying what a wonderful job Irene and I had done, and I felt quite proud. I really enjoyed doing up those cottages, but it drove me away from Irene; it was a cottage too far I think.

The shop was my idea; Irene knew it wouldn't work but I would not listen to her. I opened it up as a hobby shop, selling fur fabric, matchstick kits and fur animals, but it didn't work. My nephew came to see me, he had been made redundant from the Co-op as manager of the delicatessen section, and he said if I change my shop into a cooked meats shop he would teach me the trade. He taught me well.

Then the recession hit, and I went broke and had to sell our cottages to pay off the debts. We had just enough money left to buy a council house. We sold the cottages for twenty one thousand five hundred pounds, and we left in July 1982.

We moved to Tile Cross in Birmingham, where we paid nineteen thousand pounds for a council house. We redecorated that house top to bottom. We sold it in May 1983, and moved to Whitebeam Road, Chelmsley Wood.

Irene found out she was pregnant, and that was a shock to both of us. She gave life to our third child, Matthew, on the 28th October 1983, two days before my fortieth birthday. Irene spent 44 hours in Marston Green Maternity Hospital. While she was in hospital I decorated some of the rooms for her to come home to with our new son. We paid £17,750.00 for that house, in May 1983. I made a pond and a waterfall in the back garden and I built a little wall with a lion's mask in the middle of it spurting water from its mouth. I laid down a plastic sheet from the bottom of the wall and into the pond. I went into the countryside around the Coleshill area, where the river Blythe flowed through, and paddled in that river and found big rocks. I did that trip three times, and back home I mixed up the concrete and threw it on the plastic sheet and after a while when the concrete was going off, looking at the rocks, I thought: when rocks fall and tumble down hillsides and mountainsides, they stop wherever, so I got the rocks, held them above my head and threw them in quick succession. They rolled and fell just as they would have in natural surroundings – the result was amazing. I placed plants in between the crevasses with a little soil and I placed some plants in pots in those crevasses – it looked so natural, all my friends loved it, in fact a couple of them tried to copy it but they tried placing the rocks in their ponds instead of just throwing them. I was just lucky; I made no fuss of it like I did with all the other waterfalls in my gardens. We sold that house in March 1985, for twenty one thousand five hundred pounds £ 21,500.

We bought a semi-detached house in Castle Bromwich, number 65, Hawthorne Road, for £23,500. It needed lots of tender loving care, as the saying goes, so I thought I would be clever and start working on the house before contracts were signed. I went back to the agent who was selling the house to me and asked, "May I take another look around the house and take some measurements?"

"Yes, seeing as it is empty you can let yourself in, is that all right? And then when you have finished if we are closed just pop the keys through our letterbox," he told me.

"No problem," I replied. That's just what I was hoping he would say. I took the back door key off the ring and left the back gate unlocked, I knew the agent wouldn't notice, I popped the rest of the keys back through the letterbox as I had been asked. The next day I went back to the house and ripped out the bathroom suite, I took up the carpets, and over the next two weeks I fitted in a new bathroom suite, new carpets, cleaned up, and did lots of work in that house, and all before contracts were signed. On the day we were leaving Whitebeam Road, the lady that was buying our house came to pay me for a carpet we left. She said, "That was a scary moment this morning, wasn't it?"

I knew nothing. "What was?" I asked her.

She said, "The first-time buyers in the chain said they had changed their minds and weren't going to move." Her solicitor went to see the couple and explained if they didn't move they would have to pay all the expenses to everyone in the chain. This, I was told, frightened them, so they said they would move. I thought, and all that work and money I've spent on that house in Hawthorne road, I won't do that again. Well we moved and all went well for us, it was an easy move that day. We sold that house in March 1987.

Our next house that we bought was 24, Bentley Road, Castle Bromwich, and it was a repossession house – shame, they were a nice couple, just like us at Warton they ran out of money, but unlike us they just stopped paying their mortgage. We hadn't a mortgage, but we sold up to get out of trouble, they didn't. It's hard to leave a house that you have worked hard on for years, and then lose it, one has to take a deep breath and get on with life.

This house had been extended, I loved it; we decorated it top to bottom and landscaped the garden at the back. While I was sorting out the garden there was a large hole that used to be a pond, with a couple of inches of water in the bottom of it – all around the edge of the hole at the bottom were more frogs than I had ever seen before, they were shoulder to shoulder and every female had a male on her back. My son Matthew was looking at them, I said, "Don't stand on the edge of the hole, sit then you won't fall in." I turned my back, heard a splash, turned around and Matthew was sitting in the hole. He wasn't upset at all. I said to him with a smile, "What are you doing in there?"

He replied, "I'm talking to the frogs." I love that boy of mine. I set to, put all the frogs in a bucket and took them to Kingshurst Water Park. I filled in that hole. At the back of the house was a patio laid in 2x2 slabs, eight feet wide about eighteen feet long, so I set to to lengthen and widen it by putting more 2x2 slabs down. In the meantime we bought Matthew a little three-wheeled bike. Well I tried to show him how to peddle that bike but he just couldn't get the hang of it, so I carried on laying the patio slabs. It took me a week to get to lay the last slab. I stood up, and to my shocked surprise, just as I laid the last slab, Matthew got on his bike and peddled round and round that patio; he pedalled for ages! He rode that bike on that patio daily; I was so pleased; it was worth all the hard work, in fact I was so pleased I took a photo of him.

Sometime after that, I've no idea why, I decided I wanted a divorce. I gave Irene a hard time, and I upset her more than words can say. I regret that time in my life. We are still the best of friends and we still help each other when it's needed. All the houses, rooms, shop, going broke and losing everything we had, worked for and lost, and built up again, I suppose it took its toll on me, I just lost the plot at that time in my life. We were divorced in 1992.

I bought a house in the same road, number 31 Bentley Road, and my then ex-wife bought a house in Hurst lane, Shard End, in December

My son Matthew riding his bike for the very first time as I laid the very last slab. It was worth all that hard work to see him riding his bike.

Matthew two years later on. A bigger bike and still riding around the patio. It gave me much pleasure to see him enjoying his young life.

1994. We helped each other to move houses. She made curtains for me and cleaned my house, and I bought a pack of central heating, boiler and all that goes with it for her. I got and paid a plumber to put in the central heating system, and I prepared the house ready for the heating so it would be quicker and Irene and Matthew wouldn't have to live in a mess for long. I fitted the kitchen sink in for her and bought her a new Metro car for her birthday so she could run my son about in a car that was reliable, and she did lots and lots for me.

I started on my house, and I was missing Irene something awful but I never told her. I was in my house for three weeks when the solicitor phoned me and told me I didn't own the head lease, there were eight people that owned it and they lived in America, Australia, New Zealand, Canada and Spain. It wasn't worth anything to them so they all signed and gave it to me. It cost me my solicitor's fees plus ten pounds, and I still don't know what a head lease is all about. Any road up, I bought the freehold; it cost me £3,000. As I walked over the front room floor downstairs I noticed it looked a little suspect so I got my crowbar and tried to prise up a floor board – the whole floor caved in, it was rotten, even the joists were too. To my surprise there was seven inches of water all over the ground under the floor so I went into the back room and inspected under the floor boards – it had been concreted and the floor was new, I'm glad to say.

After looking through the deeds and maps I found that the house had been built over a stream. It had been piped up, but it must have broken because it wasn't working, so I dug two long trenches the length of the room, five feet deep and filled them with rubble. In the kitchen I noticed the concrete floor was sagging, so with my sledge hammer I hit it in the middle, and it too caved in with me standing on it! There was an eighteen inch void under that concrete, the stream had washed all the soil away over the years. So again I dug a trench and filled it in with rubble. Outside in the back garden I dug two trenches ten feet in length and six feet deep and filled those with rubble, the reason I did them in the garden was that in the winter the bottom half of the garden flooded really bad because the gardens either side of me were higher, it was the path the stream was in. One very early morning I heard a very loud crack – the guttering at the back had fallen off, so I went into the loft, and the twelve by three purling had snapped in half. I had a hole in the roof so I got a carpenter friend to help me erect a dormer, and we were doing that at a quarter to seven on Christmas Eve. When the summer came I had no washing facilities at all, no bathroom or tanks, only one floor downstairs, the only water I had was a stand pipe in the foundation that once was my kitchen floor, so I bought a new dustbin filled it with water and that's where I washed myself, in the garden in my underpants. I did that night after night for more weeks than I care to remember. There was a brick built air raid shelter built against the house with a slab of concrete on top, eight inches thick and six feet square. My younger brother John helped me knock it down. The slab of concrete we barred it on rollers to the bottom of the garden. We built two layers of bricks in a square, jacked up the concrete and got it on to the brick wall. I built a shed on it, built two steps up to it, built a two tier wall all around it on the concrete at the side of the shed, and filled it with soil. I then put flowers all around the shed – it looked great, everyone loved it. While I was doing that I had the house rewired and central heating installed, I made a shower room with black and gold tiles, I replaced all the floors, converted the coalhouse into a laundry room and fitted in a toilet so I had a toilet upstairs and down. I did a loft conversion, and finished the garden, so a rebuild and complete redecoration that had taken three and a half years was finished.

New neighbours moved in next door to me with two children. The little boy on the first morning they lived there was throwing stones at my front door. I had a leaded light window in it, and he cracked the glass. I chased him to his house, I was furious, the woman came out and I demanded to see her husband, but he wouldn't come out to see me. They had no control over their kids, so I put my house up for sale.

I got back with my wife, and we bought a house together – that was in 1998. The house was a large detached house in Springfield Road, Castle Bromwich, just round the corner from my house. We paid £124,000 for that house and, it had every modern fitting that one requires these days – his and hers fitted bedroom furniture, a luxurious fitted shower, bathroom, a converted loft, polished wood everywhere, that house wanted for nothing. It had better carpets than we had ever had, a long rear garden all laid out, shed and a greenhouse, block paved front drive, walled all round, even a utility come laundry room. We again redecorated top to bottom, just to put our mark on it really but Irene couldn't settle there, nor my son Matthew, in fact none of us could, so it went back on the market. We had only lived there for three weeks. It sold in the hour for £135,000, then we parted company once more. I bought a house thirty yards away, 10, Oaston Road, while Irene moved to Laburnum Avenue in Kingshurst, just across from Castle Bromwich.

In my new house I dug up the floors, fitted central heating and a burglar alarm, changed and ripped out the old fireplaces and fitted new fireplaces, decorated top to bottom, I built a half brick conservatory, fitted a toilet in it, fitted a new kitchen and put new carpets down and parquet floor tiles down the hall and right through to the kitchen, sanded and used Ronseal floor sealer – it looked great. In the meantime I moved Irene from Laburnum Avenue to Hawthorn Road, Castle Bromwich in July 2003. I did a lot of work for her; all the back garden as it was very overgrown, I cut down trees, weeded and tided up, and I fitted a new sink and toilet in the bathroom, but after a while she found it hard to run, as there were still lots of jobs to do. She put it on the market, but had some silly offers, the house boom had ended and she just couldn't sell it, so to help her out I sold mine and bought it off her. That was in January 2005 and I'm still here. The work I have done so far is, I have ripped out the entire bathroom and the airing cupboard, boarded all the walls and got them plastered, and run a cable from the meter board in the garage to the bathroom for a shower. I have fitted a new bathroom suite with the shower over the bath, painted and tiled around the shower, knocked a wall down in the kitchen into the extension, ripped out all the plumbing and the toilet that was in there and stripped all tiles from walls. I've replastered, fitted a new kitchen and divided part of the garage to make a laundry room, put a toilet in, a sink and washing machine, had it plastered, and it's now painted and tiled.

All the downstairs rooms are finished. I re-laid the patio with Irene's help and I've landscaped the back garden but not yet finished. I've had a new roof fitted, and put a new roof on the side entrance and fitted roof tiles instead of glass. In the garden is a brick built shed, which I have put roof tiles on instead of felt. There is still a lot to do but I am riddled now with arthritis, plus I've lost the will to do it anymore, I've lost complete interest – where I go from here, I have no idea. What makes it worse is I don't like it here, mind you I want for nothing, and my life is easier now I'm retired. Tired is the word.

I must add, without the help and support, even though we are divorced, from Irene, I wouldn't have this house as complete as it is today – thank you, Irene.

SIMPLE PLEASURES

A friend of mine passed his test and got his H.G.V. heavy goods vehicle licence class one. He drove all around Europe. After about a year, he asked me if I would like to see Rome, and a lot of Italy – would I go with him to keep him company for a couple of weeks. His load was fifty-two tons of skins, sheep and cowhides.

We got the ferry at Dover early in the morning, hit France, travelled through to Italy, almost to Sicily, and we arrived at a lovely little village.

The skins didn't smell too sweet, I can tell you. When they were being unloaded it was dinnertime and a beautiful sunny day. The four ladies that worked there were gorgeous looking – that's all the workforce there was, four ladies. After the trailer was unloaded it had to be washed out and a perfume sprayed. The reason for this was we were picking up fifty-two tons of pasta, and the bosses of the factory inspected the trailer before they would load it. The drivers had to make sure there wasn't any blood anywhere. We met up with a driver from the same firm delivering a load of skins to the same firm; he too had to collect a lorry load of pasta.

When back on the road we followed the other driver. His artic was faster than ours, it had just come out of the workshop after being repaired and painted. He'd also had a new grill and an engine overhaul – he was very proud of his wagon. Any road up, we lost him and we took the wrong turning. We went through a town during rush hour, five p.m, and we were going over flyovers that had weight restrictions on them – the Italians were hanging out of their car windows crossing their wrists to indicate we could be arrested. We passed a police car at the bottom of the flyover, but as luck would have it they turned and were looking the other way.

We eventually got to a massive lorry park in Belgium where we met up with the other driver; it was a hotel for drivers, and I had a shower, and then washed and dried all my clothes. I had a lovely chicken dinner and spent some time in the rest room, it was very cosy and relaxing, then we returned back to the wagon, that's where we slept – it had two bunks inside the cab.

I was woken up in the middle of the night with what felt like an earthquake. While we slept the air brakes had failed, and we had rolled backwards nearly two hundred yards! It's hard to believe, but we passed a few wagons and hit the lorry from the same firm, the one that had just come out of the work shop. I asked my mate why he didn't leave it in gear, to which he replied, "I wasn't taught to leave it in gear." I couldn't believe what he had told me; I told him everyone knows leaving the wagon in gear acts as a brake. We had been sleeping on the top of mountains; the thought of that now makes me shudder!

When the other driver saw the damage to his cab, he had a fit and asked Andrew the same question I did. "Why didn't you leave it in gear!" he screamed. Andrew told him the same as he told me, he wasn't taught that way. "You never do! Are you mad? Look at my cab. I've only just had this back a few days and because of your stupidity it's got to go back in the workshop!"

The next day we loaded up with pasta. Andrew said, "You see all those boxes of pasta on the bottom layer, they will all be completely flattened by the time we get back in England," and sure enough, with the vibration and the bumping of the trailer, it did completely ruin the whole of the bottom layer the length of the trailer.

A simple pleasure we enjoyed on some Friday evenings was we sat in the car with our children eating fish and chips opposite the chip shop on a car park in the Tile Cross area of Birmingham. On occasions we sat in a lane that backed on to the Elmdon Airport, eating our fish and chips and watching the planes landing and taking off. We did this for our children to see the planes; it was lovely to see the excitement in their little faces when a plane took off.

Some years later when we lived in the countryside, we found a lane that overlooked old fashioned looking farm buildings that were deep in a dell. We were high up on a hill – it was so picturesque looking

In Italy
Getting a full load of pasta to take back to England

over that farm with rolling countryside all around. We loved that view so much. We sat in our car many times over the years, enjoying those beautiful views; Mother Nature is truly a wonderful thing.

Another place we used to visit with our children was called Little Packington. It was an isolated spot, and the river Blythe ran through it. At the side of the ford was a packhorse bridge that we crossed into a lane to walk and enjoy Mother Nature in all her glory. When it was a beautiful sunny day with the river glistening in the sunshine it was a very tranquil and peaceful place to be. It was on occasions a very popular place for families, who often took picnics when they took their children to paddle and catch fish with their nets. We made our nets from my wife's old stockings on occasions attached to a cane that I got from the pet shop – the joy of seeing our children enjoying life whilst paddling and catching fish, seeing water voles and kingfishers plus many different types of butterflies and wild flowers. We took a jam jar with string tied around the top for a handle; they got so excited when they caught a fish and put it in the jam jar so they could see what they looked like. We always put the fish back in the river, we never took them home. We taught our children to be gentle and kind to animals and the wildlife.

My children are grown up now, but while I'm writing this I'm wishing they were small again so I could take them to that river and see them enjoying life. My wife and I sometimes went to that same spot on our own, and as I stopped to look over the bridge that went across the river, I could see in my mind's eye my little children. What a wonderful feeling I have – while I'm writing this down I can see my little ones in that river enjoying life to the full. I loved those times and memories. As you can see in the picture Matthew had a proper fishing net.

My son Matthew fishing in the river at Little Packington in Warwickshire where his older brother and sister fished many years before

My son Matthew with my granddaughter Holly, fishing in the River Blythe at Packington

CHRISTMAS MORNING

One pleasure I had when I was young, just like most youngsters, was eating. One evening talking to my wife about life and the hardships that we had at times, Christmas came up. We were talking about food, well she was actually, and she said it was a struggle to feed me normally, not just on Christmas day. So we sat down and analysed what I used to eat on a Christmas morning. I was shocked, even horrified. When she actually went through the list of food I ate on a Christmas day this is how it went: After getting up, I went and sat down at the table, sometimes in an easy chair, and started to eat nuts, my favourite ones at that time were hazelnuts, plus sweets and fruit. When Irene brought in my breakfast it consisted of two rashers of bacon, two eggs, mushrooms, two sausages, a piece of fried bread, beans, tomatoes, black pudding plus four pieces of bread and butter and many cups of tea. All plates washed up and put away (by my wife, always by my wife) I would play with my children and their toys, and I would be eating more nuts, apples and oranges plus I would be eating sweets as well. Irene would be in the kitchen preparing the dinner and baking while I was filling myself with food.

As the table was laid for dinner, my plate would be piled high with a turkey leg and slices off the breast, a slice of pork, sprouts, peas, roast potatoes and boiled potatoes, but not stuffing, I don't like that. After all that was eaten, out came the Christmas pudding and custard. I love my Christmas pudding, I always had a dishful, and I love custard, and then I had many cups of tea. Back to the easy chair to watch the television, I would start again to eat sweets and fruit and nuts. I would eat right through to teatime, when again Irene would lay the table with a Christmas cake and mince pies, and she always made jelly, blancmange, sliced peaches, pears, trifle, a jug of cream, pork pie, sandwiches of turkey and not forgetting the Christmas crackers – we loved pulling the crackers at teatime. The children left the table when they had finished eating, and if they left anything like fruit or jelly I would eat that as well as any fruit, jelly or blancmange left in the big bowls. I must add at this moment in time, that my wife Irene loved her family so much, she never stopped running around after us; the perfect mother and a wonderful wife, she wouldn't let me anywhere near her kitchen; fantastic woman.

Back to the easy chair again to watching the television eating fruit, sweets and nuts, and then at suppertime I had turkey sandwiches. I ate all day long – nonstop, right up to bedtime. How did I do it? I have no idea, but I did it for many years. I don't drink beer or spirits, I'm teetotal, but I do drink tea by the gallon, even to this day. I must add, as a sixty-seven year old now my portions are much smaller, but I've never lost my taste for those jellies, blancmanges and trifles – I still have a very sweet tooth (well if I had any teeth, that is). My intake is still quite large at times (ha, ha), so am I; fat is probably a better word.

My son Anthony and my daughter Wendy
Wonderful children.

This is the street where my dad was born.
Number 16 Queen's Street, Blaina, Wales.
Unfortunately some of the houses have been demolished. Dad's house was one of them. It was the house to the right of the blue car.

Serial No. 36817 Army Form B.108D.

Certificate of discharge from (a) Territorial Army

No. 756661 Rank Gunner

Name PROSSER William John
(Surname) (Christian names in full)

Corps from which discharged } Royal Artillery

N.B.—The following particulars refer only to the engagement from which the man is now being discharged :—

Enlisted at Worcester on 20. 6 1924

Medals, Clasps, Decorations, Mentions in Despatches. Any special acts of gallantry or distinguished conduct brought to notice in brigade or superior orders. (b)

Discharged in consequence of Termination of Engagement.

Para 199 (i) T. A. Regs

AFTER HAVING SERVED :—

(c) with the Colours (h) years. days.

(d) in Section "B" ARMY RESERVE (h) years. days.

(e) in Section "D" ARMY RESERVE (h)
(f) in the SUPPLEMENTARY RESERVE (h) Eight yrs.
(g) in the TERRITORIAL ARMY (h) — dys.

Date of discharge 19. 6. 1932

Description of the above-named man on Enlistment :—

Year of birth 1906 Marks or Scars

Height 5 ft. 1 ins.

Complexion Sallow

Eyes Blue Hair Brown

Place Woolwich

Date 3/6/32 for Officer i/c Royal Artillery Records. Signature and Rank.

Special attention is directed to the Notes on reverse.

*(41490X) Wt. W1763/79 65,000 12/30 *H. J. R. & L., Ltd.* Gp. 121 Forms/B.108D/4 [P.T.O

My dad's army papers 1924-1932.
Eight years training in readiness for the defence of England.

NOTES :—

(a) Here insert Section "B" Army Reserve, Section "D" Army Reserve, "Supplementary Reserve," "Territorial Army," as the case may be.

(b) The word "Nil" to be inserted where necessary.

(c) To be struck out if inapplicable.

(d) Applies to a Section "B" Army Reservist who fails to return to the O.i/c Records his A.F. B.108 for completion as to discharge. To be struck out if inapplicable.

(e) Applies only to men who enlisted direct into Section "D" Army Reserve and are discharged from that section and NOT to Section "D" Reservists who re-engage into that Section either from the Colours or from Section "B" Army Reserve. To be struck out in ink if inapplicable.

(f) Applies only to men who are being discharged from the Supplementary Reserve. To be struck out in ink if inapplicable.

(g) Applies only to men who are being discharged from the Territorial Army. To be struck out in ink if inapplicable.

(h) Each space is to be filled in and the word "Nil" inserted where necessary: numbers to be written in words.

(i) This Certificate is to be issued without any alterations in the manuscript.

WARNING.—The person to whom this Certificate is issued should on no account part with it or forward it by post when applying for a situation but should use a copy attested by a responsible person for the purpose. If the Certificate is lost it will be replaced only when its loss can be proved to have been due to very exceptional circumstances.

Application should be made to the Officer in charge Records.

Any alteration of the particulars given on the reverse of this certificate may render the holder liable to prosecution under the Seamen's and Soldiers' False Character Act, 1906.

DISCHARGE CERTIFICATE.

ANY PERSON finding this Certificate is requested to forward it in an unstamped envelope to the Under Secretary of State, The War Office, London, S.W. 1.

My Dad's Army papers 1924-1932 – eight years traning in readiness for the defence of England.

Granddad King and Grandma King
and Aunty Margaret, she was bombed and killed in WWII

The three photographs on page 493 on the previous page are of my mother's family. They all lived at number 53 Ash Road, Saltley, Birmingham 8.

Left is my granddad, Robert King. Right is my grandmother Clara King, bottom is my aunty Margaret King. In World War Two their house was bombed. My aunty Margaret was killed on the 10th April 1941. She was only 34 years old.

Her full name is Margaret Victoria Turland (nee King)
She is remembered on the Tree of Life Monument in the Bull Ring in Birmingham City Centre.

I also had an uncle Robert King, my mom's brother, I haven't a photo of him.

The monument showing my Aunty Margaret's name Turland, M.V

My parents' wedding in 1929
at
St. Saviours Church,
Ash Road,
Saltley
Birmingham 8

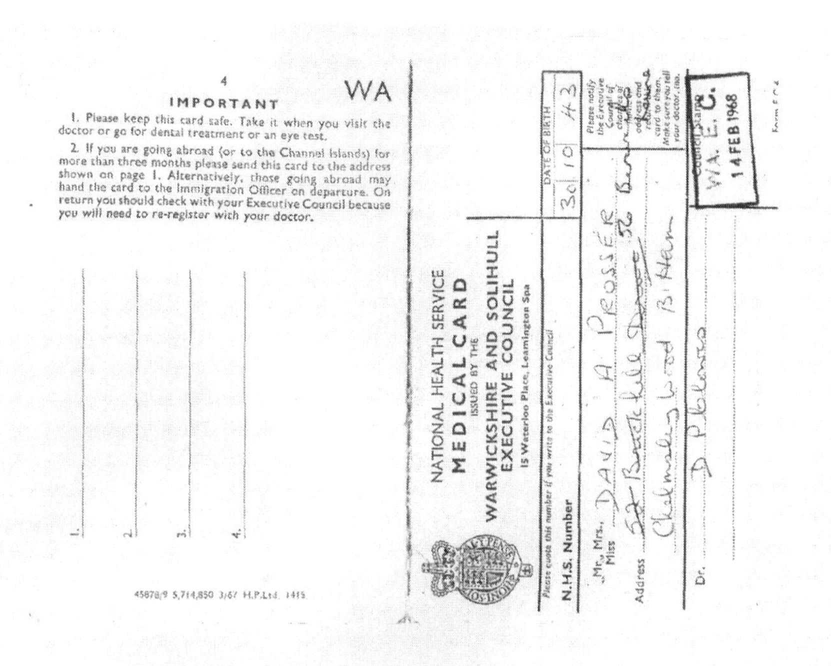

4

WA

IMPORTANT

1. Please keep this card safe. Take it when you visit the doctor or go for dental treatment or an eye test.

2. If you are going abroad (or to the Channel Islands) for more than three months please send this card to the address shown on page 1. Alternatively, those going abroad may hand the card to the Immigration Officer on departure. On return you should check with your Executive Council because you will need to re-register with your doctor.

1.

2.

3.

4.

45878/9 5,714,850 3/67 H.P.Ltd. 1415

NATIONAL HEALTH SERVICE
MEDICAL CARD
ISSUED BY THE
WARWICKSHIRE AND SOLIHULL
EXECUTIVE COUNCIL
15 Waterloo Place, Leamington Spa

Please quote this number if you write to the Executive Council

N.H.S. Number

DATE OF BIRTH 30 10 43

Mr., Mrs., Miss DAVID A PROSSER

Address 52 Brookhill Drive
Chelmsley Wood B'Ham

Dr.

Please notify the Executive Council of changes of address and return the card to them. Make sure you tell your doctor, too.

Council Stamp
W.A. E.C.
14 FEB 1968

My medical card issued on the 14th February, 1968

2

GENERAL INFORMATION

1. **Lists** of doctors, dentists and opticians taking part in the National Health Service can be seen at main Post Offices.

2. **Enquiries or complaints** about general medical, dental, ophthalmic or pharmaceutical services should be made to the Clerk of the Executive Council at the address shown on this card. A complaint should be made in writing and wherever possible within 6 weeks of the event which gave rise to it.

3. **Postage** must be paid on letters to Executive Councils.

YOUR N.H.S. DOCTOR

4. **This card** should be shown to your doctor if he asks to see it; if it is not produced he may charge a fee for which he will give an official receipt which contains instructions for the recovery of the fee.

5. **Day visits.** Please do not ask the doctor to call unless the patient is too ill to attend his surgery. Attendance at the surgery should be during surgery hours unless otherwise arranged by the doctor. When the condition of the patient does require a home visit, **please try to give notice,** if at all possible, **before 10 a.m. on the day on which the visit is required.**

6. **Night visits. Please do not call in the doctor between the hours of 8 p.m. and 9 a.m. unless you need him urgently.**

7. **In Accident or Emergency, first try to get your own doctor** (or his deputy). If he is not available, immediate treatment can be obtained from any doctor giving general medical services under the National Health Service.

8. **Temporary absence from home.** If you are away from your home district for three months or less, you can apply for treatment to any local doctor giving general medical services. Tell him you are a temporary resident *and quote your N.H.S. number.*

9. **Change of address.** If you change your address you may choose a new doctor by completing Part A on page 3. If you wish to continue to receive treatment from your present doctor, you should notify him of your new address immediately. You should also tell the Executive Council, at the same time sending this card.

3

10. **Change of Doctor.** (*a*) If you choose a new National Health Service doctor because you have changed to a new address, you and the new doctor should fill in Part A *below;* (*b*) If you wish to change your doctor for any other reason *either* (1) you may transfer at once with the consent of your present doctor and the new doctor; *Parts A and B below* should be completed by you and both doctors; *or* (2) you may write to the Executive Council (at the address on the front page of this card) saying that you intend to change. This card **must** be sent with the letter; it will be returned to you with the necessary instructions. You will not be able to transfer in this case until at least 14 days after the Council receive your letter.

Part A

*Drugs

Application to be placed on the list of

Dr...Date.......................

Signature of applicant ‡

....

†Rural Practice

Address of ....

applicant ....

Signature of accepting Doctor ....

Drs. Code No...Date.......................

Part B

Signature of consenting Doctor

I agree to this transfer.

~~Signature of accepting Doctor~~..

Drs. Code No...Date.......................

‡A person signing for the applicant should state relationship.
*If Doctor is to supply drugs he should enter D in space marked *.
†If Doctor claims a rural practice payment he should enter in the space marked † the distance from his main surgery to the patient's residence and should inform the Executive Council if he wishes to claim for units in addition to those for ordinary distance.

My medical card issued on the 14th February, 1968

THE OBJECTS OF THE ASSOCIATION

(*a*) To establish and maintain an Association Fund for the charitable purposes specified in Rule 8 and to make donations thereto out of the General Funds of the Association at the discretion of the Council.

(*b*) To promote the esprit-de-corps, mutual good fellowship and assistance between serving and ex-service members of the Royal Pioneer Corps.

In pursuance of these objects the Association shall :

(1) Perpetuate any friendships made in war and peace.

(2) Ensure that the grand record of the Royal Pioneer Corps in the War of 1939-45 is maintained also in the days of peace.

(3) Assist the authorities in every way possible to maintain a permanent Royal Pioneer Corps in the Army.

(4) Assist Members in obtaining employment and keep up-to-date lists of situations vacant.

(5) Provide useful business and other directories relating to Members and assist them by supplying travel accommodation and other details.

(6) Circulate information regarding the Service and anything which may be helpful to the Members.

(7) Co-operate with the Royal British Legion and similar well-established organisations, Department of Employment and Productivity and the recognised Employment Associations whenever advisable in the interest of Members and for the good of ex-service personnel in general.

SHERRENS - WEYMOUTH

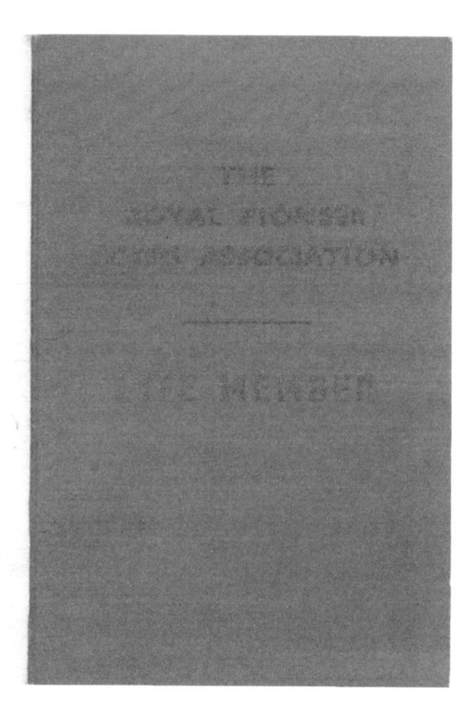

The Royal Pioneer Corps Association.
My life membership card.

The Royal Pioneer Corps Association

(Registered under
The Friendly Societies Act, 1896/48)

Registered Office :
51 ST. GEORGE'S DRIVE, LONDON,
SW1V 4DE
Tel. : 01-834 0415

President and Chairman :
General Sir NOEL THOMAS,
K.C.B., D.S.O., M.C.
(Colonel Commandant, Royal Pioneer Corps)

Patron : General Sir FRANK E. W. SIMPSON,
G.B.E., K.C.B., D.S.O.

MEMBERSHIP DETAILS

Regimental No. 24318077.

RANK Pte.

NAME PROSSER, D.A.

ADDRESS
56, Berwicks Lane,
Chelmsley Wood,
BIRMINGHAM, B37 7RE.

BRANCH H.Q.

Date of Joining 1/7/1975.

MEMBERSHIP No. L/4654.

General Secretary.

The Royal Pioneer Corps Association.
My life membership card.

…GNATURE OF PARENT, GUARDIAN OR OTHER PERSON HAVING CHARGE OR CONTROL:—

JA 281006

NATIONAL REGISTRATION

IDENTITY CARD

UNDER SIXTEEN YEARS

My National Registration Identity Card, 1943.

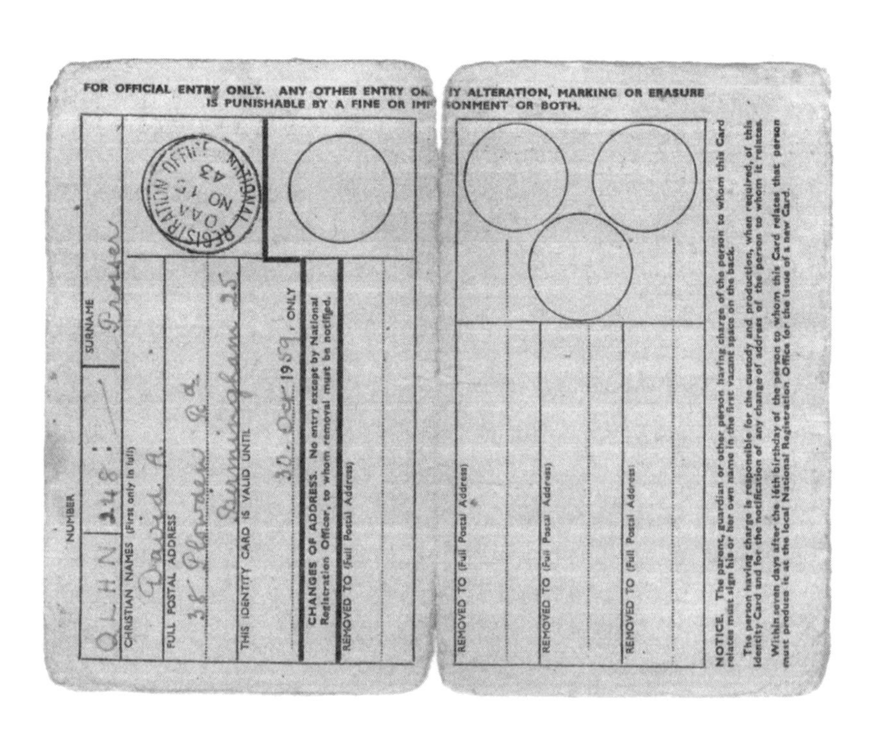

FOR OFFICIAL ENTRY ONLY. ANY OTHER ENTRY OR [illegible]Y ALTERATION, MARKING OR ERASURE IS PUNISHABLE BY A FINE OR IMP[illegible]SONMENT OR BOTH.

NUMBER QLHN 248

SURNAME Prosser

CHRISTIAN NAMES (First only in full) David A.

FULL POSTAL ADDRESS 38 Plowden Rd. Birmingham 25

THIS IDENTITY CARD IS VALID UNTIL 30. Oct 1959, ONLY

CHANGES OF ADDRESS. No entry except by National Registration Officer, to whom removal must be notified.

REMOVED TO (Full Postal Address)

REMOVED TO (Full Postal Address)

REMOVED TO (Full Postal Address)

REMOVED TO (Full Postal Address)

NOTICE. The parent, guardian or other person having charge of the person to whom this Card relates must sign his or her own name in the first vacant space on the back.

The person having charge is responsible for the custody and production, when required, of this Identity Card and for the notification of any change of address of the person to whom it relates.

Within seven days after the 16th birthday of the person to whom this Card relates that person must produce it at the local National Registration Office for the issue of a new Card.

My National Registration Identity Card, 1943.

These are my brothers and sisters with our mom and dad.
Left to right:
Janet, Kenny, Donald, John, author David, Doreen and Kathleen

Author in the middle with my two sons
Anthony on the left and Matthew on the right

A POEM

Houses we bought houses we sold

We did this till we grew old

We dug trenches and knocked down walls

Ripped up carpets floorboards too

Papered walls so they looked new

Electric cables fitted too

Fitted bathrooms and showers new

To make our home look nice to view.

***

A BIG THANK YOU

A big thank you to my mother whose love and devotion gave me the knowledge to overcome poverty and to show respect to rich and poor alike and to always have good manners. She has had to bring up seven children with never enough money to clothe, feed or to keep us warm most of the time. She was always there for her children. Many, many times she gave us her last pennies as we came first in her life. She could make sixpence go three days by buying bones from the butchers for the dog (which we hadn't got) with a pound of potatoes costing only a 1d (one penny) and a pennyworth of carrots, and with an onion she would boil it all up, she got us through the week. My dad was no help at all, well most of the time. She lived like this well into her fifties; love and attention she gave us even after we got married. Most of her children she gave lodgings too when houses were very hard to get.

Thank you, Mother, we all love you very much.

Her children DONALD, KENNETH, KATHLEEN, DOREEN, JANET, DAVID and JOHN.

I wrote a poem for my brothers and sisters, and I've included it on the next page.

Of course in our lives each day we do things similar to the day before; this book only highlights some of the happenings in my life.

To my Brothers and Sisters

An uncommon surname have we

Prosser, it is and will always be.

Common values, common link,

As a family a true bonded link.

Seven of us grew up together,

Brothers and sisters no one can sever.

As a family there is no better.

Each of us was born unique,

None the same.

But what we share is the Prosser name,

Please always remember this.

Our wonderful Mother Dora

Blessed us all with a loving kiss.

Written for you all with love.

(Brother David Prosser, born 30th October 1943)

My family
Matthew's 18th birthday
Left to right, back row: Matthew, Mom Irene, Dad David
Front row: Anthony and Wendy

My grateful thanks to

Grace Rafael
my publisher

For her dedication and patience.

Other books written by
David A Prosser

Pumps With Holes In

Two Little Urchins

The Little Cottage Shop

Twenty-three Children's Stories

Just a Brummie

Lick Em On I'm Off